# Micro-Distilleries
# in the U.S.
# and Canada

## 2nd Edition

*Cheers!* '12

## David J. Reimer Sr.

**Micro-Distilleries in the U.S. and Canada, Second Edition**

Cover Design by: CAS Burkhart

Website:  www.microdistillerybooks.com
Email: david@microdistillerybooks.com, sales@microdistillerybooks.com
Facebook:  Micro Distilleries, Micro-Distilleries in the U.S. and Canada
Twitter:  djreimersr, microdbooks

Printed in the United States of America
February 2012

Print ISBN:  978-0-9852599-0-7

eBook ISBN:  978-0-9852599-1-4

Published by:

Crave Press

www.cravepress.com

# Acknowledgements

I would like to thank everyone at the distilleries that took the time to talk with me and had the patience to answer all my questions. It was their expertise, enthusiasm, and cooperation that helped to steer me in the right direction to make this second edition possible.

A special thanks to Toby Foster, Kyle Ryan, Jason Grossmiller, Dana Kanzler, Phil Brandon, Crispin Ian Cain, Tamar Kaye, Yuseff Cherney, Rocky Cozzo, Susan Karakasevic, Wendi Webster, Kathryn Frederick, Arne Hillesland, Nicole Nollette, Dave Classick Jr., Sue Miller, Ansley Coale, Arthur Hartunian, Davorin Kuchan, Ellie Winters, Lance Winters, Jeffrey S. VanHee, Andrea Smith, Lee Palleschi, James Carling, Jennifer Querbes, Tom Cooper, Lenny Echstein, Michael Myers, Andrew Causey, Mitch Abate, Scott Leopold, Stephen Gould, Karen Hoskin, Brice Hoskin, Fred Linneman, Charles (Ted) Palmer, Russ Wall, Heather Bean, Adam von Gootkin, Nick Carbone, Richard Waters, Erik Vonk, Karin Vonk, Don Freytag, Dave Flintstone, Jeanne Toulon, Kevin Settles, Gray Ottley, Jill Koenig, Andrew Koenig, Paul Hletko, Jennifer Piccione, Sonat Birnecker, Meg Bell, Derrick C. Mancini, Stuart Hobson, Steve Ross, Luke French, Ryan Burchett, Todd Bukaty, Chase Wiseman, Jeff Wiseman, Amy Preske, Mark Brown, Paul Tomaszewski, A. Parker Schonekas, Robert Bartlett, Keith Bodine, Constance Bodine, Stacey Viera, Mike Fiore, Jeff Murphy, Bob Ryan, Jay Harman, Mat Perry, Leslie Haririan, Derrick C. Mancini, Marie-Chantal Dalese, Beth Hubbard, Chris Moersch, Kent Rabish, William (Bill) Welter, Lori Jackson, Mike Hall, Angela Braganini, John Dyer, Rifino Valentine, Richard Patrick, Suzane Shannon, Bryan Siddle, Ralph Haynes, Steve Neukomm, Nicolas Lee, Doug Throener, Holly Mulkins, Ashley Frey, Colby Frey, George Rácz, Heather Houle, R. M. (Ron) Dolin, Colin Keegan, Sean Aguilar-Thomas, Brad Estabrooke, Monte Sachs, Derek Grout, Bill Martin, Donna Lahr, Mike McGlynn, Richard Stabile, Dorit Nahmias, Rich DeVall, Ed Tiedge, Stephen Osborn, Gable Erenzo, Adam Dalton, Sarah LeRoy, Aaron Lee, Tom Lix, Ernest Scarano, Missy Duer, Rob McCulloch, Brady Konya, Greg Lehman, Linda Outterson, Alan Dietrich, Jim Bendis, Georgia Nowlin, Patrick Bernards, Lenny Gotter, Mr. Andrea Loreto, James Stegall, Jess Gallagher, Mihai Talvan, Sarah Ashton, Tom Burkleaux, Matthew VanWinkle, Laura Gaughan, Diane Paulson, Tad Seestedt, Nikki Shoemaker, Beth Gilden, John Stringer, Mike Sherwood, Ryan Webster, Michelle Ly, Lloyd Williams, Ken McFarland, Prentiss Orr, Andrew Auwerda, Laura Blackwell, Joe Fenton, Scott Newitt, Laura Coomes, Michael Joseph Flynn, Andrew Webber, Amanda Knudsen, Michael Simonis, Phil Prichards, Christian Grantham, Chip Tate, Zack Pilgrim, Courtney Volney, Dan Garrison, Kelly Railean, Matthew Railean, Deb Pickell, Lauren Kelleher, Chad Auler, Jason Malik, Bryan Plater, Bert 'Tito' Beveridge, Nicole Portwood, Beth Bellanti-Walker, David Perkins, Erik Fitchett, Michael Gulick, Tood Hardie, Joseph Buswell, Duncan Holaday, Sebastian Lousada, Mimi Buttenheim, Jeanette Miller, Scott Harris, Rick Wasmund, Jay Carpenter, Patricia Jones-McCray, Keith Barnes, Cory Duffy, Kent Fleischmann, Don Poffenroth, Berle W Figgins Jr., Ezra Cox III, Mariah White, James Caudill, Colin Levi, Mark E. Nesheim, Whitney Meriwether, Marc Bernhard, David O'Neal, Dennis Robertson, Steven Stone, Susan Watts, Orlin Sorensen, John Little, Sarah Einstein, Payton Fireman, Deb Hale, Charles McGonegal, John Kinder, Guy Rehorst, Rachel Moon, Po Lo, Nathan Greenawalt, Nick Quint, David Defazio, Michel Jodoin, Emilie Lacaille, Bob Scott, Robert J. Scott, Ken Mill, Barry Bernstein, Valerie Murray, Bryan Murray, Mia Hunt, and Bob Baxter.

I would be remiss if I didn't thank Christina Steffy, CAS Burkhart, and Enchanted Acres Photography by Roxanne Richardson for helping to bring all of this together again.

# Preface

A micro-distillery, often referred to as an "Artisan" "boutique" or "craft" distillery, is a small distillery producing premium spirits in small batches. While this term is most commonly used in the United States, micro-distilleries exist all over the world; however this book concentrates on the distilleries in the U.S. and Canada.

For a trade that dates back to the 1600s in America, it has taken a long time to recover from Prohibition. For the first time since the days of Al Capone, small distilleries are being reestablished. It was during Prohibition in the United States that most small distilleries were forced out of business, leaving only the mega-distilleries to resume operation when Prohibition was repealed. However, within the last decade, the number of micro-distilleries in the United States and Canada has rocketed from a couple dozen to more than a couple hundred. This number represents not only stand-alone distilleries, but also includes many micro-breweries and small wineries that established distilleries within their brewing or winemaking operations. The west coast of the U.S. has experienced the highest number of micro-distillery openings as these are states with more relaxed legislation.

Today's micro-distillery trend is a long way from where it was before Prohibition. After the repeal of the eighteenth amendment, what remained of the country's liquor industry was consolidated into a few large companies. While these mammoths substantially profited from Prohibition, they also greatly lowered consumer expectations. At the time, America's large but then underground drinking population wasn't fussy, and many drinkers believed they were getting the real deal from bootleggers or speakeasy bartenders, who often rebottled homemade gin or whiskey and sold it as top-shelf liquor.

Despite the recession, people with a passion for hand crafted sprits are opening micro-distilleries. And, contrary to myths about the foolishness of starting a business in a downturn, many are holding their own financially and finding audiences for their award winning, hand-crafted superior spirits.

While micro-distilleries represent a less than 5% of the overall spirits market, micro-distillers appeal to individuals who appreciate quality over mass production.

# CONTENTS

On the cover:
*Row 1:*
Bluecoat American Dry Gin – Philadelphia Distilling, PA
Huckleberry Flavored Vodka – Koenig Distillery, ID
Onyx Moonshine – Onyx Spirits Company LLC, CT
Medoyeff Vodka – Bull Run Distilling Company, OR
Clear10 Vodka – Good Spirits Distilling, KS
No. 209 Gin – Distillery No. 209, CA
Vermont Spirits Limited Release Vodka – Vermont Spirits Distilling Company, VT
Sangiovese Grappa – Soft Tail Spirits, WA
Valentine Vodka – Valentine Distilling Company, MI
Hudson Baby Bourbon Whiskey – Tuthilltown Spirits Distillery, NY
High Spirits Chili Flavored Vodka – Arizona High Spirits Distillery, AZ
Prichard's Single Malt Whiskey – Prichard's Distillery Inc., TN

*Row 2:*
Charbay Tahitian Vanilla Bean Rum – Charbay Winery & Distillery, CA
Catoctin Creek Organic Roundstone Rye™ – Catoctin Creek Distilling Co. LLC, VA
SAVVY Vodka – SAVVY Distillers L.P., TX
Deco Coffee Rum – Eastside Distlling, OR
Yerlo Rice Spirits – Lo Artisan Distillery LLC, WI
Hum – Hum Spirits Company, IL
Richland Rum – Richland Distilling Company, GA
Rogue Spruce Gin – Rogue Spirits, OR
Hawaiian Vodka – Island Distillers Inc., HI

*Row 3:*
Ocean Vodka – Hawaii Sea Spirits LLC, HI
Dark Corner Distillery Moonshine – Dark Corner Distillery, SC
Breckenridge Bourbon Whiskey – Breckenridge Distillery, CO
Dutch Harbor Breeze Grog – Ye Ol' Grog Distillery, OR
Vieux Carré Absinthe Supérieure – Philadelphia Distilling, PA
Kaua`i Rum - Kōloa Rum Company, HI

*Row 4:*
Mijiu Fire – Vinn Distillery, OR

# Alaska Distillery

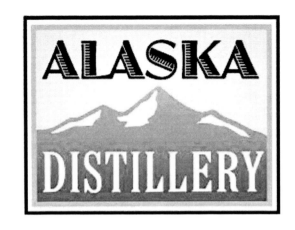

Toby Foster, CEO and President
Shawn Ansley, Owner
Scotti MacDonald, Owner
Winston Chelf, Owner

1540 North Shoreline Drive
Wasilla, Alaska  99654

*Phone:*  907-382-6250
*Fax:*  907-357-6721
*Email:*  toby@alaskadistillery.com
*Website:*  www.alaskadistillery.com
*Facebook:*  Alaska Distillery
*Twitter:*  @AK_Distillery, @permafrostvodka

*Region:*  Matanuska-Susitna Valley of Alaska

*Type*:  Micro-distillery producing 10,000 gallons annually

*Opened:*  2007

*Hours of operation:*  Monday through Friday, 8:00am to 5:00pm

*Tours:*   Tours are available.

*Types of spirits produced:*  Gin and vodka

*Names of spirits:*
- Permafrost Alaska Vodka
- Permafrost Alaska Gin
- Alaska Distillery Gin
- Alaska Distillery Smoked Salmon Vodka
- Alaska Distillery Red Raspberry Vodka
- Alaska Distillery High Bush Cranberry Vodka
- Alaska Distillery Low Bush Blueberry Vodka
- Alaska Distillery Birch Syrup Vodka
- Alaska Distillery Wild Blackberry Vodka
- Alaska Distillery Rhubarb Vodka
- Frostbite Alaska Vodka
- Purgatory Hemp Seed Vodka
- Bear Creek Alaska Whiskey

*Best known for:*  Alaska Distillery Smoked Salmon Vodka

*Average bottle price*:  $24.99 to $37.99

*Distribution:*  AK, WA, CA, TN, IL, KY, AZ, CO, IN, MT, TX, GA, British Columbia, and Alberta

*Awards and Recognitions:*
**Permafrost Alaska Vodka**
- 96 Points, 2009 Beverage Testing Institute

*Highlighted spirits:*
**Permafrost Alaska Vodka**
Permafrost Alaska Vodka is made from locally grown potatoes and Alaskan glacier ice. It is distilled three times, charcoal filtered five times and crafted in small batches to be ultra-premium and ultra-pure.

**Alaska Distillery Low Bush Blueberry Vodka**
Plump, ripe blueberries give this vodka a natural sweetness. The combination of fresh berries and pristine Alaskan glacier ice will make any drink mixed with this vodka burst with crisp flavor.

**Alaska Distillery Rhubarb Vodka**
Made with pristine Alaskan glacier ice, this handcrafted vodka is blended with the perfect amount of rhubarb for a sweet and tangy summertime cocktail any time of the year.

**Alaska Distillery Birch Syrup Vodka**
This handcrafted vodka is made with pristine Alaskan glacier ice and just enough birch syrup to have a unique rich and lightly spicy flavor.

*Events and Celebrations:* Sponsors monthly events and tastings

*Interesting facts:*
- Alaska Distillery is Alaska's first distillery.

*About:*
Not only is Alaska Distillery one of the only distilleries in Alaska, but it also collects large floating icebergs that have calved off of the glaciers in Prince William Sound. The icebergs are transported to the distillery where they are melted down to make vodka. The water is ultra-pure and leaves a very distinct taste.

*Future business plans and goals:* Increased distribution

*Suggested recipe:*
**Alaska Distillery Smoked Salmon Vodka Oyster Shooter**
- 1 raw oyster
- 1 lemon wedge
- 1 oz Smoked Salmon Vodka
- 1 tsp tomato juice
- Splash of tabasco sauce

Alaska Distillery
Wasilla, Alaska

**Arizona High Spirits Distillery**
Owned and operated by:
Mogollon Brewing Company LLC

Dana Kanzler, Managing Partner & Head Distiller/Head Brewer

4366 E. Huntington Drive, Building 2
Flagstaff, Arizona  86004

*Phone:*  928-853-1021

*Email:*   dskanzler@yahoo.com
*Website:* www.arizonahighspirits.com
*Facebook:* Mogollon Brewing Company
*Twitter:* @AZHighSpirits
*YouTube:* Arizona High Spirits

*Region:*  Southwestern U.S.

*Type*:  Micro-distillery producing approximately 1,200 gallons per year

*Opened:*  2006

*Hours of operation:*  Monday through Friday, 7:00am to 5:00pm

*Tours:*   Formal tours are not offered but can be arranged by calling in advance.

*Types of spirits produced:*    Vodka, gin, rum, and whisky

*Names of spirits:*
- Prickly Pear Vodka
- Chili Vodka
- American Vodka
- Desert Dry Gin
- Pieces of Eight Spiced Rum
- Prickly Pear Liqueur
- Single Malt Mesquite Smoked Whisky

*Best known for:*  Prickly Pear Vodka

*Average bottle price*:  $20.00 to $30.00 for 750ml bottles

*Distribution:*  Products are currently available in Arizona and are distributed to chain stores, liquor stores, bars, and restaurants.  Future distribution will include California, Nevada, and Texas.

*Awards and Recognitions:*
Arizona High Spirits has received many accolades from whisky critics, but as a rule does not enter award type programs.

*Highlighted spirits:*
**Prickly Pear Vodka**
Prickly Pear Vodka captures the true essence of the fruit from the prickly pear cactus. This little known treasure from the Arizona desert yields an aromatic, fruity bouquet with a pleasant flavor. Enjoy it on the rocks, in a Martini or with your favorite vodka cocktail.

**Chili Vodka**
High Spirits uses only the finest grain to create this high quality vodka, and infuses it with the earthy zest of serrano chili. Try it in a Martini or a Bloody Mary.

**Desert Dry Gin**
Desert Dry Gin is an ultra-smooth gin from a base of white wheat and American rye. It is flavored with select botanicals native to the Southwest and Sonora Desert, giving it a unique flavor.

**Pieces of Eight Spiced Rum**
High Spirits uses 100% blackstrap molasses to create Pieces of Eight Spiced Rum. The rum is then infused with eight exotic spices and aged to perfection in charred oak barrels. The result is a premium, luscious rum.

**Single Malt Mesquite Smoked Whisky**
Single Malt Mesquite Smoked Whisky is crafted using the finest two-row barley malt smoked gently over locally harvested mesquite. The all-malt foundation comes together with a very subtle mesquite flavor, rich in texture and well balanced.

*Services offered other than production:*
Arizona High Spirits Distillery is strictly a wholesale operation with little or no public access or retail business. It does, however, host a distilling seminar twice a year presented by Arnold-Holstein, Germany. A tasting room is planned in the near future.

*Interesting facts:*
- Arizona High Spirits is located at an elevation of 7,000 feet.

*About:*
Named after the Mogollon Rim in Arizona, Dana Kanzler and partners opened the Mogollon Brewing Company and pub in a remodeled, century old building in downtown Flagstaff, Arizona, in 1997. By 2001, Mogollon beer became the number one selling micro-brew in Arizona and the pub grew in popularity for its atmosphere and entertainment venue.

As interest in micro-distilling was gaining popularity, the company purchased a German still in 2005 to produce their own unique, small batch spirits. Since there had been no legal distilleries in Arizona, it took until 2007 to get the laws changed for Arizona High Spirits Distillery to become the first legal distillery in Arizona.

The first spirit produced was Prickly Pear Vodka, followed by American Vodka, Prickly Pear Liqueur, Pieces of Eight Spiced Rum, Desert Dry Gin, and a unique Chili Vodka infused with a serrano chili.

As the pub gained popularity and demand for Arizona High Spirits increased, time to run both became of the essence. Wanting to focus its efforts and energy on brewing and distilling, the company sold the pub in 2008 and moved to a larger facility where it could concentrate on beer and spirits production and distribution.

As of 2011, because of current laws and licensing, the new brewery/distillery location doesn't have a tasting room, though the company is working on getting those laws changed.

*Management profile:*
The staff of High Spirits is an eclectic mix of business professionals and enthusiasts who share a passion for quality craft spirits and craft beer. The staff members include distillers, brewers, world travelers, a culinary chef, a hunter and wildlife conservationist, an avid bicyclist and river runner, a motorcycle rider, rock and rollers, and country music fans as well as baseball fans. The distillers have attended several distillation seminars and are experienced brewers in a commercial micro-brewery.

*Future business plans and goals:*
Arizona High Spirits is planning to increase whisky production, expand product distribution, and explore new product development while maintaining its commitment to artisanship.

*Suggested recipe:*
**Cactus Kiss**
- 1½ oz High Spirits Prickly Pear Vodka
- ½ oz triple sec
- Splash of Chateau Monet
- Splash of cranberry juice

    Garnish with lime.
    Shake and served in a chilled martini glass.

Arizona High Spirits Distillery
Flagstaff, Arizona

## Brandon's Rock Town Distillery Inc.

**ROCK TOWN**
DISTILLERY
LITTLE ROCK, ARKANSAS
www.rocktowndistillery.com

Phil Brandon, Owner

1216 East 6th Street
Little Rock, Arkansas 72202

*Phone:* 501-907-5244
*Fax:* 501-907-1861
*Email:* phil@rocktowndistillery.com
*Website:* www.rocktowndistillery.com, www.drinkbrandons.com
*Facebook:* Rock Town Distillery
*Twitter:* @rocktowndistill

*Region:* Southern USA

*Type:* Micro-distillery producing approximately 200 gallons per month

*Opened:* July 2010

*Hours of operation:* Monday through Friday, 8:00am to 5:00pm

*Tours:* Tours are conducted on Saturdays at 1:30pm and 3:00pm. No reservation required

*Types of spirits produced:*
Un-aged whiskey, wheat whiskey, bourbon, vodka and gin

*Names of spirits:*
- Arkansas Lightning
- Arkansas Hickory Smoked Whiskey
- Arkansas Young Bourbon
- Brandon's Gin
- Brandon's Vodka

*Average bottle price:* $29.99

*Distribution:*
Tennessee, Illinois, Pennsylvania, Missouri,
Louisiana, Mississippi, and South Carolina

*Awards and Recognitions:*
**Brandon's Gin**
- Double Gold Medal, 2011 San Francisco World Spirits Competition
- Top 10 Spirit of 2010 by BevX.com

**Brandon's Vodka**
- Scored 93, Excellent Highly Recommended, 2011 Ultimate Spirits Challenge
- Received at 93/100 by Wine Enthusiast Magazine

**Arkansas Lightning**
- Gold Medal Scored 91, Exceptional, 2011 Beverage Testing Institute Chicago

*Highlighted spirits:*

**Brandon's Gin**

Brandon's Gin is distilled from Arkansas soft red winter wheat and contains complex flavors that come from the vapor infusion technique used to create it. Additionally, Brandon's Gin has a hint of juniper and wheat, and the coriander and angelica shine through with a hint of cinnamon and citrus. Brandon's Gin leaves a long, slowly fading spicy aftertaste, and it's exceptionally smooth for a 92 proof spirit. Each bottle is hand numbered and signed to reflect the care that goes into each and every one.

**Brandon's Vodka**

Brandon's Vodka is distilled from Arkansas soft red winter wheat, and its aroma is reminiscent of sweet warm wheat and vanilla. The taste also has a gentle sweetness and soft texture, and the finish fades in an easy warm glow. Each bottle is hand numbered and singed to reflect the care that goes into each and every one.

*Events and Celebrations:*
Brandon's hosts a number of events throughout the year.

*Services offered other than production:* Tours and tastings

*Interesting facts:*
- Rock Town Distillery is Arkansas' first craft distillery.

*About:*
Brandon's Rock Town Distillery was founded in 2010 with one mission - to make sure every possible element used to make Brandon's spirits - from the soft, red winter wheat for the vodka and gin to the charred, white oak barrels that store the bourbon - comes from Arkansas. Brandon's expertly crafts its vodka, gin, and bourbon in small batches using a 250 gallon copper pot still; every bottle is hand labeled. Brandon's goal is to ensure the highest quality.

*Future business plans and goals:*
Expanded distribution and to continue to produce world class spirits

Brandon's Rock Town Distillery Inc.
Little Rock, Arkansas

# American Craft Whiskey Distillery
and **Greenway Distillers Inc.**

Crispin Cain, President / Distiller / Spirits Master
Tamar Kaye, Vice President

American Craft Whiskey Distillery (ACWD)
1110 Bel Arbres Road
Redwood Valley, California 95470

Greenway Distiller Inc.
5000 Low Gap Road
Ukiah, California 95482

*Office address:*
157 E. Gobbi Street
Ukiah, California  95482

*Phone:*  707-485-2941
*Fax:*  707-463-6958 (call first)
*Email:*  acwd.1@netzero.net, crispin@greenwaydistillers.com
*Website:*  (ACWD) www.craftdistillers.com, (Greenway) www.greenwaydistillers.com
*Facebook:*  Greenway Distillers Inc.

*Region:*  Mendocino County, California

*Type:*  ACWD – A micro-distillery producing approximate 400 gallons monthly
Greenway – A micro-distillery producing approximately 600 gallons per year

*Opened:*  2010

*Hours of operation:*  Monday through Friday, 6:00am to 5:00pm

*Tours:*  Monday through Saturday by appointment

*Types of spirits produced:*
ACWD produces whiskey and Greenway Distillers produces absinthe and rose liqueur.

*Names of spirits:*
- Crispin's Rose Liqueur
- Germain-Robin Absinthe Superiure
- Low Gap Clear Whiskey

*Best known for:*
Champagne cocktail with Crispin's Rose, and White Manhattan with Low Gap Clear Whiskey

*Average bottle price:*  $45.00

*Distribution:*  See www.caddellwilliams.com

*Awards and Recognitions:*

**Germain-Robin Absinthe Superiure**
- Five Star rating from the Spirit Journal

**Absinthe**
- Rated number 9 on Spirit Journal's list of Best Spirits in the World Market

**Crispin's Rose Liqueur**
- Five Star rating from the Spirit Journal
- Highest rating by Wine Enthusiast Magazine
- Robb Report's Best of the Best, Top Ten Spirits of 2009

**Low Gap Clear Whiskey**
- Third Place (out of 19), 2011 American Distilling Institute

*Highlighted spirits:*

**Low Gap Clear Whiskey**
Low Gap Clear Whiskey is soft and smooth even though it only spends 357 minutes in a used bourbon barrel. Most of the softness comes from the distillation.

**Crispin's Rose Liqueur**
Crispin's Rose Liqueur's base spirit is made with apple juice and honey, and then is infused with fresh rose petals. While it tastes and smells like a rose, it is not soapy or perfumey but is balanced between the alcohol, the sweetness, and the tannins from the roses.

*Events and Celebrations:*
Hosts an open house at the distillery three times a year, February, June, and November

*Services offered other than production:*
Craft distillery consulting services

*About:*
Crispin Cain worked nearly two decades in the wine and distilling industry, and after suffering an almost crippling back injury he was forced to make a life change and open Greenway Distillers.

Cain's experience at Germain-Robin gave him a background in craft methods of distillation that go back to the early 1500s. He is privileged to be allowed to use a still at Germain-Robin where he can marry the distillation style of craft-method brandy with whiskey making. This allows him to craft a finely tuned spirit, paying close attention to the fire under the pot and the temperatures of the water he condenses with the spirit. Greenway Distillers spirits uses craft distillation methods, particularly the double-distillation method used to produce cognac. Double distillation allows for the careful distillation and separation of the product into precise fractions. The first pass through the still yields alcohol at about 25% alcohol by volume, and the second pass through yields the heart at 70% alcohol by volume.

*Management profile:*
**Crispin Cain**

For more than 20 years, Crispin Cain has worked in Mendocino County's best wineries. He also spent a number of years working as an assistant to Hubert Germain-Robin Distillery. Before beginning his career in wine and spirits, Cain spent two years as a VISTA volunteer in the Peace Corps. After suffering a serious back injury in 2000, Cain changed his career goals and decided to produce Crispin's Rose Liqueur. In 2005, Greenway Distillers was incorporated.

*A message from Crispin Cain:*
"One thing that makes Greenway Distillers unique is the fact that it is a farm and a distillery. We cultivate about one acre of land about a quarter mile up the hill from the distillery. My dear partner, Tamar L. Kaye, is vice president and secretary of both corporations and my assistant at Greenway Distillers. In addition to working with me at the distillery since 2005, she is responsible for the more than 160 roses growing up the hill from the distillery, and the herbs for the absinthe. We found the marriage of her skills as a horticulturist and my skills as an alchemist fit so perfectly together with the goal of capturing the essences of the plants and artfully suspending them in time itself for the enjoyment of others.

At American Craft Whiskey Distillery (ACWD), my son, Devin Cain, is my first assistant. Devin has been working with me part-time in the distillery for one year and is employed part-time at Germain-Robin Brandy. At ACWD Devin is in charge of the cellar, my assistant in the distillery, and he recently became our director of distilled spirits specialties.

The biggest kudos go to Ansley Coale, CEO of Alambic Inc, without whom none of this would be anything more than an unfulfilled dream, a good idea, or a hobby at most.

It is with the efforts of these important people in my life that I am able to make things like rose petal liqueur, absinthe, and malted wheat whiskey a reality."

*Future business plans and goals:* Expanded product line to include various whiskeys

*Suggested recipe:*
**The White Manhattan**
- 1 ½ oz Low Gap Clear Whiskey
- ½ oz bianco or dry vermouth
- ½ oz benedictine
- 2 dashes of orange bitters

American Craft Whiskey Distillery and Greenway Distillers Inc.
Redwood Valley and Ukiah, California

## Ballast Point Spirits

Jack White and Yuseff Cherney, Owners
10051 Old Grove Road, Suite B1
San Diego, California  92131

*Phone:*  858-695-2739
*Fax:*  858-695-2734
*Email:*  yuseff@ballastpoint.com
*Website:*  www.ballastpoint.com
*Facebook:*  Ballast Point Spirits
*Twitter:*  @BPbrewing

*Region:*  West Coast

*Type*:  Micro-distillery producing approximately 700 gallons a month

*Opened:*  May 2008

*Hours of operation:*   Monday through Saturday, 11:00am to 9:00pm
Sunday, 11:00am to 5:00pm

*Tours:*  Tours are available Monday through Saturday at 12:00pm, 2:00pm, and 5:00pm
Sundays at 12:00pm and 2:00pm

*Types of spirits produced:*  Bourbon, gin, rum, vodka, and whiskey

*Names of spirits:*
- Old Grove Gin
- Three Sheets Barrel Aged Rum
- Three Sheets White Rum
- Devil's Share Whiskey
- Devils' Share Bourbon
- Fugu Vodka

*Average bottle price*:  $24.00 to $65.00

*Distribution:*
Statewide in California with some East Coast distribution

*Awards and Recognitions:*
**Devil's Share Whiskey**
- Silver Medal, 2011 ADI Conference
- Gold Medal, 2010 ADI Conference

**Devil's Share Bourbon**
- Bronze Medal Best in Category, 2011 ADI Conference

**Three Sheets Barrel Aged Rum**
- 2012 Good Food Awards

*Highlighted spirits:*
**Old Grove Gin**
Old Grove Gin embodies the best of the London dry style with an emphasis on juniper. With subtle hints of rose and coriander, Old Grove is delicious on the rocks or mixed in a gin and tonic with a twist.

**Three Sheets Barrel Aged** and **Three Sheets White Rum**
Three Sheets Rum is made by fermenting organic evaporated cane sugar by a proprietary yeast strain and distilled through a custom built hybrid pot/column still.

Ballast Point Spirits offers both an aged and un-aged clear rum, each having their own signature flavors. By using raw sugar, Ballast Point Spirits has developed a rum of great distinction with subtle sweet flavors.

The aged rum spends its life in a virgin, heavily charred American oak barrel, much like the fine bourbons of Kentucky.

*Services offered other than production:* Tastings for beer only and merchandise sales

*Interesting facts:*
- First licensed distillery in San Diego since Prohibition

Photo by: John Schulz

*About:*
Jack (left) and Yuseff (right) are brewers who made the transition to distilling because of a passion for the craft. Making spirits is the natural step to make from brewing.

In 1992, Yuseff Cherney met Jack White who had just started Home Brew Mart, a local home brew supply store. Yuseff was soon hired to work in the store selling equipment and ingredients to people who wanted to brew beer at home. Jack's dream was to open a micro-brewery once the home brew shop became successful and, after three years, construction of the Ballast Point Brewing Company began in the back suite of the brew mart. By 2003, even with the acquisition of three adjoining suites, Ballast Point Brewing had already outgrown the space. Construction of a new facility began in 2004.

After Ballast Point grew to over 10,000 barrels per year, Yuseff and Jack decided to make spirits too. After attending classes and conferences on distillation, Ballast Point Spirits was born and became the first distillery in San Diego since Prohibition. Yuseff put together a hybrid pot/column still in 2008 to begin producing classic spirits. A new custom built Vendome 500 gallon copper still was then added to increase whiskey production.

*Professional associations:*  San Diego Distillery Guild

*Future business plans and goals:*  Increased production

*Suggested recipes:*
**The Real\* French 75 \*(with Gin)**
- 1 ½ ozs Old Grove Gin
- ¾ oz fresh lemon juice
- ½ oz simple syrup
- 1 cup ice cubes
- 2 oz chilled, dry sparkling wine, such as brut champagne

**The Real Singapore Sling**
- 1 oz Old Grove Gin
- ½ oz cherry brandy
- 4 ozs pineapple juice
- ¼ oz Cointreau orange liqueur
- ½ oz lime juice
- ¼ oz Benedictine liqueur
- 1/3 oz grenadine syrup
- 1 dash Angostura Bitters

Garnish with pineapple slice and maraschino cherry.


Ballast Point Spirits
San Diego, California

# Cal-Czech Distillery

Rocky Cozzo, Owner / Distiller

*Physical Address:*
1209 Hwy 49
Angels Camp, California 95222

*Mailing Address:*
P.O. Box 1296
Angels Camp, California 95222

*Phone:* 209-736-2990
*Fax:* 209-736-1909
*Email:* rocky@vodkamorava.com
*Website:* www.vodkamorava.com
*Facebook:* Cal-Czech Distillery
*Twitter:* @VodkaMorava

*Region:* Central California

*Type:* Micro-distillery producing approximately 3,000 gallons per year

*Opened:* 2012

*Hours of operation:* Monday through Friday, 9:00am to 5:00pm

*Tours:* Tours and tastings are available by appointment.

*Types of spirits produced:* Vodka

*Names of spirits:* Vodka Morava

*Average bottle price:* $30.00 to $40.00

*Distribution:* Available through distributors

*About:*
Cal-Czech Distillery is the maker of premium vodka and brandy. All spirits are hand made in small batches to assure the best quality. Located in the California gold and wine country, techniques used here were inspired by Czech and Ukrainian distillers.

*Future business plans and goals:*
To grow and expand to national distribution

Cal-Czech Distillery
Angels Camp, California

## Charbay Winery & Distillery
## Charbay Distillers

Miles and Susan Karakasevic, Owners

Miles Karakasevic, Grand Master Distiller
Susan Karakasevic, General Manager
Marko Karakasevic, Master Distiller

4001 Spring Mountain Road
St. Helena, California  94574

*Phone:*  707-963-9327
*Email:*  Susan Karakasevic:  susan@charbay.com
        Marko Karakasevic:  marko@charbay.com
        John Reagh, Tasting Room:  visit@charbay.com
*Website:*  www.charbay.com
*Facebook:*  Charbay Distillery
*Twitter:*  @Charbay
*Blog:*  www.charbayblog.com

*Region:*  Northern California

*Type:*  Winery / Micro-distillery

*Opened:*  1983

*Hours of operation:*  10:00am to 4:00pm 7 days a week, and by appointment

*Tours:*  Tours of the distillery are available.

*Types of spirits produced:*  Whiskey, vodka, rum, tequila, grappa, brandy, and liqueurs

*Names of spirits:*
- Charbay Black Walnut Liqueur
- Charbay Brandy No. 83 Folle Blanche
- Charbay Doubled & Twisted Light Whiskey
- Charbay Grappa di Marko
- Charbay Tahitian Vanilla Bean Rum
- Charbay Tequila Blanco
- Charbay Vodka
- Charbay Whiskey, Release II

*Best known for:*  Charbay Vodka and Whiskey

*Average bottle price:*  $38.00 to $350.00

*Distribution:*  Nationwide in high end shops, restaurants, and clubs

*Awards and Recognitions:*

**Charbay Clear Vodka**

- 100 Points, Wine Enthusiast
- Vodka of the Year, Food & Wine Magazine
- #1 Handcrafted Vodka in the World, Spirit Journal

*Highlighted spirits:*

**Charbay Tahitian Vanilla Bean Rum**

Rare Tahitian vanilla beans, known for their exceptional fragrance and accounting for less than 5% of the world's real vanilla supply, are used in combination with Charbay Rum to create this distinct spirit. It is great on the rocks with soda or tropical fruit juice.

**Charbay Whiskey, Release II – 110 Proof**

Charbay Whiskey Release II begins with a bottle-ready Pilsner made from two-row European barley grown and malted in British Columbia. Choice hops are added to the mash and then double distilled in a classic Alambic Charentais Pot Still. The whiskey was put up in 22 American white oak barrels charred to #3 "Gator Skin" and is being released over time. Charbay Whiskey is being release as a collection at various proof levels.

**Charbay Clear Vodka**

Charbay Clear Vodka is crafted from a blend of American Midwest corn and rye and distilled to 192 proof for purity. It is then cut to 80 proof and gently filtered to preserve the spirit's body and mouthfeel. Charbay Vodka is great on the rocks with a splash of soda water or shaken and served up.

*Events and Celebrations:* Annual Wood Roasted Pig Barbecue in the fall

*Services offered other than production:*
Spirits education, team building seminars, and custom martini bars

*Interesting facts:*

- Charbay is family owned and operated by 12th and 13th generation distillers and winemakers.

*About:*

Since 1983, Charbay has been producing small releases of handcrafted, elegant wines, ports, aperitifs, spirits, and liqueurs in Northern California. Grounded in generations of European knowledge, the Karakasevic family is committed to offering the finest wines and spirits made in the true spirit of American creativity. Miles Karakasevic, co-owner and founder, traces his family winemaking and distilling heritage back over 250 years to 1751 in former Yugoslavia.

No other known family in the U.S. produces the scope of handcrafted wines and spirits that Charbay does, having distilled and released all four of the major spirits groups.

*Management profile:*

## Miles Karakasevic

Miles Karakasevic, co-owner and founder, is a 12th generation European winemaker and master distiller. Born in old Yugoslavia, he apprenticed in the tradition followed by the Karakasevic family since the 1750s. Following in their footsteps, learning the secrets of his forefathers, he eventually became certified as a master distiller. Along the way, Miles studied enology and viticulture at the University of Belgrade.

Immigrating to the New World in 1962, Miles first stopped in Canada and Michigan before eventually settling in California in 1970. In the following years, Miles was employed by a number of wineries including Beringer Vineyards where he was the assistant winemaker. Longing to distill, he convinced a client to import an alambic pot still from Cognac. In 1983, he and Susan began making their own wines and brandy under the name Domaine Karakash. Being comfortable with all aspects of fermenting and making many wines, even champagne, Miles was excited to begin a brandy program.

Miles is also an avid reader who enjoys history, science, and philosophy.

## Susan Karakasevic

Susan Reagh Karakasevic, co-owner and founder, grew up in Michigan. Her studies of art at Western Michigan University were interrupted when she met and married Miles. In 1970, they left Michigan to jump into the budding California wine business.

In the early '80s, Susan studied the marketing aspects of the wine business and began marketing the family line of Domaine Karakash wines and brandy in 1985. In 1991, she changed the business name to Domaine Charbay. Today, Susan continues to market Charbay in addition to managing sales and packaging.

Susan says, "I am fortunate to have enough Irish-German blood to stand up to the wild Yugoslav that has made my life so colorful! We are just hitting our stride. All the long hours and all the hard work have been worth it. We've found our niche. Wait until you see what's coming."

### Marko J. Karakasevic

Marko J. Karakasevic, winemaker and distiller, grew up around pumps, hoses and tanks. This was his father's world and the family always lived close to the winery where Miles, his father, made wine. Marko began his studies in physical therapy, however harvests would lead Marko to working in various Napa Valley wineries. After working in a Napa Valley tasting room, he discovered he liked all sides of the wine business—from production to sharing his winemaking experience with visitors.

In the fall of '95, Marko realized he wanted to apprentice under his father and be the 13th generation to carry on the Karakasevic family tradition.

17

From that point on, he submitted to the same tough routine of generations of Karakasevic men and women before him - learning the winemaking, the distilling and the running of a family business. Marko conceived the idea of Charbay's whole-fruit flavored vodka program. He found the fruit and designed the packaging. In 2003, marking the 20th anniversary of Charbay, Marko received the title of distiller. In 2009, after a 26 year apprenticeship, he became a master distiller.

Give Marko a day off and he'll head out to go fishing. A couple of days will send him snowmobiling in Tahoe or fishing in Hawaii.

*Professional associations:*  Wine Institute and DISCUS

*Future business plans and goals:*
Charbay plans to continue to be innovative and distill pushing the limits of anticipated flavors

*Suggested recipes:*
**Charbay Meyer Collins** (Designed by Allan Katz)
- 2 oz Charbay Meyer Lemon Vodka
- ¾ oz St. Germain Elderflower Cordial
- ¾ oz fresh lemon juice
- Splash of Maraska Maraschino Liqueur

  Shake ingredients over ice and strain into a collins glass filled with ice.  Top with seltzer, garnish with a lemon wheel.

**Charbay Hemingway**
- 2 oz Charbay Ruby Red Grapefruit Vodka
- 2 oz pink grapefruit juice
- Splash of simple syrup
- Dash of bitters

  Shake and strain into a martini glass.
  Garnish with lime wheel.

*A note from Susan Karakasevic*
"Distilling with alambic pot stills is an old art being kept alive by old school distillers. It requires the distiller to make the call of when to make the cuts. Miles always says, 'How you make your cuts separates the men from the boys,' and, 'You must project in your mind what you want and follow through with your cuts.' This of course refers to the three cuts of the first distillation and the four cuts of the second distillation. When we run our still, it goes 24/7. The roar of the flame and the excitement of a new batch is what keeps my guys always looking for the next spirit to distill.  Independence and distilling history give us the freedom to distill as stewards of mother nature - we source premium ingredients and share with you the best flavors distilled. And we're just hitting our stride."

Charbay Winery & Distillery
St. Helena, California

## Distillery No. 209

Leslie Rudd, Founder
Samantha Rudd, Owner
Nicole Nollette, CEO
Arne Hillesland, Ginerator
Kathryn Frederick, Chief Marketing Officer

Pier 50 Shed B, Mailbox 9
San Francisco, California 94158

*Phone:*  415-369-0209
*Fax:*  415-281-8904
*Email:*  Kathryn Frederick:  kathryn@distillery209.com
               Arne Hillesland:  arne@distillery209.com
               Nicole Nollette:  nicole@distillery209.com
*Website:*  www.distillery209.com, www.209gin.com
*Facebook:*  Distillery No. 209
*Twitter:*  @distillery209

*Region:*  California

*Type*:  Craft distillery

*Opened:*  2005

*Hours of operation:*
Monday through Friday, 8:00am to 5:30pm (not open to the public)

*Tours:*  Tours are not available at this time.

*Types of spirits produced:*  Gin

*Names of spirits:*
- No. 209 Gin
- No. 209 Kosher for Passover Gin

*Best known for:*  Basil Gimlet and Last Word

*Average bottle price*:
50ml $3.99 to $4.99, 375ml $17.00, 750ml $34.99

*Distribution:*  34 states and internationally

*Awards and Recognitions:*
**No. 209 Gin**
- Gold Medal, 2010 Gin Masters Competition
- Triple Gold,  2011 MicroLiquor Spirit Awards

**No. 209 Gin**
No. 209 Gin is distilled five times with great care given to separating the heads and tails from the heart of the distillation; only the heart is used. Each batch is handcrafted using the "single shot" method, and using natural botanicals sourced from around the world. Notes of juniper, bergamot orange, cardamom, cassia, coriander and lemon peel meld together to create a citrus spice gin that Distillery No. 209 considers a truly modern spirit.

**No. 209 Kosher-for-Passover Gin**
No. 209 Kosher-for-Passover Gin is the first and only known Passover certified gin in the world. Distilled five times from a sugar cane based spirit using the "single shot" method, this gin is made using different botanicals than the standard No. 209 Gin uses. Due to Rabbinical law, cardamom is not allowed in crafting this spirit. In lieu of cardamom, California Bay leaf and several other spices were selected to maintain the citrus spice flavor.

*Interesting facts:*
- Distillery No. 209 was the 209th registered distillery permitted in the United States.
- No. 209 Kosher-for-Passover Gin is the first and only known Passover certified gin in the world.

*About:*
The No. 209 story began in New York in 1870 when William Scheffler purchased the patent for the new design of a pot still. He then decided to journey west and eventually became a distiller at Krug Winery in St. Helena, Napa Valley. In 1880, Scheffler bought his own winery, the Edge Hill Estate in St. Helena. Edge Hill, as it was named since its founding in 1867, was one of the most impressive wineries of its time. Scheffler, being a distiller at heart, added a distillery at Edge Hill in 1882. Once the stone and brick building was completed, he registered the distillery with the federal government and was given distillery license number 209, which he painted over the front door of his new distillery building. His

spirits received various awards including a medal for his efforts in the Grand Exposition in Paris in 1889.

Defunct during Prohibition, the distillery was revived in 2005 after Leslie Rudd, the new steward of the Edge Hill property, discovered the original distillery building.

While surveying the 30-acre Edge Hill Estate in 1999, Rudd found a curious brick hay barn on the property with the words "Registered Distillery No. 209" faintly visible across the face of the building over its double iron doors. Rudd didn't know it at the time, but this building would serve as the inspiration for all that would follow.

In researching the Edge Hill legacy, Rudd discovered the rich distilling tradition started by Scheffler and was inspired to restore the old distillery at Edge Hill with historical accuracy. This work resulted in preservationist awards from Napa County and the state of California. But the size and location of the building was not conducive to his plans for the revival of Distillery No. 209, so he commissioned a 24-foot high copper- pot still from Forsyths of Rothes, Scotland, and built a new home for No. 209 in China Basin on Pier 50 in San Francisco, California.

Just prior to the launch of the new Distillery No. 209, the long lost 1889 medal from Paris suddenly turned up on an auction site and Leslie was able to purchase it. He now had the final piece of the No. 209 legacy in place, which served as an affirmation of his decision to distill award-winning spirits under the Registered Distillery No. 209 banner once again.

Distillery No. 209 puts one person, the ginerator, in charge of the entire production process. The ginerator hand sorts shells and grinds the botanicals to select only the finest specimens of ingredients such as bergamot orange, juniper berries, cardamom pods, coriander seeds, lemon peel and cassia bark among others. He then fine tunes the recipe so that each batch is virtually identical. Finally the recipe is distilled in a copper alambic pot still through a single shot distillation process. The recipe was adjusted a number of times until the distillation exactly matched the flavor profile and finish that Distillery 209 was seeking.

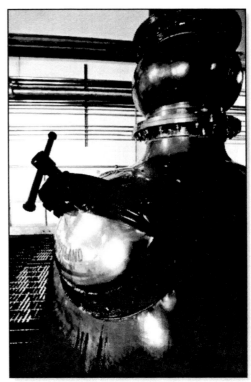

*Professional associations:* American Distilling Institute

*Future business plans and goals:*
Distillery No. 209 enjoys educating people about how gin is made by showing all of the wonderful flavors, aromas and cocktails that are associated with this unique spirit. Distillery No. 209 feels bound to show the people the advantages of drinking gin in order to expand their palette and drinking experience.

*Suggested recipes:*

**The Seder Sour**

- 1 ½ oz No. 209 Kosher-for-Passover Gin
- ½ oz warmed honey
- 1/8 oz Kosher-for-Passover horseradish
- 1 oz lemon juice
- Soda water
- Tiny pinch of Kosher salt

Add all the ingredients into a mixing tin.
Shake or stir the contents without ice until honey dissolves.
Add crushed ice, cover and shake vigorously for 15 seconds.
Strain into a chilled martini glass.
Top with a dash of soda water.
Garnish with a sprig of parsley.

**White Lady**

- 1 ½ oz No. 209 Gin
- ½ oz lemon juice
- ½ oz Cointreau
- 1 barspoon simple syrup
- 1 egg white

Shake vigorously with ice until frothy white.
Strain and serve in a cocktail glass.
Garnish with lime wheel.

Distillery No. 209
San Francisco, California

22

# Essential Spirits Alambic Distillery

Dave Classick Sr., Owner / Master Distiller
Andrea Mirenda, Owner / President
Dave Classick Jr., Distiller / ITO
Audrey Classick, Brand Ambassador

144 A&B, South Whisman Road
Mountain View, California 94041

*Phone:* 650-962-0546
*Fax:* 650-962-0653
*Email:* service@essentialspirits.com
*Website:* www.essentialspirits.com
*Facebook:* Sgt. Classick Hawaiian Rum
*Twitter:* @sgtclassick

*Region:* Northern California

*Type:* Micro-distillery producing approximately 25,000 cases per year

*Opened:* 1998

*Hours of operation:*
January to November – Monday through Friday, 10:00am to 7:00pm
December – Closed

*Tours:* Tours are offered for groups of 5 or more people for a fee.

*Types of spirits produced:*
Hawaiian rum, gin, grappa, pear eau-de-vie, and vodka

*Names of spirits:*
House Brands
- Sergeant Classick Hawaiian Rum (Silver and Gold)
- Classick Grappa di Cabernet - Stags Leap
- Classick Pure Pear Eau-de-Vie

Contract Brands
- DH Krahn Gin
- Hana Gin
- Ice Fox Vodka
- Island Rum (Silver and Gold)
- Hula Girl RTD Cocktails
- U4RIK Grape based Vodka
- Del Dotto Estates - Howell Mountain Grappa de Cabernet
- Vino Robles Grappa de Petite Syrah

*Best known for:*
Sgt. Classick Rumadillo (rum and tonic with fresh lime) and the Classick Lime Ricky

*Average bottle price:* $20.00 to $38.00

*Distribution:*
Rum is distributed in California, Washington, New York and Florida, while grappa and pear eau de vie are sold direct from the distillery.

*Awards and Recognitions:*

**Sergeant Classick Gold Hawaiian Rum**
- Nominated for Golden Rum Barrel Award 2010 Best Rum in North America
- Best In Class, 2009 New York Spirits Awards
- Gold Medal 94 Pts. "Exceptional" 2008 BTI
- Unanimous Double Gold Medal, 2008 San Francisco Spirits Competition

**Classick Pure Pear Eau-de-Vie**
- Gold Medal 92 Pts., 2007 BTI

**Classick - The Original American Bierschnaps**
- Gold Medal 91 Pts. "Exceptional" BTI
- 4 Stars F. Paul Pacult's Spirit Journal

**DH Krahn Gin**
- Gold Medal, Best Gin in America, 2009 BTI
- Gold Medal, Best Gin in America, 2006 BTI

*Highlighted spirits:*

**Sergeant Classick Gold Hawaiian Rum**
This spirit is made from 100% Hawaiian molasses and crafted in the traditional manner of fine rum makers the world over. Each batch is hand-distilled and gathered in pails a few drops at a time. At first sip you are met by unsweetened cocoa, dried cherry and new suede followed by a crème brulée crust and dark roasted spice nuts. It finishes with singed cane stalk and a peppery spice fade. Prolonged exposure to oak provides it with a medium-bodied character reminiscent of rums that have been aged for 3 to 5 years.

**Sergeant Classick Silver Hawaiian Rum**
While the silver rum is more neutral than the gold, it is by no means less complex. The distinct aromas of honey and milk chocolate find your nose first, and a hint of almost burnt caramel lingers. A cool beginning in the mouth warms slowly as the spirit moves toward the back of the palate, and you're left with the taste of a raw sugar cube or a lightly toasted marshmallow. While the liquid may be clear, it is delightfully spicy and surprisingly deep.

*About:*

Founders R. David Classick and Andrea M. Mirenda established Essential Spirits Alambic Distillery in the heart of Silicon Valley in 1998 to bring a bit of old world European quality spirits to high-tech society.

Classick and Mirenda traveled frequently in Europe and had seen many distilleries in operation. Living in one of the world's greatest fruit and wine producing areas, they realized that the tertiary industry of distilling was virtually non-existent in California. With coffee rotisseries and microbreweries on the rise, they felt the concept could be applied to spirits. They coined the term micro-distillery to describe what they intended and, with little hesitation, got started.

Using a custom built, state of the art alambic pot still from Bordeaux, France, fruit, wines, pomace, and brews are transformed into exceptionally fine spirits. After 10 years in the industry, Essential Spirits is proud to have earned the reputation for producing a spirit that, even directly off the still (at 160+ proof), has the taste and mouthfeel of a spirit that has been aged for years.

*Management profile:*

**Dave Classick Sr.** – Owner and Master Distiller
Dave (left) is a decorated veteran of the Vietnam War and a longtime resident of Mountain View, California. As owner and head of production, Dave's European training in distilling brings artistry and efficiency to his skills. His uncompromising commitment to quality guides him in a constant effort to refine the products of Essential Spirits.

**Andrea Mirenda** – Owner and President
Andrea, a lifelong resident of Mountain View, California, helps to run the business side of the operation and occasionally shares in the distilling responsibilities. With over 20 years of experience in high-tech sales and marketing, she brings the skills and creativity needed to introduce Essential Spirits' unique products to the North American market.

**Dave Classick Jr.** – Distiller and Information Technology Officer
Dave Jr. has followed in his parents' distilling footsteps. With his extensive IT background and passion for distilling, he brings not only a high-tech edge to the company but also hope for future generations in the family business, a first step in creating a dynasty, and the shared hope that distilling will run in the family for generations.

*Management profile:*
**Audrey Classick** – Brand Ambassador
Audrey studied cultural anthropology and uses her critical and analytical thinking skills as well as her enthusiasm for travel to introduce their line of spirits to diverse domestic and international markets. Being the youngest member of the family, she developed a relationship with the still through cleaning and maintenance; as a result, she shares a passion for the craft of artisan distilling.

*Professional associations:*  American Distilling Institute

*Suggested recipes:*
**Rumadillo**
- 1.5 - 2 oz Sgt. Classick Gold Rum
- 2 quartered lime wedges
- Tonic to fill

    Squeeze lime wedges in bottom of glass and add Sgt. Classick Gold Rum.
    Fill glass with ice and top with tonic water.
    * optional: Rim glass with additional lime garnish.

**Sgt. Classick Bronze Star**
- 1 oz Sgt. Classick Hawaiian Gold Rum
- 1 oz fresh lemon juice
- ½ oz Depaz dark cane syrup
- ½ oz fresh lime juice
- ½ oz fresh orange juice
- ½ oz pomegranate juice
- 1 dash Regan's Orange Bitters No. 6
- 4 whole dried star anise

    Shake all ingredients, except the pomegranate juice, vigorously over ice for approximately 15 seconds and strain into a low ball glass or tiki mug.
    Add enough freshly crushed ice until the glass or mug is nearly full.
    Pour ½ oz chilled pomegranate juice on top.
    Garnish with 1 small mint sprig, 1 star anise, and 2 small straws.

Essential Spirits Alambic Distillery
Mountain View, California

## Germain-Robin

Ansley Coale, President
Joe Corley, Distiller

1110 Bel Arbres Road
Redwood Valley, California  95470

*Phone:*  707-468-7899
*Fax:*  707-462-8103
*Email:*  alambic@pacific.net
*Website:*  www.craftdistillers.com
*Facebook:*  Craft Distillers

**craft distillers®**

pure, beautifully made spirits

*Region:*  California

*Type*:  Micro-distillery producing approximately 9,600 gallons annually

*Opened:*  1982

*Hours of operation:*  Monday through Friday, 9:00am to 5:00pm

*Tours:*  Tours are not available.

*Types of spirits produced:*  Absinthe, apple brandy, brandy, grappa, and liqueurs

*Names of spirits:*
- Germain-Robin Brandy
- Germain-Robin Apple Brandy
- Germain-Robin Grappa
- Germain-Robin Créme de Poète Liqueur
- Germain-Robin Absinthe Superieure

*Best known for:*  Grape Brandy

*Average bottle price*:  $48.00 to $350.00

*Distribution:*  Available at the distillery and retail locations nationwide

*Awards and Recognitions:*
**Select Barrel XO**
- Best Liquor In The World, 1996 Robb Report
- Best Liquor In The World, 1998 Robb Report
- 5-star review by F. Paul Pacult's Spirit Journal

**Anno Domini**
- Best Liquor In The World, 2000 Robb Report
- 5-star reviews by Paul Pacult's Spirit Journal

**Grape Brandy**
- Best on Planet, Spirits and Cocktail Magazine

*Highlighted spirits:*
**Select Barrel XO**
Only ten barrels of Select Barrel XO are produced each year. Full-bodied and complex, this cognac is comparable to $200 cognacs.

### Anno Domini
This aged pinot noir is brilliant and soft, with a creamy sherry note from a palomino component. Three different consumer magazines have named it the best pinot noir there is. Only 300 bottles of Anno Domini are produced annually.

### Single-Barrel Varietal Brandies
Each bottle is from one barrel of a single-varietal brandy chosen for its superb and distinctive quality. This brilliant brandy is intensely focused and amazingly pure.

### Apple Brandy
This brandy uses delicately distilled Anderson Valley apples including Sierra Beauty, Ben Davis, and Jonathon, creating lovely soft aromatics and long-lasting flavor. It is not widely available.

### Créme de Poète
Hubert worked on this liqueur for 16 years. Over the years, little by little, Hubert blended in tiny amounts of dried and fresh fruit, nuts, and even sandalwood.

*Services offered other than production:* Tasting room by appointment, call 707-468-7899

*Interesting facts:*
- Hubert Germain-Robin was the first known distiller to use wines from world-class varietal grapes.

*About:*
Hubert Germain-Robin (right) grew up in the business. His family owned a cognac firm, Jules Robin. When the family cognac firm was bought out by Martell Cognac, Hubert looked for a way to go back to the hand methods that had made cognac great as opposed to modern cognac stills that are built to run semi-automatically. Following a chance 1981 meeting with Ansley Coale, Hubert took an antique still from an abandoned distillery near Cognac and brought it to Coale's Mendocino County ranch where the two men built a modest distillery.

Hubert used the old still to return to ancient craft methods that had been passed for centuries from master to apprentice; however he broke with

tradition by experimenting with distillation wines made from premium wine grapes. The grapes used in Cognac, grown in that region's damp, cool weather, produce thin, relatively flavorless wines not fit for drinking. Hubert reasoned that the rich, complex, and deeply fruited grapes used to make Northern California's renowned table wines would produce correspondingly rich, complex, and deeply fruited brandies.

Hubert astonished the world of spirits when his alambic (cognac-style) brandies were released. In 1988, in a series of expert blind tastings, Germain-Robin VSOP-level brandy outscored Delamain Pale & Dry, Martell Cordon Bleu, Remy Martin VSOP and other well-known cognacs.

By the late 1990s, when Hubert's cellar had matured, his brandies began to be ranked among the world's finest spirits. The brandies are amazingly smooth, soft, and delicate, yet they are as complex and rich tasting as the finest cognacs.

*Future business plans and goals:* To keep getting better

*Suggested recipe:*
**Sazerac**
- 1 oz craft-method brandy
- 1 oz rye whiskey
- ¼ simple syrup
- 4 dashes Peychaud's
- Absinthe rinse
- Lemon peel garnish

Germain-Robin
Redwood Valley, California

# Napa Valley Distillery

Arthur and Lusine Hartunian, Owners / Operators

*Physical Address:*
225 Walnut Street
Napa, California 94558

*Mailing Address:*
4225 Solano #596
Napa, California 94559

*Phone:* 707-259-5411
*Fax:* 707-637-8270
*Email:* sales@napavodka.com
*Website:* www.napavodka.com
*Facebook:* Napa Valley Limoncello
*Twitter:* @NapaVodka

*Region:* Napa Valley, California

*Type:* Micro-distillery producing approximately 5,000 gallons per year

*Opened:* August 17, 2009

*Hours of operation:* Monday through Friday, 9:00am to 5:00pm

*Tours:* Tours are not available.

*Types of spirits produced:*
Brandy, vodka, whiskey, and a variety of liqueurs
Also produced are some private label spirits

*Names of spirits:*
- Napa Vodka
- Napa Brandy
- Napa Liqueur
- Napa California Cowboy Whiskey

*Best known for:* Japanese James Bond
Served at Iron Chef Morimoto's restaurant in Napa, CA

*Average bottle price*: $30.00

*Distribution:*
Available in California, Nevada, Louisiana, Wisconsin, Tennessee, Florida, Maryland, Washington DC, Illinois, Alberta, Canada, Montreal, Canada, Denmark, China, Hong Kong, Singapore, and South Africa

*Awards and Recognitions:*
- Gold Medal, 2011 World Spirits Competition
- Gold Medal, 2011 SIP Awards
- Bronze Medal, 2011 Hong Kong Wine and Spirits Competition
- Silver Medal, 2011 China Sommeliers Challenge
- Gold Medal, 2011 MicroLiquor Awards
- Rated 93 Highly Recommended, 2011 Wine Enthusiast Magazine
- Best Artisanal Vodka, 2011 Cooking Light Magazine Taste Test Awards
- Perfect "10" rating from Spirits Review

**Napa Vodka Vintage Reserve**
- Named one of the Top 50 Spirits in the World by Wine Enthusiast Magazine

*Highlighted spirits:*
**Napa Vodka**
This is the world's first known "vintage vodka," handcrafted entirely from premium Napa Valley Sauvignon Blanc from a single vintage and a single Napa Valley Estate.

**Napa Liqueur**
This is liqueur made from organic Meyer lemons using an Old World traditional recipe.

*About:*
Husband and wife team Arthur and Lusine Hartunian established Napa Valley Distillery in 2009 because of their creative desire to make spirits with ingredients that reflected their geographic location but had never been used before. Deciding to take their hobby of home liqueur and brandy making into a business, the Hartunians began creating premium vodka and brandy on a very small scale using premium, non-traditional ingredients. Their spirits have a unique flavor profile that cannot be found elsewhere. Aside from his duties of running Napa Valley Distillery, co-owner Arthur Hartunian is also an accomplished poker player who, in between bottling world-class spirits, can often be found playing in high-stakes cash games in Nevada and California.

*Professional associations:* American Distilling Institute and DISCUS

*Future business plans and goals:* To relocate to a larger facility in downtown Napa and open a tasting room and sales facility which will also house a small art gallery showcasing local art

*Suggested recipe:*
**Golden Cello**
- 1½ oz of Napa Liqueur
- 1½ oz of premium vodka
- ½ oz of premium brandy
- Dark chocolate

    Combine Napa Liqueur, vodka and brandy in a shaker with ice.
    Shake until cold and then strain into a martini glass.
    Top with shaved dark chocolate.

Napa Valley Distillery
Napa, California

# Old World Spirits LLC

Davorin Kuchan, President

121 Industrial Road #3-4
Belmont, California 94002

*Phone:* 650-622-9222
*Fax:* 717-924-1888
*Email:* info@oldworldspirits.com
*Website:* www.oldworldspirits.com
*Facebook:* Old World Spirits, LLC
*Twitter:* @oldworldspirits
*YouTube:* Old World Spirits Product Feature
*Yelp:* Old World Spirits
*foursquare:* OldWorldSpirits

*Region:* Northern California

*Type*: Micro-distillery producing under 50,000 gallons annually

*Opened:* 2008

*Hours of operation:* Monday through Saturday, 9:00am to 5:00pm

*Tours:* Tours are conducted on the last Friday of the month and by appointment.

*Types of spirits produced:* Whiskey, gin, absinthe, liqueurs, brandies, bitters

*Names of spirits:*
- Kuchan Eaux De Vie
    - Poire Williams
    - Indian Blood Peach
    - O'Henry Oak Aged Peach
- Kuchan Nocino Black Walnut Liqueur
- La Sorciere Absinthe Verte and Bleue
- Blade California Small Batch Gin
- Rusty Blade Barrel Aged Gin
- Kuchan Alambic Brandy
- Goldrun Rye Whiskey

*Best known for:*
Blade Gin, Rusty Blade, La Sorciere Absinthe, Kuchan Nocino and Goldrun 100% Rye Whiskey

*Average bottle price*: $30.00 to $75.00

*Distribution*: Tasting room and more than 300 locations in California, Colorado, Washington, Oregon, Idaho, and Nevada.

32

**Blade Gin**
- Gold Medal, 2011 San Francisco World Spirits Competition
- Gold Medal, 90 Pts. "Exceptional Rating," 2010 Beverage Testing Institute

**La Sorciere Absinthe Verte**
- Gold Medal, 90 Pts. "Exceptional Rating," 2011 Beverage Testing Institute
- Silver Medal, 2010 San Francisco Spirits Competition

**La Sorciere Absinthe Verte**
- Gold Medal, 93 Pts. "Exceptional Rating," 2011 Beverage Testing Institute
- Bronze Medal, 2010 San Francisco Spirits Competition

**Kuchan Indian Blood Peach Eau de Vie**
- Gold Medal, 93 Pts. "Exceptional Rating," 2011 Beverage Testing Institute

*Highlighted spirits:*

**Blade Gin**
This double gold medal winning, California-style fruit forward gin is made from wheat, California alambic brandy, fresh local citrus, ginger, cilantro, cardamom and more.

**Rusty Blade**
Rusty Blade is Blade Gin aged in select French oak barrels. It rivals the finest cognac, single malt scotch and whiskey products.

**Kuchan Alambic Brandy**
This California zinfandel is a double-distilled brandy aged in French oak and bourbon casks. It rivals the finest brandies.

**Kuchan Liqueurs**
The flagship liqueur is Kuchan Nocino, which is black walnut liqueur made from local green walnuts crushed whole, aged on California alambic brandy, and sweetened with organic tapioca.

**La Sorciere Absinthe Verte and Bleue**
This ultra-premium, pre-ban absinthe, is double-distilled alambic brandy and a dozen fine natural herbs with no coloring, sugar, or extracts added. There are two versions of this absinthe, Verte and Bleue, whose recipe is adapted from a family Croatian wormwood liqueur pelinkovac.

## Goldrun 100% Rye

Goldrun Rye is a 100% organic rye whiskey, uniquely mashed, fermented and distilled like an eau de vie. It is rich and smooth with hints of warm, freshly baked rye bread, meadow blossoms, earthly holiday spice and golden raisins.

## Kuchan Eaux De Vie

Kuchan Eaux De Vie are California brandies made from fine noble fruit.

*Events and Celebrations:* Tastings, tours, private parties, and monthly "Friday Flights"

*Interesting facts:*
- First known U.S. distillery to release "blanche" clear style absinthe and Rusty Blade Barrel Aged Gin

*About:*
Old World Spirits / Kuchan Cellars is a San Francisco Bay

artisanal distillery and winery started by Davorin Kuchan, a Croatian-born third generation winemaker and master distiller. A Silicon Valley veteran and a U.C. Berkeley Haas graduate, Kuchan grew up around family vineyards and later studied distillation at Michigan State under Dr. Kris Berglund, one of the driving forces behind the craft distillation revolution in the United States. Old World Spirit is a family legacy and is organically certified. Kuchan and his family use a combination of their own and German manufactured distillation equipment to create world class artisanal spirits.

*Future business plans and goals:* Broaden distribution

*Suggested recipe:*

## Rusty Nutcracker
- 1 oz Rusty Blade Barrel Aged Gin
- 1 oz Kuchan Black Walnut Nocino
- 4-6 drops of orange bitters

Stir for 15-20 seconds on ice.
Strain into chilled glass.
Add orange zest on top.
Garnish with orange peel.

Old World Spirits LLC
Belmont, California

34

# St. George Spirits

Lance Winters,
Owner and Master Distiller

2601 Monarch Street
Alameda, California 94501

*Phone:* 510-769-1601
*Fax:* 510-769-1666
*Email:* info@stgeorgespirits.com
        tastingroom@stgeorgespirits.com
*Website:* www.stgeorgespirits.com
*Facebook:* St. George Spirits
*Twitter:* @StGeorgeSpirits
*Flickr:* St. George Spirits
*YouTube:* St. George Spirits
*Yelp:* St. George Spirits Alameda

*Region:* California, Northwestern U.S.

*Type:* Micro-distillery

*Opened:* 1982

*Hours of operation:*
The tasting room and on-site store are open to the public year-round Wednesday through Saturday from 12:00pm to 7:00pm and Sunday 12:00pm to 5:00pm.

*Tours:*
St. George Spirits offers free educational tours year-round, Saturday at 1:00pm, 2:00pm, and 3:00pm, and on Sunday at 1:00pm. Guides lead groups around the production area of the distillery while discussing topics ranging from company history and basic distillation to bottling and barrel aging.

*Types of spirits produced:* Eaux de vie, fruit liqueurs, single malt whiskey, absinthe, agave spirit ("American tequila"), rum, vodka, tea liqueur, coffee liqueur, gin, and bourbon

*Names of spirits:*
- Aqua Perfecta (eaux de vie and fruit liqueurs)
- St. George Single Malt Whiskey
- St. George Absinthe Verte
- Agua Azul (agave spirit)
- Agua Libre Rum
- Hangar One Vodka
- Firelit Coffee Liqueur
- Qi (tea liqueur)

*Names of spirits:*
- Breaking & Entering Bourbon
- St. George Botanivore Gin
- St. George Terroir Gin
- St. George Dry Rye Gin

*Best known for:* St. George Absinthe Verte

*Average bottle price:* $20.00 to $80.00

*Distribution:* Nationwide and at on-site store

*Awards and Recognitions:*

**Aqua Perfecta Pear Eau de Vie**
- Winner, 1996 Destillata blind tasting

**Aqua Perfecta Kirsch**
- Wine Enthusiast Top 50 Spirits

**Agua Libre Fresh-Squeezed Rum**
- Gold medal, 2010 Ministry of Rum tasting competition

**Agua Libre Aged Rum**
- Silver medal, 2010 Ministry of Rum tasting competition

**St. George Gins (Terroir, Botanivore, and Dry Rye Gin)**
- Esquire Best Bottles of 2011

**Qi White Tea Liqueur**
- Wine Enthusiast Top 50 Spirits

*Highlighted spirits:*

**Aqua Perfecta Pear Eau de Vie**

St. George Spirits carefully shepherds the finest ripe Bartlett pears it can find through the distillation process to make a spirit with a deep, buttery pear flavor and a touch of spice. No sugar or artificial ingredients are added, so all you get is the pure essence of the raw

material. At 40% alcohol and with no residual sugar, this aromatic spirit makes an excellent digestif when sipped on its own and enhances any cocktail.

**St. George Single Malt Whiskey**

Distiller Lance Winters released his first bottle of St. George Single Malt Whiskey in 2000, making this one of the oldest artisanally made American whiskeys on the market today. Each batch is blended from French oak, bourbon, and port barrels, resulting in a smooth and soft sipping whiskey with notes of cocoa, vanilla, and hazelnut.

**St. George Absinthe Verte**

St. George Absinthe Verte was the first domestically produced absinthe to be released since the U.S. lifted its century-long ban on absinthe. St. George Absinthe's complex flavor and lush mouthfeel are derived from wormwood, star anise, and fennel, along with many other choice botanicals.

## St. George Gins

St. George Spirits released three new gins in 2011: Terroir, Botanivore, and Dry Rye Gin. **Terroir Gin** is distiller Lance Winters' ode to the wild beauty of the Golden State—inspired by the aromas of the coastal forests of California's Mount Tam. Douglas fir and California Bay laurel notes take the lead in creating a spirit that smells and tastes like the woods that inspired it. **Botanivore Gin**, the "botanical eater," earned its name because it's made from 20 different botanicals working in concert. Botanivore is elegant and fresh, delightful in a Gin & Tonic and all you need for a perfect martini. **Dry Rye Gin** gets its warm, malty notes from a base of 100% pot-distilled rye. Black peppercorn and caraway play up the piquant characteristics of the juniper berry, making this an intriguing and genre busting gin.

*Events and Celebrations:*
St. George Spirits hosts private cocktail parties in its tasting room for groups of 40–75 people. Additionally, it hosts two-hour cocktail education classes for groups of 10–40 people. In these classes, guests are able to taste a variety of spirits and learn how to make some of St. George Spirits' favorite cocktails.

*Services offered other than production:*
Tasting room, cocktail education classes, on-site store, hot dog stand

*Interesting facts:*
- St. George Spirits is housed in a 65,000 square foot airplane hangar on the former Alameda Naval Air Station.

*About:*
Established in 1982 by Jörg Rupf, St. George Spirits has been deemed "iconic" by F. Paul Pacult's Spirit Journal and "a leading light in the American artisanal spirits movement" by Malt Advocate. Over three decades at the vanguard of the American craft spirits revolution, St. George has earned respect and critical acclaim in the industry for creating the Hangar One line of vodkas and maintaining a portfolio of distinctive and award-winning spirits that includes Aqua Perfecta eaux de vie and liqueurs; St. George Single Malt Whiskey; St. George Absinthe Verte; Agua Libre Rum; Agua Azul; Breaking & Entering Bourbon; and Terroir, Botanivore, and Dry Rye Gin.

Located on the island of Alameda, St. George Spirits is housed in a 65,000 square foot airplane hangar on the former Alameda Naval Air Station. Because it's situated at the edge of the base with an uninterrupted westward view of San Francisco, the distillery has a frontier, edge-of-the-world feel. With many historical features persevered, the building is a masterpiece of mid-century industrial architecture.

Because of its location, nobody ends up at St. George Spirits by accident. Most people find it by word of mouth from friends who have visited it in the past, or because they've read about its products and want to try them firsthand. St. George Spirit guests come from far and wide to learn about artisanal distillation and to taste great spirits.

*Professional associations:* DISCUS

*Future business plans and goals:* St. George Spirits plans to continue making the quality spirits in its existing product line and plans to expand its rum/sugarcane distillates in the future.

*Suggested recipes:*
**The Root of All Evil**
- 1 oz St. George Absinthe Verte
- 2 oz root beer

    Add ice to rocks glass.
    Pour in St. George Absinthe Verte and root beer.

**Bobby Burns** - Christ Aivaliotis and Lucia Gonzales, Flora, Oakland, CA
- 1 ½ oz St. George Single Malt Whiskey
- 1 ½ oz sweet vermouth
- Dash of Benedictine

    Stir all ingredients with ice.
    Strain and pour into chilled cocktail glass.
    Garnish with flamed orange peel.

St. George Spirits
Alameda, California

# Tahoe Moonshine Distillery Inc.

Jeffrey VanHee, Owner and Master Distiller

1611 Shop Street #4B
South Lake Tahoe, California  96150

*Phone:*  530-416-0313
*Email:*  jeffrey@tahoemoonshine.com
*Website:*  www.tahoemoonshine.com
*Facebook:*  Tahoe Moonshine Distillery

*Region:*  East Central California

*Type:*  Micro-distillery

*Opened:*   2010

*Types of spirits produced:*  Whiskey, gin, rum, vodka, and coffee liqueur

*Names of spirits:*
- Stormin' Whiskey
- Jagged Peaks Gin
- California Dreamin' Rum
- Jug Dealer Rum
- Snowflake Vodka
- Dream Bean Coffee Liqueur
- VanHees' Mean Irish Cream
- Hot Stinkin' Garlic Vodka
- Peanut Butter Vodka

*Average bottle price:*   $23.00

*Distribution:*

Nevada distribution is handled by Encore Beverage; California distribution is handled by DBI.

*Highlighted spirits:*
## Jagged Peaks Gin
Jagged Peaks Gin is a smooth blend of natural botanicals, creating a fine balance from the rugged mountains of the juniper berry to the smooth finish of vine ripened cucumber. The ingredients consist of juniper berry, cardamom, coriander, rose petals, ginger, and cucumber.

*Highlighted spirits:*

## California Dreamin' Rum

California Dreamin' Rum is created from Costa Rican sucanat, fermented from the finest yeast and then distilled through an old pot-style still. This brings into the spirit all the sugarcane flavors you would expect from the highest quality rum.

## Jug Dealer Rum

The base of this spirit is California Dreamin' Rum. It's aged in a #4 charred oak barrel with vanilla beans and crushed macadamia nuts.

## Stormin' Whiskey

Stormin' Whiskey is a GMO free, young straight corn whiskey. It is aged in used Canadian whiskey barrels that have been cleaned and re-charred. It is smooth on the pallet with big flavors of buttery corn and oak.

## Snowflake Vodka

Snowflake Vodka starts with California wild flower honey. It is then fermented with sweet mead yeast and distilled to 190 proof. The honey flavor is very apparent.

*About:*

Tahoe Moonshine Distillery's home is in the heart of the Sierra Nevada Mountains on the Cali side of Lake Tahoe. Located at 6,200 feet, a unique blend of quality ingredients and high altitude adds a special taste to the experience found in each bottle. Lake Tahoe's majestic peaks, crystal clear water and blue skies create the passion for life that fuels the spirits of Tahoe Moonshine.

*Future business plans and goals:* Expansion and earn awards

*Suggested recipe:*

## Peanut Butter Martini

- Godiva Chocolate Liqueur
- Tahoe Moonshine Distillery Peanut Butter Vodka
- Rice milk or regular milk

Shaken, not stirred.

Tahoe Moonshine Distillery Inc.
South Lake Tahoe, California

## Treasure Island Distillery

Owned and operated by the William Smith family

990 13th Street
San Francisco, California 94130

*Phone:* 415-935-7989
*Email:* william@sfvodka.com
*Website:* www.sfvodka.com
*Facebook:* SFVodka
*Twitter:* @SFVodka

*Region:* Northern California

*Type:* Micro-distillery producing and selling approximately 55 gallons per month

*Opened:* July 2009

*Hours of operation:* Monday through Saturday, 9:00am to 6:00pm

*Tours:* Not currently open to the public

*Types of spirits produced:* Vodkas made from corn, grapes, and cane

*Names of spirits:*
- China Beach San Francisco Vodka
- Ocean Beach San Francisco Vodka
- Baker Beach San Francisco Vodka

*Best known for:* China Beach San Francisco Vodka

*Average bottle price:* $35.00

*Distribution:*
San Francisco Bay Area restaurants, bars, clubs, local fine spirit retailers and some online stores. A list of locations is available on the website.

*Awards and Recognitions:*
**San Francisco China Beach Vodka**
- Double Gold Medal, 2010 San Francisco World Spirits Competition

*Highlighted spirits:*
**China Beach San Francisco Vodka**
China Beach Vodka is made from a proprietary blend of California grapes and crystal clear snowmelt from the Sierra Nevada Mountains. This blend was designed to capture the essence of the fruit while maintaining a well-balanced, clean vodka. The fruit is squeezed, and the juice is fermented just like a wine and distilled to around 192 proof.

**Baker Beach San Francisco Vodka**

Baker Beach Vodka is made from corn and crystal clear snowmelt from high in the Sierra Nevada Mountains. Corn produces a very clean wash that makes a neutral tasting but sweet vodka that's worth the extra effort. Because only corn is used, Baker Beach Vodka is gluten free.

**Ocean Beach San Francisco Vodka**

Ocean Beach Vodka is made from sugar cane and crystal clear Sierra Nevada snowmelt. Cane produces a naturally sweet vodka. This vodka is crisp like a cold ocean breeze, and bright like a beach bonfire.

*Events and Celebrations:*

Treasure Island Distillery frequently sponsors benefits for the humanities and world conservation. Additionally, it participates in locally based events geared toward its ideals and targeted demographics.

*Interesting facts:*

- Treasure Island Distillery operates out of the old Navy brig on Treasure Island in San Francisco. The space consists of the solitary confinement cells, intake and processing areas, the guard's room, the infirmary, and one of the two exercise yards.

*About:*

The William Smith family started making beer and wine many years ago as a hobby and also had a keen interest in distilling. In 2004, family members started to explore the craft of distilling in more depth, and they quickly discovered a few micro-distilleries beginning to emerge. After a couple of years of intense investigation and planning, the family's idea of creating its own distilling business flourished to active planning and implementation. The production of Baker Beach Vodka began in July of 2009, followed by Ocean Beach and China Beach Vodkas in later months.

*Future business plans and goals:* Expanded product line

Suggested recipe:

**Ginger Mist**

- 2 oz San Francisco Vodka
- 1½ oz ginger ale
- 1 tsp of ginger simple syrup
- A dash of lime juice
- Lime garnish

Add vodka, ginger ale, simple syrup, and lime juice to a glass of ice.
Garnish with lime slice and slice of ginger.
Serve in double old fashioned glass.

Treasure Island Distillery
San Francisco, California

# Valley Spirits LLC

Lee Palleschi, Proprietor

*Physical address:*
553 Mariposa Road, Suite #1, Modesto, California  95354

*Mailing address:*
P.O. Box 1141, Modesto, California  95354

*Phone:*  209-484-0311
*Fax:*  209-572-1951
*Email:*  masterdistiller@drinkvalleyspirits.com
*Website:*  www.drinkvalleyspirits.com
*Facebook:*  Cold House Vodka

*Region:*  California

*Type:*  Micro-distillery producing approximately 1,200 gallons annually

*Opened:*  June 2010

*Hours of operation:*  8:00am to 5:00pm

*Tours:*  Tours are available.

*Types of spirits produced:*  Vodka, moonshine, and whiskey

*Names of spirits:*
- Cold House Vodka
- Moonshine Bandits Outlaw Moonshine
- Prohibition Spirits

*Average bottle price:*  $24.00

*Distribution:*  California, Nevada, and some other states

*Awards and Recognitions:*
**Cold House Vodka**
- Gold Medal, 2011 HotMixology
- Gold Medal, 2011 Beverage Testing Institute

*Highlighted spirits:*
**Cold House Vodka**
Cold House Vodka is made from clean, creamy wheat and spicy American corn.

**Outlaw Moonshine**
Outlaw Moonshine is unaged American wheat whiskey; has a smooth premium whiskey taste without the oak.

*Highlighted spirits:*
**Prohibition Spirits**
Prohibition Spirits is distilled and aged to create one of the best sipping whiskeys.

*Events and Celebrations:* Valley Spirits does host events and celebrations.

*About:*
As a young man, Proprietor Lee Palleschi remembered the days when his dad would make wine. Since then, he has learned to make wine, beer, whiskey, and vodka. He started reading as much as he could about distilling and got better and better at the craft. With the help and support of friends and fellow crafters, Valley Spirits opened to follow his dream of making the highest quality handcrafted spirits possible. While Valley Spirits can't compete with the "big guys" in terms of cost and efficiency, it excels in quality and character of spirits.

*Future business plans and goals:* Continued growth

*Suggested recipe:*
**Cold House Vodka, Lemon Drop Martini**
- 1-1½ oz of Cold House Vodka
- 4 oz of high quality lemonade made from lemons (not concentrate)
- ½ oz quality triple sec
- Add simple syrup to taste

  Shake over ice.
  Serve in a chilled, sugar rimmed Martini glass.
  Squeeze a lemon twist into it and enjoy.

Valley Spirits LLC
Modesto, California

# Ventura Limoncello Company

James Carling, President
Manuela Zaretti-Carling, Vice President

2646 Palma Drive, Suite 160
Ventura, California  93003

*Phone:*  805-658-0881
*Fax:*  805-658-0899
*Email:* General info:  info@venturalimoncello.com
           James Carling:  james@venturalimoncello.com
*Website:*  www.venturalimoncello.com
*Facebook:*  Ventura Limoncello
*Twitter:*  @vlimoncello
*YouTube:*  Ventura Limoncello Channel
*LinkedIn:*  James Carling

*Region:*  Ventura County, California

*Type:*  Micro-distillery producing approximately 2,700 gallons per year

*Opened:*  November 2007

*Hours of operation:*  Monday through Friday, 9:00am to 5:00pm

*Tours:*  By appointment only

*Types of spirits produced:*  Fruit liqueurs

*Names of spirits:*
- Ventura Limoncello Originale
- Ventura Limoncello Crema
- Ventura Orangecello Blood Orange

*Best known for:*
Ventura Limoncello Originale, America's highest rated 4-years in a row.
Limosa cocktail, Ventura Limoncello and prosecco sparkling wine.

*Average bottle price:*
Ventura Limoncello Originale: 750ml, $22 to $28. 375ml, $16 to $18
Ventura Limoncello Crema: 375ml, $17 to $19
Ventura Orangecello Blood Orange: 375ml $17 to $19

*Distribution:*
Stores and restaurants throughout California, Arizona, and Oregon

*Awards and Recognitions:*

**Ventura Limoncello Originale**
- Gold Medal, 2008 San Francisco World Spirits Competition
- Silver Medal, 2009 San Francisco World Spirits Competition
- Platinum Medal, 2010 Los Angeles SIP Awards
- Silver Medal, 2010 San Francisco World Spirits Competition
- Silver Medal, 2010 NY International Spirits Competition
- Gold Medal, 2011 San Francisco World Spirits Competition
- Gold Medal, 2011 MicroLiquor Spirit Awards

**Ventura Limoncello Crema**
- Gold Medal, 2010 LA SIP Awards

**Ventura Orangecello Blood Orange**
- Double Gold Medal Best in Class, 2011 SFWSC

*Highlighted spirits:*

**Ventura Limoncello Originale**

This is a classic lemon liqueur in the manner produced along the Amalfi Coast, Italy. There is full lemon aroma at the initial taste, followed by a nice, sweet middle and a smooth, alcohol finish.

**Ventura Limoncello Crema**

This is a lemon cream liqueur. Think lemon creamsicle in texture and taste. It's very desserty.

**Ventura Orangecello Blood Orange**

Ventura Orangecello liqueur is made from Ventura County grown, seasonal blood oranges. The sharp aroma and "bite" of a blood orange come through in this unique orange liqueur.

*Interesting facts:*
- All citrus used is grown in Ventura County, California.

*About:*

Ventura Limoncello celebrates the rich tradition of Italy while embracing the adventurous style of California living. Like all things Italian, Ventura Limoncello radiates passion and pleasure.

The Ventura Limoncello Company was founded in 2007 by James Carling and Manuela Zaretti-Carling. Their mission is to be the premier producer of all-natural, handcrafted limoncello lemon liqueur and other citrus liqueurs in the United States.

Based in the lemon growing capital of the U.S., Ventura Limoncello follows a 3-generation-old Italian family recipe and uses only locally grown fruit in the protected valleys and rolling hills of Ventura County, California. The fruit is ripened fully in steady sunshine tempered by fresh breezes from the Pacific, and then each piece of fruit is meticulously hand peeled. Hand peeling ensures only the top layer of peel containing the oils is used. This natural process produces aromatic and full flavor liqueurs.

*Professional associations:*
DISCUS, Ventura Chamber of Commerce, Greater Conejo Valley Chamber of Commerce

*Future business plans and goals:*
To identify distributors in additional states who focus on quality artisanal liquor to expand availability, and to continue to utilize the bounty of Ventura County to create additions to its product line.

*Suggested recipes:*
**Limosa**
In a sparkling wine flute, add:
- 1 oz Ventura Limoncello Originale
  Top with prosecco Italian sparkling wine.

**A-pera-tini**
In a shaker with ice, mix:
- 1 part Ventura Limoncello Originale
- 1 part pear vodka
- 2 parts white cranberry juice

  Serve in a martini glass.

**California Lemon Drop**
In a shaker with ice, mix:
- 1 part Ventura Limoncello Originale
- 1 part Hangar One Buddha's Hand Vodka
- Juice of ½ California lemon

  Serve in a martini glass.

**101 Margarita**
In a shaker with ice, mix:
- 1 part Ventura Orangecello Blood Orange
- 1 part Alquimia Reposado Tequila
- 2 parts fresh margarita mix (lime juice, orange juice, agave nectar)

  Serve on the rocks.

Ventura Limoncello Company
Ventura, California

# Breckenridge Distillery

Bryan Nolt, President
Jordan Via, Master Distiller
Jennifer Querbes, Director of Operations
Litch Polich, Head Brand Ambassador

*Physical Address:*
1925 Airport Rd, Breckenridge, CO 80424

*Mailing Address:*
P.O. Box 7399, Breckenridge, CO 80424

*Phone:* 970-547-9759
*Fax:* 970-429-5086
*Email:* Bryan Nolt:  bryan@breckenridgedistillery.com
      Jordan Via:  jordan@breckenridgedistillery.com
      Jennifer Querbes:  jen@breckenridgedistillery.com
      Litch Polich:  litch@breckenridgedistillery.com
*Website:*  www.breckenridgedistillery.com
*Facebook:*  Breckenridge Distillery
*Twitter:*  @breckdistillery

*Region:*  Western Colorado

*Type:*  Micro-distillery producing approximately 12,000 gallons per year

*Opened:*  October 2010

*Hours of operation:*
11:00am to 9:00pm - Main Street Tasting Room (closed Tuesday)
11:00am to 6:00pm - Distillery (closed Monday)

*Tours:*  Tours are available from 11:00am to 6:00pm (closed Monday)

*Types of spirits produced:*
Vodka, bourbon, single malt whiskey, rum, bitters, and various infusions

*Names of spirits:*
- Seasonal Spiced Bourbon
- Turin-Style Bitters
- Wild-Harvested Genepi Liqueur
- Dark Spiced Naval Rum
- Rocky Ford Watermelon Vodka

*Best known for:*  Breckenridge Bourbon

*Average bottle price*:  Bourbon - $40.00, Vodka - $30.00

*Distribution:*
As of October 2011: CO, TX, AR, OK, NY, CT, NJ, NE, ND, SD, IL, AL, VA, WV, MS, MO, MA, GA, FL, IA, RI, CA and NC. Currently only Breckenridge Vodka and Breckenridge Bourbon are for sale outside of Colorado.

*Awards and Recognitions:*
**Breckenridge Bourbon**
- Gold Medal, 2011 International Wine and Spirits Competition
- Silver Medal, 2011 San Francisco World Spirits Competition
- Rated "Top 3 Bourbon in the World," 2011 International Wine and Spirits Competition

**Breckenridge Vodka**
- Bronze Medal, 2011 International Spirits Competition UK

*Highlighted spirits:*
**Breckenridge Bourbon**
There's a deep honey amber hue with warm, pronounced aromas of under-ripe banana and brown sugar, with spicy notes of white pepper and toasted sesame. Breckenridge Bourbon also has a light body with a warm texture and a long sweet oak, vanilla finish with a touch of bitterness to balance. It's reminiscent of a slice of toasted rye bread with honey drizzled on it.

**Breckenridge Vodka**
This vodka is clean and brilliantly clear with mild notes of lemon cream and fragrant meadow flowers. It has a light body with a soft, warm texture and a balanced mellow finish displaying just a hint of sweetness. Minerality of the snowmelt lends to the perfect mouthfeel.

*Services offered other than production:* Tastings

*Interesting facts:*
- World's highest distillery

*About:*
Breckenridge Distillery is located 9,600 feet above sea level at the base of Peak 8 in the ski town of Breckenridge, Colorado. Under the direction of renowned master distiller and American Distilling Institute course instructor Jordan Via, Breckenridge Distillery crafts award-winning spirits with glacier and snowmelt water of America's Rocky Mountains. Fermentations are performed in traditional open top Scottish-style fermenters and the spirits are distilled using a custom-built 500 gallon Vendome copper-pot still.

Breckenridge Distillery is focused on crafting spirits with native water to preserve natural mineral notes and mouthfeel without additives, establishing a unique terroir for American spirits.

Distilling at Breckenridge is certainly unique. The lower pressure at higher elevation puts less stress on the yeast, while water boiling at a lower temperature simply uses less energy. Additionally, the extra-cold water that comes in from the tap allows the condensation process to go faster.

*Management profile:*
**Jordan Via**
Jordan Via is a former Napa Valley winemaker and a renowned master distiller that has created numerous gold medal products. He holds a Diploma of Wine and Spirits and is a course instructor for the American Distilling Institute.

*Professional associations:* American Distilling Institute and Colorado Distillers Guild

*Future business plans and goals:* New product development and expanded distribution

Breckenridge Distillery
Breckenridge, Colorado

# Colorado Gold Distillery

Tom and Pam Cooper, Owners

1290 S. Grand Mesa Drive
Cedaredge, Colorado 81413

*Phone:* 970-856-2600
*Fax:* 970-856-7900
*Email:* coop2@sopris.net
*Website:* www.coloradogolddistillers.com

*Region:* West-Central Colorado

*Type:* Micro-distillery producing 100-150 cases per month

*Opened:* 2007

*Hours of operation:* Monday through Saturday, 10:00am to 4:00pm

*Tours:* Tours are available.

*Types of spirits produced:*
Agave spirits, corn whiskey, premium gin, premium vodka, straight bourbon whiskey, and brandy

*Names of spirits:*
- Colorado Gold Premium Gin
- Colorado Gold Premium Vodka
- Colorado Gold's Own Agave Spirits
- Colorado's Own Corn Whiskey
- Colorado Gold Straight Bourbon Whiskey

*Average bottle price:* $25.00 to $60.00

*Distribution:* On-site retail store and in Texas, New Mexico, Arizona, California, Oregon, Connecticut, and Louisiana.

*Awards and Recognitions:*
**Colorado's Own Corn Whiskey**
- Bronze Medal, 2010 American Distilling Institute

**Colorado Gold Straight Bourbon Whiskey**
- Fourth Place Medal, 2010 American Distilling Institute

**Colorado Gold Premium Vodka**
- Silver Medal, 2008 Beverage Testing Institute

51

*Highlighted spirits:*

**Colorado Gold Premium Gin**

Colorado Gold Distillery uses a unique recipe of a blend of eight different herbs and orange rind giving Colorado Gold Premium Gin an aromatic and delightful, refreshing taste that appeals to both the nose and the palate. The gin is distilled using the finest locally grown grains available. Additionally, there is a distinct and flavorful taste that comes from Colorado's high mountain pure spring water.

**Colorado Gold Premium Vodka**

Colorado Gold Premium Vodka is distilled from 100% pure and locally grown grains, fermented under a controlled process, transferred into a German manufactured, state of the art 16 plate rectifying still, and distilled to only the highest quality and standards.

**Colorado Gold's Own Agave Spirits "Reposado"**

Colorado Gold's Own Agave Spirits is processed and distilled from 100% pure blue agave imported from Mexico and blended with pure Rocky Mountain spring fed water. Agave Spirits is produced "del modo Mexicano" or "in the Mexican Way" and is sold in the distillery retail store.

*Services offered other than production:*
Tastings and a gift shop

*About:*

Tom and Pam Cooper started Colorado Gold Distillery in September 2007 with the goal of producing bourbon. Bourbon is a two-year aging project, though, and the Coopers needed an immediate profit. In March of 2008, the Coopers began their first production run of their Premium Vodka and, by the end of the month, it quickly became a local favorite. Colorado Gold then put up its first two barrels of bourbon from the two-year aging process on April 15, 2000, and another two barrels in September.

In the fall of 2008, Colorado Gold produced its first bottles of Corn Whiskey. It immediately became so popular that production could barely keep up with demand. The intent was to sell it only in the distillery's retail store, but liquor stores were requesting it and it became an all-around top seller.

Premium Gin was introduced in the fall of 2008 and sold in the distillery's retail store. In October of 2009, Colorado Gold bottled its Agave Spirits and sold it in the distillery's retail store. On April 15, 2010, the long awaited first two barrels of single barrel bourbon were bottled; the first barrel was nearly sold out before it was ever bottled or tasted. Each pre-sold bottle of the first bourbon to be produced at the distillery was numbered, signed, and dated.

The latest product, brandy, was barreled in October of 2010 and sold in the distillery's store.

*Professional associations:* American Distilling Institute and Colorado Distillers Guild

*Future business plans and goals:* Expand distribution

Colorado Gold Distillery
Cedaredge, Colorado

# Downslope Distilling

Andrew Causey, Owner
Mitch Abate, Owner

6770 S. Dawson Circle
Centennial, Colorado  80122

*Phone:*  303-693-4300
*Fax:*  303-693-4302
*Email:*  General info:  spirits@downslopedistilling.com
          Media/Business:  andy@downslopedistilling.com
          Technical/Product:  mitch@downslopedistilling.com
*Website:*  www.downslopedistilling.com
*Facebook:*  Downslope Distilling
*Twitter:*  @downslopedist

*Region:*  Mountain West

*Type*:  Micro-distillery producing approximately 4,000 gallons annually

*Opened:*  2009

*Hours of operation:*  Typically 7 days a week

*Tours:*  Tours are available on Friday, Saturday and Sunday from 12:00pm to 4:00pm.

*Types of spirits produced:*
Cane vodka, grain vodka, pepper infused vodka, white rum, gold rum, vanilla rum, wine barrel aged rum, spiced rum, gin, and double diamond whiskey

*Names of spirits:*
- Downslope Cane Vodka
- Downslope Grain Vodka
- Downslope Pepper Vodka
- Downslope White Rum
- Downslope Gold Rum
- Downslope Spiced Rum
- Downslope Vanilla Rum
- Downslope Wine Barrel Aged Rum
- Downslope Double Diamond Whiskey
- Downslope Malt Whiskey

*Best known for:*  Vodka from Maui cane, Vanilla Rum, Wine Barrel Aged Rum, Pepper Vodka, and Double Diamond Whiskey

*Average bottle price*:  $25.00 to $32.00

*Distribution:*   CO, MA, OR, NE, NJ, NM, TX and WA

*Awards and Recognitions:*

**Downslope Cane Vodka**
- Gold Medal, 92 points, 2011 Beverage Testing Institute
- 3 Stars, 2011 Beverage Experts
- 9 Olives out of 10, 2011 Spirits Review

**Downslope Grain Vodka**
- Silver Medal, 88 Points, 2011 Beverage Testing Institute
- 4 Stars, 2011 Beverage Experts
- 10 Olives out of 10, 2011 Spirits Review

**Downslope Pepper Vodka**
- Silver Medal, 86 Points, 2011 BTI
- 3 Stars, 2011 Beverage Experts
- 8 Olives out of 10, 2011 Spirits Review

**Downslope White Rum**
- 3 Stars, 2011 Beverage Experts
- 9 Olives out of 10, 2011 Spirits Review

**Downslope Gold Rum**
- 3 Stars, 2011 Beverage Experts
- 9 Olives out of 10, 2011 Spirits Review
- Bronze Medal, 2011 Micro Spirits Awards

**Downslope Vanilla Rum**
- 3 Stars, 2011 Beverage Experts
- 9 Olives out of 10, 2011 Spirits Review

**Downslope Wine Barrel Aged Rum**
- 4 Stars, 2011 Beverage Experts
- 9 Olives out of 10, 2011 Spirits Review
- Finalist, 2011 Good Food Awards
- Best Sips, 2011 Boston Cocktail Summit

**Downslope Spiced Rum**
- Bronze Medal, 2011 New York World Spirits Competition

**Downslope Double Diamond Whiskey**
- Silver Medal, 2011 American Distilling Institute
- Silver Medal, 89 Points, 2011 Beverage Testing Institute
- Silver Medal, 2011 San Francisco World Spirits Competition
- 8 Olives out of 10, 2011 Spirits Review
- Bronze Medal, 2011 Micro Spirits Award

**Downslope Cane Vodka**

Downslope Cane Vodka is vodka made from the juice of Maui sugar cane before it is processed into sugar. Instead of multiple passes through the Hookah pot still, it is run through its own column still. It is then slow filtered by the Lichtenstein, a unique, self-designed apparatus. The result is an extremely smooth and infinitely mixable vodka that is also gluten free.

**Downslope Grain Vodka**

Downslope Grain Vodka is born by using the process and apparatus of the cane vodka but the same raw ingredients as Double-Diamond Whiskey. It gets one spin through the Hookah pot still and then is rectified in the column still. The result is a complex, spicy grain-flavored vodka.

**Downslope Pepper Vodka**

The basis of this extraordinary spirit is the cane vodka but it is infused with the perfect combination of New Mexico dried red chilies (roadside ristras) and black pepper from Indonesia. This complex product is excellent as a soloist and as a mixer with just about anything (try ginger…or marjoram).

**Downslope White Rum**

This, and all Downslope rums, is made from dried Maui cane juice that has not yet been processed into sugar. What that means is that none of the molasses has been removed. This rum is good on its own and as the backbone for any traditional rum cocktail. It's a tropical agricultural product made whole in the cold.

**Downslope Gold Rum**

Downslope Gold Rum is what happens when a beautiful harmony of sugar cane is aged in experienced American white oak barrels. These are the same barrels that are used for tequila, but the earthy agave flavor is replaced with the warm and comfortable flavor of unadulterated cane juice from the tropics.

**Downslope Vanilla Rum**

Downslope Vanilla Rum is produced by using two kinds of vanilla beans that have the perfect contact time in very small batches to capture an unmatched, complex vanilla flavor. These small quantities are then blended for consistency. This product stands elegantly on its own and plays well with other flavors.

**Downslope Spiced Rum**

There are many spiced rums available with very familiar flavors and easily recognizable ad campaigns. Downslope's differs in that no artificial flavors and no additives are used. The result is a complex but not overpowering citrus, spicy rum that stands alone and plays well with other flavors.

**Downslope Wine Barrel Aged Rum**

Aging rum in oak barrels certainly makes for an interesting product, but Downslope Distilling takes it to the next level by selecting some of the rum and aging it in various wine casks. Each of these rums is unique and is produced in limited quantities. In fact, there is only 60 gallons of each product in the world. Currently, some of the rum is in Hungarian Tokaji casks, a California chardonnay cask, and a Napa Valley merlot cask.

## Downslope Double-Diamond Whiskey

Downslope Double-Diamond Whiskey follows the Irish tradition of being made predominantly with malted barley. The other fraction is rye which contributes a spiciness that is Downslope's signature. The whiskey is aged in very small experienced medium toast casks and then blended. The result is a light colored, extraordinarily smooth whiskey that tastes of vanilla and honey and spice and wood.

*Services offered other than production:* Tours and tastings

*Interesting facts:*
- The barrels used at Downslope originate from wineries. They then get rum, and then whiskey. When they are retired from aging spirits, they house beer at local breweries.

*About:*

The principals established Downslope Distilling because of their passion for quality adult beverages. They began exploring their interest in distilling through home brewing, though typical home brewers they are not. While Andy was researching advanced wort production and home brewing technique, Mitch was traveling the country compiling mountains of information about how whiskey was made. They decided to combine their talents and produce limited amounts of high quality handcrafted spirits, to do so locally, and to make those products available to the local community first. Their talents combined with local ingredients and a custom designed still have allowed these men to perfect their techniques and make Centennial's first craft distillery a success.

*Future business plans and goals:* Regional growth and national exposure

*Suggested recipes:*

### Vanilla Basil Mojito
- 2 oz Downslope Vanilla Rum
- Juice of 1 lime
- Soda water
- Several fresh basil leaves
- Agave syrup

Muddle basil leaves in tall glass, add ice, agave, rum, and lime.
Top with soda water.
Garnish with sprig of basil and a sliver of sugar cane.

### Cold Killer
- Downslope Cane Vodka
- Blood orange juice
- Lemon and lime

### Hot Dog
- Downslope Pepper Vodka
- Pink grapefruit juice

Rim glass with chipotle sugar. Garnish with orange and ginger.

Downslope Distilling
Centennial, Colorado

# Maison De La Vie Ltd.
## The Village Distillery

Stephen A Gould, Owner / Distiller

412 Violet Street
Golden, Colorado   80401

*Phone:*   303-993-7174
*Fax:*   303-279-5299
*Email:*   s.gould@gouldgobal.com
*Website:*   www.village-distillery.com, www.reduxabsinthe.com, www.goldengin.com
*Twitter:*   @REDUXAbsinthe

*Region:*   Colorado

*Type:*   Micro-distillery producing approximately 1,500 proof gallons per year

*Opened:*   2008

*Hours of operation:*   Monday through Friday, 9:00am to 5:00pm

*Tours:*   Tours are available.

*Types of spirits produced:*
Absinthe, gin, grappa, eaux de vie, and liqueurs

*Names of spirits:*
- Golden Old Fashioned Distilled Gin
- Redux Absinthe
- Redux Absinthe No.2
- Cocktail Bitters product line

*Best known for:*   Redux Absinthe

*Average bottle price*:
Redux Absinthe - $85.00
Golden Old Fashioned Distilled Gin - $46.00

*Distribution:*   U.S., France, and Thailand

*Awards and Recognitions:*
### Golden Old Fashioned Distilled Gin
- Silver Medal, 2011 San Francisco World Spirits Competition
- Bronze Medal, 2011 International Wine and Spirits Competition
### Redux Absinthe
- Bronze Medal,2009 San Francisco World Spirits Competition
- Bronze Medal, 2009 International Spirits Challenge (only absinthe to medal)
- Bronze Medal, 2009 International Wine and Spirits Competition

*Highlighted spirits:*
**Redux Absinthe**
Redux Absinthe is the product of years of research using an extensive library of rare distillation texts coupled with the tasting and testing of rare vintage absinthes. The result is a premium absinthe that is both a classic traditional absinthe verte, and a unique new creation at the same time.

Redux Absinthe is made using the finest herbs and spices from around the world, all carefully selected and processed using the artisanal small-batch methods that were used by premium absinthe distillers during the height of the Belle Epoque era.

**Golden Old Fashioned Distilled Gin**
Golden Old Fashioned Distilled Gin is distilled using the finest herbs, spices and botanicals available, including wild-crafted field mint and juniper berries, and locally grown herbs and botanicals from the Front Range of the Colorado Rocky Mountains near Golden, Colorado.

*Events and Celebrations:*
A number of events are organized each year.

*About:*
Maison De La Vie Ltd. was founded by Stephen Gould in early 2008 specifically to produce premium handcrafted herbal liquors and liqueurs using the best herbs, spices and botanicals available and made with the same type of artisan production processes utilized by distillers making premium products in the mid to late 1800s.

The heart of Maison De La Vie is a world-class research library containing hundreds of rare books on distillation and related products, some dating back to the 1500s. Most of the collection dates from the late 1700s to the early 1900s.

Along with the library, Maison De La Vie currently has four antique stills and a fifth that is currently operating in France. The stills date from the early to mid-1900s.

Maison De La Vie uses environmentally friendly packaging and business practices as much as possible. As many materials as possible are sourced from local producers, reducing shipping and the related carbon footprint. The distillery is working with local wineries to utilize some of their cast-off materials in its production and packaging processes.

Maison De La Vie's French produced product is not contract distilled. Rather, the distillery owners select and procure the materials, they own the still, and do the distilling. The absinthe will be produced using the exact same recipe in both countries using the same materials. The gin, however, will not be produced in France.

*Management profile:*
**Stephen A. Gould**
Stephen Gould has worked as a saucier, as a corporate executive with extensive international trade and supply chain management experience, and as a brewer.

*Future business plans and goals:* Expanded product line and broadened distribution

*Suggested recipe:*
**Redux Absinthe Italiano**
*This is the old way that Italians drank absinthe in the late 1800s and early 1900s.*

In a tall 8oz glass, add:

- A few ice cubes
- 1 oz of Redux Absinthe
- 4 dashes of maraschino
- 4 dashes of Maison De La Vie Buddha's Hand Bitters

Fill the glass with ice-cold soda water.
Stir and serve.

Maison De La Vie Ltd.
The Village Distillery
Golden, Colorado

## Montanya Distillers LLC

Karen Hoskin, President / Co-Owner
Brice Hoskin, Vice President / Co-Owner

*Distillery and Tasting Room:*
130 Elk Avenue
Crested Butte, Colorado  81224

*Silverton Tasting Room:*
1314 Greene Street
Silverton, Colorado  81433

*Shipping Warehouse:*
398 Riverland Drive, 1D
Crested Butte, Colorado  81224
(by appointment only)

*Administrative Office:*
126 Elk Avenue, 1C
Crested Butte, Colorado  81224

*Phone:*  970-799-3206 or 800-975-6154
*Fax:*  800-975-6154
*Email:*  info@montanyadistillers.com
*Website:*  www.montanyadistillers.com
*Facebook:*  Montanya Distillers
*Twitter:*  @montanyarum
*LinkedIn:*  Montanya Distillers

*Region:*  Western Colorado

*Type:*  Micro-distillery

*Opened:*  November 2008

*Hours of operation:*  Daily from 11:00am to 8:30pm

*Tours:*  Tours are available during regular business hours and also by appointment.

*Types of spirits produced:*  Light and dark rum

*Names of spirits:*
- Montanya Oro Rum
- Montanya Platino Rum

*Average bottle price:*  $24.99 to $32.99

*Distribution:*  Currently available in 27 states

*Awards and Recognitions:*
**Oro Dark Rum**
- Silver Medal, 2011 New York World Wine and Spirits Competition
- Silver Medal, 2010 San Francisco World Spirits Competition
- Silver Medal, 2009 International Rum Tasting Competition Ministry of Rum
- Silver Medal, 2009 International Review of Spirits Beverage Testing Institute

**Platino Light Rum**
- Gold Medal, 2010 Best in Class, Rum XP Competition, Miami Rum Renaissance
- Gold Medal, 2010 San Francisco World Spirits Competition
- Gold Medal, 2009 International Rum Tasting Competition Ministry of Rum
- Silver Medal, 2009 International Review of Spirits Beverage Testing Institute

*Highlighted spirits:*
**Platino Light Rum**
Montanya Platino is a light, crisp rum distilled from high molasses content pure sugar cane, fermented with champagne yeast and aged to maturity in American oak, coconut-husk charcoal-filtered barrels. It is then blended with San Juan mountain spring water. "Notes of honey, coffee, vanilla and oak are evident in the body and finish," says Ed Hamilton, Minister of Rum. BTI 2009 says, "Aromas of coconut crème brulee and anise cookie follow through on a soft entry to a dryish medium body with slightly acidic peppery notes and a roasted nut finish. Interesting."

**Oro Dark Rum**
Montanya Oro is a dark, full-bodied sipping rum distilled from high molasses content pure sugar cane, fermented with champagne yeast and aged in once-used Stranahan's Whiskey Barrels. It is then blended with San Juan mountain spring water. "Hints of toffee in the aroma lead to a body of espresso, toffee, vanilla and honey until roasted coffee beans dominate the slightly smoky finish," says Ed Hamilton, Minister of Rum. BTI 2009 says, "Fruity caramel and poached pear tart aromas follow through on a supple, buoyant entry to a dry-yet-fruity medium body with mocha, brown spices, and cola notes. Finishes a lively coffee, toffee and pepper fade. An engaging, spicy gold rum for mixing flavorful cocktails."

*Services offered other than production:*
Tastings, full cocktail and appetizer menu, on-site retail sales

*Interesting facts:*
- Montanya Distillers is one the few U.S. distilleries owned and operated by a woman, with a female distiller and a female general manager.

*About:*
Montanya Distillers was founded in Silverton, Colorado, in 2008 by Karen and Brice Hoskin. In early 2011, they relocated to Crested Butte and opened to the public in the Historic Powerhouse on Elk Avenue in November 2011.

The original distillery (from 2008-2011) was on Blair Street in Silverton in a century old, 2,000 square foot stone building. The complete operation was on three levels, requiring a lot of heavy lifting and pumping of distilled spirits between floors. Fermentations were done in the basement, distilling and tastings on the main level, and aging and bottling on the top floor. An old box truck was used to store the rum for freight shipments.

In the summer of 2011, the Hoskins relocated Montanya Distillers to Crested Butte, Colorado, to help accommodate the company's rapid growth. Crested Butte offered the kind of commercial facilities the Hoskins were unable to secure in Silverton. The climate and approach of the local government toward small business development was very, Montanya Distillers is an authentic craft distiller of award-winning rum made from scratch and distilling in a process that dates back almost 1,000 years to the Moorish country of Spain and even to North Africa. The copper stills were handmade in Portugal by craftsman whose families have been in this business for centuries.

Both Oro and Platino Rums are made from Colorado spring and snowmelt water and pure Hawaiian sugar cane from a family farm. The process and ingredients are all-natural and unrefined. Additionally, both rums are aged in American oak barrels originally used at Stranahan's Whiskey in Denver, Colorado.

*Professional associations:* American Distilling Institute and Colorado Distillers Guild

*Future business plans and goals:*
To be the most highly respected and well-loved American rum available in the USA

*Suggested recipe:*
**Distillers Montanya Mud**
Mix in a shaker on ice:
- 2 oz iced coffee
- 1-2 oz half and half
- 2 oz Platino
- 1-2 oz cinnamon vanilla syrup
- 1-2 mint leaves muddled

    Strain into collins glass filled with ice half turbinado sugar rim.

Montanya Distillers LLC
Crested Butte, Colorado

# Mystic Mountain Distillery LLC

Fred Linneman, General Manager

11505 Spring Valley Road
Larkspur, Colorado 80118

*Phone:* 303-663-9375
*Email:* info@mysticmtnspirits.com
*Website:* www.mysticmtnspirits.com
*Facebook:* Mystic Mountain Distillery

*Region:* Western U.S.

*Type*: Micro-distillery producing approximately 50 to 75 gallons per month

*Opened:* November 1, 2005

*Hours of operation:* 9:00am to 2:00pm

*Tours:* Tours are not available.

*Types of spirits produced:* Gin, moonshine, rum, tequila, vodka, and whiskey

*Names of spirits:*
- Colorado Blue Vodka
- BOHICA Vodka
- Colorado Crystal Vodka
- Rocky Mountain Moonshine
- Colorado Fog Gin
- Blackjack Aces High Whiskey

*Average bottle price*: $20.00 to $25.00

*Highlighted spirits:*
## Colorado Blue Vodka
Colorado Blue Vodka is specifically distilled as a sipping beverage. In the distillation process, Mystic Mountain caramelizes the mash resulting in a slight butterscotch flavor and floral aroma. This unique process provides a rich and exceptionally smooth beverage.

## BOHICA Vodka
BOHICA Vodka is smooth enough to be enjoyed on its own but is versatile and mixes well with all recipes, from Bloody Marys to Vodka Tonics and the whole range of Martinis. As a tribute to the men, women, and families of the armed forces, a portion of each sale will go to support a veterans charity. It is a way for Mystic Mountain Distillery to say "Thank you" for their contribution and to help serve those who served their country.

*Highlighted spirits:*

## Colorado Crystal Vodka

Colorado Crystal Vodka is clean, crisp and lacks any distracting flavor. The bite is removed from the vodka early in the distillation process and the artesian well water is filtered over twelve times to ensure high quality. Colorado Crystal Vodka, embedded with richness and full body, is about tasting the Rocky Mountains and the natural flavor of the lemon twist or olive.

Rocky Mountain Moonshine
Sippin' Hooch

750ML · 40% ALC BY VOL (80 PROOF)

## Rocky Mountain Moonshine

Rocky Mountain Moonshine is full of flavor and body characterized with a floral aroma and a rich taste. Rocky Mountain Moonshine builds on the traditions of moonshiners who sought refuge in the Blue Ridge Mountains.

## Colorado Fog Gin

This fine gin is handcrafted at 7,000 feet in the mountains of Colorado, using water from the distillery's own well which was dug deep for clarity.

## Blackjack Aces High Whiskey

Distilled from fermented grains, Blackjack Whiskey is a natural bourbon flavor whiskey, full-bodied with a smooth, mellow satisfying taste.

*Services offered other than production:*
Some contract packaging is available.

*Suggested recipe:*

## Colorado Summer

- 1 cup Colorado Blue Vodka
- 2½ cups cranberry juice
- 1½ cups orange juice
- 3 peeled orange slices
- 1 orange wedge to garnish

Mix Colorado Blue Vodka, cranberry, and orange juice.
Pour over crushed ice, stir in and slightly muddle orange slices.
Garnish with orange wedge.

Mystic Mountain Distillery LLC
Larkspur, Colorado

65

# Roundhouse Spirits

Charles (Ted) Palmer, Owner

5311 Western Avenue #180
Boulder, Colorado  80301

*Phone:*  303-819-5598
*Email:*  ted@roundhousespirits.com
*Website:*  www.roundhousespirits.com
*Facebook:*  Roundhouse Spirits
*Twitter:*  @Shareaholic

*Region:*  North Central Colorado

*Type*:  Micro-distillery producing approximately 900 gallons annually

*Opened:*  October 2008

*Hours of operation:*  Varies

*Tours:*  Tours are available Thursday through Saturday from 3:00pm to 7:00pm

*Types of spirits produced:*  Gin and liqueur

*Names of spirits:*
- Roundhouse Gin
- Imperial Barrel Aged Gin
- Corretto Coffee Liqueur

*Best known for:*  The Roundhouse Gin Fizz

*Average bottle price*:  $25.00 to $45.00

*Distribution:*  Colorado, parts of Texas, Wyoming, and the tasting room

*Awards and Recognitions:*
**Roundhouse Gin**
- Bronze Medal, 2010 San Francisco World Spirits Competition
- Gold Medal, Beverage Testing Institute in Chicago
**Corretto Coffee Liqueur**
- Named 2010 "Best Local Liqueur" by Boulder County's Yellowscene Magazine

*Highlighted spirits:*

## Roundhouse Gin

Roundhouse Gin is a dry gin, micro-distilled, then re-distilled in a handmade Portuguese copper-pot still, and bottled by hand in exceptionally small batches. It's made with a neutral grain spirit and traditional gin botanicals of juniper berry, coriander, citrus peel, star anise, angelica, and orris root. Hints of sencha green tea, lavender, hibiscus and chamomile blossoms are added to give it a distinct, floral palette.

## Imperial Barrel Aged Gin

Imperial Barrel Aged Gin starts with Roundhouse's signature gin distilled in small batches from the finest natural botanicals, and then aged to perfection in oak casks for at least six months. Imperial is complex and smooth, and is available in very small quantities only in Colorado.

## Corretto Coffee Liqueur

In Italy, a "caffe corretto" is a coffee "corrected" with a shot of alcohol. Roundhouse Corretto is a coffee liqueur that needs no correction. Corretto is handcrafted in small batches and uses only the freshest locally roasted coffee beans from the Unseen Bean in Boulder (a 5280 Magazine coffee of the year). Then just a touch of whole vanilla bean is added to sweeten it. The end result is a dark, rich, full flavored coffee liqueur.

*Events and Celebrations:*
Roundhouse Spirits hosts numerous events.

*About:*
Roundhouse Spirits is a distiller of fine craft spirits in Boulder, Colorado. As a micro-distillery, Roundhouse handcrafts and bottles award-winning spirits in exceptionally small batches, using only the finest grain, water, spices, herbs, and coffee. It takes painstaking care to ensure that each bottle corked reflects its passions for the long traditions of spirits makers in the U.S. and abroad.

For the old railroads that crisscrossed the American West, the "roundhouse" was a special place that gave hard working steam engines and their drivers a place to rest and relax at the end of the day. Roundhouse strives to produce distinctive spirits that bring family and friends together for that same kind of R&R, and to make memories that will last a lifetime.

Most ingredients are from within 200 miles of the distillery while other ingredients are brought in from other states and countries. Since juniper berry (the principal flavor in gin) grows prevalently in the open space and mountain parks of the area, Roundhouse Gin literally has roots in Boulder.

*Professional associations:* American Distilling Institute and Colorado Distillers Guild

*Future business plans and goals:* Introduction of agave spirits

*Suggested recipe:*
**Corpse Reviver Gin Cocktail**
- 1 ¼ oz Roundhouse Gin
- 1 ¼ oz Lillet Blanc
- 1 oz Cointreau
- 1 oz lemon juice
- 8 drops absinthe

   Shake with ice.
   Strain into a chilled martini glass.

Roundhouse Spirits
Boulder, Colorado

# Spring44

Jeff Lindauer, Co-Founder and CEO
Russ Wall, Co-Founder and CMO
Jeff McPhie, Co-Founder and COO

505 West 66th Street
Loveland, Colorado  80538

*Phone:*  970-445-7109
*Email:*  info@spring44.com
*Website:*  www.spring44.com
*Facebook:*  Spring44
*Twitter:*  @spring44spirits
*YouTube:*  Spring44Distilling's Channel

*Region:*  Colorado

*Type:*  Micro-distillery

*Opened:*  May 2011

*Types of spirits produced:*  Vodka, gin, and honey vodka

*Names of spirits:*
- Spring44 Vodka
- Spring44 Gin
- Spring44 Honey Vodka

*Average bottle price*:  $24.00

*Distribution:*  Colorado, New York, New Jersey, Utah, Florida and Arizona

*Awards and Recognitions:*
## Spring 44 Vodka
- Triple Gold Award, 2011 MicroLiquor Spirit Award Competition
- 5 Star Rating, F. Paul Pacult's Spirit Journal

## Spring44 Honey Vodka
- Triple Gold Award, 2011 MicroLiquor Spirit Award Competition
- 4 Star Rating, F. Paul Pacult's Spirit Journal
- 91 Points, Tasting Panel

## Spring44 Gin
- Triple Gold Award, 2011 MicroLiquor Spirit Award Competition

*Highlighted spirits:*

**Spring44 Vodka**

Spring44 Vodka is crafted from a proprietary blend of American rye, corn, and wheat. The water comes from an artesian source in the Rocky Mountains.

**Spring44 Gin**

Spring44 took Old World-style juniper-forward gin and remixed it, adding a proprietary blend of botanicals including coriander, nutmeg and agave to give it a floral, fruity note and a balanced finish. The water comes from an artesian source in the Rocky Mountains.

**Spring44 Honey Vodka**

Spring44 Honey Vodka starts with Spring44 Vodka then an all-natural honey is added.

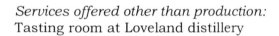

*Events and Celebrations:*

Spring44 sponsors many events including the Telluride Blues & Brews Festival. Additionally, Spring44 Gin is the official gin of the New York Rangers.

*Services offered other than production:*

Tasting room at Loveland distillery

*About:*

Spring44 handcrafts ultra-premium spirits at a different level - 9,044 feet up in the Colorado Rockies to be precise. That's where some of the earth's most superior and perfect artesian spring water can be found.

Spring44 is committed to making spirits that are good to the palate and to the planet, and it has a long legacy of commitment to the environment. The water facility in the hills, only accessible by 4X4 drive, is built from beetle-kill pine, and the works are 100% solar powered.

The terroir of the water coupled with the natural mountain botanicals allows for a magical, harmonious blend of spirit and essence. This incredible symmetry is unprecedented and very unique.

*Future business plans and goals:*  Expanded product line and broadened distribution

*Suggested recipes:*

**The Buckhorn Mule** - By Sean Kenyon
- 1 ½ oz Spring44 Vodka
- 1 medium strawberry
- 1 slice cucumber
- 3 oz ginger beer
- ½ oz fresh lime juice

In a collins glass, muddle cucumber and strawberry.
Add Spring44 Vodka, lime juice, and top with ginger beer.
Gently stir to mix.
Garnish with a cucumber and strawberry slice.

**Rocky Mountain Spritz** - By Sean Kenyon
- 1 ½ oz Spring44 Honey Vodka
- ½ oz Creme Yvette
- 2 oz sparkling wine
- 1 oz soda

Build in a large balloon glass with ice.
Add ingredients.

**The South Park Cocktail** - By Sean Kenyon
- 1 ½ oz Spring44 Gin
- ½ oz Yellow Chartreuse
- ¾ oz fresh lemon juice
- ¼ oz agave nectar
- 2 dashes Angostura bitters
- 8 mint leaves

Shake all ingredients with ice.
Double strain into a chilled coupe.
Garnish with a mint sprig.

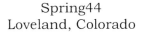

Spring44
Loveland, Colorado

# Syntax Spirits LLC

Heather Bean, Owner
Jeff Copeland, Owner

625 3rd Street, Unit C
Greeley, Colorado 80631

*Phone:* 970-352-5466 (hours and location)
*Cell:* 970-224-1248
*Email:* General info: info@syntaxspirits.com
    Heather Bean: heather@syntaxspirits.com
    Jeff Copeland: jeff@syntaxspirits.com
*Website:* www.syntaxspirits.com
*Facebook:* Syntax Spirits Distillery
*Twitter:* @SyntaxSpirits

*Region:* Northern Colorado (Weld County)

*Type:* Micro-distillery anticipating the production of approximately 2,000 cases per year

*Opened:* December 2010

*Hours of operation:*
Wednesday through Saturday, 4:00pm to 11:00pm
Hours may vary seasonally; latest hours and info, call 970-352-5466.

*Tours:*
Tours can be requested whenever the tasting room is open (staff permitting) and tours can be scheduled in advance for groups or at other times.

*Types of spirits produced:*
Vodka and flavored infused vodkas.
Rum and other spirits are under development.

*Names of spirits:* Class V

*Best known for:* Class V Vodka

*Average bottle price*: $25.00

*Distribution:*
Tasting room and across northern Colorado (Greeley, Fort Collins, Loveland, Golden, Boulder, Denver, and points between)

Photo by: Jafe Parsons

72

*Highlighted spirits:*
## Class V Vodka
Class V Vodka is a wheat-based Russian-style vodka with a sinfully smooth, clean taste. Its name is a nod to the whitewater on the wild and scenic Poudre River, the source of the distillery's mountain water. Class V Vodka is made from 100% local Weld County wheat, and nothing else.

*Events and Celebrations:* A 1,500 square foot tasting room is suitable for special events and parties. Watch for Syntax at festivals and events across Colorado.

*Services offered other than production:* Retail shop sells Syntax merchandise and bottles; tasting bar serves a full cocktail menu with Syntax's spirits.

*About:* Prior to starting Syntax Spirits, Heather Bean (below) and Jeff Copeland had been home brewing beer for more than 20 years. After school, they entered the science and engineering fields.

For many years, Heather worked for a major electronics corporation and spent about one week a month in Portland, Oregon, for her job. Portland, which hosts a thriving craft brewing culture, was beginning to spawn a few craft distilleries which Heather visited while there.

By the mid-2000s, Heather was tiring of the corporate world and took Jeff around to the Portland craft distilleries that she'd seen with the idea that the two of them might one day open their own in Colorado. Shortly thereafter, Heather quit her corporate job to start their distillery, with Jeff providing much needed support. After thousands of hours of work, along with a lot of blood, sweat and tears, Syntax Spirits was a reality.

Photo by: Eric Bellamy

The tasting room opened in December of 2010, and has been well received by the community. Additionally, they've been fortunate to receive national attention from NPR and many other publications in the short time that they've been open.

*Future business plans and goals:* Increased production and broader distribution

*Suggested recipe:*
**The Jefe' Caliente** (Named for their COO and bartender extraordinaire)
- 1 shot Class V Vodka
- 2 Tbs Ghirardelli Double Chocolate hot cocoa mix
- 1 tsp ancho chile powder (or to taste)

  Fill cup with house-roasted coffee, mix well and top with marshmallows or a cherry if desired. For an additional kick, use Class V "Perky Pepper" instead of plain vodka.

Syntax Spirits LLC<br>
Greeley, Colorado

## Onyx Spirits Company LLC

Adam von Gootkin, Co-founder
Peter Kowalczyk, Co-founder

640 Hilliard Street, Suite 3104
Manchester, Connecticut 06042

*Phone:* 860-550-1939
*Email:* contact@onyxspirits.com
*Website:* www.onyxspirits.com
*Facebook:* Onyx Spirits Company
*Twitter:* @OnyxSpirits
*YouTube:* OnyxSpirits's Channel

**ONYX SPIRITS C<u>o</u>**

PRODUCERS OF FINE LIQUOR

MANCHESTER, CONNECTICUT

*Region:* Connecticut

*Type:* Micro-distillery producing approximately 15,000 bottles per year

*Opened:* May 2011, first product released (Onyx Moonshine) October 2011

*Hours of operation:* Monday through Friday, 9:00am to 6:00pm

*Tours:* Tours are not currently available.

*Types of spirits produced:* Moonshine, vodka, and limoncello

*Names of spirits:*
- Onyx Moonshine (flagship product)
- Organic Vodka (name TBA)

*Average bottle price:* $22.00 to $28.00

*Distribution:* Statewide in Connecticut bars, restaurants, and liquor stores

*Awards and Recognitions:*
Onyx Moonshine was included in celebrity gift bags and extended to many of the biggest names in country music at the 45th Annual CMA Awards.

Onyx Moonshine was selected as the exclusive spirit for the 54th Annual Grammy Awards official gift bags.

*Highlighted spirits:*
**Onyx Moonshine**
Onyx Moonshine is the first known ultra-premium moonshine to be released commercially in the United States, and the first known moonshine to be released commercially in New England. Made from mixed corn, grain and Connecticut spring water, Onyx Moonshine is made from an authentic Prohibition era moonshine recipe and is refined into an extremely smooth, clear sipping whiskey that mixes as well as any top shelf vodka.

*Interesting facts:*
- Onyx Moonshine is the first moonshine to be produced in Connecticut since Prohibition.

*Management profile:*
**Adam von Gootkin** – Sales Management
**Peter Kowalczyk** – Production Management
Adam and Peter have been business partners since leaving college; together they have launched multiple successful businesses. Onyx Spirits Company is the result of taking their passion and enthusiasm for quality made spirits and turning it into a venture that is unique for Connecticut. The goal is to produce top shelf spirits that harken back to a New England time when things were pure, simple, and well made.

*Future business plans and goals:* Expanded product line and increased distribution

*Suggested recipes:*

**The Charter Oak**
- Warm apple cider cooked slowly with cinnamon sticks, orange slice, and brown sugar
- 1 part Onyx Moonshine
- 3 parts apple cider
- Dollop of whipped cream
- Sprinkle of nutmeg

**The Drunken Santa**
- ¾ mug of warmed whole milk
- Hot chocolate mix
- 1 shot of Onyx Moonshine

Top with whipped cream and cocoa powder.

Onyx Spirits Company LLC
Manchester, Connecticut

# Fat Dog Spirits LLC

Nick Carbone, Proprietor

3212 North 40th Street
Tampa, Florida 33605

*Phone:* 813-503-5995
*Email:* fatdogspirits@earthlink.net
*Website:* www.fatdogspirits.com, www.nicholasgin.com
*Website:* www.touchvodka.com, www.artemisiaabsinthe.com
*Facebook:* Fat Dog Spirits

*Region:* Florida

*Type*: Micro-distillery producing between 3,000 and 4,000 gallons annually

*Opened:* October 2004

*Hours of operation:* Varies

*Tours:* Tours are available upon request.

*Types of spirits produced:* Absinthe verte, gin and vodka

*Names of spirits:*
- Nicholas Gin
- Touch Vodka-Original
- Touch Red Grapefruit Flavored Vodka
- Touch Key Lime Flavored Vodka
- Touch Valencia Orange Flavored Vodka
- Artemisia Superior Absinthe Verte

*Best known for:* Nicholas Gin

*Average bottle price*: $32.00 to $34.00

*Distribution:* Florida and Chicago

*Awards and Recognitions:*
**Touch Vodka**
- Gold Medal, 2006 San Francisco World Spirits Competition
- Silver Medal, 2006 Beverage Testing Institute
- 94 Points Wine Enthusiast
- "Highly Recommended," F. Paul Pacult's Spirit Journal

**Artemisia Superior Absinthe Verte**
- Best of Class, 2008 New York Spirits Competition

**Nicholas Gin**

Individually distilled in small batches to maintain control of the delicate flavor that makes it an original artisan spirit, Nicholas Gin boldly departs from the traditional European roots of gin to forge its own American legacy. This is done with unique botanicals such as lavender, rose hips and hibiscus leaves. The result is a delightful balance of juniper and floral notes with a clean, dry finish. The fruit used in the recipe is locally harvested, while the botanicals are purchased and grown organically within the U.S.

**Touch Vodka**

Individually distilled in small batches in a pot still, Touch Vodka is produced from wildflower honey from rich pine forests and everglades and is fermented with champagne yeast. It is not filtered. The result is beautifully clear vodka with a mild whiff of honey. All of the ingredients, including key limes, oranges, grapefruit, and honey, are harvested and or purchased locally.

**Artemisia Superior Absinthe Verte**

Artemisia Superior Absinthe Verte is artisan distilled in small batches using traditional European methods adapted from an 1855 recipe from Pontarlier, France. Fat Dog Spirits uses hand selected botanicals including grande wormwood, fennel, anise, coriander, cardamom, white sage, lemon balm, and hyssop. Each batch is distilled by hand using 100% grain neutral spirits produced from premium American grain. All of the fruit used in the spirit is locally harvested, while the botanicals are purchased and grown organically within the U.S.

*About:*

Nick Carbone started Fat Dog Distillery, named for his somewhat chunky chocolate labrador, in 2004. Carbone wanted to make the first ever vodka produced from honey. After extensive testing of different distillates made from varying sources of honey, Touch Vodka was launched in August of 2005. In 2008, Key Lime and Valencia Orange flavored Touch Vodka were released along with Artemisia Absinthe. Fat Dog Distillery is the second U.S. distillery to be approved to make Artemisia Absinthe in over 100 years. Last but not least, Nicholas American Gin was released in 2009.

*Future business plans and goals:* Expand distribution and offer aged spirits

*Suggested recipes:*
**Nicholas Negroni**
- 1 oz Nicholas Gin
- 1 oz Aperol
- 1 oz Sweet vermouth
- 2 to 3 ozs chilled club soda
- 1 orange slice

Over ice in a cocktail shaker, combine Nicholas Gin, Aperol, and sweet vermouth.
Shake and strain into an ice-filled highball glass.
Top with club soda.
Garnish with orange slice.


**St. Nicholas**
- 2 ozs Nicholas Gin
- 1 oz St-Germain elderflower liqueur
- 2 ozs Lillet Blanc
- ¼ oz fresh squeezed lemon juice
- 1 lemon peel

Over ice in a cocktail shaker, combine liquids.
Shake and strain into a chilled martini glass.
Run the orange or lemon peel around the rim of the glass.
Twist peel over drink and drop it in.




Fat Dog Spirits LLC
Tampa, Florida

## Florida Farm Distillers

**PALM RIDGE**
R E S E R V E ™

Handmade Micro Batch
Florida Whiskey

Dick & Marti Waters, Owners/Distillers

Post Office Box 1070
Umatilla, Florida  32784

*Phone:*  352-455-7232
*Email:*  whiskey@palmridgereserve.com
*Website:*  www.palmridgereserve.com
*Facebook:*  Palm Ridge Reserve

*Region:*  Central Florida

*Type*:  Micro-distillery producing approximately 1,200 gallons per year

*Opened:*  2008

*Hours of operation:*  Varies

*Tours:*  Tours are not available.

*Types of spirits produced:*  Handmade micro batch Florida whiskey

*Names of spirits:* Palm Ridge Reserve

*Best known for:*  Palm Ridge Reserve

*Average bottle price*:  $50.00 to $60.00

*Distribution:*  Florida

*Highlighted spirits:*
**Palm Ridge Reserve Micro Batch Florida Whiskey**
At 90 proof, Palm Ridge Reserve is a very smooth whiskey with an intense flavor profile similar to a single malt.   The whiskey is distilled in a 60 gallon reflux-column copper still from a mash of four grains: corn, barley, malt, rye and toasted flaked rye.  Palm Ridge Reserve is then put up in small 5 gallon charred oak barrels that round out and mature the whiskey in less than one year.

*About:*
Florida Farm Distillers is a micro-distillery located on a small cattle farm near Umatilla, Florida. Owners Marti and

Dick Waters believe that their personal and detailed attention makes Palm Ridge Reserve stand out from other mass produced liquors. The boutique operation produces a 90 proof, young Florida bourbon-style whiskey distilled in a 60 gallon reflux-column copper still. This limited quantity, select whiskey (only 500 cases per year), is non-chill filtered, mellowed with toasted orange and oak woods, and left to finish in small charred oak barrels.

*Professional associations:* American Distilling Institute

*Future business plans and goals:* Manageable growth

*Suggested recipes:*

**Levi's Sunrise**
- 1 oz Palm Ridge
- ½ oz Amaretto
- ½ oz Grand Marnier
- Equal parts orange juice and ginger ale
- Splash of grenadine

**White Lady**
- 1 ½ oz Palm Ridge
- 2 oz white grapefruit juice
- 1 oz pear vodka
- Splash of simple syrup

  Shake and strain over ice.
  Finish with champagne.

**Peach Mint Julep**
- 2 oz Palm Ridge
- ¾ oz peach schnapps
- 10-12 mint sprigs
- Splash of simple syrup

  Add mint to whiskey and schnapps.
  Muddle and strain over ice.
  Finish with ginger ale.

Florida Farm Distillers
Umatilla, Florida

# Richland Distilling Company

Erik Vonk, Founder / Proprietor
Jay McCain, General Manager
Karin Vonk, Marketing and Public Relations

333 Broad Street
Richland, Georgia  31825

*Phone:*  229-887-3537 / 229-321-0678
*Email:*  cheers@richlandrum.com
*Website:*  www.richlandrum.com
*Facebook:*  Richland Distilling Company
*YouTube:*  Richlandrum's Channel

*Region:*  Southwestern Georgia

*Type:*  Micro-distillery producing approximately 10,000 gallons per year

*Opened:*  November 2011

*Hours of operation:*  Monday through Friday, 9:00am to 5:00pm

*Tours:*  Tours are available by appointment. Call 229-321-0678.

*Types of spirits produced:*  Artisan premium rum

*Names of spirits:*
- Richland Rum
- Richland Rum – Vennebroeck Velvet Proprietor's Private Reserve

*Best known for:*  Richland Rum

*Average bottle price:*  $30.00 to $50.00

*Distribution:*  Nationwide

*Highlighted spirits:*
**Richland Rum**
Richland Rum is a dark, barrel aged, full-bodied premium rum, artisan distilled in a copper-pot still from virgin, fresh sugar cane juice. The juice is won by hand pressing organically grown sugar cane that's cultivated and farmed at the proprietor's estate near Richland, Georgia. This rich, unique, velvet smooth aromatic premium rum is best enjoyed either in a sniffer or pure on the rocks.

*Events and Celebrations:*  Check www.richlandrum.com for upcoming events.

*Services offered other than production:*  Retail store

*Interesting facts:*
- All ingredients are sourced entirely in Richland, Georgia.

*About:*
Richland Distilling Company was the realization of the proprietor's longtime dream to produce artisan premium rum from fresh cane juice. When the opportunity presented itself to acquire Vennebroeck in 1998, distilling premium rum immediately came to mind. Located in Southwest Georgia, which boasts fertile soil, plenty of sunshine and an abundance of spring water from the Georgia aquifer, Vennebroeck is perfectly situated to make this dream come true.

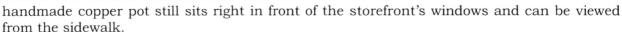

The Richland Distilling Company is a true artisan micro-distillery, which solely focuses on producing fine, premium rum, hand distilled from estate grown sugar cane juice. The company operates one 200 gallon copper- pot still hand made to order from Portugal.

The distillery is conveniently accessible and located in a restored historic storefront. The handmade copper pot still sits right in front of the storefront's windows and can be viewed from the sidewalk.

*Professional associations:* American Distilling Institute

*Future business plans and goals:* Stay small and focus on quality

*Suggested recipes:* Richland Rum should be enjoyed pure or on the rocks.

Richland Distilling Company
Richland, Georgia

# Hawaii Sea Spirits LLC

Shay Smith, President and CEO
Kyle Smith, Production Director
Don Freytag, Chief Marketing Officer/Sales Director
Sye Vasquez, Board Member and Advisor
Craig Duvall, Board Member and Advisor

250 Alamaha Street
Kahului, Hawaii 96732

*Phone:* 866-77-OCEAN (866-776-2326)
*Fax:* 808-877-8797
*Email:* Sales: sales@oceanvodka.com
      Shay Smith: shay@oceanvodka.com
      Kyle Smith: kyle@oceanvodka.com
      Don Freytag: don@oceanvodka.com
*Website:* www.oceanvodka.com
*Facebook:* Ocean Vodka
*Twitter:* @OceanVodka

*Region:* Hawaii

*Type:* Micro-distillery producing approximately 10,000 9L cases per year

*Opened:* May 2006

*Hours of operation:* Monday through Friday, 8:30am to 5:30pm

*Tours:* From time to time; some private tours are available

*Types of spirits produced:* Vodka

*Names of spirits:*
- Ocean Vodka

*Best known for:* Ocean Vodka

*Distribution:* United States, Japan, and Canada

*Awards and Recognitions:*
**Ocean Vodka**
- Gold Medal, 91 Pts., 2011 Beverage Testing Institute

*Highlighted spirits:*

**Ocean Vodka**

Handcrafted on the island of Maui, Ocean Vodka is the only known vokda in the world made from organic sugar cane and deep ocean mineral water. All 80 proof vodkas are comprised of 60% water, so the quality of the water source dramatically influences the quality of the vodka. Hawaiian deep ocean mineral water originated as Greenland glacier melt over 2,000 years ago, traveling gradually around the globe through deep ocean currents until arriving in Hawaii. The water is then 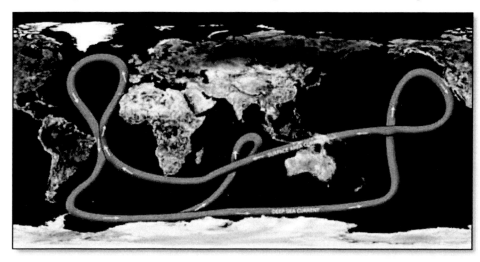 sourced from 3,000 feet below the big island of Hawaii, where it is ice cold, deeply pure, and full of naturally occurring minerals. Once the water is brought to the surface on the Kona coast, it is organically purified and desalinated through reverse osmosis. Natural filtration removes sodium while retaining rich minerals such as potassium, calcium, and magnesium. The high mineral content of Ocean Vodka water imparts a unique character and adds great depth of flavor to the traditional vodka cocktail, making Ocean Vodka a delicious choice for cocktail enthusiasts.

Since there is no organic sugar cane available in the Hawaiian Islands at this time, organic sugar cane for Ocean Vodka comes from Paraguay.

*Interesting facts:*
- 100% Gluten Free
- Uses only 100% USDA certified organic sugar cane
- The only known vodka in the world made from organic sugar cane
- The only known spirit in the world made from deep sea mineral water, sourced 3,000 feet below the Big Island

*About:*

Hawaii Sea Spirits was founded in 2006 based on a family passion for fun, care for the environment and conservation of the ocean.

The idea of creating Ocean Vodka came from Founder Shay Smith (right), sitting on his patio on Maui, Hawaii, wondering why he was drinking something made in and imported from Europe.

Growing up on an island, Smith knew the value of conserving scarce local resources and he sought to make something really cool and unique right near his home. The result - a 100% USDA certified organic vodka made with deep sea mineral water. The bottles are made largely from recycled glass and are decorated with water-soluble inks. The production facility at Hawaii Sea Spirits utilizes energy efficient lighting, recycles all shipping materials, and uses only natural cleaning products.

Hawaii Sea Spirits donates a portion of proceeds every year to multiple oceanic causes, including Oceana, Surfrider Foundation, Reef Check, Ocean Institute, Save Our Seas and Ocean Foundation

*Future business plans and goals:*
Growth and broadened distribution

*Suggested recipes:*

**Ocean Cosmo**
- Organic Ocean Vodka
- Cranberry juice
- Splash of lime juice or passion fruit purée

  Garnish with a slice of lime.

**Ocean Pom Beach Martini**
- Organic Ocean Vodka
- 1 oz cranberry juice
- 1 oz pomegranate juice
- Squeeze of orange

  Garnish with orange slice.

**Ocean Mai Tai**
- Organic Ocean Vodka
- Pineapple juice
- Orange juice
- Splash of dark rum

  Garnish with a slice of orange.

Hawaii Sea Spirits LLC
Kahului, Hawaii

# Island Distillers Inc.

Dave Flintstone, Proprietor and Sole Employee

220 Puuhale Road #B3
Honolulu, Hawaii  96819

*Phone:*  808-626-5798
*Email:*  dave@islanddistillers.com
*Website:*  www.hawaiianvodka.com
*Facebook:*  Hawaiian Vodka
*YouTube:*  Hawaiianvodka's Channel

*Region:*  Hawaii

*Type:*  Micro-distillery producing approximately 3,000 proof gallons per year

*Opened:*  December 2009

*Hours of operation:*  Open daily, hours vary

*Tours:*  Tours are not offered at this time due to Hawaiian regulations.

*Types of spirits produced:*  Vodka

*Names of spirits:*
- Hawaiian Vodka
- COCONUT Hawaiian Vodka

*Average bottle price:*  $22.00 to $26.00

*Distribution:*  Hawaii

*Awards and Recognitions:*
**Hawaiian Vodka**
- "Highly Recommended," 2011 International Review of Spirits
- "Powerful and smooth," Honolulu Magazine

*Highlighted spirits:*
**Hawaiian Vodka**
Hawaiian Vodka is an 80 proof, super smooth vodka.

**COCONUT Hawaiian Vodka**
COCONUT Hawaiian Vodka is a 70 proof fresh ripe coconut flavored vodka,
reminiscent of Hawaiian haupia.  Hawaiian Vodka is handcrafted in small batches, distilled from sugar cane and filtered through lava.  Only natural ingredients and pure Hawaiian water are used to produce a vodka like no other.

*Interesting facts:*
- Island Distillers is Oahu's only licensed distillery.

*About:*
Island Distillers was born from the idea that excellent spirits could be made in Hawaii from the abundant natural resources found there and combined with the perfect climate.

Founder Dave Flintstone spent years in the Caribbean learning about sugar cane alcohol, then spent years on the Big Island of Hawaii learning about lava filtration and purification.

After years of planning, Island Distillers was launched and now produces uncomparable vodkas. Each batch is handcrafted with an approach that guarantees perfection every time.

*Future business plans and goals:* Expanded product line and addition of a tasting room

*Suggested recipes:*
### Cucumber Breeze
- 1 ¼ oz Hawaiian Vodka
- ¾ oz Stirrings Ginger Liqueur
- 1 ¼ oz fresh lime sour
- 3 cucumber wheels
- Ginger ale

Muddle cucumber with sour.
Add liquors and ice.
Shake and strain over ice into highball.
Top with ginger ale.
Garnish with thin cucumber ribbons floating throughout glass and candied ginger perched on rim.

### Skinny Chi Chi Tini
- 1 ½ oz Hawaiian Coconut Vodka
- 1 ½ oz pineapple juice
- Squeeze fresh lime

Squeeze lime and drop into glass.
Add pineapple juice and vodka with ice.
Shake and strain into martini glass.
Garnish with pineapple wedge.

Island Distillers Inc.
Honolulu, Hawaii

# Kōloa Rum Company

Bob Gunter, President
Alicia Iverson, Controller
Jeanne Toulon, Director of Public Relations
Michael Riley, Operations Manager

Board of Directors:
Bob Weist, Chairman of the Board
John Stein, Corporate Secretary
Christopher Wolf, Director

2-2741 Kaumualii Highway, Suite C
Kalaheo, Hawaii  96741-8346

*Phone:*  808-332-9333
*Fax:*  808-332-7650
*Email:*  info@koloarum
*Website:*  www.koloarum.com
*Facebook:*  Koloa Rum Company
*Twitter:*  @KoloaRumCompany

*Region:*  The Hawaiian Islands

*Type*:  Single batch craft distiller

*Opened:*  2009

**PREMIUM HAWAIIAN RUM**

kaua'i • hawaii

*Hours of operation:*  Kōloa Rum Tasting Room and Company Store Hours

Monday and Wednesday 9:30am to 5:00pm
Tastings every half hour between 10:00am and 4:00pm
Last Tasting 4:00pm

Tuesday and Friday 9:30am to 9:00pm
Tastings every half hour between 10:00am and 8:00pm
Last Tasting 8:00pm

Thursday 9:30am to 6:30pm
Tastings every half hour between 10:00am and 5:30pm
Last Tasting 5:30pm

Saturday 9:30am to 5:00pm
Tastings every half hour between 11:00am and 4:00pm
Last Tasting 4:00pm

Sunday 9:30am to 3:00pm
Tastings every half hour between 11:00am to 2:00pm
Last Tasting 2:00pm

*Tours:*  Tours are not available.

*Types of spirits produced:*  Rum and related spirits products

*Names of spirits:*
- Kaua`i White
- Kaua`i Gold
- Kaua`i Dark Rum
- Kaua`i Spice Rum
- Kōloa Hawaiian ready-to-drink Mai Tai Cocktail
- Hawaiian Kaua`i non-alcoholic Mai Tai Mix

*Best known for:*  Kaua`i Dark Rum

*Average bottle price*:  $29.95 to $32.95

*Distribution:*
Kōloa Rum Company spirits are distributed throughout Kaua`i and the Hawaiian Islands by Johnson Brothers as well as at the Kōloa Rum Company's tasting room and company store. Additionally, Kōloa Rum is distributed by Western States Beverages, California; Southern Wine & Spirits, Nevada; Distillery Geeks, Illinois; Prime Wine & Spirits, Georgia; and by special order through State Liquor Boards in Washington, Oregon, Utah, Wyoming, and Montana.  Kōloa Rum is also distributed by Marram Wines in Western Canada.

Additional outlets include: Hi-Time Wine Cellars www.hitimewine.net, Mel and Rose www.melandrose.com, Holiday Wine Cellar www.holidaywinecellar.com, Beverages 4 Less www.beverages4lessinc.com

*Awards and Recognitions:*
**Kaua'i Dark**
- Gold Medal Best in Class, 2011 Miami Rum Renaissance Festival, Miami, FL
- Gold Medal, 2011 Miami Rum Renaissance Festival, Miami, FL
- Gold Medal, 2010 Miami Rum Renaissance Festival, Miami, FL
- Silver Medal, 2010 5th Annual International Rum Festival, Ybor City, FL

**Kaua`i Spice**
- Bronze Medal, 2011 Miami Rum Renaissance Festival, Miami, FL

**Kaua`i Gold**
- Silver Medal, 2010 5th Annual International Rum Festival, Ybor City, FL

**Kaua`i White**
- Bronze Medal, 2010 5th Annual International Rum Festival, Ybor City, FL

*Highlighted spirits:*
**Kaua`i White**
Kaua`i White is a clean and inviting rum.  It's dry and crisp with hints of oak and toasted sugars.

**Kaua`i Gold**
Kaua`i Gold has a vivid golden oak appearance.  It is slightly sweet with hints of molasses and vanilla and a burnt sugar finish.

*Highlighted spirits:*

**Kaua`i Dark**

Kaua`i Dark has rich coffee hues with notes of vanilla, cotton candy, roasted nuts, and caramel apple.

**Kaua`i Spice Rum**

Produced from a proprietary spice blend, golden wheat in color with hints of spice cake on the nose, Kaua`i Spice Rum is extremely well-balanced with a hint of caramel and vanilla and a long, smooth finish.

*Services offered other than production:*

The tasting room offers complimentary tastings of up to one ounce per person per day, and complimentary samples of other proprietary products including rum cake and chocolate rum fudge sauce. The company store, adjacent to the tasting room, features a comprehensive selection of logo products and unique gift items from Kaua`i, the other Hawaiian Islands, and beyond.

*About:*

Kōloa Rum Company was founded in 2001 to produce and market world class, single batch micro-distilled, authentic Hawaiian rum on the island of Kaua`i. In September of 2009, the Kōloa Rum Company opened its tasting room and company store and commenced bottling operations. It then established state-wide distribution in Hawaii and entered into the

California and western Canada markets. Collectively, the fermentation, distillation and blending specialists have nearly sixty years experience in the alcohol beverage industry.

The tasting room and company store are located on the grounds of the historic Kilohana Plantation in Puhi. The beautiful plantation-style building was designed in harmony with the historical feel of the plantation, and the design is authentic Hawaiiana. The history of Hawaii's first sugar plantation lives within each bottle of Kōloa Rum. The rum is carefully handcrafted in single batches from Kaua`i grown raw crystal sugar from the west side of the island and from pure mountain rainwater that is captured and slowly filtered through layers of volcanic strata before finally reaching vast underground aquifers from Mt. Wai`ale`ale and the nearby mountain peaks and rainforests. It is distilled in a 1,210 gallon vintage copper-pot still that was manufactured in New England shortly after World War II.

*Future business plans and goals:*

The location of the Kōloa Rum Company provides it with the a unique opportunity to develop a high prestige rum brand that bridges the Far East, South Pacific and North America. Its goal is to be a widely sought-after brand that is inextricably linked to and associated with the Hawaiian Islands. Additionally, it is working steadily to enhance its brand identity, expand production, and develop distribution in California and throughout North America and Canada.

*Suggested recipe:*

**Poipu Cooler** - Created by Hoku Gordines, Brennecke's Beach Boiler, Kaua`i

- 1 ½ oz Kōloa Rum Company Kaua`i Spice Rum
- ½ cup fresh mint
- ½ lime squeezed
- 1 oz soda water

  Muddle ingredients together.
  Add ice to fill glass then add:

- 3 oz pineapple juice
- 1 oz cranberry juice to float

Kōloa Rum Company
Kalaheo, Hawaii

91

# Bardenay Inc.

Kevin Settles, Owner

610 Grove St.
Boise, Idaho 83702

*Phone:* 208-426-0538
*Fax:* 208-426-8168
*Email:* info@bardenay.com
*Website:* www.bardenay.com
*Facebook:* Bardenay
*Twitter:* @Bardenay
*UrbanSpoon:* Bardenay
*Yelp:* Bardenay Restaurant & Distillery
*Trip Advisor:* Bardenay Restaurant & Distillery

*Region:* Idaho

*Type*: Micro-distillery producing approximately 2,000 cases or 4,759 gallons per year

*Opened:* Boise, ID – 1999; Eagle, ID – 2004; Coeur d'Alene, ID – 2007

*Hours of operation:* Varies

*Tours:* Tours are available.

*Types of spirits produced*: Gin, rum, and vodka

*Names of spirits:*
- Bardenay London Dry Gin
- Bardenay Vodka
- Bardenay Small Batch Rum

*Average bottle price*: $10.00 to $20.00

*Distribution:* Bardenay Distillery sells everything it makes to the state of Idaho and buys most of it back for sale in cocktails in its bars. What it does not sell in drinks is sold by the state of Idaho in its state stores. Idaho law does not allow Bardenay to sell bottles to the public.

*Highlighted spirits:*
## Bardenay London Style Dry Gin
Bardenay London Style Dry Gin is clear with a platinum cast, orange spice tea, meringue, floral juniper, and sweet anise aromas. A soft, round entry leads to a glycerous medium-to-full body of creamy citrus custard, bold reedy juniper, and honeyed orange peel flavors. It finishes with a creamy vanilla, sweet lemon, pepper, and floral talc fade. It's a round, flavorful, nicely balanced gin that will be excellent with tonic or in martinis.

## Bardenay Vodka

Bardenay Vodka is clear with aromas of fresh buttercream frosting and white cake that follow through on a round, satiny entry to a dryish medium-to-full body. It finishes with a long, powdered sugar and wet stone fade. It's a tasty, creamy, and appealing vodka for cocktails or for sipping on the rocks.

## Bardenay Small Batch Rum

Bardenay Small Batch Rum is pale golden silver in color. Interesting aromas of anise seeds, tarragon, and caramelized pecans follow through on a round, soft entry to a dryish medium body with Milk Duds and pink peppercorn notes. It finishes with a crisp, lively spicy finish.

*Events and Celebrations:*
Bardenay hosts monthly fundraising events for select charitable organizations as chosen by the staff and management.

*Services offered other than production:*
Restaurants and bars

*Interesting facts:*
* Bardenay Distillery is the nation's first restaurant distillery.

*About:*
To make Bardenay a reality, Idaho state law had to be changed and the Bureau of Alcohol, Tobacco and Firearms (BATF) had to modify its interpretation of what constituted an allowable space for a distillery.

In Idaho, it was illegal to manufacture distilled spirits and, at the same time, hold a license to sell liquor by the drink. Bardenay hired a lobbyist and crafted legislation that would eliminate this restriction under certain circumstances. Many months were spent lobbying for the bill and it passed the legislature and was signed by the governor in April of 1999.

That fall, the BATF issued a permit for a pilot distillery so recipes could be developed and the process of formula approval started.

93

Getting permission to move into the restaurant location is when the real work started. Prior to Bardenay, the BATF had never allowed a distillery to operate in a public space. This meant that the application was put under much more scrutiny than the average application and the process took months. With every step up the ladder the application took, the ability to comply with regulations and ensure that all procedures would be followed and all taxes paid had to be explained again. Eventually the application ended up at BATF headquarters in Washington D.C. The overwhelming support from Idaho helped ensure approval. The legislature had passed a law for Bardenay, the Governor had supplied a letter of support to the BATF, and one of Idaho's U.S. Senators had contacted them on the distillery's behalf. Permission to move from the pilot facility was granted during the winter of 2000 and on April 25, 2000, Bardenay Boise became the first bar in America to sell a cocktail that contained spirits made on its premises. The distillery in Eagle opened in the winter of 2005 and the distillery in Coeur d'Alene opened in the fall of 2007.

Bardenay Distillery ingredients are not native to its area but it does buy spices from a local co-op and uses local artists and printers for its labels. Additionally, the distillery reuses what it can within federal regulations. Both the restaurant and distillery recycle extensively and the menus are printed on a special paper that uses a minimum amount of water to produce and lasts four times longer than the distillery's old menu paper.

*Professional associations:* American Distilling Institute

*Future business plans and goals:*
Expand spirit production while maintaining product quality. Look for new opportunities.

*Suggested recipe:*
**Bardenay Ginger Rum Cocktail**
- 1½ oz Bardenay Rum
- ¾ oz triple sec
- 2 oz homemade sweet & sour mix

Bardenay Inc.
Boise, Eagle, and Coeur d'Alene Idaho

# Koenig Distillery

Andrew Koenig, Owner & Master Distiller

20928 Grape Lane
Caldwell, Idaho  83607

*Phone:*  208-455-8386
*Fax:*  208-455-8038
*Email:*  info@koenigdistilleryandwinery.com
*Website:*  www.koenigdistilleryandwinery.com
*Facebook:*  Koenig Distillery and Winery
*Twitter:*  @DrinkKoenig

*Region:*  Southwest Idaho

*Type:*  Micro-distillery producing approximately 12,000 gallons per year

*Opened:*  1999

*Hours of operation:*  Tasting room is open Friday through Sunday 12:00pm to 5:00pm

*Tours:*  Private tours can be arranged by calling 208-455-8386.

*Types of spirits produced:*  Flavored vodka, potato vodka, eau de vie

*Names of spirits:*
- Koenig Potato Vodka
- Koenig Huckleberry Flavored Vodka
- Koenig Pear Brandy
- Koenig Apricot Brandy
- Koenig Cherry Brandy
- Koenig Plum Brandy
- Koenig Grappa

*Average bottle price:*  $19.95

*Distribution:*
Idaho state liquor stores, the tasting room, and controlled state stores in Pennsylvania, Oregon, Washington, and Montana.   There are limited sales in California and the Northeast.

*Awards and Recognitions:*
## Huckleberry Vodka
- Silver Medal, 89 points, "Highly Recommended," Beverage Testing Institute
- Bronze Medal, 2011 San Francisco World Spirits Competition

*Awards and Recognitions:*

**Potato Vodka**
- Gold Medal, 90 points, 2009 International Review of Spirits BTI Institute
- Top 50 Spirits 2007/Superb (90-95)/Highly Recommended, Wine Enthusiast Mag.
- Silver Medal, 2007 San Francisco World Spirits Competition
- Four Stars & "Highly Recommended," F. Paul Pacult's Spirit Journal

**Pear Brandy**
- Gold Medal, 2001 New World International Wine Competition
- Silver Medal, 2001 Intervin International Wine & Spirits Competition
- Silver Medal, 2001 LA County Fair Wine & Spirits Competition
- 88 points, "Highly Recommended," Beverage Testing Institute

**Grappa**
- Silver Medal, 2001 Northwest International Wine Competition
- 86 points, "Highly Recommended," 2001 Beverage Testing Institute

**Cherry Brandy**
- Silver Medal, 2001 Northwest Wine Summit
- Bronze Medal, 2002 New World International Wine Competition
- Bronze Medal, 2001 LA County Fair Wine & Spirits Competition

**Plum Brandy**
- Gold Medal, 2001 Intervin International Wine & Spirits Competition

**Apricot Brandy**
- Silver Medal, 2002 Taster's Guild
- Bronze Medal, 2002 LA County Fair Wine & Spirits Competition

*Highlighted spirits:*

**Koenig Huckleberry Flavored Vodka**
Koenig Distillery macerates handpicked, wild huckleberries in vodka and then slowly distills them in custom made copper stills. The resulting all-natural spirit has a ripe berry aroma and a slightly sweet flavor that blends extremely well with other spirits, champagne and freshly squeezed fruit to make unusual and elegant cocktails.

**Koenig Potato Vodka**
Using the world's finest potatoes, Rocky Mountain water and unique, hand hammered copper- pot stills from Germany, Koenig Distillery carefully crafts a super-premium potato vodka slowly, one batch at a time.

**Koenig Pear Brandy**
Koenig Pear Brandy begins with locally grown, tree-ripened Bartlett pears. Either estate grown or purchased from local farmers, the fruit is picked at its ripest, hand sorted and gently mashed to begin fermenting. Once the fruit is carefully fermented, it is slowly distilled in small, copper-pot stills. The final step is aging in clear glass carboys for a minimum of two years to preserve the flavor of the fruit. While this is not the simplest or the most cost effective way to make the product, the end result is an award-winning brandy. The finished spirit has an incredible aromatic pear essence.

*Services offered other than production:* Tasting room and small retail store

*Interesting facts:*
- It takes more than 15 pounds of fresh fruit to make each bottle of brandy.

*About:*

Designed and built by brothers Andrew and Greg Koenig, Koenig Distillery and Winery combines old world brandy, vodka, and winemaking traditions with some of the Northwest's finest fruit to produce classic eau de vie fruit brandies, premium varietal wines, and vodka.

The idea to establish a distillery and winery in southwest Idaho has roots in Europe, where the brothers lived for three years in their father's hometown of Lustenau, Austria. There, pears, apples, and plums were transformed into clear, distinctive spirits through the age old art of distillation. At home in Idaho, some of the Northwest's finest fruit was being grown on the Sunny Slope, near where their mother's family had homesteaded and made wine during the Great Depression two generations earlier. The concept of traditionally distilling high quality fruit into world class brandies provided the foundation on which the Koenig brothers slowly built the Koenig Distillery and Winery.

For over four generations, the Sunny Slope area has been synonymous with the highest quality fruit. Long summer days, cool nights and the temperate influence of the Snake River create an ideal climate for growing aromatic fruit and premium wine grapes. Fertile, sandy soils and high altitude add an extra dimension exclusive to the Snake River Valley.

Aware of the potential quality of brandy distilled from fruit grown in this area, Andy and Greg set out to establish a small orchard and vineyard near the river. Peach, apricot, plum, pear, and cherry varieties known for their flavor were planted in 1995, with a small vineyard of Merlot, Semillon, and Chardonnay being added a year later. Harvests from these plantings comprise the majority of Koenig brandies and wines. In 2006, the Koenigs added a new and much larger 2-column, 50-plate still specifically for the production of potato vodka. The original hand hammered, coppe- pot stills were custom built by a fourth generation German coppersmith specifically for the production of eau de vie and vodka.

With the tremendous growth of flavored vodkas, Koenig introduced a huckleberry flavored vodka to the market in 2008.

*Management profile:*
Andrew Koenig trained in a 400 year old facility in the Austrian Alps where careful methods and traditions of distilling have been perfected for centuries. Additionally, Andrew is a consultant for other craft distilleries. His services include providing assistance with set-up and production.

Greg Koenig created the watercolor artwork that is used on the labels.

Jill Koenig used her design background to develop the labels, logos and marketing materials.

*Professional associations:* American Distilling Institute

*Future business plans and goals:* Expansion while maintaining high quality standards

*Suggested recipes:*

## The Frozen Peach
- 8 oz Koenig Potato Vodka
- 4 oz Koenig Apricot Brandy
- 1 12 oz can of frozen lemonade
- 4 ripe Idaho peaches, skin removed and chopped or 2 cups frozen peaches
- 8-12 ice cubes or 1-2 cups crushed ice

Blend all ingredients until ice is reduced to small pieces.
Serve in cocktail glasses.
Serves 4-6.

## Huckleberry Blast
- 2 parts Koenig Huckleberry Vodka
- 2 lemon wedges
- Ginger ale

Garnish with 3 to 4 berries.
Pour over ice and stir.

## Hucktini
- 2 parts Koenig Huckleberry Vodka
- ½ part of simple syrup
- Muddled lime

Combine the ingredients in a martini shaker.
Shake well.
Strain and serve with garnished lime.

Koenig Distillery
Caldwell, Idaho

## Few Spirits LLC

Paul Hletko, Founder

918 Chicago Avenue
Evanston, Illinois 60202

*Phone:* 847-920-8628
*Email:* info@fewspirits.com
*Website:* www.fewspirits.com
*Facebook:* Few Spirits
*Twitter:* @fewspirits
*Blog:* fewspirits.tumblr.com

*Region:* Northeastern Illinois

*Type:* Micro-distillery producing less than 5,000 proof gallons of spirits annually

*Opened:* 2011

*Hours of operation:* By appointment

*Tours:* Tours are offered on Saturdays at 2:00pm and by appointment.

*Types of spirits produced:* Gin and whiskey

*Names of spirits:*
- Few American Gin
- Few White Whiskey
- Few Bourbon
- Few Rye

*Average bottle price*:
White spirits range from $35.00 to $45.00.
Bourbon and rye range from $70.00 to $80.00.

*Distribution:* Products are distributed through the tasting room and retail outlets.

*Highlighted spirits:*

### Few American Gin

Nuanced by notes of vanilla and citrus peel, American Gin slowly reveals its more subdued juniper flavor awash in a house-distilled grain spirit. Equally satisfying sipped with ice or blended into a craft cocktail, this is a gin essential to any stalwart of fine drinking.

### Few White Whiskey

White Whiskey is bottled exactly as it comes from the still with no frills. Clean and crisp, White Whiskey is unkissed by the barrel as part of the distillery's revitalization of the Prohibition era staple. More refined and intentionally left unfiltered to preserve flavor, this throwback is a showcase of Few Spirits' quality grains and craftsmanship.

*Services offered other than production:* Few Spirits offers tastings and tours.

*Interesting facts:*
- Few Spirits is the first legal alcohol ever produced in Evanston, Illinois.

*About:*
Evanston, a dry community, was home to many influential advocates for Prohibition who effectively kept the city free of alcohol for more than one hundred years.

Though the city legalized drinking in the late nineties, it took the perseverance of Founder and Master Distiller Paul Hletko to reverse the antiquated liquor laws. With roots going back to some of Europe's fabled brewing families, Paul and Few Spirits have marked the end of Evanston's Prohibition and given the city its very own craft distillery.

Few Spirits uses as many local ingredients as possible and may be one of the only distilleries in the country that grows its own hops for its gin.

*Professional associations:*
American Distilling Institute, DISCUS, and Midwest Distillers Guild

*Future business plans and goals:*
Continued growth, expanded product line and broadened distribution

*Suggested recipes:*
**White Manhattan**
- 2 oz Few White Whiskey
- ½ oz Sweet Vermouth
- 2-3 dashes Angostura Orange Bitters

   Garnish with maraschino cherry.

**American Trade Winds**
- 2 oz Few American Gin
- ½ oz Orange Curacao
- ½ oz lemon juice

   Garnish with lemon twist.

Few Spirits LLC
Evanston, Illinois

100

# Hum Spirits Company

Jennifer Piccione, Chief Executive Officer
Adam Seger, Chief Innovative Officer
Bryce Williford, Chief Financial Officer
Erin Ramsay, Social Media Coordinator and Executive Assistant

676 N. LaSalle Drive, Unit 329
Chicago, Illinois 60654

*Phone:* 312-735-1838
*Email:* info@humspirits.com
*Website:* www.humspirits.com
*Facebook:* The Hum Spirits Company
*Twitter:* @humspirits
*YouTube:* Hum Channel

*Region:* Northeastern Illinois

*Type:* Liqueur

*Opened:* November 2009

*Hours of operation:* 9:00am to 6:00pm

*Tours:* Tours are available.

*Types of spirits produced:* Liqueur

*Names of spirits:* Hum Botanical Spirit

*Best known for:* Hum Botanical Spirit

*Average bottle price:* $36.00

*Distribution:*
Illinois, Minnesota, Tennessee, New York, New Jersey, Delaware, Virginia, Washington DC, Maryland, Florida, Atlanta, Louisiana, Arizona, Nevada, California, Montana, Washington, Idaho and Texas

*Awards and Recognitions:*
**Hum**
- Gold Medal, 2011 MicroLiquor Spirit Awards
- 94 Points "Exceptional," September 2009 Beverage Testing Institute
- 5 Stars, Highest Recommendation, September 2009 F. Paul Pacult's Spirit Journal
- 140 Best Spirits in the World, 2011 F. Paul Pacult's Spirit Journal
- Hum was the only spirit featured at Oprah Winfrey's Wrap Party at the Four Seasons in Chicago, 2011

Hum is a 70 proof liqueur that is strong enough to stand alone as a base spirit, but has the versatility to blend with every other base spirit, wine and even beer to make unique cocktails. Hum has a pot still rum base infused with four incredibly rich botanicals - hibiscus, ginger, cardamom and kaffir lime - to produce a perfectly balanced spirit. Hum uses 100% natural ingredients.

Technically a liqueur, Hum has a striking crimson red color from fair trade hibiscus, a peppery kick from organic ginger, heady aromatics from cardamom and the intoxicating fragrance of kaffir lime. This unparalleled spirit ironically tastes like a bold red wine.

Hum is best enjoyed on the rocks or with a splash of soda and lime or your favorite cola. Enjoy it tall with tonic, ginger ale, lemon/lime or citrus soda. Add Hum to your favorite beer or sparkling wine. Replace sweet vermouth or orange liqueur with Hum to kick up the classic Negroni, Manhattan or Margarita. Shake it with sour mix to make an incredible Martini. Brew your favorite tea, add Hum and seasonal produce and make a killer punch. Cook with Hum like you would with brandy. Then, end your evening with your favorite ice cream drizzled with Hum. The applications are only limited by your imagination.

*About:*

Inspired by the French Caribbean and modeled after the great amaros of Italy, celebrated Mixologist and Founder Adam Seger of Chicago infuses pot still hum with fair trade hibiscus, ginger root, green cardamom and kaffir lime to create the beautifully balanced American botanical spirit called Hum.

All ingredients for Hum are from California and it is produced at Pennsylvania Pure Distilleries in Glenshaw, Pennsylvania. Bottles used for samples and R&D are re-purposed into hummingbird feeders.

*Management profile:*

**Adam Seger**

CIO Adam Seger is a mixologist, advanced sommelier and certified culinary professional.

**Jennifer Piccione**

CEO Jennifer Piccione is an attorney and graduate of the Advanced Academy of Southern Wine and Spirits Academy of Fine Wine and Spirits.

*Future business plans and goals:* Continue growth and increased distribution

Hum Spirits Company
Chicago, Illinois

# Koval Distillery

Robert Birnecker, Owner / Master Distiller
Sonat Birnecker, Owner / President

5121 N. Ravenswood Avenue
Chicago, Illinois 60640

*Phone:* 312-878-7988
*Email:* info@koval-distillery.com
*Website:* www.koval-distillery.com, www.lionspridewhiskey.com
*Facebook:* KOVAL Distillery
*Twitter:* @kovaldistillery

*Region:* Midwest

*Type:* Micro-distillery producing approximately 3,000 gallons annually

*Opened:* 2008

*Tours:* Tours are offered every Wednesday, Saturday, and Sunday; private tours for large parties and special events

*Types of spirits produced:*
Brandy, beer spirit, aged whiskey, white whiskey, and liqueurs

*Names of spirits:*
**White Whiskey:**
KOVAL Rye Chicago, KOVAL Midwest Wheat, KOVAL American Oat, KOVAL Levant Spelt, KOVAL Raksi Millet

**Aged Whiskey:**
Lion's Pride Rye, Lion's Pride Dark Rye, Lion's Pride Oat, Lion's Pride Dark Oat, Lion's Pride Wheat, Lion's Pride Dark Wheat, Lion's Pride Millet, Lion's Pride Dark Millet, Lion's Pride Spelt, Lion's Pride Dark Spelt

**Liqueurs:**
KOVAL Rose Hip, KOVAL Ginger, KOVAL Chrysanthemum Honey, KOVAL Jasmine, KOVAL Coffee, KOVAL Orange Blossom

**Brandy:**
KOVAL Pear Brandy (Williams), KOVAL Apple Brandy (aged in American oak)

**Beer spirit:** KOVAL Bierbrand

103

*Best known for:* The Rose Hipster cocktail

*Average bottle price*: $25.00 to $45.00

*Distribution:* California, Colorado, Illinois, Indiana, Kentucky, Maryland, Missouri, New Jersey, New York, Tennessee, Washington DC, and Wisconsin

*Awards and Recognitions:*

**KOVAL Rye Chicago**
- Gold Medal, 2010 American Distilling Institute
- Gold Medal, 2010 Destillata

**KOVAL American Oat**
- Gold Medal, 2011 American Distilling Institute
- Silver Medal, 2010 Destillata

**KOVAL Chrysanthemum Honey Liqueur**
- Silver Medal 89 points, Beverage Testing Institute
- Bronze Medal, 2010 Destillata

**KOVAL Ginger Liqueur**
- Gold Medal, 2011 SIP Awards
- Silver Medal, 89 points, Beverage Testing Institute
- Bronze Medal, 2010 Destillata

**KOVAL Rose Hip Liqueur**
- Silver Medal 88 points, Beverage Testing Institute

**KOVAL Midwest Wheat**
- Bronze Medal, 2010 Destillata

**KOVAL Raksi Millet**
- Bronze Medal, 2010 Destillata

Bottle photos by: Alan Gagne

*Highlighted spirits:*

**Rye Chicago**

This distillate has been compared to aquavit because of its peppery and floral notes. Rye Chicago is smooth, round, and warm, with a hint of vanilla. Peppery and floral notes abound in this distillate with a hint of sweet vanilla. However, it is really a traditional American drink – George Washington is said to have made it. Rye Chicago is perfect sipped or mixed, political aspirations optional.

**Lion's Pride Rye Whiskey**

This single-barrel, 100% rye whiskey is aged in new American oak just long enough to unleash the fruitiness, softness and vanilla in each distillate. Lion's Pride Rye Whiskey is extremely smooth and easy to sip.

**Lion's Pride Organic Whiskey**

Named after the distillers' eldest son, Lion's Pride Organic Whiskey is a single-grain, single-barrel whiskey. This whiskey contains only the pure heart cut distillate of the single-grain white whiskeys and is aged in new American oak barrels. The wood for each barrel is carefully selected for the fineness of its grain and its tannin content. Additionally, these barrels are only used once and are available for sale throughout the year.

## Ginger Liqueur

Each batch of Ginger Liqueur requires 60 pounds of hand peeled organic ginger. Because of its spicy and satiny flavor, this liqueur can be used for cooking, mixed with rum or lemonade, or enjoyed straight.

## Coffee Liqueur

Organic coffee beans for this liqueur are roasted to perfection at a carbon-neutral facility in Brazil. The beans have a rich flavor with a subtle dark chocolate finish. Add it to hot chocolate or coffee, mix it into a martini, or use it to make the best ever tiramisu.

*Services offered other than production:*
Aside from production, Sonat and Robert teach distilling and serve as consultants for prospective distillers, www.kotheconsulting.com. Since Robert grew up distilling, he has extensive experience that many new distillers lack. The Birneckers' efforts as educators and consultants are their contribution to help improve the craft industry. They offer one of the most comprehensive courses for prospective distillers in the U.S., and it is the only course that brings together professors of distillation and fermentation from Europe and the U.S. Students also have a chance to get hands on experience. Finally, the Birneckers are also representatives for Kothe Destillationstechnik, one of the leading producers of distillation equipment in the world.

*Interesting facts:*
• Koval Distillery is first boutique distillery located in Chicago since Prohibition.

*About:*
When their son was born, Sonat and Robert Birnecker decided they wanted a quality of life that their careers as a professor and an Austrian Embassy press secretary could not provide. They wanted to live in the city they loved, close to family and friends, and to be able to walk to work, to eat lunch as a family daily, and to have their children with them all the time. Robert grew up in Austria helping his grandparents make brandy, white whiskey, and liqueurs, and soon it became clear that distilling was a family tradition that they could carry on in Chicago that would give the quality of life they wanted.

The name Koval is Yiddish for blacksmith, but the word also refers to a black sheep or someone who does something unexpected or out of the ordinary. Sonat's great-grandfather earned Koval as his nickname when, at the age of 17, he surprised his family and emigrated from Vienna to Chicago in the early 1900s. Coincidentally, the surname of Robert's grandfather (at whose side Robert learned the art of distilling) is Schmid - German for smith. Sonat and Robert chose the name Koval to honor both men and to reflect their own extraordinary decision to give up comfortable jobs in DC, to relocate to Chicago, and to build a family business from the ground up.

*Management profile:*
### Robert Birnecker
Robert Birnecker is one of America's leading consultants on craft spirits. He not only teaches distilling at the prestigious Siebel Institute of Technology, but he also has a spirits certificate from Austria's leading distilling and brewing university. Robert has been setting up distilleries across America and Canada for many years now and has personally taught many of the craft distillers listed in this book. In addition to private consulting, Robert also offers two workshops a year, one in the spring and one in the winter. Information about workshops and consulting can be found at www.kotheconsulting.com. Robert also runs www.kothedistilling.com and www.kothecomplete.com, resources for those interested in buying distilling equipment.

### Sonat Birnecker
Sonat Birnecker is a Chicago native and has an MSt from Oxford and a PhD from the University of London.

Both can answer any questions you may have about German literature of the 20th century, Jewish history in Germany or Austria, or the political and economic culture of North Africa. Also, if the mood struck, they could lindy hop around the distillery while saying sweet nothings to each other in about five languages.

*Professional associations:*   Midwest Distillers Guild

*Future business plans and goals:*  Broadened distribution of current portfolio

*Suggested recipe:*
### Rose Hipster
- 2½ oz Koval Rose Hip Liqueur
- 2½ oz gin

    Mix in a shaker and garnish with an orange slice.

Koval Distillery
Chicago, Illinois

# Quincy Street Distillery

Derrick C. Mancini, Owner

*Physical Address:*
39 E. Quincy Street
Riverside, Illinois  60546

*Mailing Address:*
91 Lawton Road
Riverside, Illinois  60546

*Phone:*  708-870-5987
*Email:*  manager@quincystreetdistillery.com
*Website:*  www.quincystreetdistillery.com
*Facebook:*  Quincy Street Distillery

*Region:*  Northeastern Illinois

*Type:*  Micro-distillery producing approximately 2,500 gallons per year

*Opened:*  February 2012

*Hours of operation:*  Friday and Saturday, 5:00pm to 9:00pm

*Tours:*  Tours are available by appointment.

*Types of spirits produced:*  Gin, eau de vie, absinthe, vodka, and whiskey

*Names of spirits:*
- Taliesin™
- Strindberg™
- Old No. 176
- Water Tower White Whiskey

*Average bottle price*:  $25.00 to $55.00

*Distribution:*  Illinois

*Highlighted spirits:*
**Taliesin™**
This honey eau de vie is produced by distilling mead made from midwestern honey.

**Strindberg™**
This absinthe verte is a green absinthe made using traditional herbal flavorings and coloring.

**Old No. 176**
Old No. 176 is a traditional dry gin.

*Services offered other than production:* Tasting room and retail sales

*About:*
Quincy Street Distillery was opened in historic Riverside, Illinois, to produce and sell fine artisanal spirits.

*Management profile:*
Derrick C. Mancini is a Ph.D. scientist

*Professional associations:*
American Distilling Institute

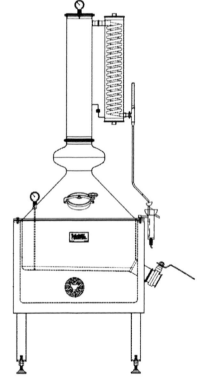

Sketch of still custom fabricated by Vendome Copper & Brass Works for Quincy Street Distillery. Copyright 2011 Derrick Mancini, all rights reserved.

Quincy Street Distillery
Riverside, Illinois

## Heartland Distillers

Stuart Hobson, Owner / Distiller

9402 Uptown Drive, Suite 1000
Indianapolis, Indiana  46256

*Phone:*  800-417-0150
*Fax:*  800-417-0150
*Email:*  stuart@heartlanddistillers.com
*Website:*  www.heartlanddistillers.com
*Website:*  www.indianavodka.com, www.indianainfusions.com
*Facebook:*  Indiana Vodka, Indiana Infusions
*Twitter:*  @Indiana_Vodka
*Region:*  Midwestern U.S.

*Type*:  Micro-distillery

*Opened:*  January 2009

*Hours of operation:*  Heartland Distillers is closed to the public.

*Tours:*  Tours can be arranged.

*Types of spirits produced:*  Gin, vodka, and whiskey

*Names of spirits:*
- Heartland Distiller's Reserve Vodka
- Heartland Distiller's Reserve Bourbon
- Indiana Vodka
- Indiana Infusions
- Prohibition Gin

*Best known for:*  Indiana Vodka

*Average bottle price*:  $17.00 to $25.00

*Distribution:*
Heartland Distillers is prohibited by law to sell directly to the public.
The spirits are, however, distributed in several U.S. states.

*Awards and Recognitions:*
**Indiana Vodka**
- Gold Medal, 2010 San Francisco World Spirits Competition
- Bronze Medal, 2010 Los Angeles International Wine & Spirits Competition

*Highlighted spirits:*

## Indiana Vodka

Handcrafted in small batches utilizing a time tested copper-pot still process, Indiana Vodka is distilled six times with only the finest Midwestern grain for maximum flavor and smoothness. It is then filtered twice and hand bottled. Each distilled batch is cold filtered, producing a clean and crisp vodka.

## Prohibition Gin

Prohibition Gin is made with fresh herbs and botanicals using an old nineteenth century technique. The gin base is distilled six times for maximum smoothness. During the final distillation, the herbs and botanicals are placed in a botanical extraction vessel and their essences are gently extracted as the alcohol vapor rises up through the still. This process produces a smooth and aromatic gin.

## Indiana Infusions

Indiana Infusions is made from Indiana Vodka and comes in seven flavors including honey lemon, cherry vanilla, orange cream, raspberry citrus, double vanilla, chocolate espresso, and chai tea.

*Events and Celebrations:*
Heartland Distillers hosts numerous tastings and events year-round and often donates its time and products to many local charity events and fundraisers.

*Interesting facts:*
  * Heartland Distillers is Indiana's first new distillery since Prohibition.

*About:*
Heartland Distillers was founded in 2008 by Stuart Hobson who wanted to revamp Indiana's 200 year old distilling heritage that had died out during Prohibition.

With nearly two decades of experience in the spirits industry and a longing to get back to his family roots in manufacturing, Hobson applied for and was issued the first new beverage distillery license in Indiana since Prohibition, and he set up the distillery.

In January of 2009, the appropriately named Indiana Vodka was the first product to be crafted. Heartland Distillers utilizes time tested Old World techniques, hand-selected ingredients and modern technology to create all of its unique and flavorful spirits.

*Future business plans and goals:* Introduction of Heartland Distiller's Reserve Vodka, Heartland Distiller's Reserve Bourbon, and several liqueurs

Heartland Distillers
Indianapolis, Indiana

# Virtuoso Distillers LLC

Steve Ross, Owner

4211 Grape Road
Mishawaka, Indiana 46545

*Phone:* 574-876-4450
*Fax:* 574-391-3828
*Email:* steve@18vodka.com
*Website:* www.18vodka.com
*Facebook:* 18 Vodka
*Twitter:* @18Vodka

*Region:* North-Central Indiana

*Type:* Craft-distillery producing approximately 150 gallons per month

*Opened:* February 2008

*Hours of operation:* 10:00am to 5:00pm

*Tours:* Tours are available by appointment.

*Types of spirits produced:* Vodka, whiskey, and lemoncello

*Names of spirits:*
- 18 Vodka

*Best known for:* Vodka

*Average bottle price:* $23.00 to $28.00

*Distribution:* Indiana, District of Columbia, and Illinois

*Awards and Recognitions:*
- Spirit Journal, March 2009

*Highlighted spirits:*
**18 Vodka**
18 Vodka is an all-natural spirit made from 100% rye. The purity of its ingredients is apparent in its silky smoothness. The rye is of the highest quality and is American grown. The water used is crystal clear and is sourced from a natural, underground aquifer

*About:*

Inspired by early American distillation, the masters at Virtuoso Distillers handcrafted batch after batch until they found the perfect smoothness and light body for their 18 Vodka.

The production of 18 Vodka incorporates a number of sound monitoring practices. These practices allow the master distiller the ability to select the true hearts of the distillation cycle at the same point in every batch. 18 Vodka derives its name from their German copper- pot still which contains 18 distillation chambers within two copper columns and harmonizes traditional, trusted distillation methods with state of the art technology. Only after running through all 18 chambers of the still can it be called 18 Vodka. Right through to bottling, 18 Vodka is meticulously handcrafted to ensure superior quality. Additionally, every bottle is inspected before it goes out the door.

*Future business plans and goals:* Broaden distribution

*Suggested recipes:*

**Raspberry 18 Vodka Collins**

Muddle 4 raspberries in ¾ oz simple syrup then add
- 1 oz lemon juice
- 2 oz 18 Vodka

  Combine ingredients and shake.
  Pour over ice in a Collins glass.
  Top with soda water.
  Garnish with two speared raspberries and a lemon twist.

**18 Vodka Gimlet**
- 2 oz 18 Vodka
- ½ oz fresh lime juice

  Combine ingredients in a shaker with ice.
  Shake and strain into a chilled cocktail glass.
  Serve with a lime twist.

**18 Chocolate**
- 3 oz of 18 Vodka
- ½ oz Crème de Cacao

  Dip the rim of a martini glass in powdered chocolate.
  Combine ingredients in a shaker with ice.
  Shake and strain into the glass, and serve.

Virtuoso Distillers LLC
Mishawaka, Indiana

## Cedar Ridge Distillery

Jeff Quint, Owner

1441 Marak Road
Swisher, Iowa 52338

*Phone:* 319-857-4300
*Fax:* 319-857-4301
*Email:* info@crwine.com
*Websites:* www.crwine.com, www.clearheartspirits.com, www.crdistillery.com
*Facebook:* Cedar Ridge Winery & Distillery

*Region:* East-Central Iowa

*Type*: Micro-distillery producing 600 to 3,000 gallons monthly

*Opened:* 2005

*Hours of operation:*　Wednesday through Friday from 11:00am to 9:00pm
　　　　　　　　　　　Saturday and Sunday from 11:00am to 5:00pm

*Tours:* Tours are available upon request.

*Types of spirits produced:* Brandy, bourbon whiskey, gin, grappa, liqueur, rum, vodka

*Names of spirits:*
- ClearHeart Vodka
- ClearHeart Gin
- ClearHeart Light Rum
- Cedar Ridge Dark Rum
- Cedar Ridge Iowa Bourbon Whiskey
- Cedar Ridge Apple Brandy
- Cedar Ridge Grape Brandy
- Cedar Ridge Lemoncella (lemon liqueur)
- Cedar Ridge Lamponcella (raspberry liqueur)
- Cedar Ridge Grappa

*Distribution:* Iowa, Illinois, Missouri, and Nebraska

*Awards and Recognitions:*

**Cleara Heart Vodka**
- International Gold Medal, Best in Category, Los Angeles Spirits Competition

**Cedar Ridge Dark Rum**
- International Gold Medal, Los Angeles Spirits Competition

**Cedar Ridge Iowa Bourbon Whiskey**
- Gold Medal, Los Angeles Spirits Competition

**Lemoncella**
- Silver Medal 87 points, Beverage Testing Institute

**Cedar Ridge Grappa**
- Silver Medal, San Francisco World Spirits Competition

*Highlighted spirits:*

**Cedar Ridge Bourbon Whiskey**
Cedar Ridge Bourbon Whiskey is Iowa's first bourbon whiskey. Because it's handcrafted in small batches with a European-engineered, custom pot still, it's a smooth, premium bourbon.

**Cedar Ridge Apple Brandy**
Cedar Ridge Apple Brandy is crafted from fresh apple juice from a local orchard, aged for two to three years in American oak barrels, and then finished in limousine oak barrels for three months.

**Clearheart Vodka**
Clearheart Triple Distilled Fruit & Grain Vodka is handcrafted ten gallons at a time. The distillation process begins by using light fruit wine to capture a faint hint of fruit in the final product. With each step in the distillations process, Cedar Ridge retains only the heart of the batch, resulting in a crisp, clear vodka that finishes very clean.

**Cedar Ridge Grappa**
Cedar Ridge Grappa is the only grappa available in Iowa and is a true grappa made with the leftovers of wine making.

**Cedar Ridge Lamponcella Liqueur**
Cedar Ridge Lamponcella is a sweet, intense raspberry liqueur.

**Cedar Ridge Lemoncella Liqueur**
Cedar Ridge Lemoncella bursts with super sweet and super lemony flavor.

*Interesting facts:*
- Cedar Ridge Distillery is Iowa's first micro-distillery.

Cedar Ridge Distillery
Swisher, Iowa

# Mississippi River Distilling Company

Ryan and Garrett Burchett, Owners

303 North Cody Road
Post Office Box 801
LeClaire, Iowa 52753

*Phone:* 563-484-4342
*Fax:* 563-289-4455
*Email:* info@mrdistilling.com
Distiller's: ryan@mrdistilling.com, garrett@mrdistilling.com
*Website:* www.mrdistilling.com
*Facebook:* Mississippi River Distilling Company
*Twitter:* @mrivrdistilling
*YouTube:* Mississippi River Distilling

*Region:* Eastern Iowa and Western Illinois

*Type*: Micro-distillery producing approximately 6,000 gallons annually

*Opened:* December 2010

*Hours of operation:*
Monday through Saturday from 10:00am to 5:00pm
Sunday 12:00pm to 5:00pm

*Tours:*
Tours are offered daily on the hour from 12:00pm to 4:00pm.

*Types of spirits produced:* Bourbon whiskey, gin, and vodka

*Names of spirits:*
- River Pilot Vodka
- River Rose Gin
- River Baron Artisan Spirit
- Cody Road Bourbon Whiskey

*Average bottle price*: $25.00 to $30.00

*Distribution:*
Iowa, Illinois, Missouri, Minnesota, and on-site retail store

*Awards and Recognitions:*
## River Pilot Vodka
- Gold Medal, 2011 International Review of Spirits , Beverage Testing Institute
- Bronze Medal, 2011 New York International Spirits Competition
- Silver Medal for Taste, 2011 MicroLiquor Spirit Awards
- Bronze Medal for Packaging and Design, 2011 MicroLiquor Spirit Awards

*Awards and Recognitions:*

**River Rose Gin**
- Silver Medal for Taste, 2011 MicroLiquor Spirit Awards
- Bronze Medal for Packaging and Design, 2011 MicroLiquor Spirit Awards

**River Baron Artisan Spirit**
- Silver Medal, 2011 Top 10 in the Nation: The Fifty Best.com
- Silver Medal for Taste, 2011 MicroLiquor Spirit Awards
- Bronze Medal for Packaging and Design, 2011 MicroLiquor Spirit Awards

*Highlighted spirits:*

**River Pilot Vodka**

River Pilot Vodka is crystal clear vodka of unparalleled smoothness. It is distilled slowly in small batches retaining the sweetness and fragrance of 100% Iowa ingredients. This full flavored vodka has the flowery aroma of wheat and the sweet, smooth finish of corn. Each bottle is hand numbered to reflect the handcrafted dedication each bottle receives.

**River Rose Gin**

River Rose honors a time when life along the river was gracious and inspiring. Reflecting the deep respect for local expertise, River Rose is distilled with fresh grains from local farmers. The unique blend of botanicals dates back to a recipe from the late 1800s. Highlighted with traditional juniper, River Rose Gin jumps from your palette with a full body of citrus including orange, grapefruit and lemon. Lavender, rose petals, and locally grown cucumbers provide a distinctive finish that makes your martini swirl with aroma. The slow, small batch process ensures a consistently clean and smooth finish.

**River Baron Artisan Spirit**

In the era when grand steamboats were the lifeblood of the Mississippi, powerful traders enhanced the life of communities; known as river barons, they were the keepers of life's luxuries. As the big steamers powered from New Orleans to St. Paul and back, these barons directed the flow of fine goods, including wine and spirits. Reflecting their demand for premium quality, River Baron is full flavored with the flowery aroma of wheat and the sweet, smooth finish of corn. This signature spirit is distilled and filtered in small batches ensuring the outstanding quality river barons demanded.

**Cody Road Bourbon Whiskey**

Cody Road Bourbon is named in honor of LeClaire, Iowa, native William "Buffalo Bill" Cody. Born in 1846, Buffalo Bill inspired and entertained many during his life. This spirit reflects his spirit, charisma and passion for life. Handmade from local heartland grains, Cody Road Bourbon is bottled at 90 proof and has a distinctive aroma with a beautifully smooth finish. Each barrel is handmade from white American oak trees, many of which are harvested in Iowa and Illinois. That oak is then cut and assembled into barrels at a cooperage just south of the headwaters of the Mississippi River in Minnesota.

*Events and Celebrations:*
Mississippi River Distilling Company features special limited bottlings each year for TugFest, a tug of war across the Mississippi River between LeClaire, Iowa, and Port Byron, Illinois.

*Services offered other than production:*  Small retail shop selling merchandise and souvenirs

*Interesting facts:*
- 100% of the grain is sourced from within 25 miles of the distillery.

*About:*  The Mississippi River Distilling Company started in 2010 after two brothers decided to take a chance on a dream.  What started out as a crazy idea grew into an opportunity to create something that LeClaire, Iowa, hadn't seen since Prohibition - a chance to create truly home grown, handmade spirits. Ground breaking took place along the banks of the Mississippi in July of 2010.  In December, the doors of the Mississippi River Distilling Company opened to the public and the first bottle of MRDC's River Baron Vodka was sold.  The products made at Mississippi River Distilling are all about the local grain and the farmers who produce it.  Guiding the process through every phase from grain to glass, the distillers intentionally leave plenty of the sweetness of the corn and wheat in their spirits.  This creates a finished product that is extremely smooth and very unique to the distillery.

*Future business plans and goals:*
Continued success and an expanded facility

*Suggested recipes:*
### Steaming Rose
- 1 oz  River Rose Gin
- ¼ oz Cointreau
- ¼ oz Kahlua
- 5 oz hot coffee
- 1 ½ oz whipping cream

  Pour all ingredients except for cream into glass coffee cup.
  Float cream and lightly drizzle with Cointreau.  Garnish with cherry.

### Mississippi Mud Pie
- 1 oz River Pilot Vodka
- 1 oz Dark Creme de Cacao
- 2 oz chocolate milk
- ¼ oz Amaretto

  Mix with ice in a shaker.
  Drizzle chocolate syrup into a martini glass for a unique presentation.
  Fill martini glass.

Mississippi River Distilling Company
LeClaire, Iowa

# Templeton Rye Distillery

Kevin Boersma, Distillery Manager

209 East 3rd Street
Templeton, Iowa 51463

*Phone:* 712-669-8793
*Email:* info@templetonrye.com
*Website:* www.templetonrye.com
*Facebook:* Templeton Rye
*Twitter:* @TempletonRye
*YouTube:* Templeton Rye Whiskey

*Region:* Midwest

*Type:*
Micro-distillery producing 100 barrels annually. Primary product is contract distilled by LDI of Lawrenceburg, Indiana.

*Opened:* 2005

*Hours of operation:* 8:00am to 5:00pm

*Tours:*
Tours are available and include a guided walk through the production area, barrel warehouse, bottling line, and tasting room.

*Types of spirits produced:* Whiskey

*Names of spirits:*
- Templeton Rye Whiskey

*Best known for:* Templeton Rye

*Average bottle price:* $39.00

*Distribution:*
Iowa, Illinois, New York, and San Francisco

*Awards and Recognitions:*
**Templeton Rye Whiskey**
- Gold Medal, 2010 San Francisco World Spirits Tasting
- Gold Medal, 2009 San Francisco World Spirits Tasting
- "Rye Whiskey of the Year" in the 2009 Whiskey Bible by Jim Murray

*Events and Celebrations:*
Templeton Rye Distillery hosts an annual Rock & Rye music festival in conjunction with the town of Templeton.

*Services offered other than production:* Tastings and merchandise sales

*Interesting facts:*
- Templeton Rye was Al Capone's whiskey of choice.

*About:*
When Prohibition outlawed the manufacture and sale of alcoholic beverages in 1920, many enterprising residents of Templeton, Iowa, chose to become outlaws. They produced a high caliber and much sought after whiskey known as Templeton Rye.

Because of its extremely smooth finish, the American rye whiskey earned the nickname of "The Good Stuff" and it made a small town with a population of 350 famous. As the premium brand of the era, Templeton Rye fetched an impressive $5.50 per gallon, or approximately $70 by today's standards.

Templeton Rye became Al Capone's whiskey of choice, quickly finding its way to the center of his bootlegging empire. Hundreds of kegs per month were supplied to Capone's gang who, in turn, filled the demand of speakeasies throughout Chicago, New York, and as far west as San Francisco.

After Capone was convicted on charges of tax evasion and sent to prison, legends suggest that a few bottles even found their way inside the walls of Alcatraz to the cell of prisoner AZ-85.

Although most American whiskeys ceased production after Prohibition ended, Templeton Rye continued to be produced illegally in small quantities for loyal patrons. In 2006, more than eighty-five years later, the infamous small batch rye whiskey was finally available legally.

Although building a distillery from scratch was a slow and expensive process, the team at Templeton Rye Distillery has made great strides to increase production capabilities in Templeton. The company maintains a strong presence in the community and eventually hopes to move all production to Templeton.

As the largest employer in Templeton, the distillery has invested more than $1 million in the local economy and has hosted more than 5,000 visitors since opening to the public.

Each year, the distillery partners with the Templeton Community Betterment Association to put on a local summer music festival called Rock & Rye.

The Templeton Rye Distillery recently spearheaded the Templeton Archive Project. This is a campaign to document the history of its product through interviews with the older residents of the Templeton area to capture their stories and preserve their unique memories of Templeton Rye, the Prohibition era, and the role Templeton Rye played in Templeton, Iowa.

*Future business plans and goals:* Continued success and growth

*Suggested recipes:*

**Blinker**
- 2 oz Templeton Rye
- ½ oz fresh grapefruit juice
- 1 bar spoon raspberry syrup or spoon of raspberry preserves

Combine all ingredients, including ice, in a mixing glass and shaker.
Shake vigorously.
Strain into a chilled cocktail coupe and garnish with grapefruit twist.

**Ward 8**
- 2 oz Templeton Rye
- ½ oz orange juice
- ½ oz lemon juice
- 3 dashes grenadine

Combine all ingredients, including ice, in a mixing glass and shaker.
Shake vigorously.
Strain into a chilled coupe cocktail glass.

**Pecan Pie**
- 2 oz Templeon Rye
- 1 oz Dark Creme de Cocoa
- 1 oz Frangelico
- ½ oz Irish cream liqueur

Shake all ingredients.
Strain and serve up in a martini glass.

Templeton Rye Distillery
Templeton, Iowa

120

## Good Spirits Distilling

Todd Bukaty, President
Ron Bailey, Vice President

2019 E. Spruce Circle #A
Olathe, Kansas  66062

*Phone:*  913-397-8815
*Fax:*  913-397-8815
*Email:*  tbukaty@goodspiritsdistilling.com
*Website:*  www.goodspiritsdistilling.com
*Facebook:*  Clear10 Vodka
*Twitter:*  @CLEAR10Vodka

*Region:*  East-central Kansas

*Type:*  Micro-distillery producing approximately 1,500 proof gallons per year

*Opened:*  2008

*Hours of operation:*   9:00am to 5:00pm

*Tours:*  Tours are not available.

*Types of spirits produced:*  Vodka, triple sec, flavored vodka, private label

*Names of spirits:*
- CLEAR10 Vodka
- Czar
- Miss Kitty's Velvet Vodka
- Twister Vodka

*Best known for:*  Asian Mahito

*Average bottle price*:  $20.00

*Distribution:*  Kansas, Missouri, and Oklahoma

*Awards and Recognitions:*
**CLEAR10 Vodka**
- Gold Medal 92 Pts., Beverage Testing Institute

*Highlighted spirits:*

**CLEAR10 Vodka**

CLEAR10 Vodka is locally crafted in small batches, distilled six times and slow-filtered ten times. This meticulous process allows the distillers to create a vodka free of additives or preservatives. The result is an exceptional taste, a clean finish and uncommon clarity.

*Interesting facts:*
- CLEAR10 Vodka is gluten free.

*About:*

CLEAR10 Vodka is the vision of three Midwest friends who decided local grains and naturally filtered water was the perfect recipe for nature's clear libation. A background in farming, mixology, chemistry, and 50 combined years consuming quality and not so quality vodka provided the founders with an extremely fastidious palate and a knack for crafting amazing vodka.

*Suggested recipes:*

**Asian Mahito** - Created by Gene Mah
- 2 oz CLEAR10 Vodka
- 6-8 oz ginger ale
- 2 fresh mint leaves
- 2 orange slices
- Ice

Muddle 1 mint leaf and 1 orange slice in the bottom of a pint glass.
Fill glass with ice.
Pour CLEAR10 Vodka slowly over ice.
Fill glass with cold ginger ale.
Stir and garnish with remaining mint leaf and orange slices.

**CLEAR10 Blue Sea**
- 2 oz CLEAR10 Vodka
- ½ oz Blue Curacao Orange Liqueur
- Lemon lime soda

Mix CLEAR10 and Blue Curacao in a cocktail shaker.
Shake well.
Add a shot of lemon lime soda.
Garnish with orange slice.

Good Spirits Distilling
Olathe, Kansas

# Barrel House Distilling Co.

Barrel House Distilling Co.

Jeff Wiseman, Owner
Peter Wright, Owner
Frank Marino, Owner

1200 Manchester Street
Lexington, Kentucky 40504

*Phone:* 859-259-0159
*Fax:* 859-259-0159
*Email:* barrelhousedistillery@yahoo.com
*Website:* www.barrelhousedistillery.com, www.purebluevodka.com
*Facebook:* Barrel House Distilling Company

*Region:* Kentucky

*Type:* Craft-distillery producing approximately 5,000 gallons per year

*Opened:* June 2008

*Hours of operation:* Varies

*Tours:* Fridays and Saturdays between 12:00pm and 5:00pm, or by appointment

*Types of spirits produced:* Moonshine, rum, vodka, and whiskey

*Names of spirits:*
- Pure Blue Vodka
- Devil John Moonshine
- Kentucky Honey (rum)

*Best known for:* The Winchester and the KY Martini

*Average bottle price:* $20.00 to $25.00

*Distribution:*
Kentucky, Tennessee, Maryland, Washington DC, and Illinois

*Highlighted spirits:*
**Pure Blue Vodka**
Pure Blue Vodka is a 100% corn vodka. It is gluten free and is cut with Kentucky mountain spring water. This is a clear clean vodka with a subtle sweet finish.

**Kentucky Honey**
Kentucky Honey is a traditional rum recipe with a twist-it has a small amount of honey that is fermented and distilled, and then aged in used, freshly dumped Kentucky bourbon barrels.

123

*Highlighted spirits:*
**Devil John Moonshine**
Devil John Moonshine is a traditional Kentucky moonshine. The moonshine recipe dates back to the mid-1800s and is named after Devil John Wright, Civil War soldier, lawman and moonshiner from the Cumberlands in Kentucky. John Wright is the great-great uncle of co-founder Peter Wright. This small batch spirit is reminiscent of a time when many a still ran in the hills of Kentucky to quench the thirst of men like Devil John and his crew.

Made from an old fashion mountain "secret" recipe, Devil John moonshine is handcrafted at 90 proof. Cane sugar is combined with just the right amount of milled corn to enhance the flavor while not overpowering the palate. The combination of corn and cane sugar allows for the best of both worlds - a pure, clean moonshine with a subtle sweetness.

*Services offered other than production:*
Tasting room and gift shop

*Interesting facts:*
- Barrel House Distilling is spearheading stream and watershed cleanup in Kentucky as a service to its community.

*About:*
Barrel House Distilling was started in 2008 by three childhood friends to renew Kentucky's pre-Prohibition heritage of craft distilling. The idea came about during a poker game; the three tossed around the idea of starting a small batch distillery in Lexington, and then they went all in and established their new company in the barreling house of the Old Pepper Bourbon Distillery. All of their products are distilled 100 gallons at a time in a spot that has a distilling tradition that dates back to the late 1700s; in fact, James E. Pepper, who ran the Pepper Distillery on the same site, is said to have invented the Manhattan cocktail.

*Management profile:*
**Jeff Wiseman**
Jeff attended the University of Kentucky and Georgetown College prior to starting an air freight company which eventually covered most of the eastern United States. He sold the business in 2005 to pursue construction and distilling. He is also the father of two boys with his wife of many years, Kathryne.

124

*Management profile:*
**Peter Wright**

Pete spent a year in the back country of the Gambia working in AIDS prevention, is a veteran of the US Army (Military Police), and graduated from Davidson College. A neurologist, he earned his medical degree at the University of Kentucky and trained at Wake Forest University before returning to his hometown of Lexington. He enjoys flying planes, motorcycling, and is an avid sailor and yachtsman.

*Future business plans and goals:* Broaden distribution

Suggested recipes:

**The Winchester**
- 1 ½ oz of Pure Blue Vodka
- 1 ½ oz of ginger ale
- A splash of orange juice

**The Twizzler**
- 1 ½ oz Pure Blue Vodka
- 3 oz cranberry juice
- Lime wedge
- Twizzler

  Pour Pure Blue Vodka and cranberry juice over ice.
  Add a squeeze of lime juice.
  Garnish with a lime wedge.
  Add Twizzler - use as a straw.

**Blue Bloody Mary**
- Pure Blue Vodka
- V8 or tomato juice
- Lemon juice
- Chunk of banana pepper

  Pour Pure Blue Vodka into a tall glass over ice.
  Add tomato juice, lemon juice, pepper and salt to taste.
  Add a banana pepper chunk, and add its juice to taste.

Barrel House Distilling Company
Lexington, Kentucky

# E.H. Taylor, Jr. Old Fashioned Copper Distillery
Microstill is located at Buffalo Trace Distillery

113 Great Buffalo Trace
Frankfort, Kentucky 40601

*Phone:* 502-223-7641
*Fax:* 502-875-5553

*Website:* www.buffalotrace.com

*Region:* Bluegrass

*Type:* Micro-distillery

*Opened:* 2009

*Hours of operation:* Monday through Friday, 7:00am to 5:00pm

*Gift shop hours:* Monday through Friday, 9:00am to 4:30pm
Saturday, 10:00am to 3:00pm

*Tours:* Tours are available.

*Types of spirits produced:* Bourbon Whiskey

*Names of spirits:*
- E.H. Taylor, Jr. Straight Kentucky Bourbon Whiskey

*About:*
Edmund Haynes Taylor, Jr., 1830-1923, is the Father of the modern bourbon industry.

Although the early days of bourbon making in Kentucky are often recounted with legends and lore, E.H. Taylor, Jr., left an undisputed and invaluable legacy for America's favorite spirit.

One of Kentucky's original bourbon aristocrats, Taylor was an industry leader who greatly advanced the quality of Kentucky bourbon and safeguarded the bourbon label from bogus producers. Called the "father of the modern bourbon industry," Taylor started and/or owned seven different distilleries throughout his career, the most successful being the O.F.C. and Carlisle distilleries, the forerunners of today's Buffalo Trace Distillery.

A native of Columbus, Kentucky, Taylor was orphaned at an early age and sent to New Orleans to live with his great uncle, Zachary Taylor, who would become the 12th U.S president. He was educated at Boyer's French School in New Orleans before coming to Frankfort, Kentucky, where he was adopted and raised by another uncle, Col. Edmund H. Taylor, one of Frankfort's most prominent community leaders. Taylor finished his education at B.B. Sayre's Academy and followed in his uncle's footsteps in the banking profession.

Taylor's real passion, however, was bourbon making. During his banking days in the 1860s, Taylor helped organize several area distilling companies and came to know many of the early whiskey makers personally. His direct involvement with the development of these whiskey ventures exposed him to all aspects of the whiskey trade, which proved to be invaluable when he decided to begin his own bourbon-making operation.

In 1869, Taylor purchased a small distillery on the banks of the Kentucky River. The distillery was located on the same site as the pioneer settlement of Leestown —the first settlement north of the Kentucky River where distilling had been taking place since 1787— which sprung up nearly 100 years earlier. Interestingly, Taylor's ancestors had been instrumental in the development of Leestown, and his great-grandfather, Commodore Richard Taylor, built his home there. Known as "Riverside," the house still stands today and is the oldest existing structure in Franklin County.

Taylor quickly started to renovate the distillery property, raising its production capabilities to state of the art levels. One of his initial improvements was the substitution of copper fermentation vats for the wooden tubs that had been used in the past—a unique technique for his time. He also bought new grinding machinery and massive columnar copper stills for which he built larger, more modern structures to house them and, subsequently, he demolished the original distillery building. His capital investment and overriding attention to detail demonstrated his commitment to producing a bourbon whiskey of unparalleled quality.

Taylor named the new distillery O.F.C. derived from "Old Fire Copper," the traditional distilling method he adopted. From the time the grain was ground until the time it was barreled, Taylor's whiskey came into contact only with copper. Eventually, Taylor became recognized as the maker of first rate bourbon whiskey in the old fashioned, handmade, sour mash, fire copper method. The O.F.C. name was so synonymous with quality whiskey that several other producers tried to pass their wares off under the same name. O.F.C.'s quality came from Taylor's whiskey making innovations, including the nation's first climate controlled aging for whiskey, which incorporated the use of steam in brick covered rick warehouses.

Another Taylor innovation was a patented mash technique which he helped develop during the 1870s. Taylor used a strained-slop process that filtered out dead meal to recreate a rich creamy liquid instead of an inert mass, which other distilleries used to cook the mash. According to Taylor, "Properly handled by the skilled distiller, the use of this spent beer is a valuable aid in the attainment of a faultless fermentation." (It also produced almost a gallon more of whiskey per bushel of grain!)

Taylor built Carlisle, a second distillery, adjacent to O.F.C. between 1879 and 1880. Consisting of the two distilleries, the property was among the largest and the finest in the world. Both Carlisle and O.F.C. whiskies bore the famous E.H.Taylor signature, a trademark recognized throughout the United States and Europe as a guarantee of high quality.

127

In addition to advancing the quality of bourbon within his own distilleries, Taylor worked to pass legislation that required accuracy in labeling consumer products, like bourbon, to prevent fraud; this was a radically progressive concept in the 1880s. Taylor was also a staunch advocate of the Bottled in Bond Act (1879). This act provided that whiskey must be aged for a minimum of four years in warehouses supervised by federal agents. To qualify as a bonded whiskey, it had to be distilled at one place at one time, it had to be at least 100 proof, and its actual maker had to be identified on the label.

It is said that, during Taylor's career, he bridged the classic and modern eras of bourbon making. He was a traditionalist yet an innovator. He was a proud, competitive distiller, yet he championed the entire bourbon industry and left a legacy that has benefited bourbon makers and bourbon lovers for generations.

Today, Buffalo Trace Distillery carries on Col. E. H. Taylor Jr's spirit of innovation through its E.H. Taylor Jr. Old Fashioned Copper Distillery, a microstill located on the grounds of Buffalo Trace Distillery. This microstill allows the distillery to conduct experiments on a smaller scale and has received many awards for its creations. The Experimental Collection, as the product line is called, has been responsible for such ground breaking experiments as unique mash bills, various types of wood, and barrel toasts. Currently there are more than 1500 experimental barrels of whiskey aging in the warehouses of Buffalo Trace Distillery.

E.H. Taylor, Jr. Old Fashioned Copper Distillery
Frankfort, Kentucky

## MB Roland Distillery

Paul Tomaszewski, Owner
Merry Beth (Roland) Tomaszewski, Owner

137 Barkers Mill Road
Pembroke, Kentucky 42266

*Phone:* 270-640-7744
*Fax:* 270-640-7740
*Email:* paul@mbrdistillery.com, mb@mbrdistillery.com
*Website:* www.mbrdistillery.com
*Facebook:* MB Roland Distillery
*Twitter:* @mbrdistillery

*Region:* Southwestern Kentucky

*Type:* Micro-distillery producing approximately 100 to 300 gallons per month

*Opened:* November 2009

*Hours of operation:* Open year-round Wednesday through Friday, 10:00am to 5:00pm
Saturday, 10:00am to 6:00pm

*Tours:*
Tours are available during hours of operation.

*Types of spirits produced:*
Shine, bourbon whiskey, corn whiskey, and rum

*Names of spirits:*
- True Kentucky Shine
- Strawberry Kentucky Shine
- Apple Pie Kentucky Shine
- Blueberry Kentucky Shine
- Kentucky Pink Lemonade
- Kentucky Mint Julep
- White Dog Whiskey
- Black Dog Whiskey
- Bourbon Whiskey
- Malt Whiskey
- Barrel Aged Kentucky Shine
- Black Patch Whiskey
- X Barrel Whiskey

*Best known for:* Black Dog and True Kentucky Shine

*Average bottle price:* $15.00 to $25.00

*Distribution:*
MB Roland spirits are available in Kentucky, Tennessee, and Illinois as well as at the on-site gift shop. Products will soon be available in California, Indiana, Louisiana, and New York.

*Highlighted spirits:*

**White Dog and Black Dog Corn Whiskies**
White Dog and Black Dog Corn Whiskies are made from locally-grown white corn. Using white corn sets MB Roland Distillery products apart from other similar ones because this imparts a sweeter, floral taste and aroma.

**True Kentucky Shine**
True Kentucky Shine is made in a similar fashion as White Dog Corn Whiskey except that sugar is added to the mash prior to fermentation, just like moonshiners do. Due to the combination of the white corn and sugar, an aroma and flavor of apple peels and citrus notes comes through.

*Events and Celebrations:* MB Roland hosts a monthly "Pickin on the Porch" festival from May to September. No admission is charged and it offers well-priced concessions.

*Services offered other than production:* Retail gift shop and tasting room

*Interesting facts:*
• MB Roland Distillery was built on a former Amish dairy farm.

*About:*
MB Roland Distillery was the vision of Paul Tomaszewski (left) and his wife, Merry Beth (Roland) Tomaszewski, supported it. Paul is a West Point graduate and served five years in the Army, including service in Iraq, and didn't want to simply work for corporate America.

After extensive research and studying the possibility of opening a distillery, a promising site became available.

Paul knew his name wasn't exactly the best fit for the business, so he used his wife's; it sounds more like a whiskey, plus he gets to blame any bad things on her because it's her name on the label. Merry Beth jokes that while most women drive their husbands to drinking liquor, she drove hers to making it.

*Professional associations:* American Distilling Institute, Kentucky Distillers Association

*Future business plans and goals:*  To continue to make superior quality products

*Suggested recipes:*

**Self Diagnosis**
- 1½ parts Dr. Pepper
- 1½ parts cream soda
- 1 part true Kentucky Shine

**Strawberries & Cream**
- 1 part Strawberry Kentucky Shine
- 1 part cream soda

**Apple Pie Manhattan**
- 1 part Apple Pie Kentucky Shine
- 1 part True Kentucky Shine
- Dash of bitters
- Dash of Sweet vermouth

Shake over ice and pour.

MB Roland Distillery
Pembroke, Kentucky

## Celebration Distillation

James Michalopoulos, Founder / Owner
Parker Schonekas, Operations Manager
Erick Leowko, Sales Manager
Kim Jones, Marketing Manager

2815 Frenchmen Street
New Orleans, Louisiana 70122

*Phone:* 504-945-9400
*Fax:* 504-947-4446
*Email:* General info: info@oldneworleansrum.com
   Parker Schonekas: parker@oldneworleansrum.com
   Erick Leowko: erick@oldneworleansrum.com
   Kim Jones: kim@oldneworleansrum.com
*Website:* www.neworleansrum.com
*Facebook:* Celebration Distillation Corporation
*Myspace:* Old New Orleans Rum
*Twitter:* @NewOrleansRum

*Region:* Louisiana

*Type:* Micro-distillery producing approximately 700 gallons per month

Opened: 1996

*Hours of operation:* Monday to Friday, 9:00am to 5:00pm, and Saturday, 1:30pm to 5:00pm

*Tours:* Tours are available Monday through Friday at 12:00pm, 2:00pm and 4:00pm and on Saturday at 2:00pm and 4:00pm.

*Types of spirits produced:* Rum

Names of spirits:
- Old New Orleans Crystal Rum
- Old New Orleans Amber Rum
- Old New Orleans Cajun Spice Rum

*Best known for:* Cajun Spice Rum

*Average bottle price:* $17.00 to $21.00

*Distribution:*
Celebration Distillation spirits are available in its tasting room and through its distributor in Louisiana, New York, Mississippi, California, Colorado, Wisconsin, Missouri, Minnesota, Illinois, and Florida.

**Old New Orleans Amber Rum**
- Silver Medal, 2008 International Rum Festival
- Silver Medal, 2007 Ministry of Rum Competition, New Orleans
- Gold Medal - Aged Rum, 2007 American Distilling Institute
- Bronze Medal, 2004 International Review of Spirits
- Bronze Medal, 2001 Ministry of Rum Competition, Barbados

**Old New Orleans Crystal Rum**
- Gold Medal, 2008 International Rum Festival
- Gold Medal, 2007 Ministry of Rum Competition, New Orleans
- Silver Medal, 2007 and 2004 International Review of Spirits

**Old New Orleans Cajun Spice Rum**
- Highest Rated Flavored Rum, 2010 and 2009
- Silver Medal, 2008 International Rum Festival
- Highest BTI Rating-Flavored Rum, 2008 and 2007 International Review of Spirits
- Bronze Medal, 2007 Ministry of Rum Competition, New Orleans

**10 Year Special Edition Rum**
- Bronze Medal, 2008 International Rum Festival
- Silver Medal, 2007 Ministry of Rum Competition, New Orleans

*Highlighted spirits:*

**Old New Orleans Crystal Rum**

Old New Orleans Crystal Rum is a light-bodied white rum with balanced flavors of sweet molasses, vanilla, caramel and a hint of pure vanilla.

**Old New Orleans Amber Rum**

Old New Orleans Amber Rum is a blend of three rums and is aged for three years. It is medium bodied with hints of vanilla and molasses with deep caramel notes.

**Old New Orleans Cajun Spice Rum**

Old New Orleans Cajun Spice Rum is a rum blend combined with the kick of cayenne and cinnamon, hints of nutmeg, ginger, and cloves to create this truly unique, truly New Orleans flavor.

**10 Year Special Edition Rum**

Aged 10 years and only sold at the distillery, this rum survived Hurricane Katrina.

*Events and Celebrations:*

Celebration Distillation is a unique venue hosting many parties and celebrations throughout the year. It offers private party packages, happy hours for groups of 10 or more, and seasonal public parties with music, food and spirits.

*Services offered other than production:* Tasting room, product and merchandise sales

*Interesting facts:*
- Celebration Distillation is the oldest continuously licensed and operating rum distillery in the continental United States.
- Cajun Spice Rum has been the highest rated flavored rum four years in a row from 2007 to 2010 by the Beverage Testing Institute.
- Celebration Distillation is the only liquor manufacturer in Louisiana that is allowed to sell its product from the tasting room.
- All Celebration Distillation rums are made with pure Louisiana black strap molasses delivered to the distillery from a sugar refinery in Gramercy, Louisiana. The distillery also grows its own ginger.

*About:*
James Michalopoulos, a celebrated New Orleans-based artist, is the founder of Celebration Distillation. Inspired by a Swiss friend who entertained guests with spirits she made with fruit picked from her garden, Michalopoulos decided to use the regional crop of sugar cane to create his own spirits in Louisiana. After a successful European painting tour, he invested in a rum fabrication experiment. Michalopoulos, along with several artist and musician friends, cobbled together a still in a 9th Ward kitchen.

After two years of distillation and engineering studies and plenty of trial and error, it was time to scale up. They constructed their own unique combination pot and column still which

enabled the crew members to create robust flavor and also to achieve purity and control over the process.

In 1995, the crew members purchased an old cotton warehouse on Frenchmen Street. They refitted it and designed and built new equipment. Eventually, after many experiments, a fermentation process was found that produced the savor they craved. In 1999, the first white rum was put on the market; over time it became known as Old New Orleans Crystal. Soon thereafter came Old New Orleans Amber Rum and then Old New Orleans Cajun Spice Rum. By the millennium, Celebration Distillation had become one of the world's best rum makers with gold medals to prove it.

The crew at Celebration Distillation has always been composed of artists and musicians with an engineer or two thrown in for balance. It continues to search for excellence with the eyes of an artist, always committed to a creative process and great quality. Honing technique and craft with never-ending experimentation, the entire range of Old New Orleans Rums are subtle and sophisticated and witnesses to the virtuosity of the distillers.

*Distiller profiles:*

**Bryan "Cromag" Carroll,** Master Distiller – is a former Dixie Brewer, trained mechanic, and fiddle player. Bryan ensures that only the highest quality distillate is cut from the stills and brought on to further processing. With his trained nose and taste, Bryan has improved the rum's consistency and quality.

**Dave Rudd,** Distiller – A long time bartender, Dave became interested in the manufacturing processes behind all the spirits he poured and consumed. After months of training, Dave switched full-time gigs; now he makes spirits Monday through Friday and only pours them on an occasional Saturday.

**Benjamin Hunt (Bengy),** Distiller – With a background in chemistry and experience with more than a couple illicit spirit producers, Bengy has brought some outside grassroots experience to the operation.

**Jascha Jacobson,** Distiller – is a jack of all trades - tattoo artist, tall-bike fabricator, and blighted homes renovator. Jascha is also an experienced still designer.

*Professional associations:* American Distilling Institute

*Future business plans and goals:* Increase production capacity and efficiency with new equipment installations. Continue to grow sales in distributed areas.

*Suggested recipes:*

**Partly Cloudy**
- ½ oz Old New Orleans Amber Rum
- 4 oz ginger ale

  Serve on the rocks.

**Louisiana Lemonade**
- 2 oz Old New Orleans Crystal Rum
- Equal parts sour mix, club soda, and lemon-lime soda

**Banana's Foster**
- ½ oz Banana Liqueur
- 1½ oz Old New Orleans Cajun Spice Rum
- 1 dap of a banana
- 2 scoops vanilla ice cream

  Blend until smooth and pour into a brandy snifter.
  Sprinkle cinnamon on top.

Celebration Distillation
New Orleans, Louisiana

# Spirits of Maine Distillery

Robert and Kathe Bartlett, Owners

175 Chicken Mill Road
Gouldsboro, Maine 04607

*Phone:* 207-546-2408
*Fax:* 207-546-2554
*Email:* info@bartlettwinery.com
*Website:* www.bartlettwinery.com

*Region:* Mid-coast Maine

*Type:* Micro-distillery producing 500 to 1,000 gallons per year

*Opened:* 2007

*Hours of operation:*
Open June to mid-October - Monday through Saturday, 10:00am to 5:00pm
Closed Sundays and holidays. Open by appointment after season.

*Tours:* No tours

*Types of spirits produced:*
Brandy, eau de vie, light and dark rum, geists, and liqueurs

*Names of spirits:*
- Fine Apple Brandy
- Pear Eau-De-Vie
- Peach Eau-De-Vie
- Honey Eau-De-Vie
- Raspberry Geist
- Light Rum and Dark Rum

*Average bottle price:* $30.00 to $40.00

*Distribution:* Throughout Maine and at the tasting room

*Awards and Recognitions:*
**Apple Brandy**
- Silver Medal, 2011 San Francisco World Spirits Competition
- Silver Medal, 2010 Beverage Testing Institute
- 88 Points, 2010 Ultimate Cocktail Challenge
- 93 Points, 2010 Ultimate Spirits Challenge
- Silver Medal, 2009 Beverage Testing Institute
- Bronze Medal, 2009 International Eastern Wine Competition

*Awards and Recognitions:*
**Pear Eau-De-Vie**
- Double Gold Medal, 2011 San Francisco World Spirits Competition
- 89 Points, 2010 Ultimate Cocktail Challenge
- 87 Points, 2010 Ultimate Spirits Challenge
- Gold Medal, 2009 Beverage Testing Institute
- Silver Medal, 2009 International Eastern Wine Competition
- Bronze Medal, 2009 International Indy Wine Competition

*Highlighted spirits:*
**Bartlett Pear Eau-De-Vie**
This spirit is made in the European tradition, dry and full bodied with very ripe pear aromas.

**Bartlett Fine Apple Brandy**
This medium bodied, dry brandy has understated notes of green apple and mineral dust and French oak complexity.

*Events and Celebrations:* Private parties are hosted by the distillery.

*Services offered other than production:* Tasting room and retail store

*Interesting facts:*
- Bartlett Maine Estate Winery became Maine's first licensed winery in 1982.
- Spirits of Maine Distillery became Maine's second distillery in 2007.

*About:*
Bob and Kathe Bartlett are the proprietors and vintners of Bartlett Maine Estate Winery, and making quality wine is their calling. Emphasizing quality over quantity, they continuously tinker with their process and try new aging techniques and blends to produce fresh, exciting wines.

In 1981, the Bartletts wrote Maine's Farm Winery Bill and were responsible for changing the law to allow wineries to offer tastings and sales at the winery and to self-distribute on the wholesale level statewide. Two years later, Bartlett Maine Estate Winery opened its doors with only 600 gallons of wine. Today it presses almost 7,000 cases a year and offers more than twenty varieties. As its reputation spread, so did the pressure to industrialize; but at heart, Bob and Kathe wanted to remain a homegrown, locally owned business.

Going from winemaking to distilling was a natural evolution, and Spirits of Maine Distillery became Maine's second distillery in 2007.

*Future business plans and goals:*
- Broaden distribution and more aged products

*Suggested recipes:*
**The Jeff Smith Sidecar**
- 2 oz Bartlett Fine Apple Brandy
- 1 ½ oz fresh organic sweet and sour (Made from organic limes and lemons sweetened with organic raw agave nectar)
- ¾ oz Cointreau

Mix ingredients.
Finish with lime and sugar rim.

Spirits of Maine Distillery
Gouldsboro, Maine

# Sweetgrass Farm Winery & Distillery

**Sweetgrass Farm**
WINERY AND DISTILLERY

Keith and Constance Bodine, Owners

347 Carroll Road
Union, Maine 04862

*Phone:* 207-785-3024
*Email:* info@sweetgrasswinery.com
*Website:* www.sweetgrasswinery.com, www.backrivergin.com
*Facebook:* Back River Gin

*Region:* Maine

*Type:* Micro-distillery

*Opened:* 2005

*Hours of operation:* 11:00am to 5:00pm daily from Mother's Day through December 31

*Tours:* Yes

*Types of spirits produced:*
Gin, rum, apple brandy, whiskey, liqueurs, wines, vanilla extract, and bitters

*Names of spirits:*
- Back River Gin
- Three Crow Rum
- Maple Smash Liqueur

*Best known for:* Back River Gin

*Average bottle price:* $21.49 to $34.49

*Distribution:*
Throughout Maine and at the tasting room

*Highlighted spirits:*

**Back River Gin**
Back River Gin is a smooth, American style, dry gin with a hint of spice and blueberries. It's great on the rocks but also makes a fine gin and tonic or a mean martini.

**Three Crow Rum**
Three Crow Rum is a light rum with tastes of vanilla, caramel and butterscotch.

**Maple Smash Liqueur**
Maple Smash Liqueur is a unique blend of brandy and the distillery's own maple syrup.

*Services offered other than production:* Tasting room, retail store and consulting services

*About:*
Sweetgrass Farm Winery & Distillery produces wines and spirits with a distinct Maine character on a farm in Union, Maine. Creating fine wines, ports, and distinctive spirits, Sweetgrass Farm Winery & Distillery hand crafts its spirits in Old World tradition with a copper alambic still capturing the full flavors of the Back River Gin, Cranberry Gin, Three Crow Rum, and Apple Brandy. Sweetgrass Farm is a family run business firmly rooted in the community, supporting local sustainable agriculture, and donating 10% of profits to organizations which support families, children, and rural life.

*Future business plans and goals:* Expand distribution of spirits

Sweetgrass Farm Winery & Distillery
Union, Maine

# Blackwater Distilling Inc.

Christopher Cook, CEO
Jon Cook, COO
Mark Troxler, VP of Business Development
Jon Blair, Production Manager

184 Log Canoe Circle
Stevensville, Maryland 21666

*Phone:* 443-249-3123
*Email:* info@blackwaterdistilling.com
*Website:* www.blackwaterdistilling.com, www.sloopbetty.com
*Facebook:* Sloop Betty
*Twitter:* @sloopbetty
*YouTube:* sloopbetty

*Region:* Mid-Atlantic

*Type:* Micro-distillery

*Opened:* 2010

*Tours:* Tours are not offered.

*Types of spirits produced:* Vodka

*Names of spirits:*
- Sloop Betty

*Best known for:* Sloop Betty

*Average bottle price:* $29.99

*Distribution:* Maryland, Delaware, and DC

*Awards and Recognitions:*
**Sloop Betty**
- Gold Medal, November 2011 International Review of Spirits
- 94 Points, Tasting Panel
- Gold Medal, Fiftybest.com
- Gold Medal and 91 Points, Beverage Testing Institute

*Highlighted spirits:*
**Sloop Betty**
Sloop Betty, the flagship product of Blackwater Distilling, is a handcrafted wheat vodka made in Maryland. Smooth with a crisp undertone, the pure, natural ingredients of a small batch vodka come through as you savor every drop. Designed with both vodka connoisseurs and those new to the pleasure of the cocktail hour in mind, Sloop Betty can be enjoyed alone or mixed in a drink.

*Interesting facts:*
- Blackwater Distilling is the first fully licensed distillery in MD in nearly 40 years.
- Blackwater Distilling is the only Maryland-based micro-distillery.

*About:*
Blackwater Distilling became incorporated in 2005, after which the principals spent several years attending symposiums, conferences, and classes to learn the craft as well as the nuances of the industry.

Using state of the art and proprietary equipment and high quality wheat and sugar cane, each production batch of Sloop Betty is carefully handcrafted. The distillers have also developed a detailed production and quality assurance process to ensure that Sloop Betty vodka is consistently flavorful. Additionally, Blackwater Distilling is working with the Maryland Organic Certification Program to obtain recognition as an official organic handler. Furthermore, the water that is the basis for Sloop Betty has been nationally recognized for its purity and excellence in taste; it's sourced from the ShoreGood Water Company in Federalsburg, Maryland. Maintaining the integrity of the land from which it crafts its products is a cornerstone of the company's values. It also gives back to the community. Dubbed the "Everglades of the North," the Blackwater National Wildlife Refuge that is the distilling company's namesake will receive a percentage of all Blackwater Distilling proceeds.

*Management profile:*

**Christopher Cook** – Chief Executive Officer
Christopher Cook (photo center), along with his brother Jon Cook, began navigating the complex waters of handcrafted spirits in 2005. Christopher received a bachelor's degree at Lynchburg College and has enjoyed a career in the information technology field for many years. After years of business planning and training through seminars and formal courses in the art of distilling, Christopher plays a key role in reviving Maryland's fine heritage of custom, handcrafted spirits at the helm of Blackwater Distilling.

Blackwater Distilling was founded on the principles of fashioning a super-premium local product with respect for the environment from which it draws resources. Cook and his business partners named their new venture to pay homage to a treasured Eastern Shore wildlife refuge. A longtime Maryland resident, Christopher enjoys hiking and camping.

**Jon Cook** – Chief Operating Officer
A student of leading distilling industry experts and scientists skilled in spirits production, Jon Cook (photo right) is Blackwater Distilling's chief operating officer.

In addition to planning the business with his brother Christopher, Jon is responsible for ensuring the production of a consistently smooth and balanced batch of super-premium spirits every time. Jon's training in the art of handcrafting fine spirits combined naturally with the entrepreneurial experience he gained at a start-up firm in Annapolis, Maryland.

142

The entrepreneurial spirit and interest in distilling that Jon shares with his business partners drive his passion for handcrafting Blackwater Distilling's flagship product, Sloop Betty vodka. Jon has been integral in developing a detailed production and quality assurance process to ensure that Sloop Betty is consistently flavorful so that the superior craftsmanship is tasted in every sip.

**Mark Troxler** – Vice-President for Business Development
A friend and business partner of Christopher and Jon Cook for more than two decades, Mark (photo left) blends his business acumen and expertise in commercial real estate with training in handcrafted spirit distillation. As the head of Blackwater Distilling's business development, Mark is focused on growing the distillery and increasing the more than $1.1 billion of economic activity Maryland and the Washington area represent in the production, distribution and sale of distilled spirits.

**Jon Blair** – Production Manager
Jon Blair lends his award-winning talents in distillation and fermentation to the Blackwater Distilling team as production manager for Sloop Betty. Jon has extensive experience in plant sanitation, recipe and product development, and quality control. Prior to working for mainland distilleries, Jon worked as assistant production manager at Hawaii's Kolani Distillers.

*Professional associations:* American Distilling Institute, DISCUS

*Future business plans and goals:*
Broaden distilled spirits product line. Additionally, Blackwater Distilling hopes to offer tours, tastings, and products available for sale; this is, however, contingent on legislation in Maryland.

*Suggested recipe:*
Sloop Betty is a super-premium beverage made to be savored on the rocks or shaken with ice and served neat in a glass.

**Daily Pinup**
- 2 oz Sloop Betty
- 1 oz lemon juice
- 1 oz simple syrup
- ½ oz honey
- 3 oz iced tea

    Shake with ice and dump into large pint glass.
    Garnish with a lemon wedge on a skewer.

Blackwater Distilling Inc.
Stevensville, Maryland

Blackwater Distilling Inc. photos courtesy of Stacey Viera

143

# Fiore Winery & Distillery

Mike Fiore, Owner
Rose Fiore, Owner
Eric Fiore, Owner

3026 Whiteford Road
Pylesville, Maryland 21132

*Phone:* 410-879-4007, 410-452-0132
*Fax:* 410-452-0021
*Email:* mike.fiore@fiorewinery.com
*Website:* www.fiorewinery.com
*Facebook:* Fiore Winery
*Twitter:* @FioreWinery

*Region:* Mid-Atlantic

*Type:* Micro-distillery producing approximately 150 gallons per month

*Opened:* 2009

*Hours of operation:*   Monday through Saturday, 10:00am to 5:00pm
Sunday, 12:00pm to 5:00pm

*Tours:* Tours are available.

*Types of spirits produced:*
Brandy, grappa, and limoncello

*Names of spirits:*
- Fiore Grappa
- Fiore Limoncello

*Best known for:* Wine and grappa

*Average bottle price:* $15.00 to $25.00

*Distribution:* Maryland

*Highlighted spirits:*
**Fiore Limoncello**
Fiore Limoncello is crafted from a generations old family recipe. The same traditional methods used in Fiore's home region of Calabria in southern Italy are used to produce this liqueur. Limoncello can be served after a meal or with dessert and is best served chilled in cordial glasses to better experience the flavor.

**Fiore Grappa**
The Fiores use traditional family methods for distilling grape pomace to produce this smooth spirit.

*About:*

Fiore Distillery opened its doors in 2005 when the Maryland General Assembly passed legislation permitting distillery operations at wineries. Mike Fiore led the effort by Maryland winemakers to lobby for the law, which limits the amount of beverage that can be produced to 200 gallons.

The distillery's story begins much earlier than 2005, though. In 1975, Mike and Rose Fiore bought a small farm in northern Harford County, Maryland, and decided to grow grapes.

Formerly a vineyard owner in Italy, Mike wondered if it was the right location to bring a little bit of the old country to his new country. He joined a Wine Growers Association to learn about French-hybrid grapes, which were the grapes popular with most growers at the time. Mike and Rose eventually planted a small experimental vineyard behind their house and it slowly grew in size.

In 1986, Mike and Rose opened Fiore Winery and named the vineyards La Felicetta. Although he and Rose held onto their day jobs, Mike's enthusiasm towards the vineyard started to flourish. Over the next twenty years, the pair turned their passion into prosperity. They gradually moved from 1,500 to 35,000 gallons. Their commitment to produce a quality product has earned them hundreds of awards, including 50 international medals between 2005 and 2008.

The addition of the distillery was a natural evolution since the byproducts used from winemaking are distilled. Recently, Maryland passed a law that allows for distillation of up 1,900 gallons a year. Because of that, Fiore Winery & Distillery purchased a new Vendome as a finish still. This allows them to produce 150 gallons a month.

*Future business plans and goals:* Crafting a vodka made from 100% grape skins

Fiore Winery & Distillery
Pylesville, Maryland

# Ryan & Wood Inc.

Bob Ryan and Dave Wood, Owners
Kathy Ryan and Maryann Wood, Owners

15 Great Republic Drive
Gloucester, Massachusetts 01930

*Phone:* 978-281-2282
*Fax:* 978-281-2202
*Email:* Bob Ryan: bob@ryanandwood.com
        Kathy Ryan: kathy@ryanandwood.com
*Website:* www.ryanandwood.com
*Facebook:* Ryan & Wood Inc., Distilleries

*The Spirit of Cape Ann*

*Region:* Northeastern Massachusetts

*Type:* Micro-distillery producing approximately 7,000 gallons per year

*Opened:* Incorporated April 2006

*Hours of operation:* 8:00am to 5:00pm

*Tours:* Tours are available Monday through Saturday at 10:00am and 1:00pm.

*Types of spirits produced:*
Gin, rum, vodka, and whiskey

*Names of spirits:*
- Beauport Vodka
- Folly Cove Rum
- Knockabout Gin
- Ryan & Wood Straight Rye Whiskey
- Ryan & Wood Straight Wheat Whiskey

*Average bottle price:* $28.00

*Distribution:*
On-site retail space and self-distributing to eastern Massachusetts

*Highlighted spirits:*
**Folly Cove Rum**
Folly Cove Rum is produced using molasses fermented on site. It is distilled in a 600 liter still and barrel aged for up to 18 months in previously experienced American whiskey barrels.

**Knockabout Gin**
Knockabout Gin begins with Beauport Vodka and ten botanicals. These are steeped in the still to make a "gin tea" that is distilled.

146

*Highlighted spirits:*
## Straight Rye Whiskey and Straight Wheat Whiskey
Straight Rye Whiskey and Straight Wheat Whiskey are barrel aged in an ever changing Massachusetts coastal climate.

*Services offered other than production:* On-site retail shop

*About:*
Ryan & Wood Inc., is pleased to call Gloucester, America's oldest seaport, its home. Its products are named to honor local history. The knockabout, the gin, was a vessel design change to the traditional fishing schooner to save fisherman's lives at sea. Beauport, the vodka, is taken from the first name of Gloucester, "Le Beau Port" or "the beautiful port," given by Champlain in 1606. Folly Cove, the rum, is a section on the northeast part of Gloucester Island at the Rockport boarder that is historically known as a significant rum smuggling area.

Gloucester has been a world leading fishing port for almost 400 years. It is also a popular tourist destination. As part of an effort to be a part of Gloucester's "agri-tourism," Bob and Dave named their fermentation tanks after historic and current schooners that helped make Gloucester famous. The Lannon is an excursion vessel, daily taking tourists out to experience life on a schooner. The Adventure is the last of the Grand Bank Dory Schooners, built in Essex, MA, and fished out of Gloucester.

*Management profile:*
## Bob Ryan
A native of Gloucester, Massachusetts, Bob (left) spent many years working on the historic waterfront. In discovering craft distilling, Bob returned to the Gloucester business scene pouring his entrepreneurial spirit into Ryan & Wood Inc.'s world class spirits.

## Dave Wood
A lawyer by trade, Dave (right) has put his expertise to work ensuring that the distilling dream became a reality. He believes that a hard day's work should be rewarded with a top notch drink and envisions Ryan &d Wood Inc.'s labors of love to be just that - top notch drinks.

*Future business plans and goals:* Continued growth and wider distribution

Ryan & Wood Inc.
Gloucester, Massachusetts

# Triple Eight Distillery

Jay Harman, Owner
Dean Long, Owner
Randy Hudson, Owner

5 Bartlett Farm Road
Nantucket, Massachusetts  02554

*Phone*:  508-325-5929
*Fax:*  508-325-5209
*Email:*  jay@ciscobrewers.com
*Website:*  www.ciscobrewers.com/distillery

*Region:*  Massachusetts

*Type:*  Micro-distillery producing 8,000 gallons annually

*Opened:*  2000

*Hours of operation:*  10:00am to 7:00pm

*Tours:*  Tours are available by appointment.

*Types of spirits produced:*
Gin, rum, notch single malt whisky, and vodka

*Names of spirits:*
- Triple Eight Vodka
- Hurricane Rum
- Gale Force Gin
- Notch Single Malt Whisky

*Distribution:*  East Coast and Colorado

*Interesting facts:*
- One of the first micro-distilleries in Massachusetts

*About:*
Triple Eight Vodka is a super premium liquor produced on Nantucket by the Triple Eight Disillery.  The distillery, Nantucket's first legal spirits producer, gets its name from Nantucket Well #888 from which it draws the water to distill its spirits.

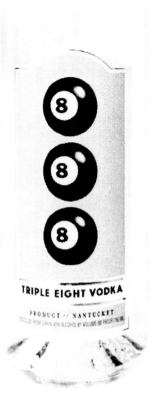

Triple Eight Distillery
Nantucket, Massachusetts

148

# Chateau Chantal

Robert Begin, Founder
James Krupka, CEO
Mark Johnson, Winemaker
Brian Hosmer, Winemaker

15900 Rue de Vin
Traverse City, Michigan 49686

*Phone:* 231-223-4110
*Fax:* 231-223-4130
*Email:* General Info: wine@chateauchantal.com
       Mark Johnson: mjohnson@chateauchantal.com
*Website:* www.chateauchantal.com
*Facebook:* Chateau Chantal Winery
*Twitter:* @chateauchantal
*Blog:* chateauchantal.wordpress.com

*Region:* Old Mission Peninsula, Michigan

*Type:* Micro-distillery producing 500 gallons annually

*Opened:* 2001

*Hours of operation:*
June through August:
    Monday through Saturday, 11:00am to 9:00pm

September through October:
    Monday through Saturday, 11:00am to 7:00pm

November through mid-June:
    Monday through Saturday, 11:00am to 5:00pm

Sundays year round: 11:00am to 5:00pm

Closed: Thanksgiving, Christmas, New Year's, and Easter

*Tours:*
Tours are conducted June through August at 1:00pm, 2:00pm, and 3:00pm. Other tour times can be scheduled for large groups.

*Types of spirits produced:*
Brandy, eau de vie (cherry, pear and plum)

*Names of spirits:*
- Chateau Chantal Cherry Eau de Vie
- Chateau Chantal Pear Eau de Vie
- Chateau Chantal Plum Eau de Vie
- Chateau Chantal Brandy – "Cinq à Sept"
- Chateau Chantal Cerise
- Chateau Chantal Cerise Noir
- Chateau Chantal Entice

*Best known for:*  Chateau Chantal Cerise

*Average bottle price:*  $24.99 to $34.00

*Distribution:*
Eaux de vie and Cerise Noir are only available in the tasting room. Cerise and Entice are distributed throughout Michigan and Illinois.

*Awards and Recognitions:*
**Chateau Chantal Cerise**
- Gold Medal, 2009 Taster's Guild International Wine Competition
- 2006 Wine Library Award for Best Dessert Wine

**Chateau Chantal Entice**
- Silver Medal, 2010 Taster's Guild International

*Highlighted spirits:*
**Chateau Chantal Cherry Eau de Vie**
Cherry Eau de Vie is distilled from carefully selected tart Michigan cherries.  The cherries are harvested when ripe, fermented, crushed, distilled, and quickly bottled in order to preserve their freshness and aroma.

**Chateau Chantal Entice**
Entice is made from frozen grapes and fortified with Chateau Chantal grape brandy.

**Chateau Chantal Cerise**
Cerise is a blend of Cherry Eau de Vie and cherry wine made in the traditional port wine method.

**Chateau Chantal Brandy – "Cinq à Sept"**
Distilled from fermented Northern Michigan grapes, this brandy spent five years mellowing in a French oak barrel, gaining a golden color and rich caramel flavor. Displaying notes of honey, spice, and butterscotch, this sipper is best served in a Brandy snifter, or other wide bottomed glass, to promote the release off the fine aromas.

*Events and Celebrations:*
The tasting room can accommodate groups of up to 50 people for wine tasting and other small group activities. Additionally, the hospitality room overlooking the Grand Traverse Bay can accommodate larger groups.

The first weekend in October is Chateau Chantal's annual Harvest Fest featuring tours, grape stomping, tasting, and other activities.

*Services offered other than production:*
Tasting room and tours

*About:*
Chateau Chantal is located on a 65 acre estate on Old Mission Peninsula, in one of the most scenic areas of the Great Lakes. Chateau Chantal has vineyards, a winery, and a bed and breakfast. Views of East and West Grand Traverse Bays, Power

Island, and rolling vineyards abound from each window. Focusing on Michigan wines, Chateau Chantal produces Riesling, Chardonnay, Pinot Grigio, Pinot Noir, Merlot, Cabernet Franc and other varietals.

As a Catholic diocesan priest for 12 years, Robert Begin worked in his home area of Detroit until 1972 when he decided to head a construction business. Nadine Begin had taken a similar path by entering the Felician Sisters in 1950. After earning her master's degree in home economics and teaching for 22 years, she too decided to seek a different life.

Married in 1974, the couple followed Robert's dream of building a European style winery chateau. In December 1983, Robert and Nadine formed Begin Orchards and purchased 60 acres of cherry orchards on the estate property. Located in the cherry capital of the U.S., where 75% of the nation's tart cherries are produced, the Begins felt it was a natural connection to use local cherries and fruit to create their spirit products.

Between 1984 and 1991, the Begins cleared much of the land, planted various grape varieties and purchased additional land. In July 1990, Robert received a Special Use Permit to operate the Chateau and, in June of 1991 the company was incorporated. In 1993 construction of the Chateau was completed.

In 1993, the Begin family opened the doors of Chateau Chantal after the completion of a French style bed and breakfast, winery, and vineyard estate. Evidence that their years spent in service to others shines through to every visitor and employee of the Chateau with their caring and enthusiastic spirit molding the Begins into the perfect hosts.

*Management profile:*
**Mark Johnson**
Following a three year apprenticeship, founding winemaker Mark Johnson (left) became only the third American to receive his Masters Degree in Viticulture and Enology from the Technical University and Research Station in Geisenheim, Germany.

**Brian Hosmer**
Winemaker Brian Hosmer (right) is a graduate of Michigan State University's enology program.

**Marie-Chantal Dalese**
Marie-Chantal Dalese is a graduate of the University of Adelaide (AUS) graduate program in wine business.

*Professional associations:* Wine America

*Future business plans and goals:* Increased hospitality events

*Suggested recipes:*
**Brandy Sour**
- 2 oz Chateau Chantal Cherry Eau de Vie
- Juice of 1-2 lemons
- ½ tsp powdered sugar
- ½ slice of lemon
- 1 cherry

   Shake brandy, lemon juice, and powdered sugar with ice.
   Strain into a whiskey sour glass.
   Decorate with lemon slice, top with the cherry and serve.

Chateau Chantal
Traverse City, Michigan

Photos courtesy of: Brian Confer, Chateau Chantal

## Corey Lake Orchards

Dayton Hubbard, Owner

12147 Corey Lake Road
Three Rivers, Michigan  49093

*Phone:*  269-244-5690
*Email:*  coreylakeorchards@gmail.com
*Website:*  www.coreylakeorchards.com
*Facebook:*  Corey Lake Orchards

*Region:*  Southwest Michigan

*Type:*  Micro-distillery

*Opened:* 1999

*Hours of operation:*  Farm market is open May through October, 8:00am to 6:00pm

*Tours:*  Tours of the distillery are conducted Saturday afternoons and by appointment.

*Types of spirits produced:* Brandy and a brandy/juice blend

*Names of spirits:*
- Hubbard's Apple Brandy
- Hubbard's Cherry Brandy
- Hubbard's Grape Brandy
- Hubbard's Peach Brandy
- Hubbard's Pear Brandy

*Average bottle price:*  $10.00 to $30.00

*Distribution:*
All of the brandies are produced and sold exclusively at Corey Lake Orchards.

*Highlighted spirits:*  Both Apple and Pear Brandy are 120 proof.

*Events and Celebrations:* Special tours are available for various traveling groups.  Corey Lake Orchards has a U-Pick and Picked produce farm market as well as many other activities.

*Interesting facts:*
- All Hubbard's brandies are made from fruit grown on its farm.

*About:*
Located in Three Rivers, Michigan, Corey Lake Orchards Distillery was opened in 1999 by Dayton Hubbard in order to manufacture brandy to take advantage of excess produce grown on its farm.

True to the motto "from seed to sip," all varieties of Hubbard's Brandy are made from the Corey Lake Orchard's harvest. Brandy production begins in the orchards and vineyards where premium apples, cherries, grapes, peaches, and pears are hand-picked at the peak of flavor and ripeness. The fruit is then gathered, blended, and pressed and the juices are fermented in huge barrels. The juices are then distilled in a copper Christian Carl Still imported from Germany. The clear spirit is drawn off in this process and is trickled into the barrels. The brandy is then aged in oak for several years to develop its flavor. The barrels play an important role in the aging process, but it is the fruit, soil and the climate of southwest Lower Michigan that give Hubbard's Brandy its unique character.

*Management profile:*
## Dayton Hubbard
Dayton Hubbard has a bachelor's degree in horticulture from Virginia Tech and a master's degree from Rutgers.

In the 1950s, Dayton and his wife Allene moved to southwest Michigan searching for that perfect piece of farmland. In 1962, they found it and went on to raise a myriad of fruits and vegetables as well as four daughters. Dayton attributes his success to "a lot of luck, repeat customers, and help from above."

Hubbard's daughter Beth helps to manage the farm.

*Future business plans and goals:*
Expand product line by adding other types of brandies, wines and hard ciders

Corey Lake Orchards
Three Rivers, Michigan

154

## Entente Spirits LLC
Round Barn Distillery

Moersch Family, Owners

10983 Hills Road
Baroda, Michigan 49101

*Phone:* 269-422-1617
*Email:* info@roundbarndistillery.com
*Website:* www.roundbarndistillery.com
*Facebook:* the Round Barn Winery
*Twitter:* @RoundBarnWinery

*Region:* Heart of the Midwest

*Type:* Micro-distillery producing 4,000 gallons annually

*Opened:* 1999

*Hours of operation:* Open year-round

*Tours:* Tours are not available.

*Types of spirits produced:*
Bourbon, eau de vie, grappa, rum, vodka, calvados style and cognac style brandies

*Names of spirits:*
- DiVine Bourbon
- DiVine Rum
- DiVine Vodka
- Other products are labeled under Round Barn

*Best known for:* DiVine Vodka

*Average bottle price:* $15.00 to 35.00

*Distribution:*
Entente Spirits sells through its tasting rooms and through distributors in Michigan, Indiana, and Illinois.

*Awards and Recognitions:*
**DiVine Vodka**
- Gold Medal, 2010 San Francisco World Spirits Competition
- Silver Medal, 2009 Los Angeles International Wine & Spirits
- Gold Medal, 2009 Beverage Testing Institute

*Services offered other than production:* Tasting room and retail shop

*Interesting facts:*
- Entente Sprits tasting rooms are located in turn of the century barns, including an Amish-built round barn.
- DiVine Vodka is made from grapes.

*About:*

Born out of a passion to create domestic, ultra-premium vodka from grapes, DiVine Vodka hit the spirits market this past year. DiVine is the first and only estate vodka to be distilled and bottled in the United States and made from grapes. It is produced in southwest Michigan, one of the Midwest's richest fruit belts, using grapes harvested from the Lake Michigan Shore American Viticultural Area (AVA). Not only is it truly unique for premium vodka to be produced in the U.S., but it is also unique for vodka to be distilled from grapes instead of from grains or potatoes. Drawing on tradition, Master Vintner and Distiller Matthew Moersch takes pride in hand crafting the product in a European copper-pot still. He and his staff are hands-on for the entire process, from harvesting grapes to distilling to bottling.

*Future business plans and goals:* Expanded product line

*Suggested recipes:*

**DiVine's "Little Lebowski"**
- 2 oz DiVine Vodka
- 1 oz brandy
- 3 oz French vanilla creamer

Shake with ice, pour into rocks glass.

**Cranberry DiVine**
- 1 oz DiVine Vodka
- ½ oz Raspberry Pi
- 3 oz Round Barn Cranberry Wine

Shake with ice, strain into martini glass.
Garnish with lime twist.

Entente Spirits LLC
Baroda, Michigan

156

## Grand Traverse Distillery

Kent Rabish, Owner/Distiller
George Wertman, General Manager/Distiller

781 Industrial Circle, Suite 5
Traverse City, Michigan 49696

*Phone:* 231-947-8635
*Fax:* 231-947-7713
*Email:* kent@grandtraversedistillery.com
*Website:* www.grandtraversedistillery.com
*Facebook*: Grand Traverse Distillery

*Region:* Midwest

*Type:* Micro-distillery selling about 2,500 cases per year

*Opened:* 2007

*Hours of operation:*
Thursday and Friday from 12:00pm to 5:00pm, Saturday from 11:00am to 4:00pm
Expanded hours during peak seasons
Retail sales room at the distillery is open Monday through Friday from 11:00am to 5:00pm

*Tours:* Tours are available.

*Types of spirits produced:* Vodka and whiskey

*Names of spirits:*
- True North Vodka
- True North Cherry Flavored Vodka
- True North Chocolate Flavored Vodka
- Wheat Vodka
- Ole George Whiskey
- Bourbon Whiskey

*Distribution:*
Grand Traverse Distillery tasting room, Colorado,
Michigan, and the Chicago area

*Awards and Recognitions:*
**True North Vodka**
- Top 50 Spirits, 2010 Wine Enthusiast Magazine
- Top 50 Spirits, 2009 Wine Enthusiast Magazine
- Gold Medal, 2009 International Review of Spirits
- Gold Medal, 2008 San Francisco World Spirits Competition
- 4 Star Review, Beverage X
- 4 Star Review, F. Paul Pacult's Spirit Journal

*Highlighted spirits:*
**True North Vodka**
This vodka is sweet with the spicy essence of rye. The ingredients in True North Vodka originate from the Grand Traverse region, including the crystal clean glacial waters of the Great Lakes.

**Ole George Whiskey**
Ole George Whiskey is distilled from a 100% rye mash bill and is bottled at 93 proof. Rye has a unique character that no other grain can provide in that the rye imparts a spicy flavor. Ole George Whiskey is bottled straight from the barrel.

*Services offered other than production:*
Tasting room and retail store. Additionally, Grand Traverse Distillery does custom whiskey blending for customers. Customers purchase a small whiskey barrel and the customers decide what they like. The whiskey is crafted with their mash bill and then taken home and aged in their barrel.

*Interesting facts:*
- Grand Traverse Distillery is northern Michigan's oldest micro-distillery.

*About:*
Grand Traverse Distillery is the vision of Michigan native Kent Rabish. After visiting micro-distilleries on the West Coast, Kent saw the opportunity to bring handcrafted spirits to Michigan.

*Future business plans and goals:* Put up more whiskey and work on a nice gin

*Suggested recipes:*
**The Silver Bullet** – Drink designed by Trattoria Stella, Traverse City Michigan
- 2 oz of True North Vodka
- ¼ oz of Springbank 15 year single malt whiskey

   Mix, stir with ice and a long cocktail spoon to chill.
   Serve in a chilled martini glass.

**Pamalicious** - Drink designed by Jon Damhof
- 1 oz True North Cherry Flavored Vodka
- 1 oz Malibu Rum
- 1 oz Peach schnapps
- 2 oz Pama pomegranate liquor
- 2 to 3 oz or to taste cranberry/pomegranate juice

   Mix ingredients and serve over crushed ice.

Grand Traverse Distillery
Traverse City, Michigan

# Journeyman Distillery

Bill Welter, Founder
Nick Gurniewicz, Partner

109 Generations Drive
Three Oaks, Michigan  49128

*Phone:*  269-820-2050
*Fax:*  269-820-2045
*Email:*  info@journeymandistillery.com
*Website:*  www.journeymandistillery.com
*Facebook:*  Journeyman Distillery
*Twitter:*  @JourneymanDist
*YouTube:*  JourneymanDistillery's Channel

*Region:*  Southwestern Michigan

*Type:*  Micro-distillery producing approximately 7,000 gallons per year

*Opened:*  October 7, 2011

*Hours of operation:*
Winter Hours
Friday 5:00pm to 11pm, Saturday 11:00am to 11:00pm, and Sunday 12:00pm to 8:00pm

Summer Hours:  Check website

*Tours:*
Tours are available on Saturdays at 1:00pm, 3:00pm, 5:00pm, and 7:00pm.  Sign up on website.

*Types of spirits produced:*
White whiskey, wheat whiskey, rye whiskey, vodka, gin and bourbon

*Names of spirits:*
- W.R. Whiskey (White Whiskey)
- Ravenswood Rye (Rye Whiskey)
- Buggy Whip Wheat (Wheat Whiskey)
- Red Arrow Vodka
- Road's End Rum
- Bilberry Black Heart's Gin
- Featherbone Bourbon
- Three Oaks Single Malt
- Michigan Spirit Whiskey

*Best known for:* E.K. Warren

In the 1880s, E.K. Warren invented a product called the Featherbone that revolutionized the way corsets were made. He was also a staunch Prohibitionist that attempted to buy up all the liquor licenses in the county pre-Prohibition. Additionally, he built the factory building in which the distillery is located.

*Average bottle price:* $19.99 to $49.99

*Distribution:* Currently products are only available at the distillery.

*Highlighted spirits:*

**W.R. Whiskey**

At 90 proof, W.R. Whiskey is aged for less than 24 hours in new white oak. Its mash bill is the same as the Ravenswood Rye, which is to say it's a heavily wheated organic rye. The notes on this fresh light product are bright and floral and it's surprisingly soft on the pallet.

**Red Arrow Vodka**

Distilled from 100% organic wheat, Red Arrow Vodka is clean, crisp, smooth and 90 proof.

**Bilberry Black Hearts Organic Gin**

Indigenous to Britain and northern Europe, the Bilberry highlights the juniper and eight other botanicals found in Bilberry Black Hearts Organic Gin. A cousin to the huckleberry and blueberry, the bilberry is smaller and has a fuller taste. The bilberry is dark in color and usually appears black, thus the berry was commonly referred to as a black heart in 19th century southwestern England.

At 90 proof, Bilberry Black Hearts Organic Gin is clean, bright, and fruity with subtle hints of black licorice.

*Events and Celebrations:*
Journeyman Distillery has a 3,500 square foot tasting bar and event facility able to host events of all types.

*Services offered other than production:*
Cocktail bar and retail store

*Interesting facts:*
- Journeyman Distillery is certified organic by Midwest Organic Services Association.

*About:*
Journeyman Distillery is located in a historic manufacturing building. The distillers mill, mash, ferment, distill, bottle and barrel all their products on site.

*Professional associations:* American Distilling Institute

*Future business plans and goals:* Expanded product line

*Suggested recipes:*
**E.K. Warren**
- 1 ½ oz Ravenswood Rye
- ¾ oz simple syrup
- ¾ oz lemon juice
- 2 dashes Angostura

**Whiskey Sour**
A classic cocktail popularized during the mid to late 1800s with a twist

- 2 oz Ravenswood Rye
- 1 oz vanilla simple syrup
- ¾ oz lemon

**Bees Knees**
The "bees knees" was a popular saying during the 1920s, meaning the height of excellence. Additionally, it's a pre-Prohibition era cocktail made with honey to help mask the smell of alcohol. Bilberry Black Hearts Gin adds a hint of juniper and bilberry to accentuate the flavor of the honey.

- 1 oz Bilberry Blackhearts Gin
- 1 spoonful of freshly squeezed lemon juice
- 1 spoonful of freshly squeezed orange juice
- 1 spoonful of honey

Journeyman Distillery
Three Oaks, Michigan

# Northern United Brewing Company & Distilling

Mike Hall, Head Distiller
Michael Wooster, Manager
Josh Lentz, Supervisor
Kaleb Longworth, Assistant Distiller
Sam Maxbauer, Assistant Distiller
Charles Psenka, Sr., Chief Liaison

13512 Peninsula Drive
Traverse City, Michigan  49686

*Phone:*   231-223-8700
*Fax:*   231-223-8702
*Email:*  jpbrewery.traverse@nubco.net
*Website:*  www.civilizedspirits.com
*Facebook:*  Civilized Spirits
*Twitter:*  @DrinkCivilized

*Region:*   Old Mission Peninsula, Grand Traverse County, Traverse City Michigan

*Type:*   Micro-distillery

*Opened:*   December 2010

*Hours of operation:*   As demand dictates

*Tours:*   Tours are available by appointment.

*Types of spirits produced:*
Vodka, rum, gin, cherry spirit, agave, whiskies, and apple spirit

*Names of spirits:*
- Civilized Vodka
- Civilized Sakura
- Civilized Whiskey
- Civilized White Dog
- Civilized Single Malt Whiskey
- Civilized Rum
- Civilized Gin

*Average bottle price*:  $30.00 to $40.00

*Distribution:*  Michigan

*Highlighted spirits:*

**Civilized Vodka**

Civilized Vodka is as smooth as the bay waters at daybreak and as subtle as a fleeting wisp of cool summer breeze. Descended from wine borne of northern Michigan Riesling vines, this vodka graciously hints at its ingredients with a bouquet of grape and a clean finish. Distilled in the ways of the north woods, every bottle of Civilized Vodka has the social graces to complement and enhance the flavors of any cocktail or to confidently stand alone.

**Civilized Sakura**

Mike Hall handcrafts this cherry flavored vodka in the custom built still. With each level of distillation, the purest spirit rains though the 23 caps and trays of the still. The distillation of cherries from Traverse City's finest orchards is expensive, but it produces a character that is unmatched. The distilled cherries blend well with the distilled wheat vodka, and the natural cherry flavor renders it delightfully smooth with a cherry nose and distinct cherry sweetness. This cherry flavored vodka is perfect for sipping.

**Civilized White Dog Whiskey**

Moonshine, white lighting, and white dog have a strong history throughout Michigan during the years of Prohibition. Mike Hall pays tribute to that bygone era and has created an incredibly refined white whiskey. Mike works with local farmers to select the perfect Old Mission Peninsula rye. With each level of distillation, the purest spirit rains through each of the 23 caps and trays of the custom built still, producing a character that is unmatched. The distilled rye is pure, and the wheat lends a sweet finish to this smooth tasting classic.

**Civilized Gin**

Mike works with local farmers to select the perfect Old Mission Peninsula juniper for use in the distillation of Civilized Gin and, as with the other spirits, with each level of distillation the purest spirit rains through each of the 23 caps and trays of the custom built still. The distillation grain and perfectly selected juniper produce a classic London Dry style gin. This gin is smooth with a distinct juniper finish.

*Highlighted spirits:*

**Civilized Whiskey**

This whiskey follows the simple etiquette of the north — never be harsh or subtle. Locally grown rye and pure, pH-neutral water drawn from the distillery's well lay the foundation for a spirit of uncommon smoothness. White oak barrels cellared in a hi-tech, climate controlled storage facility impart straight-forward tastes of toffee, dark dried fruit, and leather.

**Civilized Rum**

Unspoiled by flavoring adjuncts of any kind, Civilized Rum gains its taste from the fruits of the earth — locally grown sugar beets — and its color from the ingenuity of the red-blooded American spirit. It takes an entire Michigan summer to grow the sweet 2g Michigan sugar beet, planted in the spring and harvested in the autumn. Through clear Michigan water and sugar beet fermentation and distillation, the result is a clean elixir whose subtle, sweet and warming nuances are exposed with every hearty swig.

**Civilized Single Malt**

This malt has a subtle and sweet nose with oak and peat as well as a smooth palate with a malt finish.

*Services offered other than production:*
Tasting room in adjacent restaurants

*Professional associations:* American Distilling Institute

*Suggested recipes:*

**Civilized Sour Dog**
- 1 ½ Civilized White Dog Whiskey
- ¾ oz Cointreau
- ½ a fresh lemons juice
- 4 lemon wedges
- 1 splash of lemon-lime soda

In a shaker combine whiskey, Cointreau, lemon juice, 3 lemon wedges and ice.
Shake vigorously and pour into a rocks glass.
Add a lemon-lime soda.
Garnish with the additional lemon wedge.

**Northern United Brewing Company & Distilling**
**Traverse City, Michigan**

164

## St. Julian Winery

David Braganini, President
Larry Gilbert, Resident Distiller

716 S. Kalamazoo Street
Paw Paw, Michigan 49079

*Phone:* 800-732-6002
*Fax:* 269-657-5743
*Email:* wines@stjulian.com
*Website:* www.stjulian.com
*Facebook:* St. Julian Winery
*Twitter:* @stjulianwinery

*Region:* Lake Michigan Shore AVA

*Type:* Micro-distillery producing 150 cases per month

*Opened:* 2000

*Hours of operation:*
Monday through Saturday, 9:00 am to 6:00pm
Sunday, noon to 5:00pm

*Tours:* Free tours are offered every hour on the hour.

*Types of spirits produced:* Brandy and vodka

*Names of spirits:*
- A & G Brandy
- Grey Heron Vodka

*Best known for:* Grey Heron Vodka

*Average bottle price:* $34.99

*Distribution:*
St Julian spirits are only available at the Michigan tasting locations in Paw Paw, Union Pier, Frankenmuth, and Dundee.

*Awards and Recognitions:*
**A & G Brandy**
- Gold Medal, 2009 Taster's Guild
- Gold Medal, 2008 Taster's Guild
- Gold Medal, 2008 Indy International
- Voted "Best Winery" 2008-2010 from Kalamazoo Gazette Readers

**Grey Heron Vodka**

Grey Heron Vodka is made from 100% grape spirits. It is distilled and filtered five times to achieve its smooth texture and rich palate. This vodka opens with neutral wet stone and cream aromas, then leads to a round dryish medium-to-full body and finishes with warming anise and sweet cream.

**A & G Brandy**

A & G Brandy brings together years of patience and perseverance with a product that showcases the world class quality of Michigan's fruit belt. It has an alluring nose of vanilla, hazelnut and butterscotch intertwined with toast, chocolate and anise.

*Events and Celebrations:*
St. Julian Winery hosts a variety of parties for its Wine Club members and hosts an annual Wine & Harvest Festival every September.

*Services offered other than production:* Tastings and four retail locations

*About:*
Founded by Mariano Meconi in 1921 along the southern shore of Lake Michigan, St. Julian is Michigan's oldest, largest and most awarded winery.

Today, grandson David Braganini has adopted the family tradition of wine making and has turned St. Julian into Michigan's most renowned winery. Family owned and operated, St. Julian produces all of its wines and spirits from 100% Michigan grown fruit. It's A & G Brandy is aged in Michigan oak.

*Suggested recipe:*
**Sparkling Pomegranate-Blueberry Mojito**
- St. Julian Pomegranate-Blueberry Juice
- St. Julian Grey Heron Vodka
- Ginger ale
- Crushed ice
- Fresh mint
- Lime

Place 4 mint leaves at bottom of glass.
Cut ¾ of lime and squeeze lime juice into the glass.
Using a spoon, gently smash the mint into the lime juice. Add crushed ice.
Add 1-2 shots of Grey Heron.
Fill the remainder of the glass with Pomegranate-Blueberry juice.
Finish with a splash of ginger ale and stir.
Garnish with mint.

St. Julian Winery
Paw Paw, Michigan

# Valentine Distilling Company

Rifino Valentine, President & Founder
161 Vester Street
Ferndale, Michigan  48220

*Phone:*  248-629-9951
*Email:*  info@valentinevodka.com
*Website:*  www.valentinevodka.com
*Facebook:*  Valentine Vodka
*Twitter:*  @valentinevodka

*Region:*  Southeastern Michigan

*Type:*  Micro-distillery / cocktail lounge

*Opened:*  2007

*Hours of operation:*  Wednesday through Saturday, 4:30pm until ?

*Tours:*  Tours are available by appointment.

*Types of spirits produced:*  Vodka, flavored vodka, and infused vodka

*Names of spirits:*
- Valentine Vodka
- White Blossom

*Best known for:*  Cucumber Chill

*Average bottle price*:  $30.00

*Distribution:*  Products are available at the distillery and at nearly 1,000 liquor stores, bars and restaurants throughout Michigan and Chicago. Online purchases from www.binnys.com

*Awards and Recognitions:*
**Valentine Vodka**
- Double Gold Best Domestic Vodka, The Fifty Best 2011
- Gold Medal, 2011 Beverage Testing Institute
- Gold Medal, 2010 Beverage Testing Institute

*Highlighted spirits:*
**Valentine Vodka**
"Exceptional," wrote Beverage Testing Institute, adding, "Clear. Mild aromas of banana and coconut pudding and pastry aromas with a silky off-dry medium-to-full body and a creamy, peppery spice and talc finish. Very lively and tasty."

## Valentine White Blossom

Valentine White Blossom is Valentine Vodka with a careful blend of natural elderflower and a touch of grapefruit. A sip of White Blossom opens with a bright bouquet layered with hints of citrus; it hovers over a slightly honeyed, velvety structure and finishes soft and clean.

*Events and Celebrations:*
Valentine Distilling Company hosts a number of charity and private events.

*Services offered other than production:*
Valentine Distilling offers a full service cocktail lounge.

*About:*
As one of the first distilleries in the world to use a multi-grain recipe utilizing a blend of red Michigan wheat, two-row malted barley and corn, Valentine Vodka is well on the way to setting the standard for ultra-premium handcrafted vodka.

Crafted in copper-pot stills one batch at a time, the limited quantities and process is carefully overseen by Rifino Valentine. In each batch, the fermented mash is carefully created from the proprietary recipe. The mash is then triple distilled to arrive at one of the cleanest and smoothest products. Finally, the vodka is hand filtered using naturally based carbons derived from coconut shells and wood, another break from the traditional producers who use carbon derived from coal.

*Management profile:*
### Rifino Valentine

Rifino Valentine is a native of Leelanau County, Michigan, and a graduate of Glen Lake High School. He attended Cornell University where he was a member of the wrestling team and lightweight football team. After graduating from Cornell University in 1993 with a BA Economics, he worked on Wall Street from 1994-2005. In 2005, he realized that one of his favorite pastimes was enjoying a great tasting martini.

After failing to find handcrafted, ultra-premium vodka made in America, Rifino Valentine envisioned a locally crafted product where consumers could indulge in a premium product craft distilled on American soil, using American grown grains. And thus Valentine Vodka was born.

### Nicholas Brancaleone

Nicholas Brancaleone, the cocktail lounge general manager, has worked in the service industry for over 15 years. He experiments with new flavors using simple, local, fresh ingredients revealing the best flavors and develops new cocktails with such skill that the term "mixologist" sells him short. He is known as the "liquid chef" or "liquid engineer."

*Professional associations:*  American Distilling Institute

*Future business plans and goals:*
Expand distribution to Colorado, Tennessee, Canada, and throughout the Midwest

*Suggested recipes:*
**Cucumber Chill**
- Cucumber Infused Vodka
- Muddle fresh mint
- Sugar
- Splash of soda

  Garnish with fresh mint and lime.

**Pink Blossom**
- Valentine White Blossom Vodka
- Cranberry
- Splash of soda

*Closing remarks:*
"I have always believed in the quality of handmade, premium products. Whether it is jam made with fresh fruit on a small family farm or a pint from my favorite microbrewery, I've always appreciated the care and quality of ingredients that a small, local producer uses in their products. It is also a good feeling knowing that I'm not only getting a better product, but that my hard earned money is going to a true artisan rather than a faceless corporation in a far away country. So when I found myself craving a premium martini, with imported vodka being my only option, I made it my mission to create one of the world's best vodka, right here in the USA!" - Rifino Valentine, President and Founder, Valentine Distilling Co.

Valentine Distilling Company
Ferndale, Michigan

## Cathead Distillery LLC
Bottle Tree Beverage Company

Austin Evans, Owner
Richard Patrick, Owner

Gluckstadt, Mississippi  39110

*Phone:*  601-667-3038
*Fax:*  601-667-3065
*Email:*  info@catheadvodka.com
*Website:*  www.catheadvodka.com
*Facebook:*  Cathead Vodka
*Twitter:*  @CATHEADVodka

*Region:*  Southeast

*Type:*  Micro-distillery producing 200 to 300 gallons a month

*Opened:*  May 2010

*Hours of operation:*  Monday through Friday, 9:00am to 5:00pm

*Tours:*  Tours are not available.

*Types of spirits produced:*
Vodka, gin, schnapps, moonshine, and whiskey

*Names of spirits:*
- Cathead Vodka

*Best known for:*  Lazy Cat

*Average bottle price:*  $19.99 to $21.99

*Distribution:*
Cathead Vodka is available statewide in Mississippi and Arkansas as well as in the Memphis and Chattanooga areas.

*Highlighted spirits:*
**Cathead Vodka**
Cathead Vodka is distilled six-times, is charcoal filtered and is made from the highest quality grains.  It's described as being "one bad cat."

*Interesting facts:*
- The first legal commercial distillery in Mississippi

*About:*

The owners of Cathead Vodka LLC have a passion for craft distilled products and a mutual appreciation for small business. They opened the doors to produce quality products and to represent Mississippi as a craft distillery for the renaissance of craft products being offered on the market today.

*Suggested recipes:*

**Lazy Cat**
- 1 cup Cathead Vodka
- 12 oz pink lemonade concentrate
- 3, 12 oz bottles of Lazy Magnolia Indian Summer or any pale ale ice

    Garnish with fresh fruits.
    Makes 6-8 servings.

**Siberian Cat**
- 2 oz Cathead Vodka
- 1 oz Kahlua®
- 1 oz cream
- ½ oz shot of espresso
- ½ oz Guiness®

    Serve in cocktail glass over ice.

**Urbane Cat**
- ¾ oz Cathead Vodka
- ¾ oz Rosso vermouth
- ¼ oz cherry brandy
- Dash or two of orange juice

    Add ice and serve in a low ball glass.
    Garnish with a lemon twist.

Cathead Distillery LLC
Bottle Tree Beverage Company
Gluckstadt, MS

## Crown Valley Distilling Company

Joe and Loretta Scott, Owners
Bryan Siddle, Director of Operations
Suzane Shannon, Manager

13326 State Route F
Ste. Genevieve, Missouri  63670

*Phone:*  573-756-9700
*Fax:*  573-756-1421
*Email:*  Suzane Shannon: sshannon@crownvalleywinery.com
Bryan Siddle:  bsiddle@crownvalleywinery.com
Distiller:  seckl@crownvalleywinery.com
*Website:*  www.crownvalleybrewery.com
*Facebook:*  Crown Valley Brewing and Distilling, Crown Valley Vodka
*Twitter:*  @CrownValleyBrew
*Blog:*  blog.crownvalleybrewery.com

*Region:*   Ste. Genevieve County, Missouri

*Type:*
Micro-distillery producing approximately 5,000 proof gallons per year

*Opened:*  May 2, 2009

*Hours of operation:*
January through March
Wednesday through Sunday, 11:00am to 5:00pm

April through October
Wednesday through Thursday, 11:00am to 6:00pm
Friday through Sunday, 11:00am to 8:00pm

November through December
Wednesday through Sunday, 11:00am to 6:00pm

*Tours:*
Tours are conducted on the hour during regular business operations.

*Types of spirits produced:*  Whiskey and vodka

*Names of spirits:*
- Crown Valley Vodka
- Missouri Moonshine

*Average bottle price*:  $30.00

*Distribution:* Products are only available for purchase on site.

*Highlighted spirits:*
**Crown Valley Vodka**
Crown Valley ultra-premium, triple-distilled vodka is handcrafted from the finest estate grown grapes, sharing both their unique character and authentic essence. It is made in a custom still, cold filtered and produced in small batches to achieve the ultimate level of purity. With a distinct, fresh nose and subtly sweet overtones, Crown Valley Vodka exhibits a genuine presence of luxury, resulting in an ultra-smooth finish.

**Missouri Moonshine**
Missouri Moonshine is a cuttingly fragrant, double-distilled white whiskey. Unlike white whiskey produced by bootleggers during Prohibition using sugar water and corn feed, this Crown Valley spirit is made from a blend of rye and barley, rendering a uniquely raw and chewy sweetness. Served neat with a splash of water or on the rocks, this white whiskey signifies a sense of the good old days in every glass.

*Events and Celebrations:* Musical entertainment every weekend beginning in May and ending in October with sporadic events following throughout the remainder of the year

*Services offered other than production:*
Country store, coffee shop, retail shop, and food service

*About:*
Located in the lush green countryside of Coffman, Missouri, Crown Valley Brewing and Distilling Company specializes in the production of regional wine, beer, and distilled spirits.

Once an old schoolhouse, the operations inside the building are state of the art and include a rustic, dark Alder wood bar, retail shop and outdoor patio complete with a stone fire pit.

Reflecting a very green approach, Crown Valley Distilling produces two unique spirits of which the ingredients used were byproducts of previously used materials from the winery and brewery. The vodka, Missouri's very first vodka since Prohibition, is distilled from grape skins used for winemaking that were grown within the Crown Valley's Estate. The white whiskey, Missouri Moonshine, is distilled from rye and barley used during the beer making process at Crown Valley Brewing.

Crown Valley also offers its own line of gourmet foods such as spices, sauces and coffee. Additional offerings include beer, chocolates, pastries and pretzels.

*Professional associations:* American Distilling Institute

*Future business plans and goals:* Expansion and broadened distribution

*Suggested recipes:*

**Izzy-Tini**
A refreshing blend of Crown Valley Fizzy Izzy Root Beer and a splash of Crown Valley Vodka

**The Coffman Tornado**
A fruity blend of juices (pineapple, grape, cranberry and grapefruit) with a splash of sprite and Crown Valley Vodka

**General Lee**
Missouri Moonshine and ginger ale

Crown Valley Distilling Company
Ste. Genevieve, Missouri

## Pinckney Bend Distillery

Jerome Meyer, President and CEO
Thomas Anderson,
VP Production & Product Development
Ralph Haynes, VP Sales & Marketing

*Physical Address:*
1101B Miller Street
New Haven, Missouri  63068

*Mailing Address:*
1101B Miller Street
Post Office Box15
New Haven, Missouri  63068

*Phone:*  573-237-5559
*Email:* ralph@pinckneybend.com
*Website:* www.pinckneybend.com
*Facebook:* Pinckney Bend Distillery
*Twitter:* @Pinckney_Bend, @ardentspirits

*Region:*  East Central Missouri

*Type*:  Micro-distillery producing approximately 1,000 proof gallons per year

*Opened:* June 2011

*Hours of operation:*  Not currently open to the public

*Tours:*  Tours are not available at this time.

*Types of spirits produced:* Gin

*Names of spirits:* Pinckney Bend American Gin

*Average bottle price*: $26.00 to $29.00

*Distribution:* Distributed locally and in the St. Louis, Missouri area

*Awards and Recognitions:*
### Pinckney Bend American Dry Gin
- Gold Medal for Taste, 2011 MicroLiquor International Competition

*Highlighted spirits:*
## Pinckney Bend Gin
At 94 proof, Pinckney Bend Gin is smooth and balanced, premium quality American gin with nuanced layers of flavor and aromatics. Pinckney Bend Gin is excellent on its own in a martini, but it also plays exceptionally well with others as a mixer.

*About:*
Pinckney Bend was a navigational hazard well-known to generations of Missouri River boatmen. Located at mile marker 83 above St. Louis, it is the site of a once thriving town that's long since disappeared, and a stretch of river where at least five 19th century steamboats were wrecked, including the famous side-wheeler Spread Eagle.

Today its namesake, the Pinckney Bend Distillery in New Haven, Missouri, celebrates the legend and lore of this vanished town. The river has changed course since those early days but, standing on the levee not far from the distillery's front door and looking westward, you can almost see where the town of Pinckney once stood.

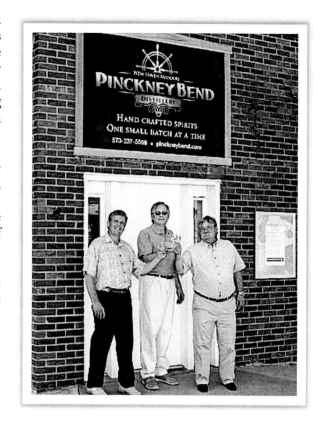

Pinckney Bend brandy and eau de vie products are all produced from locally grown fruit within a 75 mile radius of New Haven. The water is sourced from a deep limestone aquifer that is similar in chemistry to that of Kentucky.

The nine botanicals used in Pinckney Bend Gin are all certified organic and grown in the USA.

*Professional associations:*
American Distilling Institute and Agri-Missouri

*Future business plans and goals:* Tasting room in September 2012 and expanded product line

Pinckney Bend Distillery
New Haven, Missouri

# Square One Brewery and Distillery

Steve Neukomm, Owner

1727 Park Avenue
St. Louis, Missouri 63104

*Phone:* 314-231-2537
*Fax:* 314-588-8050
*Email:* steve@squareonebrewery.com
*Website:* www.squareonebrewery.com
*Website:* www.spiritsofstlouisdistillery.com
*Facebook:* Square One Brewery & Distillery
*Twitter:* @SquareOneBrews

*Region:* East Central Missouri

*Type:* Micro-distillery

*Opened:* Brewery opened in 2006; distillery opened in 2008

*Hours of operation:*
Monday through Saturday 11:00am to 1:30am, Sunday 10:00am to 12:00pm

*Tours:* Tours are available upon request.

*Types of spirits produced:* Agave blue, gin, liqueurs, rum, and whiskey

*Names of spirits:*
Under the brand name "Spirits of St. Louis"
- JJ Neukomm American Malt Whiskey
- Vermont Night Whiskey Liqueur
- Island Time Amber Rum
- Regatta Bay Gin
- Agave Blue

*Average bottle price:*  $25.00 to $48.00

*Distribution:*  Square One spirits are, at this time, only distributed in Missouri.

*Awards and Recognitions:*
**JJ Neukomm Malt Whiskey**
- Bronze Medal, 2011 American Distilling Institute (ADI) Conference

**Vermont Night Whiskey Liqueur**
- Gold Medal and Best of Category, 2011 ADI Conference Whiskey Competition
- Silver Medal, American Distilling Institute Conference

*Highlighted spirits:*
**JJ Neukomm Whiskey**
JJ Neukomm Whiskey is a complex malt whiskey with four types of malts, including a cherry wood smoked malt, and is aged in Missouri oak barrels.

**Vermont Night Whiskey Liqueur**
Vermont Night Whiskey Liqueur is made with fresh citrus vanilla beans, cloves, and cinnamon, and is sweetened with pure Vermont maple syrup.

**Agave Blue**
Agave Blue is American style tequila made from 100% blue agave aged in used whiskey barrels.

**Regatta Bay Gin**
Regatta Bay Gin is made with eight different botanicals, including hops.

*Services offered other than production:*  Square One has a brewery and a restaurant.

*Interesting facts:*
- Square One was the first legal distillery in St. Louis since Prohibition.
- Square One was the third restaurant in the U.S. to have a distillery added to its brewpub.

*About:*
In 2006, Square One opened with the goal of being a distillery pub to provide its customers with a unique and different tasting experience.

Using a Vendome 50 gallon column still, Square One is constantly changing and refining what it offers in distilled products.

All of the spirits are full flavored, with a unique taste that comes from the finest and best quality grain, agave, molasses and herbs available.

Square One Brewery and Distillery
St. Louis, Missouri

## Glacier Distilling Company

Nicolas Lee, Distiller

*Physical Address:*
10237 HWY 2 E
Coram, Montana  59913

*Mailing Address:*
Post Office Box 593
West Glacier, Montana 59936

*Phone:*  406-387-9887
*Fax:*  406-387-9889
*Email:*  info@glacierdistilling.com
*Website:*  www.glacierdistilling.com
*Facebook:*  Glacier Distilling Company

*Region:*  Montana

*Type:*  Micro-distillery producing approximately 3,000 cases per year

*Opened:*  January 2011

*Hours of operation:*
Summer hours - daily, noon to 8:00pm
Winter hours – Thursday through Sunday, noon to 6:00pm

*Tours:*
Tours are available during normal hours and by appointment.

*Types of spirits produced:*  Whiskey

*Names of spirits:*
- Glacier Dew
- North Fork Flood Stage Whiskey
- Bad Rock Rye
- Wheatfish Whiskey

*Best known for:*  Glacier Dew

*Average bottle price:*   $28.00 to $64.00

*Distribution:*  Montana liquor stores

*Highlighted spirits:*
### Glacier Dew
Glacier Dew is very briefly rested whiskey distilled from a mash of barley, corn and rye. Because it is not aged long enough to get color and flavor from the barrel, what remains is a clear whiskey that showcases the natural flavors of the grains. It is a perfect light whiskey for sipping neat or mixing in a cocktail.

### Bad Rock Rye
Bad Rock Rye is a spicy rye, oak finished whiskey released one barrel at a time.

### North Fork Flood Stage Whiskey
North Fork Flood State Whiskey is the perfect blend of rye, barley and corn mellowed in charred American oak barrels. The result is a whiskey that ebbs and flows on your palate like something that is always new but has been there forever.

*Events and Celebrations:*
Events are hosted periodically during the summer.

*Services offered other than production:* Tasting room and tours

*Interesting facts:*
- The recipe for Glacier Dew was inspired by legendary moonshiner Josephine Doody who produced some renowned shine in Glacier Park back in the early 1900s.

*About:*
Glacier Distilling Company is a locally owned, small batch distillery located on the doorstep of Glacier National Park. All of its spirits are handcrafted and hand bottled in The Whiskey Barn.

Photo By Kelley Christensen (2011)

The Whiskey Barn was built in 2010 and production began in early 2011.

The first release was Glacier Dew, a clear, unaged whiskey, in March of 2011. North Fork Flood Stage, a barrel-aged whiskey, was released in May and a single barrel of Bad Rock Rye was released in July. The whiskey has a unique flavor because of the locally grown grains and relatively high mineral content water from a nearby glacial aquifer.

To make a smooth whiskey that is aged such a short time, Glacier Distilling uses distilling techniques adopted from eau-de-vie distillers in Europe. Additionally, its German-made still allows great control over the flavors in the distillate. Cuts off the still are based on what the distiller's senses tell him, relying on the technical parameters only as a guideline.

*Professional associations:* American Distilling Institute

*Future business plans and goals:* Expanded product line

*Suggested recipes:*
**Glacier Sunrise**
In a rocks glass with ice, pour:
- 1 oz or more Glacier Dew
- Splash of grenadine
- Orange juice to top it off

Garnish with an orange slice.

**River Sex**
In a shaker filled with ice, pour:
- 1 oz or more of Glacier Dew
- ½ oz peach syrup
- ½ oz grenadine
- 4 oz pineapple juice
- 4 oz orange juice

Shake and pour in a sugar rimmed glass.
Garnish with a cherry.

**Grand Dad's Tea**
- Pour a healthy splash of Glacier Dew into a glass of peach iced tea.
Garnish with a peach wedge if you have it.

**Mule Kick Martini**
In a shaker, pour:
- 2 oz Glacier Dew
- ½ oz Dry vermouth
- Jalepeño and olive juice to taste

Shake and pour into a martini glass.
Garnish with olive and jalepeño pepper.

Glacier Distilling Company
Coram, Montana

# Sòlas Distillery

Zac Triemert, Founder/President/Master Distiller
Jason Payne, Vice President
Holly Mulkins, Spirits Ambassador / VP of Sales & Marketing

11941 Centennial Road Suite #1
La Vista, Nebraska 68128

*Phone:* 402-763-8868
*Fax:* 402-763-8656
*Email:* Zac Triemert: zac@solasdistillery.com
  Jason Payne: jason@solasdistillery.com
  Holly Mulkins: holly@solasdistillery.com
*Website:* www.solasdistillery.com
*Facebook:* Sòlas Distillery
*Twitter:* @SòlasDistillery

*Region:* Midwest

*Type*: Micro-distillery

*Opened:* December 2009

*Tours:* Tours are available on Saturdays from 10:00am to 1:00pm.

*Types of spirits produced:* Vodka, rum, and single malt whisky

*Names of spirits:*
- Joss Vodka
- Chava Rum
- Sòlas Single Malt Whisky

*Average bottle price*: $20.00 to $60.00

*Distribution:* Nebraska

*Awards and Recognitions:*
**Joss Vodka**
- Bronze Medal, 2010 San Francisco International Spirits Competition
- Double Gold Medal, 2010 San Francisco International Spirits Competition

*Highlighted spirits:*
**Joss Vodka**
Joss Vodka is made from locally grown, organic wheat that is distilled in a custom and proprietary distillation column. It's then brought down to bottling strength with Nebraska Sandhills water. The end product is light on the palate with a unique earthy taste and a smooth, slightly sweet finish.

182

*Highlighted spirits:*

## Chava Rum

Chava Rum is made of rich, thick refiners grade molasses and is matured for a year in a combination of brand new charred barrels and used bourbon barrels. It is a Cuban style rum with great flavor and complexity designed to be enjoyed neat.

## Sòlas Single Malt Whisky

Sòlas Single Malt Whisky is made from 100% two-row malt and is double-pot distilled in the traditional Scottish fashion. The heart of the whisky is matured for a minimum of three years in a combination of brand new charred barrels, used bourbon barrels, and used wine barrels. It is set for release in February 2013.

*Events and Celebrations:*
Sòlas Distillery has at least one big event per quarter at the distillery, including a Speak Easy party, a summer Beer-B-Q, and a Halloween party with costume contests, pumpkin smashing and a fortune teller.

*Services offered other than production:*
Brewery, tasting room, rental hall, and vodka infusion classes

*About:*
Sòlas Distillery is located in La Vista, Nebraska. The company originated when two brewers, Zac Triemert and Jason Payne, found they shared a similar dream - to start a premium quality craft distillery.

*Management profile:*

## Zac Triemert

Zac Triemert earned his bachelor's degrees in microbiology and chemistry and master's degrees in brewing and distilling from Heriot-Watt University in Edinburgh, Scotland. He designed Sòlas' unique vodka distillation column for his master's thesis. After studying, Triemert worked as a fermentation microbiologist for six years and was head brewer at Upstream Brewing Company for another six years. He also helped rewrite Nebraska's Prohibition-era liquor laws to open the doors to craft brewers and spirits distillers.

*Future business plans and goals:*
To be a successful regional craft distillery and expand distribution

Sòlas Distillery
La Vista, Nebraska

# Churchill Vineyards and Distillery

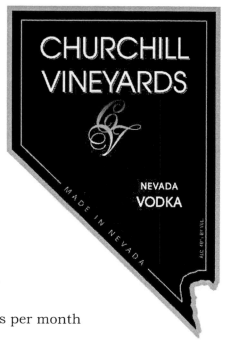

Colby Frey, Owner/Winemaker/Distiller
Ashley Frey, Owner/Marketing

1045 Dodge Lane
Fallon, Nevada 89406

*Phone:* 775-423-4000
*Fax:* 775-423-3338
*Email:* General information: info@churchillvineyards.com
      Ashley Frey: Ashley@churchillvineyards.com
      Colby Frey: Colby@churchillvineyards.com
*Website:* www.churchillvineyards.com
*Facebook:* Churchill Vineyards

*Region:* High desert region, West Central Nevada

*Type:* Micro-distillery producing approximately 200 gallons per month

*Opened:* Experimental license 2006, federal license January 2010

*Hours of operation:* Open by appointment only

*Tours:* By appointment only

*Types of spirits produced:*
Whiskey, vodka, brandy, and grappa

*Names of spirits:*
- Nevada Vodka
- Nevada Brandy
- Nevada Single Malt Whiskey

*Best known for:*
Churchill Vineyards Grappa and Coke

*Average bottle price*: $20.00 to $50.00

*Distribution:*
Nevada distribution through Southern Wine and Spirits

*Highlighted spirits:*
**Nevada Vodka**
Nevada Vodka is distilled from fruit and grain grown on the historic Frey Ranch in Fallon, NV.

*Highlighted spirits:*
**Nevada Brandy**
Nevada brandy is distilled from Syrah grapes and aged in French oak for three years.

**Nevada Single Malt Whiskey**
This whiskey is distilled from malted barley grown on the historic Frey Ranch in Fallon, NV.

*Events and Celebrations:*
Churchill Vineyards and Distillery participates in the annual Tractors and Truffles event highlighting agriculture in Fallon through a farm to plate dinner. The goal of the event is to feature the freshest locally grown produce, meats and alcoholic beverages.

*Interesting facts:*
- Churchill Vineyards is Nevada's first legal, and oldest, distillery.

*About:*
Churchill Vineyards and Distillery is located on the historic Douglass Island/Frey Ranch in Churchill County, and is considered one of the oldest farms in Nevada. 100% of the grains and fruit used in the spirits are grown on premise by the Frey family.

*Management profile:*
**Colby Frey**
Colby Frey is a fifth generation Nevada farmer and the primary winemaker of Churchill Vineyards. Through his current knowledge of farming and practices of the past, Colby is successfully growing quality grain crops from the same fertile ground of earlier generations and producing premium vodka, brandy and grappa in northern Nevada. Producing alternative crops is the future of agriculture in Nevada, and Colby is eager to accomplish his goals.

*Professional associations:* Nevada Grown, Made in Nevada Inc.

*Future business plans and goals:*
Continue to produce high quality spirits and broaden distribution.

Churchill Vineyards and Distillery
Fallon, Nevada

## Las Vegas Distillery

Katalin and George Rácz, Owners

7330 Eastgate Road, Suite 100
Henderson, Nevada 89011

*Phone:* 702-629-7534
*Fax:* 212-517-2196
*Email:* info@lasvegasdistillery.com
*Website:* www.lasvegasdistillery.com
*Facebook:* Las Vegas Distillery
*Twitter:* @VegasDistillery

*Region:* Nevada

*Type:* Micro-distillery

*Opened:* March 2011

*Tours:* Tours are available.

*Types of spirits produced:* Vodka, rumskey

*Names of spirits:*
- Nevada Vodka
- Seven Grain Vodka
- White Rumskey

Future releases include:
- The "WHISKEYSMITH" copper-stilled boutique whiskey collection
- Barrel Aged Rumskeys
- Gin
- Rum
- Fruit Distillates

*Interesting facts:*
- Las Vegas Distillery is one of the first legal distilleries in the history of Nevada.

*About:*

Located in Henderson, Nevada, Las Vegas Distillery LLC was founded in July 2008 by George and Katalin Rácz. This small family enterprise is Nevada's first artisan boutique distillery and it participates in founding a new agricultural-type manufacturing industry in Nevada. Utilizing swan-neck and an alambic Carl artisan copper-pot stills, George and Katalin bring their Hungarian and Transylvanian family traditions into their business by handcrafting their spirits in the old fashioned way, from grain to bottle. Through passion, hard work and distilling in small batches, their goal is to manufacture great quality and

great value products and to become good "smiths" who, through craftsmanship, aim to achieve excellence in American artisan distilling.

*Management profile:*

### George Rácz

George Rácz has a bachelor's degree in film making from Hunter College and received his distillery training from Cornell University Artisan Distilling Workshop, Dry Fly Distilling School and Christian Carl. George's dream is to sail around the world and he enjoys good food and drinking with good friends.

### Katalin Rácz

Katalin Rácz has a bachelor's degree in business administration from Baruch College. She enjoys art and art history and would like to find a way to connect art, artists and artisan spirits.

Las Vegas Distillery
Henderson, Nevada

## Flag Hill Winery & Distillery

Frank W. Reinhold, Jr, Owner

297 North River Road
Lee, New Hampshire 03861

*Phone:* 603-659-2949
*Fax:* 603-659-5107
*Email:* wine-info@flaghill.com
*Website:* www.flaghill.com
*Facebook:* Flag Hill Winery & Distillery
*Twitter:* @flaghillwinery

*Region:* New England

*Type:* Winery and distillery producing
approximately 1,622 gallons per year

*Opened:* 2004

*Hours of operation:*
Wednesday through Sunday, 11:00am to 5:00pm

*Tours:* Tours are available on weekends from
June to September.

*Types of spirits produced:* Absinthe, brandy,
grappa, gin, liqueurs, and vodka

*Names of spirits:*
- General John Stark Vodka
- Josiah Bartlett Barrel Aged Apple Brandy
- Karner Blue Gin
- Moonshine
- Graham's Grappa
- Sugar Maple Liqueur
- Blueberry Liqueur
- Raspberry Liqueur
- Cranberry Liqueur
- Strawberry Liqueur
- Edward III Modern Absinthe
  (produced and bottled by Flag Hill for Edward III of New York)

*Average bottle price:* $15.00 to $26.00

*Distribution:*
Liquor stores in Massachusetts, New Hampshire, Pennsylvania, and in the tasting room

*Awards and Recognitions:*

**Sugar Maple Liqueur**
- Bronze Medal, 2010 NY International Spirits Competition

**Cranberry Liqueur**
- Gold Medal, International Review of Spirits by the BTI

**Karner Blue Gin**
- Gold Medal, International Review of Spirits by the BTI

**General John Stark Vodka**
- Rated Very Good/Recommended, Wine Enthusiast Magazine
- 3 stars and a review of "Recommended" by Spirit Journal

**Josiah Bartlett Barrel Aged Apple Brandy**
- Gold Medal / Best of Category, ADI
- Bronze Medal, International Review of Spirits by BTI

**Flag Hill Winery and Distillery**
- Appeared in a feature article, Wine and Spirits Magazine 2006
- Appeared in a feature article, Yankee Magazine 2006

*Highlighted spirits:*

**General John Stark Vodka**
General John Stark Vodka is made from crisp New Hampshire apples and is triple distilled for an ultra-smooth taste with a hint of caramel.

**Josiah Bartlett Barrel Aged Apple Brandy**
Josiah Bartlett Barrel Aged Apple Brandy is made from New Hampshire apples and aged in oak barrels with an initial bouquet of apple, pear and butterscotch.

**Sugar Maple Liqueur**
Strong and sweet, Sugar Maple Liqueur is made from sweet New England maple syrup blended with General John Stark Vodka.

**Cranberry Liqueur**
A mouth pucker, Cranberry Liqueur combines the tart taste of Massachusetts cranberries with General John Stark Vodka.

*Services offered other than production:*
Tasting room and gift shop, private events and weddings for up to 250 guests

*Interesting facts:*
- In 2004, Flag Hill became the first distillery in New Hampshire.

*About:*
Established in 1990, Flag Hill Winery and Distillery has grown from a family operated business to the largest vineyard in New Hampshire.

In March of 1995, Frank Reinhold, owner, purchased a 25 gallon alambic pot still to make brandy for the production of New Hampshire's first port, North River Port. After years of research on the viability of using apples and potatoes as the base product for distilled spirits, Frank secured Flag Hill as the first distillery in New Hampshire in 2004, producing spirits such as General John Stark Vodka and Josiah Bartlett Barrel Aged Apple Brandy. Since it was already fermenting on site, it seemed a natural progression to expand the company's presence from a local winery to a regional distillery and he purchased a handcrafted still from Christian Carl Inc., located in Goppingen, Germany, in 2004.

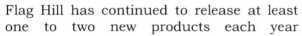

Once the staff of Flag Hill was trained by the Carl brothers about the process and nuances of their new equipment, quality control batches were run and tested and a final product was bottled. General John Stark Vodka entered the market in December of 2004 and was an immediate success.

Flag Hill has continued to release at least one to two new products each year including vodka, grappa, apple brandy, gin, moonshine and a line of five liqueurs made with natural ingredients: Sugar Maple Liqueur, Raspberry Liqueur, Blueberry Liqueur, Strawberry Liqueur and Cranberry Liqueur.

Approximately 10% of Flag Hill Distillery ingredients are from Flag Hill's vineyard; 65% come from within 40 miles of the winery, mainly from Concord, NH; 15% of the ingredients come from the New England region; and 10% of the ingredients come from other places around the U.S. The base of many of the products is apples which are purchased as "seconds" or "dropped" from local orchards who would otherwise have a hard time selling them.

Flag Hill Winery & Distillery has a radiant heat floor and a solar thermal roof to preheat or pre-chill the water it uses in various aspects of operating the still. Additionally, it recently installed photovoltaic cells to the building to help add energy back to the grid

*Management profile:*
**Frank W. Reinhold Jr.**
Owner Frank Reinhold received his degree in viticulture and enology from UC Davis. Prior to opening Flag Hill, he was a nuclear submariner for 26 years in the Navy.

*Professional associations:* American Distilling Institute, NH Winery Association, NH Made, NH Lodging & Restaurant Association, Exeter Area Chamber of Commerce

*Future business plans and goals:* Expand distribution

Flag Hill Winery & Distillery
Lee, New Hampshire

# Don Quixote Distillery & Winery

Ron and Olha Dolin, Owners

236 Rio Bravo
Los Alamos, New Mexico 87544

*Phone:* 505-695-0864
*Email:* ron@dqdistillery.com
*Website:* www.dqdistillery.com
*Facebook:* Don Quixote Distillery and Winery

*Region:* High desert mountains of Northern New Mexico

*Type*: Craft distillery manufacturing approximately 4,000 gallons per year

*Opened:* 2003

*Hours of operation:* Tuesday through Sunday, 12:00pm to 6:00pm, or by appointment

*Tours:* Tours are available at both the distillery and the winery.

*Types of spirits produced:* Eau de vie, vodka, bourbon, gin, whiskey, brandy, and grappa

*Names of spirits:*
- Don Quixote Angelica
- Don Quixote Blue Corn Vodka
- Don Quixote Blue Corn Bourbon
- Don Quixote Gin
- Don Quixote Pisco
- Don Quixote Qalvados – Apple Brandy
- Don Quixote Grappa
- Don Quixote Malvasia Bianca Grappa
- Don Quixote Mon Cherie Cherry Eau de Vie
- Spirit of Santa Fe Gin
- Spirit of Santa Fe Brandy
- Spirit of Santa Fe Vodka – American style wheat vodka

*Best known for:* Blue Corn Vodka, Pisco, Angelica, and Gin

*Average bottle price*: $25.00 to $50.00

*Distribution:* New Mexico in various regional outlets and online

*Awards and Recognitions:*
- Don Quixote Distillery & Winery featured on the Travel Channel, May 2010
- Don Quixote Distillery on Martha Stewart Living radio show, February 2010
- Named "Worlds Best Vodka" by New York Restaurant Owners

**Don Quixote Blue Corn Vodka**

Don Quixote Blue Corn Vodka is made using organic New Mexico Blue Corn and an all-natural fermenting and distilling process. This is a European style vodka that retains the subtle overtones of blue corn.

**Don Quixote Pisco**

Don Quixote Pisco is made in the New Mexico tradition using Muscat grapes and aged two years in French oak barrels. It is smooth and slightly sweet.

**Don Quixote Angelica**

Don Quixote Angelica is made by mixing unfermented Muscat juice with Don Quixote Pisco brandy and aged in French oak barrels for six years. This is a very sweet port style wine at 20% alcohol. Angelica was the most popular beverage in America during Prohibition.

**Spirit of Santa Fe Gin**

Spirit of Santa Fe Gin is Blue Corn Vodka infused with native New Mexico herbs including juniper, pinon, sage, chamisa, and rose hips.

**Spirit of Santa Fe Brandy**

Spirit of Santa Fe Brandy is a blended brandy made from a host of New Mexico fruits including grapes, apples, cherries, and plums. It is rich in flavors and aromas and is barrel aged for six years.

*Events and Celebrations:*

Don Quixote Spirits offers private tastings that include wine, spirits, food, and entertainment; these are by appointment for groups of ten or more. On the second Saturday of each month, it offers a three hour wine and spirits appreciation class. Additionally, once a month during the summer, it offers Drinking Under The Stars, a magical evening of wine and spirits enjoyment around a pinon campfire.

*Services offered other than production:* Tasting room

*Interesting facts:*

- Don Quixote Distillery is New Mexico's first and only distillery specializing in premium spirits made from New Mexico agricultural products.

*About:*

Founded in 2001 and located in Los Alamos, New Mexico, Don Quixote Distillery & Winery is a craft distillery and boutique winery specializing in limited production, high quality spirits, ports, and wines. Distilling at an elevation of 7,500 above sea level, spirits cook off the wine or mash about 14 degrees cooler than at sea level giving Don Quixote spirits a gentle smoothness and slightly sweet taste. Additionally, it employs old European fermenting and distilling techniques as well as a moonshine era thumper (doubler) in production.

*Management profile:*

## Ron and Olha Dolin

As a Ph.D. engineer at one of the world's most prestigious research laboratories, Ron has spent years using his free time to experiment with various wine fermentation and spirits distillation techniques.

Ron built his first still at age 19 when he was a freshman in college. His solar powered, corn based ethonol/methonol fuel design still was a generation ahead of what was in vogue at the time. Unfortunately, Ron was unable to convince campus security that his dorm still was "purely for research." As his confiscated still was hauled away a security guard commented, "You can buy your booze like the rest of us."

In 1999 while on a trip to the Ukraine, Ron met his future wife Olha and, only after they were married, did he discover Olha shared his passion for wine and spirits creation.

Olha grew up in a family of distillers learning the ancient Eastern European secrets to fine vodka and brandy production from her grandfather and father. Ron's technical curiosity combined with Olha's inherited knowledge and passion for spirits production formed the backbone of what has become Don Quixote Distillery & Winery

Together they smuggled their first still out of Ukraine and their first brandies were produced from wines Ron had made over the years while experimenting. With the exception of almost starting their home on fire during their first spirits run, their humble beginnings laid the ground work for the distillery they have today.

Ron designs and builds all of the stills used at Don Quixote. The first still he designed and built was a five gallon copper alambic pot still engineered to maximize the advantages of distilling at 7,500 feet above sea level. In the ensuing years, Ron's quest for perfection led him to continually experiment and design newer improved stills. He is currently on his seventh design generation and believes he has finally optimized his design to blend production efficiency with smooth spirit taste and delicate aroma. The trademark characteristics of all Don Quixote stills are their gentle even heating that renders soft, slightly sweet spirits with pleasantly balanced aromas.

*Future business plans and goals:* Broaden distribution

Don Quixote Distillery & Winery
Los Alamos, New Mexico

# Santa Fe Spirits

Colin Keegan, Owner
Nick Jones, Master Distiller

7505 Mallard Way Unit I
Santa Fe, New Mexico  87507

*Phone:*  505-467-8892
*Email:*  info@santafespirits.com
*Website:*  www.santafespirits.com
*Facebook:*  Santa Fe Spirits
*Twitter:*  @SantaFeSpirits

*Region:*  Southwest

*Type:*  Micro-distillery producing approximately 3,000 proof gallons per year

*Opened:*  February 2011

*Hours of operation:*  Wednesday and Friday, 3:00pm to 7:00pm
Saturday, 3:00pm to 5:00pm

*Tours:*  Tours are available Wednesday, Friday and Saturday from 3:00pm to 5:00pm.

*Types of spirits produced:*  Un-aged, pure malt whiskey and apple brandy

*Names of spirits:*
- Santa Fe Silver Coyote Pure Malt Whiskey
- Santa Fe Apple Brandy

*Best known for:*  The Whiskeyrita
A margarita that substitutes tequila with Silver Coyote

*Average bottle price*:  $29.99 to $45.99

*Distribution:*  Currently only in New Mexico

*Highlighted spirits:*
**Silver Coyote Pure Malt Whiskey**
A combination of Scottish yeast, European and American malts, traditional distilling techniques, and precision-crafted equipment are essential to the production of this exceptionally pure malt whiskey. These ingredients combine to produce a subtle spirit expressing hints of fruit aromatics followed by a smooth mouth feel complemented with sweet, malty notes that gradually yield to a dry, earthy finish.

194

*Highlighted spirits:*
**Santa Fe Apple Brandy**
Overtones of apple peel, vanilla, fruit, and cinnamon yield to hints of granitic earth, sweet water, and dry air.

*Services offered other than production:*
A tasting room with a retail store

*About:*
Founded by Colin Keegan, an Englishman and whiskey aficionado, Santa Fe Spirits uses local, organic ingredients to bring high quality Scotch-style whiskies and Calvados-style apple brandies to the Southwest.

Located 7,000 feet above sea level at the foot of the Sangre de Cristo mountain range, Santa Fe Spirits is a small distillery producing exceptional spirits designed to capture and accentuate the essence of the Southwest. By blending his own apples with the fruit of neighboring New Mexico orchards, Colin is dedicated to showcasing the flavors of the southwest.

*Management profile:*
**Colin Keegan**
Colin has always appreciated good scotch and brandy. When the economy took a turn in 2009, he closed down his architectural business and built a distillery where he could produce his own style of these traditional spirits. For Colin, the birth of Santa Fe Spirits in 2010 was the dream of a lifetime.

**Nick Jones**
Nick Jones has always had a reverence for water and its life-giving qualities. This reverence led him to the study and production of aqua vitae, uisge beatha, or eau de vie, literally meaning the "water of life." A passionate commitment to local flavors and ingredients, a healthy respect for time honored recipes and techniques, and a constant study of modern distilling science are key to Nick's distilling philosophy.

*Professional associations:*
American Distilling Institute and DISCUS

Santa Fe Spirits
Santa Fe, New Mexico

# Breuckelen Distilling Company Inc.

Brad Estabrooke, Founder

77 19th Street
Brooklyn, New York 11232

*Phone:* 347-725-4985
*Email:* info@brkdistilling.com
*Website:* www.brkdistilling.com
*Facebook:* Breuckelen Distilling

*Region:* New York

*Type:* Micro-distillery producing less than 10,000 gallons

*Opened:* 2010

*Hours of operation:* Tasting room Saturday, 12:00pm to 6:00pm or by appointment

*Tours:* Saturday between 12:00pm and 6:00pm

*Types of spirits produced:* Gin and whiskey

*Names of spirits:*
- Glorious Gin
- 77 Whiskey

*Average bottle price:* $35.00

*Distribution:* New York City, IL, NV, and NJ

*Services offered other than production:* Tasting room

*About:*
Breuckelen Distilling is an artisan distillery located in Brooklyn, New York, making gin from organic New York grains. Breuckelen is a fraction of the size of typical distilleries, but its production methods create high quality products.

*Management Profile:* **Brad Estabrooke**
Brad Estabrooke, Breuckelen's founder, is an ordinary guy with an extraordinary love of distinctive wines and spirits. His idea for the distillery formed after reading an article about micro-distilleries in an in-flight magazine. The article discussed some of the new laws that had been put into place that made it easier for micro-distilleries to open. Estabrooke started looking into the idea and, after he was laid off from his finance job in December of 2008, he began working full time on the distillery project.

Breuckelen Distilling Company Inc.
Brooklyn, New York

## Catskill Distilling Company LTD

Monte Sachs, President
Stacy Cohen, Vice President

*Physical Address:*
2037 Route 17B
Bethel, New York  12720

*Mailing Address:*
Post Office Box 345
White Lake, New York  12786

*Phone:* 845-583-3141
*Fax:* 845-583-8566
*Email:* msachs@hvc.rr.com
*Website:* www.catskilldistillingco.com
*Facebook:* Catskill Distilling Company

*Region:*  Southeastern New York

*Type:*  Micro-distillery

*Opened:*  September 2011

*Hours of operation:*  Friday through Sunday, 2:00pm to 8:00pm

*Tours:*  Tours are available daily.

*Types of spirits produced:*  Vodka, aged whiskeys (bourbon, rye, wheat and buckwheat), white whiskeys and muscat grappa.

*Names of spirits:*
- Peace Vodka

*Average bottle price*:  $34.99

*Distribution:*  On site

*Highlighted spirits:*
**Peace Vodka**
Peace Vodka is distilled from locally grown wheat.

*Services offered other than production:*  Dancing Cat Saloon on site

*Future business plans and goals:*  Expanded product line

Catskill Distilling Company LTD
Bethel, New York

# Harvest Spirits LLC

Derek Grout, Owner

3074 US Route 9
Valatie, New York 12184

*Phone:* 518-261-1625
*Email:* info@harvestspirits.com
*Website:* www.harvestspirits.com
*Facebook:* Harvest Spirits Farm Distillery
*Twitter:* @HarvestSpirits

*Region:* New York State

*Type:* Micro-distillery

*Opened:* 2008

*Hours of operation:* Saturday and Sunday, 12:00pm to 5:00pm

*Tours:* Tours are available.

*Types of spirits produced:*
Vodka, brandy, grappa and applejack. In development: Himbeer Geist, frozen applejack, bacon-washed applejack, fruit-in-bottle and various fruit and herbal infused spirits

*Names of spirits:*
- Core Vodka
- Cornelius Applejack
- Apple Eau de Vie
- Pear Eau de Vie
- Grappa
- Rare Pear Brandy

*Best known for:* Applejack and vodka

*Average bottle price:* $25.00 to $40.00

*Distribution:*
Harvest Spirits products are available at the distillery for off-premises consumption, and are independently distributed in New York state.

*Awards and Recognitions:*
**Cornelius Applejack**
- Double Gold Medal, 2010 San Francisco World Spirits Competition

**Pear Brandy**
- Gold Medal, 2010 San Francisco World Spirits Competition

**Core Vodka**
- Silver Medal, 2010 San Francisco World Spirits Competition
- "Best in Class" Vodka, 2009 New York Spirits Awards
- Gold Medal, 2009 Beverage Testing Institute
- Gold Medal, 2008 Beverage Testing Institute

*Highlighted spirits:*

**Core Vodka**

Core Vodka is a neutral, handcrafted vodka made from home grown apples and filtered water.

**Cornelius Applejack**

Cornelius Applejack is made from 100% Hudson Valley apples, is triple distilled and is aged in bourbon barrels. Each bottle is made from more than 60 lbs. of fresh apples and offers a smooth, satisfying take on an American classic.

**Pear Eau de Vie**

Pear Eau de Vie is made from the freshest pears grown in the Hudson Valley. Each bottle captures the full flavor of these ripe Bartlett pears.

**Apple Brandy**

Similar in style to the pear brandy, apple brandy is made from fresh Hudson Valley apples

**Grappa**

Released in October of 2011, Harvest Spirits teamed up with Hudson-Chatham Winery to produce this incredibly smooth grappa. The spirit opens up with a bouquet of fresh grape skins and earth. A rich mid palette transforms to a satisfying finish of dried Thompson raisins, white pepper and talc. Bone dry and bottled at 80° proof, this is an exquisitely made expression of the local grapes the grappa originated from.

**Rare Pear Brandy**

Rare Pear Brandy was released in October of 2011 after the Pear Brandy spent two years in new American oak barrels. The barrel aging imparts bold oak flavors, amber hues and mellows the spirit over time. Very few pear brandies are ever aged, so this is very rare indeed with a brilliant floral nose of pear skins and ripe fruit. A dry but dense mid-palette leads to a sustained baked pear finish.

*Services offered other than production:* Tasting room with retail sales

*About:*

Harvest Spirits is a small distillery crafting 100 gallons at a time. It is flexible and precise enough to create fine vodka. Additionally, Harvest Spirits grows its own apples and makes its own fermentation. The pears are from Columbia County, New York.

*Future business plans and goals:* Introduction of a hard cider and perry fortified ciders

*Suggested recipes:*
**Core Swoon -** Swoon Kitchen Bar, Hudson, NY
- 3 oz Core Vodka
- 1 oz Campari
- Splash of lime

Shake with ice and strain in a chilled martini glass.

**The Michigan Rag**
Pour over ice:
- 3 oz Core Vodka
- 1 Tbs cherry juice concentrate
- Finish with Michigan Vernor's Gingerale or comparable

Garnish with mint sprig.

Harvest Spirits LLC
Valatie, New York

# Hidden Marsh Distillery

George, Ginny, Bill & Ed Martin, Owners

2981 Auburn Road (U.S. Route 20)
Seneca Falls, New York  13148

*Phone:* 315-568-8190
*Fax:* 315-568-8607
*Email:* info@beevodka.com
*Website:* www.beevodka.com
*Facebook:* Montezuma Winery & Hidden Marsh Distillery

*Region:*  Finger Lakes Region, New York

*Type*:  Micro-distillery

*Opened:*  2008

*Hours of operation:*  Daily from 9:00am to 6:00pm

*Tours:*  Tours are not available.

*Types of spirits produced:*  Vodka, brandy, whiskey, and liqueurs

*Names of spirits:*
- BEE Vodka
- Queen's Flight
- Apple Brandy
- Raspberry Liqueur
- Maple Liqueur

*Best known for:*  BEE Vodka

*Average bottle price:*  $24.99 to $48.99

*Distribution:*  BEE Vodka is only available in liquor stores throughout New York state.  All other spirits are only available in the tasting room.

*Awards and Recognitions:*
**BEE Vodka**
- Double Gold Medal, 2011 New York State Fair
- Best of Class Distilled Spirits, 2011 New York State Fair
- Silver Medal "Highly Recommended" 88 points, Beverage Testing Institute

**Queen's Flight**
- Gold Medal and Best Of Class at the Indy International
- Silver Medal, "Highly Recommended" 87 points, Beverage Testing Institute

*Awards and Recognitions:*
## Apple Brandy
- Silver Medal, Finger Lakes International Competition
## Maple Liqueur
- 91 Points, Ultimate Spirits Challenge
- Two Gold Medals & Beverage Testing Institute "Exceptional" 91 points

*Highlighted spirits:*
## BEE Vodka
BEE Vodka is a unique specialty vodka made from the purest honey in the Finger Lakes region. It's triple distilled in individual batches for a flawless finish. BEE Vodka has an initial rich velvety mouthfeel, followed by smooth character and purity. It then finishes with undertones of caramel and distant notes of honey. BEE Vodka is 40% alcohol (80 proof).

## Queen's Flight
Queen's Flight is distilled 100% from honey. Distinctive aromas of caramel and vanilla come from the new charred oak it is aged in. Soft and sweet like a premium bourbon, Queen's Flight Honey follows through with notes of caramel, honey and a toasted almond finish. This spirit is 40% alcohol (80 proof).

## Apple Brandy
With aromas of vanilla and butterscotch, this single barrel brandy has been distilled from fresh local apples and aged in American oak for one year. With subtle apple character up front, it finishes with tones of caramel and oak. Enjoy straight as an aperitif or on the rocks as an after dinner drink.

## Maple Liqueur
Maple Liqueur is 20% alcohol (40 proof). It is produced from a blend of premium New York state maple syrup and ultra-premium BEE Vodka. This sweet liqueur has notes of maple and a toasty warm finish.

*Events and Celebrations:* Hidden Marsh Distillery hosts events for the winery but plans on hosting more distillery related events in the near future.

*Services offered other than production:* Tasting room and gift shop

*About:*
George Martin had been a bee keeper for more than thirty years and, along with his wife Virginia and son Ed, maintained and built a honey production and pollination business which contained two thousand hives in Maine, New York, Florida, and South Carolina.

In 1998, due to dropping honey prices and increasing costs, the Martin family began niche marketing its honey. Bill had always dabbled in mead making and home brewing and, in 1999, applied for a farm winery license. The commercial production of honey wine was born when Martin's Honey Farm and Meadery opened in Sterling, New York.

In 2001, the Martins realized the importance of their location in the fruit belt of New York and decided to try their hand at making fruit wines. They opened Montezuma Winery and it was such a success that they moved their production facilities and gift shop to a 14,000 square foot building in Seneca Falls. Although they continue to produce grape wines, the focus of their product line is fruit and honey wines. Always looking to expand their offerings, the Martins added a distillery to feature premium liqueurs plus vodka and brandy made with honey, apples, and other seasonal fruits.

Custom built in Germany, the 400 liter Christian Carl column-pot still has two columns consisting of a 4-plate column for high end brandy production and a 21-plate column for premium vodka production. With this distillery being the first of its kind in the Finger Lakes region, the Martins are proud to be a pioneer in the field of artisan distilling in New York state.

The distillery may have opened to be a nice addition to the winery, but it has now taken on a life of its own by attracting people just for the spirits.

*Future business plans and goals:* Expanding the distillery and product line

*Suggested recipes:*

**Bee Sour**
- 2 oz BEE Vodka
- 2 oz fresh lemon juice
- 1 oz simple syrup or agave syrup or ½ - ¾ oz honey
- 1 oz egg white
- 2 dashes Angostura bitters

    Shake vigorously with or without ice (no ice makes better foam).
    Pour into glass with ice.
    Garnish with slice of lemon and maraschino cherry.

**Bit O'Honey:  Smooth, Rich & Creamy**
- 2 oz BEE Vodka
- 1 oz butterscotch schnapps
- 1 oz coffee liqueur
- 1 oz Irish cream
- 1 oz cream

    Mix ingredients, shake and pour over ice.

Hidden Marsh Distillery
Seneca Falls, New York

# Lake Placid Spirits LLC

Ann Stillman O'Leary, Owner
Twig McGlynn, Manager

Post Office Box 227
Lake Placid, New York 12946

*Website:* www.lakeplacidspirits.com
*Facebook:* P3 Placid Vodka
*YouTube:* Lake Placid Spirits--Cool Runnings

*Region:* New York State

*Type:* Micro-distillery producing approximately 5,000 liters per year

*Opened:* 2008

*Hours of operation:* 24/7/365

*Tours:* Tours are not available.

*Types of spirits produced:* Vodka

*Names of spirits:*
- 46 Peaks Potato Vodka
- P3 Placid Vodka

*Best known for:* P3 Placid Vodka

*Average bottle price:* $28.00 to $32.00

*Distribution:*
Lake Placid Spirits is available in New York state through local community wine and liquor stores, restaurants, bars, clubs, and resorts.

*Highlighted spirits:*
## 46 Peaks Potato Vodka
46 Peaks Potato Vodka is a 100% potato neutral spirit. It uses potatoes grown at Tucker Farms on the North Slope of the High Peaks of the Adirondack Mountains. This vodka is blended with crisp, clean water drawn directly from Lake Placid, and a final filtration is done with Herkimer diamonds from Herkimer, New York, in the southern Adirondack Park region.

## P3 Placid Vodka
P3 Placid Vodka is 100% grain vodka with final filtration using Adirondack garnet crystals from the Barton Mines in the southern Adirondack Park region.

*About:*
In the vibrant heart of the Adirondack Park is Lake Placid Spirits. Creating fine liquor from nature's best grains, potatoes and fruit, Lake Placid Spirits crafts its products in small batches using the centuries old method of pot-still distillation.

*Management profile:*
**Ann Stillman O'Leary**
Ann Stillman O'Leary, owner, has authored two books on interior design – "Adirondack Style" and "Rustic Revisited" - has a local TV series on PBS showcasing homes called "Rustic Living," and has put together a futuristic look of Adirondack style architecture and furniture. Additionally, Ann directs the packaging and artwork needs of Lake Placid Spirits and is the head mixologist.

*Future business plans and goals:*  Expand product line

*Suggested recipes:*

**The Black Fly-tini**
- 1 ½ oz 46 Peaks Potato Vodka
- ½ tsp Rosemary Vodka infusion
- Splash of vermouth

    Shake and garnish with 3 capers.

**Wink and a Pear**
- 1 ½ oz P3 Placid Vodka
- ½ oz pear liqueur
- ½ oz Canton Ginger Liqueur
- 2 oz lemonade

    Garnish with crystallized ginger strips.

Lake Placid Spirits LLC
Lake Placid, New York

# Long Island Spirits

Richard Stabile, Owner / Founder / Master Distiller

2182 Sound Avenue
Baiting Hollow, New York 11933

*Phone:* 631-630-9322
*Fax:* 631-630-0246
*Email:* info@lispirits.com
*Website:* www.lispirits.com
*Facebook:* LiV® Vodka
*Twitter:* @LiVGUY

*Region:* North Fork, Long Island, New York

*Type:* Micro-distillery producing approximately 12,000 gallons per year

*Opened:* 2007

*Hours of operation:* Monday through Friday, 1:00am to 5:00pm
Saturday and Sunday, 11:00am to 5:00pm

*Tours:* Available by appointment

*Types of spirits produced:* Potato vodka, brandy, and liqueuers

*Names of spirits:*
- LiV Vodka
- Sorbetta
- Pine Barrens Whiskey

*Best known for:* LiV Vodka

*Average bottle price:* $27.00

*Distribution:*
Products are distributed in the tasting room as well as in New York, New Jersey, Rhode Island, District of Columbia, Connecticut, Massachusetts, Pennsylvania, Illinois, Georgia, and Colorado.

*Awards and Recognitions:*
**LiV Vodka**
- Gold Medal, 2011 NY International Spirits Competition
- Scored 92 by Anthony Dias Blue Tasting Panel
- Won "Best in Class," New York Spirits Awards

*Highlighted spirits:*

## LiV Vodka

LiV Vodka is artisan distilled from 100% Long Island Marcy potatoes, so it's gluten free. Long Island potatoes are smaller (more skin to fruit) which contributes to a buttery and extremely smooth taste profile. LiV Vodka is embraced by the New York City cocktail culture and supported by a number of members of the United States Bartenders Guild.

"LiV Vodka has a wonderful vanilla nose, creamy textured mouth feel followed by lovely rich banana and vanilla flavors balanced with just enough fire on the finish; overall crisp, clean just pure style. I am big fan of LiV Vodka, it's unique character shines through," said Dale Degroff, master mixologist and "King Cocktail."

## Sorbetta™

Launched in the spring of 2010, Sorbetta™ is a family of all-natural fruit liqueurs (lemon, orange, lime, strawberry and raspberry) that are crafted from the base spirits of LiV Vodka.

**Lemon:** The fragrance is pure, fresh and sultry with the proper amount of sweetness for a fresh finish.

**Lime:** This has incredibly sweet lime aromatics with a dynamic front end. The complex layered finish with sweetness gives way to a delightfully pleasing, subtle but light peppery back end.

**Strawberry:** This liqueur is clean, alluring, and has a rich subtle strawberry flavor. Pure vine ripened fruit shines through with an uncommonly regal finish.

**Raspberry:** Sweet raspberry aromatics with delicate hints of spice and chocolate are present in this liqueur. Its creamy sweetness fruit flavor is followed by a delicate, smooth finish

### Pine Barrens Whiskey

Long Island Spirits and Blue Point Brewery have combined their rich artisan legacy in distilling and brewing to create the first American Single-Malt Whiskey to be distilled on Long Island. Pine Barrens Whiskey takes its inspiration from the old world, and then takes it in a new direction by capturing the rich heritage of its European cousins and adding a craft beer styling to the depth, complexity and richness of the velvety smooth taste profile. Pine Barrens is pot distilled and hand crafted in small batches and then delicately aged in petite charred American Oak casks.

207

*About:*

Located in Baiting Hollow, New York, in the heart of Long Island's renowned wine growing region, Long Island Spirits is the first distillery on the island since the 1800s. Surrounded by over 5,000 acres of potato farms, the distillery is located on the North Fork of Long Island. The distillery is rich in history and tradition dating back to the early 1900s. Long Island Spirits has become a popular destination for many tourists that come to the East End's North Fork to explore the wine trail.

*Management profile:*

**Richard Stabile**

Richard Stabile, owner and head distiller, grew up on Long Island. He spent most of his summers in Nassau Point on the North Fork of Long Island where wine making and the close connection with local farming was and continues to be a way of life.

Growing up in an Italian household, Stabile was exposed to wine making at an early age; he helped his family crush grapes in his grandfather's Brooklyn basement. Following the end of Prohibition in 1933, his grandfather was one of the first in the state of New York to receive a Beer Wholesaling License under the name "Sunbeam Beverage Distribution."

Richard traveled the world visiting wineries and distilleries and sampled many fine spirits including rum in the Caribbean and scotch in northern Japan. He also received several years of formal training at workshops and distilleries and obtained certification in the field of spirits. For more than twenty years, he has been a results oriented business executive with a proven track record of entrepreneurial success in being part of three high-tech startup companies as well as holding key management positions at two different major multinational corporations.

In the late 1990s, his employer relocated him and his wife to California where his appreciation and interest in fine wine and spirits greatly matured. Upon returning home to Long Island in 2000 to start a family, Richard combined all of his skills to develop a new business.

*Future business plans and goals:* Broaden distribution and expand product line

*Suggested recipe:*

**Pacific Palm -** Created by Jill Schulster at JoeDoe in the Lower East Side of Manhattan
- 1¼ oz LiV Vodka
- 2 oz coconut water
- ¼ oz fresh lime juice
- ¼ oz simple syrup
- 1 tsp lime zest

    Shake all ingredients.
    Strain over ice into double rocks glass.

Long Island Spirits
Baiting Hollow, New York

## Nahmias et Fils

Dorit Nahmias, President
David Nahmias, Master Distiller

201 Saw Mill River Road, Building C
Yonkers, New York  10701

*Phone:*  914-294-0055
*Email:*  Dorit Nahmias:
dorit@baronnahmias.com
        David Nahmias:  david@baronnahmias.com
*Website:*  www.nahmiasetfils.com
*Facebook:*  Nahmias et Fils distillery

*Region:*  Southeastern New York

*Type:*  Micro-distillery producing approximately 5,000 gallons per year

*Opened:*  2012

*Hours of operation:*  Monday through Friday, 8:00am to 6:00pm

*Tours:*  Tours are not available yet.

*Types of spirits produced:*
Mahia and unaged rye whiskey

*Names of spirits:*
- Mahia
- Legs Diamond Whiskey

*Average bottle price:*  $34.99 to $44.99

*Distribution:*
New York state liquor stores, restaurants, bars and clubs

*Highlighted spirits:*
**Mahia**
Distilled according to the old traditions of Morocco, Mahia is a spirit made from figs or dates and herbs. It literally translates to "water of life."

*Highlighted spirits:*

## Legs Diamond Rye Whiskey

Legs Diamond Rye Whiskey starts with locally grown rye from sustainable farms. The grain is then mashed, fermented and carefully distilled, resulting in a white whiskey that is incredibly smooth with a touch of sweetness.

*About:*

Opening a distillery had been a long time dream of David Nahmias. David's family members were distillers in Morocco where they distilled Mahia, a traditional Moroccan spirit distilled from figs and anise.

*Professional associations:*
American Distilling Institute

*Future business plans and goals:*
Tasting room

Nahmias et Fils
Yonkers, New York

## StilltheOne Distillery LLC

Ed and Laura Tiedge, Owners

1 Martin Place
Port Chester, New York 10573

*Phone:* 914-217-0347
*Email:* ed@stilltheonedistillery.com
*Website:* www.combvodka.com
*Facebook:* COMB Vodka, StilltheOne Distillery

*Region:* Southeastern New York

*Type:* Micro-distillery

*Opened:* August 2010

*Hours of operation:* 7:00am to 5:00pm

*Tours:* Tours are available by appointment.

*Types of spirits produced:* Vodka, gin, and brandy

*Names of spirits:*
- COMB Vodka
- COMB 9 Gin
- COMB Blossom Brandy

*Best known for:* COMB Vodka

*Average bottle price:* $34.00

*Distribution:*
Select New York liquor stores and fine restaurants

*Awards and Recognitions:*
**COMB Vodka**
- Gold Medal, 2010 Beverage Testing Institute
- Silver Medal, 2010 New York International Spirits Competition

**COMB 9 Gin**
- Bronze Medal, 2010 New York International Spirits Competition

COMB VODKA • COMB 9 GIN

## COMB Vodka

Like different grapes for wine, honey can provide a large number of varietal options. Clover, wildflowers, raspberry, citrus, tulip poplar and tupelo are just a few of the nectar sources that bees use to make honey. Each one contributes its unique character and allows StilltheOne Distillery to create a perfectly balanced spirit. COMB is pure and flavorful and requires no filtering.

*Events and Celebrations:* By special arrangement

*Interesting facts:*
- This is the first legal distillery in Westchester since Prohibition.

*About:*

While navigating a career change, Ed Tiedge landed on the simple idea of making something people enjoy.

Having a liking for making homemade wine, Ed never thought about going pro until the annual licensing fees for small distilleries dropped to $1,500 from $50,000. The former hedge fund portfolio manager knew he could do this, and he also knew that, to sell well, his spirits would have to be unique. His wife, Laura, pointed out that anyone can make liquor, but not everyone can make good liquor. The business would later be named for her since, after 26 years of marriage, she is "still the one."

After a 10 day course at the American Distilling Institute in California, Ed proved to his wife that he could create something good.

Rather than laying down their life savings to fund his new venture, Laura suggested the Ed sell his Porsche. With little hesitation-he was tired of it anyway-he listed the car for sale. Little did he know that fate would put him in touch with a Swiss buyer who possessed the distillation education Ed needed. He learned that the inquirer's family had been in the wine making business for more than 800 years and was branching out into brandy. Before long, the car was sold and Ed found himself standing in a distillery in Cognac, France, communicating courtesy of a translation iPhone app.

For the next month, he joined the French crew as they got the stills running each morning, broke for lunch, and then checked on its product in the afternoon. Ed filled all other available hours with trips to neighboring distilleries to "sniff out the competition" and was amazed by the variations. Despite using the same type of still and having neighboring vineyards, the cognac was distinctly different. Reinforcing what he had learned at the distilling institute, this experience impressed upon him the importance of minutiae like yeast-strain selection and temperature.

Upon returning to Port Chester, Ed set up two makeshift pot stills. A short time later and with the help of a friend, Ed engineered a larger, more conventional copper-pot still that replaced the now idle, column-pot hybrid.

Ed put his money on honey from the start and he credits his success to the fine mead that is made right on site. Ed starts with vats of Florida orange blossom honey because of the distinct flavor that comes from the flower. He then dilutes it with water, impregnates it with yeast, and ferments the solution in three steel fermentation tanks for about two weeks before transferring it to the stills.

Despite their sweet beginnings, the finished sprits are classifiably dry, clean and sharp.

*Future business plans and goals:* Broaden distribution

*Suggested recipes:*
## COMB Pink Lemonaide
- 1½ oz COMB Vodka
- 6 oz pink lemonaide

  Stir well in tall glass with ice.
  Add your favorite garnish.

## Beach COMBER
- 1½ oz COMB Vodka
- ¼ oz triple sec
- 2 dashes maraschino liqueur
- ¾ oz lime juice

  Add all ingredients to a shaker and shake about 10 times.
  Pour into a chilled glass.

## COMB Martini
- 1½ oz COMB Vodka
- Dash of dry vermouth
- Ice
- Lemon or lime twist

  Add COMB Vodka and vermouth into a shaker with ice.
  Shake, shake, shake.
  Strain into a martini glass and garnish.

StilltheOne Distillery LLC
Port Chester, New York

# Stoutridge Distillery

Stephen Osborn, Owner / Operator
Kimberly Wagner, Owner / Operator

10 Ann Kaley Lane
Marlboro, New York 12542

*Phone:* 845-236-7620
*Fax:* 845-236-7621
*Email:* steve@stoutridge.com
*Website:* www.stoutridge.com

*Region:* Mid-Hudson Valley New York

*Type:* Micro-distillery

*Opened:* 2009

*Hours of operation:* Friday through Sunday, 11:00am to 6:00pm year-round

*Tours:* Tours are available.

*Types of spirits produced:* Brandy, grappa, vodka, gin, corn, and rye whiskey

*Names of spirits:*
- Northern Threat Yankee Bourbon
- Wagner's White Lightning
- Stoutridge Vodka
- Stoutridge Gin

*Distribution:* All of the wines and spirits are sold exclusively at the winery.

*Events and Celebrations:* Multiple venues are available for events of up to 100 people.

*Services offered other than production:* Tours and tastings

*Interesting facts:*
- The distillery is built on the site of a Prohibition era distillery.

*About:*
Stoutridge Vineyard is a premium estate winery located in Marlboro, New York, 70 miles north of Manhattan in the Hudson Valley AVA. The vineyards are half a mile from the Hudson River on the southeast facing slopes of a ridge of land on which grapevines and fruit trees have been continuously planted for 200 years.

The Marlboro area has a rich history of fruit and wine production and, during the 1800s, was the principal supplier of fresh fruit for New York City.

Stoutridge Vineyards is built on the historical foundations of vineyards planted in the late 1700s, a winery established in 1902 which was closed by Prohibition, and a bootleg era distillery which operated until 1956.

In 2001, the vineyards were replanted and a state of the art winery and micro-distillery were built utilizing the same foundation walls of the earlier distillery.

The winery opened in 2006 and the distillery opened in late 2009.

The fruits and grains used for the wines and spirits at Stoutridge are all sourced from New York State. Stoutridge has a strong commitment to sustaining agriculture in the Hudson Valley.

*Future business plans and goals:* Successful sales of products

Stoutridge Distillery
Marlboro, New York

## Tuthilltown Spirits Distillery

Ralph Erenzo, Founder / Distiller
Brian Lee, Founder / Distiller
Gable Erenzo, Distiller / Ambassador / Manager
Joel Elder, Production Manager / Distiller

14 Grist Mill Lane
Gardiner, New York 12525

*Phone:* Tuthilltown office: 845-255-1527
          Retail store / Tour reservations: 845-633-8734
*Email:* info@tuthilltown.com
*Website:* www.tuthilltown.com
*Facebook:* Tuthilltown Spirits
*Twitter:* @Tuthilltown

*Region:* New York

*Type:* Craft-distillery producing approximate 14,000 gallons per year

*Opened:* 2005

*Hours of operation:* Thursday through Monday, 11:00am to 6:00pm,
          Sunday 12:00pm to 6:00pm

*Tours:*
Tours are conducted on Saturdays and Sundays at 12:00pm,
2:00pm and 4:00pm by reservation.

*Types of spirits produced:* Bourbon, rum, whiskey, vodka,
seasonal liqueurs and eau de vie

*Names of spirits:*
- Hudson Whiskeys
  - Single Malt
  - Baby Bourbon
  - Four Grain Bourbon
  - Manhattan Rye
  - New York Corn Whiskey
- Heart and Spirit of the Hudson Vodka
- Rogen's Rum

*Best known for:* Hudson Baby Bourbon

*Average bottle price:* $28.00 to $45.00

*Distribution:* International

- Craft Whiskey Distillery of the Year, 2011 Whisky Magazine
- Artisan Distillery of the Year, 2010 American Distilling Institute
- Best New American Whiskeys, 2010 Food and Wine Magazine

*Highlighted spirits:*

## Hudson Single Malt Whiskey

Hudson Single Malt Whiskey is made in the classic fashion with whole ground malted barley and nothing else. Aged in small American oak casks, this whiskey is a departure from popular single malt scotches. The new oak lends a deeper woody affect to the spirit which is rich in color and full flavored.

## Hudson Baby Bourbon

Hudson Baby Bourbon is single grain bourbon made from 100% New York corn and aged in special small American oak barrels. This unique aging process produces a mildly sweet, smooth spirit with hints of vanilla and caramel. The Baby is Tuthilltown's first whiskey. Each bottle is hand waxed and numbered, and it is the distillery's most sought after spirit.

## Hudson New York Corn Whiskey

Hudson New York Corn Whiskey is distilled the old fashioned way - one batch at a time from 100% New York corn. No sugar is added. This unaged sipping whiskey is clear and soft to the tongue, with the faint aroma of corn fields at harvest. The foundation for this whiskey is Hudson Baby Bourbon.

Coming soon is a new line of small batch eaux de vie (peach, pear, apple), brandy, cassis, bitters, vodka and gin. These will be sold only at Tuthilltown for the first year.

*Interesting facts:*
- Tuthilltown Spirits is New York's first whiskey distillery since Prohibition.
- Hudson Baby Bourbon was the first bourbon whiskey to be distilled in New York.

*About:*

Before Prohibition, more than 1,000 farm distillers produced alcohol from New York grains and fruits. Today, Tuthilltown Spirits Distillery is bringing back traditional batch-distilled spirits.

For 220 years, Tuthilltown Gristmill, listed on the National Register of Historic Places, used waterpower to render local grains to flour. In 2001, Ralph Erenzo and Vicki Morgan acquired the property and, with the help of partner Brian Lee, they converted one of the mill granaries into a micro-distillery.

The partners worked tirelessly to teach themselves the craft of small-batch distillation while navigating the legal and administrative aspects of building the company. Two and a half years later, Tuthilltown Spirits produced its first batches of vodka from scraps collected at a local apple slicing plant; now the distillers use fresh cider from nearby orchards. Production includes vodkas, whiskeys, rum, eaux de vie, brandy, and infusions.

In 2007, Gable Erenzo joined the team and the distillery sent its first international shipment to Paris. The team has continued to grow and it's thrilled to bring the craft of small-batch spirits distilling back to New York.

Tuthilltown captures waste alcohol from the distillation process and uses it to power furnaces that create steam and run the stills and mash tuns. It also uses reed bed systems to process its agricultural gray water and compost solid waste. Solar panels are set to be installed within a year. Tuthilltown's ten year goal is to be completely off the grid.

*Management profile:*
### Ralph Erenzo
Ralph brings 35 years of production and development experience to the distillery. Prior to starting Tuthilltown Spirits, his business ExtraVertical Inc. provided technical services to corporate and media clients. Ralph built and managed New York City's first public climbing gyms including The ExtraVertical Climbing Center on Broadway. His dream of a "climber's ranch" near the largest rock climbing area in the East was set aside in favor of producing high quality spirits. Additionally, Ralph wrote and lobbied for the passing of legislation for the DD license which allows sales by small producers on site at the production facility. This is now a benefit for all NY distilleries

Ralph's writing and commentary have been featured in national media, including op-ed columns for the New York Times. His work at the state level has resulted in the passage of the Farm Distillery Act, which permits New York farms to establish distilleries on site and sell their agricultural spirits at the farm.

218

## Brian Lee

Brian designed and built the technical facilities for Tuthilltown Spirits. He is responsible for engineering and all technical aspects of fermentation and distillation for the company. Brian also serves as CFO for the company. Prior to his work with Tuthilltown Spirits, Brian was a senior technical designer for a company building high-end broadcast television facilities. His clients included SKY Latin America, CBS, and NBC. He served as the on-site technical consultant for ESPN's conversion to high definition television (HDTV). Brian's technical and mechanical skills ensure all the systems at the distillery continue to function. He is also constantly searching for more efficient methods of functioning. He is currently working on hydro and solar power as supplemental energy sources.

## Gable Erenzo

As Distiller and Brand Ambassador, Gable divides his time between production and the national roll out of Tuthilltown Spirits. With over 15 years experience in production and national event management, an associate's degree from CU, and a BS business management from SUNY New Paltz, he brings considerable business knowledge and experience to the company. Gable's prior position as head distiller and production manager at the distillery educated him about all aspects of the Tuthilltown Spirits' production process and prepared him for his role as brand ambassador. A rock climber and outdoor enthusiast from the very start, Gable has been climbing in the "Gunks" for over 20 years.

*Professional associations:* American Distilling Institute and DISCUS

*Suggested recipe:*

**Hudson Valley Sunrise** - Recipe courtesy of Nathan Storey
- 1 oz Hudson New York Corn Whiskey
- 2 oz fresh apple cider
- ½ oz fresh lemon juice
- ¼ oz cherry infused brandy (optional)
- 2 drops Fee Brothers Orange Bitters

Shake over ice and strain into a fancy glass.
Garnish with a kumquat peel.

Tuthilltown Spirits Distillery
Gardiner, New York

# Warwick Valley Distillery

Jason Grizzanti, Owner
Jeremy Kidde, Owner
Joseph Grizzanti, Owner

114 Little York Road
Warwick, New York 10990

*Phone:* 845-258-6020
*Fax:* 845-258-6055
*Email:* wvwinery@warwick.net
*Website:* www.wvwinery.com
*Facebook:* Warwick Valley Winery and Distillery

*Region:* Hudson River Region

*Type:* Micro-distillery producing approximately 2,400 gallons per year

*Opened:* 2002

*Hours of operation:* Daily from 11:00am to 6:00pm

*Tours:* Tours are available by appointment only.

*Types of spirits produced:* Bourbon, gin, apple brandy, pear brandy, and fruit liqueurs

*Names of spirits:*
- American Fruits™ Apple Brandy
- American Fruits™ Pear Brandy
- American Fruits™ Black Currant Cordial
- American Fruits™ Bartlett Pear Liqueur
- American Fruits™ Sour Cherry Cordial
- American Fruits™ Burbon Barrel Aged Apple Liqueur
- Warwick Rustic American Gin

*Distribution:* Throughout the U.S.

*Awards and Recognitions:*
**American Fruits™ Apple Brandy**
- 89 Points, 2009 Beverage Testing Institute

**American Fruits™ Black Currant Cordial**
- 88 Points, 2010 Beverage Testing Institute

**American Fruits™ Pear Brandy** (Eau de vie de Poire)
- Double Gold Medal, 2011 Finger Lakes International Wine Competition
- Double Gold Medal, 2009 Finger Lakes International Wine Competition

*Highlighted spirits:*
## American Fruits™ Apple Brandy
American Fruits™ Apple Brandy (Eau de vie de Pomme) is aged for a minimum of 2 years in New York oak, offering an aroma of apple and a spirit with a smooth and clean finish.

## American Fruits™ Pear Brandy
American Fruits™ Pear Brandy (Eau de vie de Poire) offers ripe pear aromas up front and remains strong through the finish.

## American Fruits™ Black Currant Cordial
American Fruits™ Black Currant Cordial is an infusion of locally grown organic black currants and Warwick Valley Distillery's own distilled spirit. The resulting liqueur has supple currant, honey and jam notes.

## American Fruits™ Sour Cherry Cordial
American Fruits™ Sour Cherry Cordial is an infusion of fresh Montmorency cherries and their own distilled spirit. The resulting cherry cordial boasts aromas and flavors of ripe cherry and cinnamon.

*Events and Celebrations:* Hosts private parties and weddings

*Services offered other than production:*
Tasting room, restaurant, and a retail store

*Interesting facts:*
- In 2002, Warwick Valley Winery & Distillery became the first licensed distillery in the Hudson Valley since Prohibition.

*About:*
Warwick Valley Winery & Distillery is located in the foothills of the Hudson Valley, nestled between Mt. Eve and Mt. Adam. It was started as a result of abundant apple crops that lead its owners to experiment with making hard cider.

Once hooked, they applied for a farm winery license and opened the doors to the public in 1994 with three wines and one cider.

As the passion and enthusiasm for creating wines and ciders evolved, so did the idea of beginning the first distillery in the Hudson Valley since Prohibition. In 2001, the owners applied for and received a grant to develop New York's first fruit micro-distillery. Using the same principle that had brought success to the wine and cider, Warwick Valley created a line of fruit brandies and liqueurs. American Fruits™ brandies and liqueurs are made to capture and preserve the essence of the fruit at its peak ripeness.

Renovated from an old apple packing house and overlooking a goose pond and the orchards, its setting is perfect for enjoying some great wine, food and music. The post and beam tasting room of the distillery provides visitors with a unique environment to explore the many wines, ciders, brandies, and liqueurs. When the weather is nice, the barn doors open up to two patios for dining, relaxing and sipping wine. During the cooler months the owners fire up wood burning stoves and bring the music indoors.

*Suggested recipes:*

**Pear Brandy Sidecar**
- American Fruits™ Pear Brandy
- Fresh lemon
- Simple syrup
- Grand Marnier

Serve in martini glass.

**Warwick Bramble**
- Warwick Gin Sour with American Fruits™ Black Currant Cordial
- Splash club soda (optional)
- Blackberry garnish

Serve in a collins glass.

**Queen Villager**
- Rye or bourbon with American Fruits™ Sour Cherry Cordial and Grand Marnier

Serve on rocks or up in martini glass.

Warwick Valley Distillery
Warwick, New York

# Adam Dalton Distillery

Adam Dalton, Owner/Manager/Distiller
Joan Dalton, Owner/Manager/CFO

251 Biltmore Avenue
Asheville, North Carolina  28801

*Phone:*  336-413-1657
*Email:*  adamdaltondistillery@gmail.com
*Website:*  www.addistillery.com
*Facebook:*  Adam Dalton Distillery

*Region:*  West Central North Carolina

*Type:*  Micro-distillery producing approximately 2,500 gallons per year

*Opened:*  2011

*Hours of operation:*    Monday through Friday, 5:00pm until close
                                   Saturday and Sunday, 3:00pm until close

*Tours:*  Tours are available by appointment.

*Types of spirits produced:*  Rum, blue agave, vodka, moonshine, and whiskey

*Names of spirits:*
- White Widow

*Average bottle price*:  $19.99

*Distribution:*  North Carolina

*Services offered other than production:*  Full service bar and retail store

*About:*
Family owned and operated, Adam Dalton Distillery is a small start-up with big ideas for modernizing old style distilling with a creative twist.

*Future business plans and goals:*  Expanded product line and broadened distribution

Adam Dalton Distillery
Asheville, North Carolina

# Piedmont Distillers

Joe Michalek, Founder
Junior Johnson, Co-Owner

203 East Murphy Street
Madison, North Carolina 27025

Phone: 336-445-0055
Fax: 336-445-9955
Email: info@piedmontdistillers.com
Website: www.piedmontdistillers.com
Facebook: Junior Johnson's Midnight Moon, Catdaddy Carolina Moonshine
Twitter: @JJMidnightMoon, @Catdaddy2005

Region: Northcentral North Carolina

Type: Micro-distillery

Opened: 2005

Tours: Tours are conducted the last Friday of every month from 2:00pm to 4:00pm. Tours are free of charge. Space may be limited. Minors must be accompanied by a parent or guardian.

Types of spirits produced: Moonshine

Names of spirits:
- Junior Johnson's Midnight Moon
- Catdaddy Carolina Moonshine

Best known for: Junior Johnson's Midnight Moon and Catdaddy Carolina Moonshine

Average bottle price: $20.00 to $30.00

Distribution: Products are sold in most states in the U.S.

Highlighted spirits:
## Catdaddy Carolina Moonshine
True to the roots of moonshine, Catdaddy is inspired by traditional moonshine recipes and distilling processes. It's a premium spirit made from American corn that's handcrafted in very small batches in a copper still and triple distilled to be ultra-smooth. Catdaddy's one of a kind taste comes from a secret recipe; only the founder and master distiller know the secret ingredients. Its flavor is best described as a little sweet with a little spice.

224

## Midnight Moon

Midnight Moon is a premium spirit based on Junior Johnson's legendary family moonshine recipe. It's made from American corn, handcrafted in small batches, and born in a copper still. Midnight Moon is triple distilled to deliver a smooth, clean-tasting spirit. Midnight Moon does not have the harsh, heavy corn taste that is often associated with illegal moonshine.

## Midnight Moon Fruit Inclusions

Midnight Moon Apple Pie, Midnight Moon Strawberry, Midnight Moon Cherry, Midnight Moon Blueberry and Midnight Moon Cranberry each begin with the handcrafted, ultra-smooth Midnight Moon recipe. Real fruit and Midnight Moon are then placed in mason jars by hand (just like moonshiners have done for generations), and are aged for several weeks to ensure each bottle reaches the peak of all-natural fruit flavor before leaving the distillery.

*Events and Celebrations:* Check website for dates and times

*Services offered other than production:* Gift shop

*Interesting facts:*
- The distillery is housed in the town's former train station which was built in 1915.

*About:*
Piedmont Distillers is a small distillery in Madison, North Carolina, founded by Joe Michalek, a native New Yorker who moved to North Carolina in 1995.

Through his job in marketing, Joe had the opportunity to travel the South attending events like music festivals and NASCAR races. On one such adventure, Joe found himself in a cabin in the woods listening to a jam session by local blues legends when someone handed him a jar of peach moonshine. At first, Joe was apprehensive to take a sip; after all, he didn't know where it came from or who made it. He did not hesitate long - this was the stuff of legends. He took a sip of the illicit brew and was surprised that it tasted great and was very smooth.

Over the next several years, moonshine became Joe's passion. He read books, tasted all sorts of recipes, watched documentaries, and eventually earned the trust of local moonshiners. These old timers shared their recipes, distilling techniques and general tricks of the trade. Once he had learned as much as he could, Joe decided it was time to share North Carolina moonshine with the rest of the world.

Piedmont Distillers opened its doors in 2005 with the first spirit, Catdaddy Carolina Moonshine. Catdaddy harkens back to the moonshining days of old with its corn recipe, secret flavors, copper still and small batch process. In May of 2007, moonshine and racing legend Junior Johnson became part owner of Piedmont Distillers and together they introduced Junior Johnson's Midnight Moon. Midnight Moon is made from the Johnson family's generations old moonshine recipe. It is also born in a copper still, made from corn, crafted in small batches and triple distilled.

Junior grew up tending to the family's stills during the day and running 'shine at night. Junior's ability to make a car run flat-out combined with his incredible skills behind the wheel made him a bootlegging legend. He went on to become one of the greatest drivers and team owners in racing history.

Although its first two spirits are moonshines, Piedmont Distillers does not consider itself strictly a moonshine distillery. Rather, the focus is on handcrafted, superior quality spirits that are made one small batch at a time. The distillers are constantly innovating new spirits that embrace distilling traditions and ingredients of the region, excite the palate and the senses, and offer people something different than what's typically on the store shelves.

*Future business plans and goals:* Broaden distribution

*Suggested recipe:*
**Moonshine Smash**
- 1½ oz Catdaddy
- ½ oz fresh lemon
- 3-4 sprigs of mint
- 1-2 oz club soda

    Muddle the mint in the lemon juice.
    Add Catdaddy and a level scoop of ice.
    Shake and strain over fresh ice.
    Top with soda.
    Garnish with mint sprig and lemon wheel.

Piedmont Distillers
Madison, North Carolina

# Cleveland Whiskey LLC

Tom Lix, CEO

1768 E 25th Street
Cleveland, Ohio  44114-4420

*Phone:*  216.881.8481
*Fax:* 216-579-9225
*Email:* tlix@clevelandwhiskey.com
*Website:* www.clevelandwhiskey.com
*LinkedIn:* www.linkedin.com/in/tomlix

*Region:*  Northern Ohio

*Type*:  Experimental distilled spirits plant

*Opened:* 2009

*Hours of operation:*  24/7

*Tours:*  Invitation only

*About:*
Bringing 21st century science and technology to an industry steeped in traditional practices, Cleveland Whiskey is an experimental distilled spirits plant (EDSP) with a focus on technologies associated with accelerated aging of distilled spirits.

With a patent-pending process of thermal and pressure change, Cleveland Whiskey dramatically accelerates production while reducing overall costs.

Cleveland Whiskey, with funding assistance from the North Coast Opportunities Technology Fund, the Lorain County Community College Innovation Fund and the Cuyahoga County New Product Development and Entrepreneurship Loan Fund, has finished prototype development and is currently working on bringing product to market.

*Management profile:*
**Tom Lix**
CEO and Founder Tom Lix was most recently the president and founder of application services provider Public Interactive®. Prior to founding Public Interactive in 1995, Lix was president of Market Pulse™, a Cambridge-based database software company and subsidiary of Computer Corporation of America. Previously, he was President of Yankelovich Partners, where he consulted for leading food, beverage and hospitality companies including Guinness PLC, Proctor & Gamble, H. J. Heinz Company, Unilever, PepsiCo, The Clorox Company and Burger King.

*Professional associations:*  American Distilling Institute

Cleveland Whiskey LLC
Cleveland, Ohio

# Ernest Scarano Distillery

*Physical Address:*
1989 County Road 62
Gibsonburg, Ohio 43431

*Mailing Address:*
Post Office Box 213
Elmore, Ohio 43416

*Phone:* 419-205-8734
*Website:* www.esdistillery.com

*Region:* Northwest Ohio

*Type:* Micro-distillery producing approximately 100 gallons per year

*Opened:* March 17, 2010

*Hours of operation:* Monday through Sunday, 7:30am to 8:00pm

*Tours:* Tours are not available.

*Types of spirits produced:* 4 year, 160 proof, 100% straight rye

*Names of spirits:*
* Old Homicide
* Whiskey Dick

*Best known for:* Old Homicide

*Average bottle price:* Old Homicide $95.00/12oz, Whiskey Dick $45.00/12oz

*Distribution:* To be announced

*Highlighted spirits:*

**Old Homicide**
Old Homicide is currently aging. This rye whiskey will sit in oak to age and mellow until approximately May 1, 2014. It will then be placed in sugar maple charcoal for 30 days and then bottled.

**Whiskey Dick**
Whiskey Dick is an unaged rye whiskey. It is mellowed in sugar maple charcoal resulting in a very smooth and mellowed flavor.

*Professional associations:* American Distilling Institute

Ernest Scarano Distillery
Gibsonburg, Ohio

228

# Indian Creek Distillery

Joe and Melissa Duer, Owners
7095 Staley Road
New Carlisle, Ohio  45344

*Phone:*  937-846-1443
*Email:*  jmduer76@gmail.com
*Website:*  www.staleymillfarmanddistillery.com

*Region:*  Mid-Ohio

*Type:*  Micro-distillery producing approximately 5,000 gallons per year

*Opened:*  April 2012

*Hours of operation:*  9:00am to 5:00pm

*Tours:*  Tours are available by reservation.

*Types of spirits produced:*  Rye whiskey and unaged whiskey

*Names of spirits:*
- Staley Rye Whiskey
- Lady Liberty Moonshine

*Best known for:*  Rye Whiskey

*Average bottle price*:  $40.00 to $80.00

*Distribution:*
On premises and throughout the U.S.

*Highlighted spirits:*
**Staley Rye Whiskey**
Unique to its heritage and rich in the flavors of history, Staley Rye Whiskey is the spirit of America in a bottle.

**Lady Liberty Moonshine**
Freedom never tasted so good.

*About:*
To visit Indian Creek Distillery is to step back in time to an early American farm and to experience the vision of an early American

man.  It's a rare glimpse into the only remaining pioneer agricultural/industrial complex remaining in the same family in the United States today.   History is alive and well at the legendary Staley Mill Farm and Distillery.

Melissa is the 6th generation to own her family's historic Staley Mill Farm. Her great-great-great grandfather Elias Staley, an early American entrepreneur, purchased this 160 acre farm after he built a grist mill and mill races for a Mr. Rench. A distillery was built in 1820 and bold frontier rye whiskey was distilled for 100 years until Prohibition. Today, a new distillery has been built and once again Staley Rye Whiskey is flowing from the stillhouse. Distilled using the exact same copper-pot stills that Elias used almost 200 years ago, the same limestone water and the same mash bill, Staley Rye Whiskey is truly distinct in that it is the only historic family owned artisan distillery in the U.S. using the old fashioned double copper distilling method that the family used for generations.

*Professional associations:*
American Distilling Institute

*Future business plans and goals:*
To consistently produce high quality spirits that are historic in nature and are unique, remarkable and rare

*Suggested recipe:*
**The Maple Leaf**

- 2 ozs Staley Rye
- ¾ oz local maple syrup
- ¾ oz lemon juice

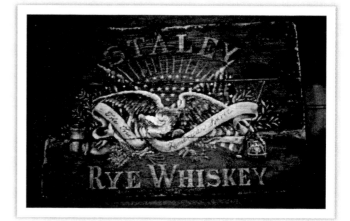

Shake with ice and strain into a glass over ice. Garnish with a cinnamon stick.

Indian Creek Distillery
New Carlisle, Ohio

# Woodstone Creek

Donald Outterson, Owner / Distiller

3641 Newton Avenue
Cincinnati, Ohio 45207

*Phone:* 513-569-0300
*Email:* woodstonecreek@yahoo.com
*Website:* www.woodstonecreek.com
*Facebook:* Woodstone Creek

*Region:* Ohio

*Type*: Micro-distillery producing 20 barrels per year

*Opened:* January 1999

*Hours of operation:* Not open to the public

*Tours:* Not open to the public

*Types of spirits produced:*
Bourbon, single malt (peated and unpeated), white dogs, varietal whisky (barley, rye, wheat, corn), vodka, rum, gin, grape brandy, honey brandy, bierschnaps

*Names of spirits:*
- Woodstone Creek 5 Grain Straight Bourbon Whiskey
- Woodstone Creek Vodka
- Woodstone Creek Single Barrel Peated Single Malt Whisky

*Best known for:* Bourbon and Single Peated Malt Whisky

*Average bottle price*: $20.00 to $117.00 /750 mL bottle

*Distribution:*
Tasting room, Ohio, Illinois, Indiana, Kentucky, and Colorado

*Awards and Recognitions:*
**Woodstone Creek 5 Grain Straight Bourbon Whisky**
- Bronze Medal, American Distilling Institute
- Bronze Medal, 2008 Beverage Testing Institute

**Woodstone Creek Vodka**
- Silver Medal, 2007 Beverage Testing Institute

**Woodstone Creek Single Barrel Peated Single Malt Whisky**
- 92 points, 2009 Murray's Whisky Bible

*Highlighted spirits:*

## Woodstone Creek 5 Grain Straight Bourbon Whisky

This bourbon whisky is a deep dark amber color. Curious aromas of iodine tincture, buttery caramel apple, baked prunes and lemons, dried pine needle, and Spic n' Span follow through on a bold entry to an off-dry full body with peat moss, caramelized nuts, honeyed cornbread, and star anise notes. It finishes with a silky textured buttery toffee, iodine, and charcoal fade. Beverage Testing Institute says it's an "interesting amalgamation of scotch and bourbon whisky characteristics".

## Woodstone Creek Single Barrel Peated Single Malt Whisky

Murray's Whisky Bible of 2009 says "the nose is earthy, salty peat; much more redolent of Islay than of Cincinnati just beautifully constructed with excellent layering of gentle smoke, grapey fruit and toasted oak. The silkiness on the palate stuns. All taste is understated yet the clarity of the riches never fades. There's lots of fruit, but the even sweeter peat circles in clouds and dovetails with drier, oak-led incursions. A tantalizing saltiness gives this a coastal dimension which belies the distillery's location some 1,000 miles inland. It's surprisingly brittle at the finish, but the smoke shows little sign of abating. Overall balance and complexity: What a wonderful whisky! Islayfiles will be confused by this one because it displays so many coastal characters. A massive well-done for a first bottling from this new distillery."

## Woodstone Creek Vodka

This clear vodka, crème anglaise and mild anise cookie aromas follow through to a soft, silky and delicate entry and lead to a creamy, off-dry medium-to-full body with notes of minerals, toasted nuts, and vinyl. It finishes with a peppery sweet mineral ore and balsa fade. Beverage Testing institute calls it a nice artisanal vodka with a pot still character.

*Services offered other than production:* Tasting room

*Interesting facts:*
- Woodstone Creek is Ohio's first licensed micro-distillery.
- Donald originated the microdistillery license in Ohio in 1998. Additionally, he worked to change the liquor law in 2008 when he introduced legislation to allow self-sales for micros in the state.

*About:*

Since its beginnings in a barn north of Cincinnati in 1999, Woodstone Creek has used fine ingredients and it modestly produces 100–200 cases of wine, mead and distilled spirits annually.

Woodstone Creek is a true single-barrel spirit, produced in a 238 gallon, direct fired pot still designed by the distiller. Its spirits are made much the same way they were made prior to the Industrial Revolution. Each barrel is distilled, aged and bottled individually, not blended with other barrels; this results in an individual character that cannot be duplicated.

*Management profile:*
## Donald Outterson

Donald Outterson, a champion homebrewer and past president of the New York Homebrewing League, decided to go "pro" in 1982.

His family ancestry spurred an interest in spirits which started in college while he was an exchange student in Scotland. He served an apprenticeship in English ales and graduated in 1986 from the Siebel Institute of Technology in Chicago. Upon graduation, he traveled all over the United States, Australia and Germany as a certified brewmaster. He won several awards at Great American Beer Festival, wrote numerous articles, reviewed books, and conducted seminars at craft-brewing tradeshows nationwide. In 1988, Don moved to Cincinnati where he met his wife, Linda, and opened the city's first brewpub, Wallaby Bob's.

Shortly thereafter, he launched a commercial consulting/equipment business geared to start-up brewpubs, microbreweries, wineries and micro-distilleries.

Within the first five years, Don consulted, devised recipes and sourced equipment for fifty-three start-up brewpubs and microbreweries. He also sold parts and equipment to wineries and small distilleries. Additionally, he built a small pilot plant to demonstrate equipment. When the brewpub fad peaked, he closed the consulting business. The pilot plant was then expanded and licensed to become a fully functioning winery.

Donald originated the micro-distillery license in Ohio in 1998. In 2008, he helped change the liquor law by introducing legislation to allow self-sales for micros in the state.

*Professional associations:* American Distilling Institute

*Future business plans and goals:* Expand public space to include food and entertainment, and expand production to include beer

*Suggested recipes:*
## Pomme Lovely
- 8 oz Woodstone Creek Pomegranate Honey Pyment
- 1 oz Woodstone Creek 94 Proof Premium Dry Gin

    Shake with ice, strain and serve.

## Raspberry Blast
- 8 oz Woodstone Creek Raspberry Honey Pyment
- 1 oz Woodstone Creek 100 or 80 proof Vodka
- Simple syrup to taste and dash of lime juice

    Shake with ice, strain and serve.

Woodstone Creek
Cincinnati, Ohio

# Bendistillery

Jim Bendis, Chief Executive Officer
Alan Dietrich, Chief Marketing Officer
Jennah Padilla, Operations Manager
Makency Camreta, Private Label Director
Hannah Routon, Production Manager

19330 Pinehurst Road
Bend, Oregon 97701

*Phone:* 541-318-0200
*Fax:* 541-318-1886 (Bend OR Office)
*Fax:* 760-832-7656 (So. CA Office)
*Email:* info@bendistillery.com
*Website:* www.bendistillery.com
*Facebook:* Crater Lake Vodka, Bend Distillery
*Twitter:* @bendistillery

*Region:* Central Oregon

*Type*: Micro-distillery producing approximately 35,000 cases per year

*Opened:* Fall 1995

*Hours of operation:*
Monday through Thursday, 9:00am to 5:00pm
Friday, 9:00am to 6:00pm
Saturday, noon to 6:00pm

*Tours:* Tours of the facility are available.

*Types of spirits produced:* Gin, vodka and flavored vodkas, rum, distilled spirit specialties

*Names of spirits:*
- Crater Lake Vodka
- Diamond 100 Vodka
- Cascade Mountain Gin
- Cofia Hazlenut Espresso Vodka
- Mazama Infused Pepper Vodka
- Approximately 20 private label spirits

*Average bottle price*: $22.95 to $29.95

*Distribution:* Distribution is primarily focused in Oregon, Washington, California, and Idaho; however, the spirits are available in other states.

*Awards and Recognitions:*

**Crater Lake Vodka**
- Platinum Medal, 2010 Sip Awards International Spirits Competition
- Four Stars, 2009 Beverage Experts
- Gold Medal and 92 Points, 2008 Beverage Testing Institute
- Gold Medal and 92 Points, 2003 Beverage Testing Institute
- Silver Medal, 2000 San Francisco World Spirits Competition

**Cascade Mountain Gin**
- Four Stars, 2009 Beverage Experts
- Silver Medal, 2006 World Beverage Competition "World's Best Gin"
- Bronze Medal, 2006 International Review of Spirits
- Bronze Medal, 2000 San Francisco World Spirits Competition

**Cofia Hazelnut Espresso Vodka**
- Gold Medal, 2011 The Fifty Best Flavored Vodkas
- Platinum Medal Best of Show, 2006 World Beverage Competition "Best Flavored Vodka in the World"
- Gold Medal and 93 Points, 2003 Beverage Testing Institute
- Silver Medal, 2003 San Francisco World Spirits Competition

**Mazama Infused Pepper Vodka**
- Gold Medal, 2004 San Francisco World Spirits Competition
- Four Stars, 2004 Spirit Journal

**Diamond 100 Vodka**
- Double Gold Medal, 2007 San Francisco World Spirits Competition
- Gold Medal, 2007 International Review of Spirits

*Highlighted spirits:*

**Crater Lake Vodka**
Crater Lake Vodka is slowly filtered ten times through charcoal and crushed volcanic rock and then aged briefly in oak. Though long and painstaking, this technique makes Crater Lake Vodka one of the smoothest vodkas in the world with a soft, spring water feel that hints slightly of vanilla. Crater Lake Vodka is 80 proof.

**Cascade Mountain Gin**
Cascade Mountain Gin is a return to the original flavor and spirit of gin. It's crafted with wild, handpicked juniper berries from the central Oregon high desert plateau. While most gins use extracts and artificial flavorings, Cascade Mountain Gin is made with only fresh, natural ingredients; this gives it a subtle and full flavor. The aroma of Cascade Mountain is clean and pure without the perfume or chemical smells that come with the use of extracts and commercial flavorings. Cascade is the gin for the serious martini connoisseur and is 95 proof.

**Cofia Hazelnut Espresso Vodka**
Cofia Hazelnut Espresso Vodka is created from two of the most well-known flavors of the Northwest - fresh-brewed coffee and hazelnuts. Unlike most flavored vodkas, the coffee and hazelnut in Cofia are rich, strong and all natural. Cofia day at the distillery means the whole neighborhood is steeped in the aroma of fresh brewed coffee and roasted hazelnuts. Cofia Hazelnut Espresso Vodka is 50 proof.

**Diamond 100 Vodka**
Filtered over 100 times through charcoal and crushed lava rock and aged slightly in new American oak, Diamond 100 Vodka is 80 proof and very smooth.

*Highlighted spirits:*
## Mazama Infused Pepper Vodka
Named after Mt. Mazama, the volcano that erupted to become Crater Lake, Mazama Infused Pepper Vodka is handcrafted using only fresh natural ingredients. Starting with the same spirit used to make Crater Lake Vodka, the distillery infuses a blend of no fewer than six different sweet and hot peppers. The result is a pepper vodka that delivers balanced flavor along with heat. Mazama Infused Pepper Vodka is 80 proof.

*Services offered other than production:* Tastings where allowable by law

*About:*
Located in Bend, Oregon, Bendistillery was founded in 1996 with the goal of reviving the tradition of handcrafted American gin and vodka and, in the process, it helped launch the boutique spirits revolution. Founder Jim Bendis opened Bendistillery to create the first micro-distillery in the county using fresh, handpicked, wild juniper berries.

*Future business plans and goals:*
To produce the world's first organic estate gin, single-barrel tequila, and a double malt porter whiskey in conjunction with Deschutes Brewery

*Suggested recipes:*
## Mazama Bloody Mary
- 2 oz Mazama Infused Pepper Vodka
- 4 oz tomato juice
- ½ oz Demetri's Bloody Mary Spice Blend

    Mix ingredients over ice in a cocktail shaker.
    Shake to mix and pour contents, including ice, into a celery salt rimmed glass.
    Garnish with celery stalk, lime, olive and pickled asparagus spear.

## Ski Lift
- 2 oz Hazelnut Espresso Vodka
- 1 oz brandy
- 6 oz hot chocolate

    Combine all ingredients in a coffee mug, nudge or wine glass.
    Top with whipped cream and chocolate shavings.

Bendistillery
Bend, Oregon

236

## Brandy Peak Distillery

David and Georgia Nowlin, Owners

18526 Tetley Road
Brookings, Oregon   97415

*Phone:*  541-469-0194
*Fax:*  541-469-0194
*Email:*  distiller@brandypeak.com
*Website:*  www.brandypeak.com

*Region:*   Southern Oregon

*Type*:   Micro-distillery

*Opened:*  Began production in 1994, opened tasting room 1995

*Hours of operation:*
Open March through the first weekend of January
Tuesday through Saturday, 1:00pm to 5:00pm and other times by appointment

*Tours:*   Tours of the distillery are available.

*Types of spirits produced:*  Brandies, eaux de vie, grappa and a blackberry liqueur

*Names of spirits:*
- Brandy Peak Natural Pear Brandy
- Brandy Peak Aged Pear Brandy
- Brandy Peak Aged Pinot Noir Brandy
- Brandy Peak Spirit of Muscat Brandy
- Brandy Peak Aged Muscat Brandy
- Brandy Peak Grappa
- Brandy Peak Aged Grape Brandy
- Brandy Peak Blackberry Liqueur

*Average bottle price*:  $20.00 to $32.00

*Distribution:*  Brandy Peak spirits are available in the tasting room as well as in liquor stores in Oregon, and in select fine liquor stores in California.

*Awards and Recognitions:*
**Brandy Peak Natural Pear**
- Gold Medal and Best of Show, 2002 Oregon State Fair

**Brandy Peak Aged Pear**
- Double Gold, 2009 American Distilling Institute
- Gold & Double Gold, 1997 San Francisco International Wine Competition

*Awards and Recognitions:*

**Brandy Peak Grappa**
- Gold Medal and Best of Class, 2004 Oregon State Fair

**Brandy Peak Aged Grape Brandy**
- Silver Medal, 2005 Oregon State Fair
- Silver Medal, 1997 Los Angeles County Fair

*Highlighted spirits:*

**Brandy Peak Natural Pear Brandy**
This brandy exhibits enticingly ripe and earthy fruit flavors, with polished aromas of pear and vanillin.

**Brandy Peak Aged Pear Brandy**
Mellowed in French and Oregon oak casks, this brandy exhibits polished aromas of pear and vanillin along with flavors of ripe earthy fruit.

**Brandy Peak Muscat Brandy**
Muscat has an intense perfume of spring flowers, a touch of natural sweetness and a lingering finish of anise.

**Brandy Peak Aged Grape Brandy**
Traditional pot-still grape brandy aged in French Limousin oak, it has a charming bouquet of citrus and cloves with a smooth, dry finish.

**Brandy Peak Grappa**
Brandy Peak Grappa is a zesty blend of varietal grape distillates with a very light touch of Oregon oak. It is smooth and pleasant with a very clean finish.

**Brandy Peak Blackberry Liqueur**
The Blackberry Liqueur is lusciously sweet with the sunshine ripeness of wild blackberries in a bottle. Wild, local handpicked blackberries are used in making this liqueur.

*Events and Celebrations:* Brandy Peak Distillery does not host events.

*Services offered other than production:* Tasting and tours

*Interesting facts*
- Spirits are distilled in wood-fired pot stills that are unique in the industry.
- It takes fourteen pounds of pears to make a 375ml bottle of the pear brandy.
- No artificial additives, colorings or flavorings are used.
- Brandy Peak is named after the highest mountain in Curry County.

238

*About:*

In the hills of the temperate rainforests of the southern Oregon coast, R.L. Nowlin, with his son David, built his dream distillery "to capture the varietal characteristics of fruit as brandy."

In 1984, Nowlin challenged the wine and spirits industry with his dissertation "Distilled Beverages - A Challenge for Tomorrow," given when he received the prestigious James F. Guymon Award from the American Society of Enology and Viticulture for his 50 years of contributions to the industry. In 1993, the distillery arose from what had been a tangle of blackberry bushes, shrubs, and fir trees. Drawing on his fifty years of experience in the spirits industry, Nowlin designed and built the country's only two legal wood-fired pot stills at that time. A year later, brandy production began and the tasting room opened to the public the following year. Brandy Peak was named for the highest mountain in Curry County where the distillery is located and also from where many of the blackberries are gathered.

Brandy Peak Distillery has a product line of ten brandies and one liqueur. Nowlin works on developing new products, while his son, David (below right), and wife, Georgia (below left), are involved with the day-to-day operations.

*Professional associations:* Oregon Distillers Guild

Brandy Peak Distillery
Brookings, Oregon

239

# Bull Run Distilling Company

Lee Medoff, Co-Founder and Head Distiller
Patrick Bernards, Co-Founder and Chief Enthusiast
John Rudi, President

2259 NW Quimby Street
Portland, Oregon  97210

*Phone:*  503-224-3483
*Email:*  patrick@bullrundistillery.com
*Website:*  www.bullrundistillery.com
*Facebook:*  Bull Run Distilling Company
*Twitter:*  @BullRunSpirits
*YouTube:*  BullRunDistillingCo. Channel

*Region:*  Pacific Northwest

*Type:*  Micro-distillery producing approximately 6,700 proof gallons per year at full production

*Opened:*  Monday, December 5, 2011, the 78th Anniversary of the repeal of Prohibition

*Hours of operation:*  Monday through Friday, 9:00am to 5:00pm
Tasting Room and Retail Store Hours:
>    Sunday: 12:00pm 4:00pm
>    Monday and Tuesday: Closed
>    Wednesday through Friday: 1:00pm to 6:00pm
>    Saturday: 1:00pm to 6:00pm

NOTE:
*Please check their website for seasonal changes to hours prior to visiting.*

*Tours:*
Tours are offered Thursday through Sunday between 1:00pm and 6:00pm by reservation only.

*Types of spirits produced:*
rum, whiskey, vodka, and a limited release line of sweet and bitter liqueurs, schnapps, aquavit and other interesting libations

*Names of spirits:*
- Pacific Rum
- Oregon Whiskey
- Medoyeff Vodka
- Temperance Trader Straight Bourbon Whiskey
- Temperance – A limited release line of spirits sold exclusively at Bull Run Distillery that may include, but may not be limited to: Aquavit, Sweet & Bitter Liqueurs, Flavored Vodka, Absinthe, Flavored Rums, and Schnapps

240

*Best known for:*
The Medoyeff Mule, Bull Run Distillings take on the famous Moscow Mule, the cocktail that put vodka on the map in the U.S. back in the 1950's

*Average bottle price:*
Medoyeff Vodka, $27.95 to $32.95;  Temperance Trader Bourbon, $29.95 to $32.95

*Distribution:*
Bull Run products can be found in California, Illinois, Kansas, New York, Oregon, Texas, Washington, and the District of Columbia.

*Awards and Recognitions:*
**Medoyeff Vodka**
- "Very Highly Recommended," July 2011 DrinkSpirits.com

**Temperance Trader Bourbon**
- "Highly Recommended," August 2011 DrinkSpirits.com

*Highlighted spirits:*
**Medoyeff Vodka** – 80 Proof

Medoyeff Vodka is an all grain vodka made in an Eastern European style.  Bearing Lee Medoff's original Russian family name, this vodka is flavor forward; the flavor not only comes from the grain, but it also comes from the proprietary filtering process which Medoff picked up on his travels through Eastern Europe.  As with Eastern European vodka, Medoyeff Vodka was designed to be appreciated straight, but it will certainly enhance any vodka cocktail.

**Temperance Trader Bourbon** – 84 Proof (varies by batch)
Temperance Trader Bourbon is "high-rye" bourbon made from a blend of four year - old barrels. While this "found spirit" was conceived in bourbon country, it was born in Oregon.

*Events and Celebrations:*
The distillery holds several annual events celebrating its founding, products and the history of the industry.  Details are available on the website.

*Services offered other than production:*
Bull Run Distillery has a tasting room and retail store where all of its products can be tasted and purchased. Bull Run merchandise and other unique bar related items are also available for purchase. Additionally, Bull Run provides a number of on-site classes and workshops.

*About:*
Bull Run Distilling Company provides a glimpse into America's spirited past – back to the time of the Temperance movement and Prohibition. The tasting room has the feel of an old bar with walls covered in period documents such as the prescription for whiskey from 1929 – the only way one could "legally" get whiskey during Prohibition. Conversely, the distillery production area is large (6,000 square feet), bright and airy with gleaming steel and copper lining one end of the distillery.

241

Bull Run was the brainchild of Co-Founder and Head Distiller Lee Medoff. Lee's vision for Bull Run is to produce dark, craft spirits in volume, with a focus on Pacific Rum and Oregon Whiskey. Many of the ingredients are local and organic. The water is sourced from the Bull Run Wilderness watershed.

*Management profile:*
## Lee Medoff
Lee Medoff (standing) has more than 20 years of experience in brewing, wine making and distilling. Medoff's resume of distilling includes: first distiller for McMenamins, co-founder of House Spirits, co-founder of Bull Run Distilling Company and founder of the Oregon Distillers Guild. He is also known to be an amazing cook.

## Patrick Bernards
Patrick Bernards (seated) has more than 20 years of experience in business-to-business and business-to-consumer sales and marketing. In addition to co-founding Bull Run Distilling Company, Patrick is on the Board of Directors for the Oregon Distillers Guild. Patrick also arguably makes the world's best Moscow Mule.

*Professional associations:* American Distilling Institute and Oregon Distillers Guild

*Future business plans and goals:* Increased production and broadened distribution.

*Suggested recipes:*
## Medoyeff Mule
- 2 oz Medoyeff
- 3 oz Blenheim's Old #3 Red Cap Ginger Ale
- ¼ fresh squeezed lime juice
- 5 drops Bittermens Tiki Bitters

   Serve over ice and garnish with a wedge of lime.

## Preacher's Daughter
- 2 oz Temperance Trader Bourbon
- 3 oz Blenheim's Old #3 Red Cap Ginger Ale
- 2 slices of fresh peach
- 1 small handful of fresh mint

   Muddle peaches and mint in a glass.
   Add bourbon and ginger ale, ice and serve.
   Garnish with a sprig of mint.

Bull Run Distilling Company
Portland, Oregon

# Cascade Peak Spirits Distillery
Home of Organic Nation

Diane Paulson, Co-founder / Owner
David Eliasen, Co-founder / Owner / Distiller

Post Office Box 1198 (mail)
280 E. Hersey Street (site)
Ashland, Oregon  97520

*Phone:*  541-482-3160
*Fax:*  541-552-9310
*Email:*  spirits@organicnationspirits.com
*Website:*  www.organicnationspirits.com
*Facebook:*  Organic Nation Spirits
*Twitter:*  @OGNationSpirits
*LinkedIn:*  Diane Paulson
*YouTube:*  Certified Organic Spirits

*Region:*  Pacific Northwest

*Type*:  Certified organic micro-distillery producing approximately 50 to 100 cases per month

*Opened:*  September 2007

*Hours of operation:*  Open year-round on a short schedule and by appointment

*Tours:*  Tours are available by appointment only.

*Types of spirits produced:*  Certified organic vodka, gin, and a rye whiskey (out in early 2012)

*Names of spirits:*
- Organic Nation Vodka
- Organic Nation Gin
- Oldfield Rye Whiskey

*Best known for:*  Organic Nation Gin and Vodka, and a Bees Knees cocktail

*Average bottle price*:  $30.00 to $55.00

*Distribution:*
Products are available at the distillery and in Oregon liquor stores as well as in bars and restaurants throughout Oregon and California.  Recently released in Japan and Sweden.

*Awards and Recognitions:*
**Organic Nation Vodka**
- Silver Medal, 2009 San Francisco World Spirits Competition
- Gold Medal, 2011-2012 Good Food Awards, CA

**Organic Nation Gin**
- Silver Medal, 2009 (packaging) & 2010 San Francisco World Spirits Competition
- Silver Medal, 87 Points, Highly Recommended, Beverage Testing Institute

*Highlighted spirits:*
**Organic Nation Gin**
Certified organic, Organic Nation Gin is handcrafted using 12 organic botanicals including coriander, basil, lemon balm and black pepper. The gin is twice distilled from organic rye, wheat and corn.

**Organic Nation Vodka**
Organic Nation Vodka is distilled from organic rye, wheat, and corn and is filtered seven times filtered. It's certified organic.

**Oldfield Rye Whiskey**
Named after longtime friends and investors, Oldfield Rye Whiskey is aged in new oak barrels for 20 plus months using organic rye grown within 40 miles of the distillery and organic malt.

*Events and Celebrations:*
Cascade Peak Spirits sponsors many local and regional events.

*Services offered other than production:* Tastings and tours. Eventually fortification for southern Oregon wineries, apple brandy with local organic Thompson Organics, grappas.

*Interesting facts*
- Cascade Peak Spirits is the first certified organic artisan distiller in the Pacific Northwest creating uniquely crafted organic spirits.

*About:*
After falling in love over several Martinis in 2004, Diane Paulson and David Eliasen discovered the micro-distillery movement in Oregon and decided to make their own organic vodka. They wanted their business to be a sustainable business and focus on the "Buy Local, Buy Green" movement.

After visiting micro-distilleries in their area, instituting their own training program, and getting through the myriad of legal issues, they opened Cascade Peak Spirits in 2007 with the graces of good fortune and good friends.

The custom built Bavarian Holstein Still from Germany is named Lil' Guenther after the TTB agent who helped Diane and David get their DSP license within 40 days.
244

Cascade Peak Spirits works with many environmental non-profits such as Oregon Environmental Council. Additionally, Cascade Peak Spirits buys only local, certified organic products and the labels are the first in the spirits industry that are 100% biodegradable. Approximately 85% of all ingredients are sourced from within Jackson and Josephine Counties. The remaining ingredients come from within the Pacific Northwest.

*Management profile:*

## Diane Paulson

Diane Paulson is the president and CEO of Cascade Peak Spirits Inc. (Organic Nation) and directs business development, growth strategies, product development, and strategic partnerships. A resident of Oregon since 1975, Diane holds a master's degree in education with experience in social work, teaching, and operating a private business as a real estate broker. Diane was born a natural entrepreneur. All of the women in her family tree were entrepreneurs even during the Great Depression.

## David Eliasen

David Eliasen, vice president of Cascade Peak Spirits Inc., is responsible for product production and new product development. David received extensive training from the finest regional and national distillers and brings a wealth of expertise in water quality to Organic Nation; he worked for the City of Ashland Water Department for ten years and was also the water master in Jackson County.

*Future business plans and goals:* Expand marketing efforts and product line using locally grown pears, apples, grapes. Broaden distribution to Asia and Europe. Create a 6,000 sq. ft. state of the art sustainable and green distillery in Ashland.

*Suggested recipe:*

## Extreme Chocolate Girl

- 2 oz Organic Nation Vodka
- ½ oz Extreme Chocolates' Dark Chocolate Pinot Sauce
- ½ oz Godiva White Chocolate Liqueur
- ½ tsp Extreme Chocolates' Vanilla Extract
- 2 oz Extreme Chocolates' Dark Chocolate, melted in a squeeze bottle

Start with a chilled cocktail glass.
Squeeze a swirl design inside the glass with the melted chocolate.
In a shaker, add ice cubes, vodka, chocolate sauce, chocolate liqueur and vanilla.
Shake vigorously for 30 seconds and strain into chilled glass.

Cascade Peak Spirits Distillery
Ashland, Oregon

## Eastside Distilling
Formerly Deco Distilling

Lenny Gotter, Owner
Bill Adams, Owner

1512 SE 7th Avenue
Portland, Oregon  97214

*Phone:*  503-926-7060
*Fax:*  503-853-1163
*Email:*  General info:  info@eastsidedistilling.com
　　　　　Lenny Gotter:  lenny@eastsidedistilling.com
*Website:*  www.eastsidedistilling.com
*Facebook:*  Eastside Distilling
*Twitter:*  @eastsidedistill
*YouTube:*  Eastside Distilling Channel

*Region:*  Pacific Northwest

*Type*:  Micro-distillery producing approximately 5,000 gallons annually

*Opened:*  2008

*Hours of operation:*
Tasting room hours Friday, 4:00pm to 7:00pm
Saturday and Sunday, 12:00pm to 5:00pm

*Tours:*  Tours are available by appointment.

*Types of spirits produced:*  Rum and bourbon

*Names of spirits:*
- Deco Silver Rum
- Deco Coffee Rum
- Deco Ginger Rum
- Burnside Bourbon
- Holiday Spiced Liqueur

*Best known for:*  Ginger Lemonade and Ginger Rum

*Average bottle price*:  $19.95 to $26.95

*Distribution:*  Tasting room, Oregon and Washington liquor stores

*Awards and Recognitions:*
**Deco Coffee Rum**
- Silver Medal, 2011 San Francisco WSC
- Bronze Medal, Beverage Testing Institute

*Highlighted spirits:*
**Deco Silver Rum**
Deco Silver Rum is a clean, smooth, and slightly sweet light rum that will complement any cocktail, from tropical drinks to the classic rum and cola. As a mixing rum, Deco Silver holds its own when blended with strong citrus flavors and other mixers.

**Deco Ginger Rum**
Deco Ginger Rum is handcrafted and flavored using only natural ingredients and no sugar. It is easy enough to make it sweeter by adding simple syrup or sweetened soda.

**Deco Coffee Rum**
Locally roasted Arabica beans give Deco Coffee Rum its deep smooth richness.

**Holiday Spiced Liqueur**
Holiday Spiced Liqueur is made by mixing a very special and secret blend of cinnamon, cardamom, clove, mace, and allspice and infusing it in Deco Silver Rum at 60 proof for seven days. High quality Hawaiian turbinado sugar is then added to take the edge off. The result is a lovely and spicy liqueur. One sip and you'll swear that you just tasted the flavor of Christmas in a bottle!

*Events and Celebrations:*
Eastside Distilling hosts several events throughout the year including cocktailing classes.

*Services offered other than production:*
Tasting room and storefront

*About:*
Eastside Distilling was started in Portland, Oregon, by two lifelong friends, Bill Adams and Lenny Gotter. With both sharing a passion for distilled spirits, the pair started from the ground up in 2008, developing recipes and the company mission. Then in November of 2009, Deco fine and flavored rums started to appear on liquor store shelves. Now, Deco Rums can be found at a majority of liquor stores in Oregon and at many bars and restaurants in the Portland area.

Eastside Distilling uses Florida molasses, fair trade coffee, and ginger from China. Additionally, Bill and Lenny are working on products and flavors using Oregon resources.

*Professional associations:*
American Distillers Institute, Oregon Distillers Guild, Distillery Row

*Future business plans and goals:*
Adding new flavors, an aged rum, and a liqueurs line

*Suggested recipes:*

**Deco Ginger Lemonade**
- 1 oz Deco Ginger Rum
- 3 oz fresh squeezed lemonade

Pour over ice.

**Black Tai -** From Jason Henry of Thatch Tiki Bar
- 1 oz Deco Coffee Rum
- 1 oz dark rum
- ½ oz lime juice
- ½ oz pineapple juice
- ¼ oz orgeat
- ¼ oz curacao

Shake vigorously.
Serve in a double rocks glass.
Garnish with a pineapple tidbit.

**Deco Magic -** From Justin DuPré of Thatch Tiki Bar
- 1 oz Deco Coffee Rum
- 1 oz Deco Silver Rum
- 1 oz pineapple juice
- ¾ oz Coco Lopez
- ½ oz passion fruit purée
- ½ oz lemon juice

Blend with lots of ice and serve in a fun cup.

**Deco Espresso Martini** - From Drew Nyugen of Thatch Tiki Bar
- 1 oz Deco Coffee Rum
- 1 oz Deco Ginger Rum
- ½ oz simple syrup
- Splash of lemon juice

Eastside Distilling
Portland, Oregon

## Elixir Inc.

Mr. Andrea Loreto, President/CEO

*Physical Address:*
1050 Bethel Drive
Eugene, Oregon  97402

*Mailing Address:*
105 Deer Valley Drive
Eugene, Oregon  97405

*Phone:*  541-345-2257
*Email:*  contact@elixir-us.com
*Website:*  www.calisaya.net
*Twitter:*  @CalisayaLiqueur

*Region:*  Eugene, Oregon (Willamette Valley)

*Type:*  Micro-distillery producing approximately 5,000 gallons per year

*Opened:*  June 2011

*Hours of operation:*   Monday through Friday, 9:00am to 5:00pm

*Tours:*  Tours are not available at this time.

*Types of spirits produced:*  Liqueur

*Names of spirits:*
- Calisaya

*Average bottle price*:  $47.00

*Distribution:*  Oregon state liquor stores

*Awards and Recognitions:*
### Calisaya
- Silver Medal, 2011 San Francisco World Spirits Competition
- Silver Medal, 2010  San Francisco World Spirits Competition
- Silver Medal for packaging, 2010 San Francisco World Spirits Competition
- Silver Medal, 2010  Los Angeles International Wine and Spirits Competition
- Bronze Medal,  International Review of Spirits Competition

*Highlighted spirits:*
### Calisaya
Calisaya is handcrafted from a traditional Italian recipe using cinchona bark imported from Italy. The bitter orange essence is handcrafted from California Seville oranges. Local McKenzie River water is the primary ingredient.

249

Notes of fresh spices, effervescent citrus and bitter orange gently subside to scents of warm woods and sap laced in light caramel. This liqueur has a smooth and clean feel as well as immediate notes of incense, leather and forest floor with a pleasantly astringent and delicately lingering quinine and orange zest bitterness.

*Interesting facts:*
- Around 1630, European missionaries in South America learned about cinchona calisaya—a mysterious Peruvian shrub whose bark boasted inimitable herbal and aromatic essences. Father Barnabé de Cobo brought the plant to Rome in 1632, whereupon clergymen and laypeople alike crafted an array of imaginative liqueurs from its prized bark. Nearly four centuries later, cinchona calisaya remains a staple ingredient in aperitifs and after-dinner drinks throughout Italy. Calisaya celebrates this storied past in a subtle bittersweet liqueur derived from authentic cinchona bark enhanced with select botanicals and flowers.

*About:*
Brothers Mario and Andrea Loreto decided to open Elixir Inc. in order to celebrate Andrea's passion for historic liqueurs and "slow" production methods. After years of research in rare and out-of-print recipe books tucked away in historic Florentine libraries, and following countless experiments in both Italy and the Pacific Northwest, Andrea developed Elixir's first liqueur - Calisaya. The product is the perfect marriage of Old World wisdom and New World opportunity.

*Management profile:*
**Andrea Loreto**
Andrea Loreto grew up in Florence and earned his MBA in Italy before meeting his American wife and relocating to the U.S. In addition to his talents as a liquorista, Andrea is also a connoisseur of perfumes and essences and is an expert chef.

*Professional associations:* Oregon Distillers Guild

*Future business plans and goals:* Create another historic and all-natural liqueur

*Suggested recipes:*
**Glamis**
- 1 oz Calisaya Liqueur
- 1 ½ oz Scotch Whiskey

Stir in mixing glass with ice and strain.
Serve in cocktail glass.

**Dorando** - Named after the Italian marathon runner Dorando Pietri
- 1½ ounces Calisaya Liqueur
- 1½ ounces Tom Gin
- Dash of orange bitters

Shake well with ice, strain and serve in cocktail glass.

Elixir Inc.
Eugene Oregon

## Hard Times Distillery LLC

James Stegall, Co-Owner / Distiller
Dudley Clark, Co-Owner / Distiller

*Physical Address:*
175 S. 5th
Monroe, Oregon  97456

*Mailing Address:*
464 Laurel Street
Junction City, Oregon  97448

*Phone:*  541-357-8808
*Email:*  General Info:  info@hardtimesdistillery.com
          James Stegall:  james@hardtimesdistillery.com
          Dudley Clark:  dudley@hardtimesdistillery.com
*Website:*  www.hardtimesdistillery.com
*Facebook:*  Hard Times Distillery LLC
*Twitter:*  @hardtimesdstlry
*YouTube:*  Hardtimesdistillery's Channel

*Region:*  Southern Willamette Valley, along the eastern edge of the Coastal Range Mountain

*Type*:  Micro-distillery

*Opened:*  August 2009

*Hours of operation:*
Monday through Friday mornings
Saturday and Sunday, noon to 5:00pm

*Tours:*  Tours are available during business hours.

*Types of spirits produced:*
Fermented vodka, infused vodka, and whiskey

*Names of spirits:*
- Green Geisha
- Sugar Momma
- Sweet Baby Moonshine

*Best known for:*
Sugar Momma Lemon Drop and Green Geisha Wasabi Bloody Mary

*Average bottle price*:  $18.00 to $27.00

*Distribution:* Tasting room and Oregon liquor stores

*Awards and Recognitions:* eDev 2011 Start-up of the Year

*Highlighted spirits:*
**Sugar Momma Vodka**
Sugar Momma Vodka is a sipping vodka with a spicy nose and a long sweet finish. It has been described as smoky, peppery with hints of vanilla, a rum drinkers vodka.

*Services offered other than production:* Tastings

*About:*
James Stegall (right) and Dudley Clark (left) wanted to create spirits focused on fermentation and distillation, with a focus on local character.

This is a complete do-it-yourself facility. James and Dudley built everything in the distillery including the three pot stills (one for whiskey and two for vodka), the three liquid management reflux columns, and a vapor management reflux column. They also constructed the tasting room. The recipes were developed using old fashioned moonshine techniques and then they "up-scaled" them for production.

Hard Times Distillery is a unique experience for the home distiller or chemist who wants to see how two guys can build a distillery and make it work in these HARD TIMES.

*Future business plans and goals:*
Sourcing more local ingredients and possibly growing botanicals on site

Hard Times Distillery LLC
Monroe, Oregon

# Immortal Spirits & Distilling Company

Jesse Gallagher, Co-owner / Operator
Enrico Carini, Co-owner / Operator

3582 S Pacific Highway, Unit D.
Medford, Oregon   97501

*Phone:* 541-646-8144
*Email:* info@immortalspirits.com
*Website:* www.immortalspirits.com
*Facebook:* Immortal Spirits and Distilling Company
*Twitter:* @immortalspirits

*Region:* Southwestern Oregon

*Type:*
Micro-distillery producing approximately 500 gallons per year

*Opened:* 2010

*Types of spirits produced:* Whiskey, rum, brandies, absinthe

*Names of spirits:*
- Eau de Vie Poire
- State of Jefferson Rum (currently aging)

*Distribution:*
Distributed through the Oregon Liquor Control Commission

*About:*
Immortal Spirits & Distilling Company operates a 7 gallon copper-pot still used for recipe development, an 88 gallon copper - and stainless - pot still for second distillations and a 1,200 gallon stainless-pot still for striping low wines. It uses locally sourced ingredients whenever possible - local wines and fruit for the brandy, eau de vie, and absinthe, and Oregon grown barley for the single malt whiskey.

*Future business plans and goals:*
Product line expansion and increased production

Immortal Spirits & Distilling Company
Medford, Oregon

253

# LiL'BiT Distillery Inc.

Mihai Talvan, Chief Everything Officer
Ioan Talvan, Master Distiller

1501 NE Industrial Avenue
Woodburn, Oregon  97071

*Phone:*  503-701-5780
*Email:*  contact@lilbitinc.com
*Website:*  www.lilbitinc.com, www.milibit.com
*Facebook:*  MiLi BiT Țuica
*Twitter:*  @MiLiBiT

*Region:*  Pacific Northwest

*Type:*  Micro-distillery producing approximately 200 gallons per year

*Opened:*  September 2009

*Hours of operation:*  9:00am to 5:00pm

*Tours:*  Tours are not available.

*Types of spirits produced:*  Brandy

*Names of spirits:*  MiLi BiT Țuică

*Average bottle price*:  $25.00 to $30.00

*Distribution:*
State liquor stores and a few local restaurants and bars

*Highlighted spirits:*
**MiLi BiT Țuică**
MiLi BiT Țuică  has been described as "a tsunami in your mouth."

*Services offered other than production:*  Tastings for trade guests only

*Interesting facts:*
Romanians know MiLi BiT Țuică as tuică ('tsuj.kə), Germans call it schnapps (not to be confused with the liquored drink), Serbs know it as slivovitz, Hungarians will call this palinka, and the French insist on calling it eau de vie.  The U.S. government classifies it as brandy.

*Future business plans and goals:*  Growth and expanded product line

LiL'BiT Distillery Inc.
Woodburn, Oregon

**New Deal Distillery**

Tom Burkleaux, Owner
Matthew VanWinkle, Owner

1311 SE 9th Avenue
Portland, Oregon 97214

*Phone:* 503-234-2513
*Fax:* 503-234-2571
*Email:* info@newdealdistillery.com, tom@newdealdistillery.com
*Website:* www.NewDealDistillery.com
*Facebook:* New Deal Distillery
*Twitter:* @NewDealPDX

*Region:* Northwest Oregon

*Type*: Craft-distillery producing approximately 700 gallons a month

*Opened:* July 2004

*Hours of operation:* Tours and tastings Saturday and Sunday, 12:30pm to 5:00pm

*Types of spirits produced:* Vodka, infused vodka, liqueurs, moonshines, and rums

*Names of spirits:*
- New Deal Vodka
- Portland 88 Vodka
- Hot Monkey Pepper Vodka
- Mud Puddle Chocolate Vodka
- Coffee Liqueur
- Ginger Liqueur
- Gin No. 1
- Gin No. 3
- Clawfoot Gin
- Distiller's Workshop Moonshine
- Distiller's Workshop Rum
- Distiller's Workshop Whiskey

Photo by: Jeremy Dunham, Polara Studios, 2009

*Average bottle price:* $20.00 to $50.00

*Distribution:* Tasting room and liquor stores in Oregon and Washington

*Awards and Recognitions:*

**Hot Monkey Pepper Vodka**

- Gold Medal, 2008 San Francisco WSC

**Gin No. 3**

- 2010 DrinkSpirits.com, One of the top 5 New American Gins

*Highlighted spirits:*

**Hot Monkey Pepper Vodka**

This vodka is a fiery infusion of 5 southwestern chilis in a balance of heat and flavor.

**Mud Puddle Chocolate Vodka**

This is a bitter cacao spirit with no added sugar.

**Gin No. 1**

This is created with a special still that captures heavier essences during distillation.

**Wildcat**

Wildcat is a unique "moonshine."

*Events and Celebrations:* The distillery hosts numerous events including an artisan food market called Season's Eatings, which is a fundraiser for the Oregon Food Bank.

*Services offered other than production:* Tastings, retail shop, sponsorships, and classes

*About:*

In 2001, Tom Burkleaux and Matthew VanWinkle decided to make local spirits before they knew there was a craft distilling movement. Neither of them liked the over-branded marketing of big companies and believed if you want something good, you make it yourself.

Photo by: Marie Richie

With $5,000 and 12 credit cards, Burkleaux and VanWinkle bootstrapped their way up from a 120 square foot space into a 5,000 square foot space by sheer stubbornness. Ever since they bottled the first spirits in 2005, New Deal Distillery has continued to grow with the addition of employees and an expanded product line.

New Deal uses water from the Bull Run Reservoir, one of North America's largest gravity-fed water supplies. This water, which comes from the melted snow pack from Mt. Hood's annual accumulation of 500-600 inches of snow each season, is considered by many to be among the most pure water in the nation.

Photo by: Jeremy Dunham, Polara Studios, 2010

This same incredible resource that has kept folks skiing at Timberline longer than any other ski area in North America is wholly renewable every year. Unlike some forests, the Mt. Hood wilderness that comprises the Bull Run Reservoir is a pristine, alpine treasure that remains unspoiled.

The grains are sourced locally, the sugar comes from warmer climates, and the spices are sourced from all over the world. Additionally, the distillery uses a cooling water reclamation system to cut down on water usage.

*Professional associations:* Oregon Distillers Guild, Distillery Row Association

*Suggested recipes:*
**Princess of Whales -** By Lydia Reismueller
- 1½ oz Mud Puddle
- 1 oz aquavit
- ½ oz Madeira
- ½ oz simple syrup

  Stir and strain into a champagne flute.
  Top with champagne (or prosecco) and chocolate shavings.


**House Bloody Mary -** By the employees of New Deal Distillery
- 2 oz Hot Monkey Vodka
- 2 Tbs dill pickle brine
- ½ tsp worcestershire sauce
- ½ tsp onion powder
- ½ tsp garlic powder
- ¼ tsp lemon pepper
- 8 oz Campbell's tomato juice
- ½ oz fresh squeezed lemon juice
- ½ oz fresh squeezed lime juice

  Mix and pour over ice.
  Garnish as you wish.

New Deal Distillery
Portland, Oregon

## Ransom Spirits

Tad Seestedt, Sole Proprietor

23101 Houser Road
Sheridan, Oregon 97378

*Phone:* 503-876-5022
*Fax:* 503-876-5022
*Email:* tad@ransomspirits.com
*Website:* www.ransomspirits.com
*Facebook:* Ransom Spirits

*Region:* Northwestern Oregon

*Type*: Micro-distillery producing approximately 5,600 cases per year

*Opened:* 1997

*Hours of operation:* Not open to the public

*Tours:* Not open to the public

*Types of spirits produced:* Gin, whiskey, brandy, grappa, and vodka

*Names of spirits:*
- WhipperSnapper Oregon Spirit Whiskey
- Old Tom Gin
- Small's Gin
- Gewürztraminer Grappa
- The Vodka

*Average bottle price*: $25.00 to $37.00

*Distribution:* Oregon, Washington, California, Colorado, Illinois, Wisconsin, Missouri, New York, New Jersey, Massachusetts, Nevada, Tennessee, District of Columbia, Texas, and special order in Vermont and Montana

*Highlighted spirits:*
### WhipperSnapper Oregon Spirit Whiskey
WhipperSnapper is crafted from premium ingredients. From meticulously milling the grain, working and fermenting the mash, and making well-considered, ruthless cuts at the condenser, WhipperSnapper is only the very best fraction of distillate and is placed in oak to mature.

# RANSOM

258

### Old Tom Gin

Ransom Spirits' Old Tom Gin is a historically accurate revival of the predominant gin in fashion during the mid 1800s and the Golden Age of American cocktails. Its subtle maltiness is the result of using a base wort of malted barley combined with an infusion of botanicals in high proof corn spirits. The final distillation is run through an alambic pot still in order to preserve the maximum amount of aromatics, flavor and body.

### Small's Gin

Small's Gin brings together a combination of recipes from the 19th century with obsessive distillation techniques and the finest regional ingredients. Handmade in small pot batches, Small's Gin is intensely aromatic due to a complex infusion of juniper, orange, lemon, coriander, cardamom, angelica, caraway, star anise, and raspberry. The best of tradition, dedication to quality, and innovation come together to create a remarkable, elaborate and unrivaled spirit.

### Gewürztraminer Grappa

Made using lightly pressed Gewürztraminer pomace, Gewürztraminer Grappa is a high quality spirit with fruity and soft aromatics.

### The Vodka

The Vodka is made using expertly distilled grain spirits and the exceptional water of Oregon's coastal mountain range. It is filtered gently through a media of charcoal and limestone, yet it retains the hint of barley.

*About:*
Ransom Spirits is nestled in the Willamette Valley along the foothills of the Coastal Mountain Range is Sheridan, Oregon.

Starting out with only a small life savings and a fistful of credit cards, the Ransom Project was launched in 1997 with the distillery making small amounts of grappa, eau de vie and brandy. Still wine production began in 1999, with Ransom operating as a semi-nomadic entity. For the five years that followed, Ransom Wine Co. followed the path of its founder, Tad Seestedt, through several contract winemaking jobs and custom crushing locations.

In 2008, a forty acre farm was purchased outside of Sheridan, Oregon, where the winery, distillery and ingredients (grapes and barley) for both were all brought together at one location using one of the last hand-hammered French Cognac stills.

The name Ransom was initially chosen to represent the investment necessary to become self-employed. It has since come to represent the amount of debt owed to banks and other loaning institutions.

Ransom Spirits
Sheridan, Oregon

Photos courtesy of Ransom Spirits. Photos by: "Eye of the Lady Photography Studio"

## Rogue Spirits

Brett Joyce, President
John Couchot, Master Distiller

Rum Distillery:
1339 Northwest Flanders Street
Portland, Oregon 97209

Main Distillery:
2122 Marine Science Drive
Newport, Oregon 97365

*Phone:* 503-241-3800
*Email:* isaac@rogue.com
*Website:* www.rogue.com
*Facebook:* Rogue Ales
*Twitter:* @RogueAles
*Myspace:* Rogue Ales

*Region:* Oregon

*Type:* Micro-distillery

*Opened:* Portland in 2003, Newport in 2006

*Hours of operation:*

Portland Pub and Rum Distillery:
Sun. through Thur., 11:00am to 12:00am
Friday and Saturday, 11:00am to 1:00am

Newport Distillery and House of Spirits:
Memorial Day to Labor Day
    Wed. – Sun., noon to 8:00pm
Winter – Saturdays, noon to 6:00pm

*Tours:*   Tours of both facilities are available as follows:
        Portland: 2:00pm on weekdays or by special request
        Newport: 4:00pm daily

*Types of spirits produced:*  Whiskey, gin, and rum

*Names of spirits:*
- Rogue Dark Rum
- Rogue White Rum
- Rogue Hazelnut Spiced Rum
- Rogue Dead Guy Whiskey
- Rogue Oregon Single Malt Whiskey
- Rogue Pink Gin
- Rogue Spruce Gin

*Average bottle price:*  $30.00 to $45.00

*Distribution:*  Available at any Rogue outpost and distributed in 36 states and 5 countries

**Rogue Dark Rum**
- Silver Medal, 2010 International Review of Spirits
- Commended, 2010 International Spirits Challenge
- Silver Medal, 2010 Ministry of Rum Tasting Competition
- Silver Medal, 2010 San Francisco World Spirits Competition

**Rogue Hazelnut Spiced Rum**
- Gold Medal, 2012 World Beverage Competition
- Bronze Medal, 2010 International Review of Spirits
- Bronze Medal, 2010 International Wine & Spirits Competition
- Bronze Medal, 2010 Ministry of Rum Tasting Competition
- Gold Medal, 2009/2010 World Beverage Competition

**Rogue Dead Guy Whiskey**
- Gold Medal, 2012 World Beverage Competition
- Bronze Medal, 2010 International Spirits Challenge
- Bronze Medal, 2010 International Wine & Spirits Competition
- Bronze Medal, 2010 San Francisco World Spirits Competition
- Silver Medal, 2010 Wine & Spirits Wholesalers of America Tasting

**Rogue Oregon Single Malt Whiskey Gold**
- Gold Medal, 2010 American Distillers Institute
- Bronze Medal, 2010 International Wine & Spirits Competition
- Gold Medal, 2010 San Francisco World Spirits Competition

**Rogue Pink Gin**
- Silver Medal, 2012 World Beverage Competition
- Silver Medal, 2010 International Spirits Challenge
- Silver Medal, 2010 San Francisco World Spirits Competition

**Rogue Spruce Gin**
- Platinum Best of Show, 2012 World Beverage Competition
- Silver Medal, 2010 International Spirits Challenge
- Silver Medal, 2010 International Wine & Spirits Competition
- Silver Medal, 2010 San Francisco World Spirits Competition

*Highlighted spirits:*

**Rogue Dark Rum**
Rogue Dark Rum is handcrafted in 567 liter grundies using 100% Hawaiian cane sugar, champagne yeast, and free range coastal water. Each batch is double distilled and aged in charcoaled oak bourbon barrels from the Jack Daniels Distillery in Tennessee.

**Rogue White Rum**
Rogue White Rum is handcrafted in 567 liter grundies using 100 % Hawaiian cane sugar, champagne yeast, and free range coastal water. Each batch is double distilled and is mellowed in oak bourbon barrels from the Jack Daniels Distillery in Tennessee.

*Highlighted spirits:*

**Rogue Hazelnut Spiced Rum**

Rogue Hazelnut Spiced Rum is made from crushed, toasted hazelnuts and is handcrafted in 567 liter grundies using Hawaiian cane sugar, champagne yeast, and free range coastal water. Each batch is double distilled and aged in charcoaled oak bourbon barrels from the Jack Daniels Distillery in Tennessee.

**Rogue Spruce Gin**

Rogue Spruce Gin is the first ever spruce gin; it's made with 14 ingredients including spruce, cucumber, angelica root, orange peel, coriander, lemon peel, ginger, orris root, grains of paradise, tangerine, juniper berries, champagne yeast, grain neutral spirit and free range coastal water.

**Rogue Pink Gin**

Rogue Spirits' Spruce Gin is transformed into Pink Gin using Oregon Pinot Noir barrels, resulting in a slightly fruity, mellow gin with a pink hue.

**Rogue Dead Guy Whiskey**

Rogue Dead Guy Whiskey is made from Rogue's Dead Guy Ale and is ocean aged in American oak.

*Services offered other than production:* Tastings and tours

*Interesting facts*

* The Portland distillery was the first rum distillery in Oregon.

*About:*

Since 2003, Rogue Spirits has created unique distillates from local ingredients native to the Northwest and from Rogue's barley farm in Oregon's Tygh Valley. All spirits are handcrafted in pot stills and are ocean aged. Rogue has been brewing beer since 1988. The Rogue grow your own (GYO) barley farm is 257 acres and yielded 499,000 pounds of barley and approximately 386,725 pounds of malt during the last harvest.

*Management profile:*

**John Couchot**

From chemistry to brewing and finally to inspired alchemy, John Couchot has over 30 years of experience turning solids into liquids. He is the distiller at Rogue's House of Spirits in Newport, Oregon, where he operates a 150 gallon copper compound-pot still.

Couchot received a bachelor's degree in chemistry in 1996 from the Evergreen State College in Olympia, Washington. He was a professional chemist for 6 years, working to isolate the active ingredients from Amazonian plants that were found to have curative properties.

*Future business plans and goals:* Continued success and growth

Rogue Spirits
Portland and Newport, Oregon

# Stringer's Orchard Winery and Distillery

Joanne and John Stringer, Owners

Post Office Box 191
New Pine Creek, Oregon  97635

Location: ¾ mile south of Oregon border, Hwy 395 in California

*Phone:*  530-946-4112
*Fax:*  530-946-4194
*Email:*  winemaker@stringersorchard.com
*Website:*  www.stringersorchard.com

*Region:*  Northwestern U.S.

*Type*:  Winery / micro-distillery producing less than 1,000 gallons of spirits per year

*Opened:*  Winery opened in 1984, distillery opened in 2005

*Hours of operation:*  Closed January through March
April to December, Monday through Saturday, 10:00am to 5:00pm

*Tours:*  Tours are available.

*Types of spirits produced:*  Brandy and liqueur

*Names of spirits:*
- Wild Plum Wine
- Plum Brandy (Slivovitz)
- Pacific Plum Liqueur
- Pacific Plum Gin
- Plum Jam and Syrup

*Average bottle price*:  $19.95 to $28.00

*Distribution:*  Most products are sold locally.

*Awards and Recognitions:*
**Plum Brandy**
- Silver Medal, 2008 California State Fair

*Highlighted spirits:*

## Plum Brandy (Slivovitz)

Created from estate-grown wild plums, European "Slivovitz" brandies are rich in aromas and flavors. Stringer's Plum Brandy is handcrafted using a European copper-pot still and centuries old traditional distilling methods. For generations, Slivovitz has toasted births, weddings, successes, failures, and honored memories of lost ones and is part of the Stringer heritage.

## Plum Liqueur

Plum Liqueur is crafted from wild plums that are sorted, cleaned and soaked in spirits for six months; this process is called maceration. The result is a dark red, slightly sweet, intense fruity liqueur. Plum Brandy is also added for a finishing touch.

*Services offered other than production:* Tasting room and tours

*Interesting facts:*
- Only known distillery making alcohol from wild Pacific plum

*About:*

Stringer's Orchard Winery, founded in 1984, is mother and son owned, family operated, and specializes in wild plum products. The winery is nestled in Goose Lake Valley with rugged mountains towering to the east and the expansive Goose Lake to the west. Not only is the view spectacular, but the location is ideal for growing the region's hardy delicacy - the wild plum. It is from this plum that Stringer's Orchard Winery creates its wine and brandy.

*Future business plans and goals:* Expanded product line

Stringer's Orchard Winery and Distillery
New Pine Creek, Oregon

264

## Sub Rosa Spirits

# sub rosa spirits

Michael Sherwood, Owner

876 SW Alder Drive
Dundee, Oregon 97115

*Phone:* 503-476-2808
*Email:* sub-rosa@comcast.net
*Website:* www.subrosaspirits.com
*Facebook:* Sub Rosa Spirits

*Region:* Northeast Oregon

*Type*: Craft-distillery

*Opened:* 2007

*Types of spirits produced:* Vodka

*Names of spirits:*
- Sub Rosa Tarragon Vodka
- Sub Rosa Saffron Vodka

*Best known for:*
Sub Rosa Tarragon Vodka and Sub Rosa Saffron Vodka

*Average bottle price:* $29.95

*Distribution:* Available in OR, WA, CO, CA, IL, and D.C.

*Awards and Recognitions:*
### Sub Rosa Saffron Vodka
- Gold Medal, 2010 Beverage Testing Institute International Spirits Review
- Gold Medal, 2009 Beverage Testing Institute International Spirits Review
- 93 Points, 2007 Anthony Dias Blue for Tasting Panel Magazine

### Sub Rosa Tarragon Vodka
- Gold Medal, 2010 Beverage Testing Institute International Spirits Review
- Gold Medal, 2009 Beverage Testing Institute International Spirits Review

*Highlighted spirits:*
### Sub Rosa Tarragon Vodka
At 90 proof, Sub Rosa Tarragon Vodka is delightfully herbal with the slightest hint of licorice. Made with fresh certified organic tarragon leaves and just a touch of mint for flavor dynamics, this pale green spirit is all natural.

*Highlighted spirits:*

## Sub Rosa Saffron Vodka

Smooth but intense, Sub Rosa Saffron Vodka is a bold blend of eight spices combined into a unique distillate that is not for the faint of palate. Inspired by Indian and Asian food and at 90 proof, this distillate is beguiling with toasted cumin on the nose, lemony coriander on the mid-palate, and a hint of ginger, just a touch of heat, and the aromatics of saffron at the end.

*Interesting facts:*

- Sub Rosa Saffron Vodka is the first commercial savory spiced vodka that captures the flavors of India and Asia.

*About:*

Sub Rosa Spirits, located in Dundee, Oregon, is a craft micro-distillery producing non-traditional distillates that carry great intensity and flavor.

The words "sub rosa" come from the Latin "under the rose," from the association of the rose with confidentiality. Use of a rose at secret meetings was a symbol of the sworn confidence of the participants. The ceilings of ancient banquet rooms were often decorated with roses to remind guests that what was spoken within was private.

Lovers of Sub Rosa distillates carry on the tradition of elixirs consumed in private, a shared secret with a select few. Anyone who is familiar with secret societies such as the Illuminati, Freemasons, Priory of Scion, or Knights Templar will be familiar with the concept of "sub rosa." By sampling Sub Rosa elixirs, you become part of the cadre. Membership is open to a select few who quest after the true spirit.

*Management profile:*

## Mike Sherwood

Mike Sherwood is an Oregon modern day Renaissance man. He paid his dues as a commercial logger and commercial fisherman, a neighborhood advocate, an energy conservation geek, a music promoter, a software developer, an off-shore sailor, a craft beer guy, a city planning commissioner, a food and wine writer, a cellar rat, a winemaker, a distiller, the founding executive director of the Oregon Brewers Guild, and the co-founder of the nation's first craft distillers guild.

He now works in the cellar of the Sineann Winery in Oregon's Willamette Valley and, when he's not working the harvest or topping off barrels, he distills small batches of spirits for his Sub Rosa Spirits brand at Integrity Spirits Distillery in Portland, Oregon.

Alcohol is in Mike's blood it seems, as his family owned a beer and wine distributorship in a small, southern Oregon logging town in the 60s. At a young age he ascended to the roll of bartender at family parties, learning to make a mean Manhattan at lightening speed. While helping make wine at the Sineann Winery, Mike was recruited to manage Rogue Ale's Rum Distillery and to design a new distillery-bar-restaurant in 2005; he was director of distillates there for a year. Together with his wife Linda Lausmann, who provides culinary inspiration, Mike has created a line of incredibly fresh and vibrant vodka infusions worth savoring.

*Future business plans and goals:* Development of gin, rum and liqueurs

*Suggested recipes:*

**Fairy Tarragon -** by Chris Hannah of Arnaud's French 75 bar – New Orleans
- 1½ oz Sub Rosa Tarragon vodka
- 1 oz Galliano
- ½ oz lemon juice
- ¼ oz absinthe
- 1 dash Peychaud's Bitters

Shake and strain into chilled Martini glass.

**Ginger Snap**
- 1½ oz Sub Rosa Saffron Vodka
- ¼ tsp grated fresh ginger (just a pinch)
- ½ oz fresh lime juice
- 1 oz orange juice
- ½ oz simple syrup

Shake vigorously in a mixing glass filled with ice.
Pour over crushed ice in a short glass.
Garnish with a sprig of fresh cilantro that you "spank" between your palms.

**Kashmir**
- 2 oz Sub Rosa Saffron Vodka
- 3 oz apricot nectar
- ½ oz fresh lime juice
- 2 grinds black pepper
- ½ oz simple syrup or Canton Ginger Liqueur

Chill over ice, shake vigorously, and serve up.
Alternatively, build and serve on the rocks.

Sub Rosa Spirits
Dundee, Oregon

# Superfly Distilling Company

Ryan Webster, Owner

16399 Ste. B Lower Harbor Road
Brookings, Oregon 97415

*Phone:* 530-520-8005
*Email:* ryanwebster@msn.com
*Website:* www.superflybooze.com
*Facebook:* Superfly Distilling Company

*Region:* Southeastern Oregon

*Type:* Micro-distillery

*Opened:* 2008

*Tours:* Tours are occasionally offered.

*Types of spirits produced:* Vodka, flavored vodkas, rum, and whiskey

*Average bottle price:* $20.00

*Awards and Recognitions:*
**Potato Vodka**
- Silver Medal, 2010 World Spirits Competition

*Interesting facts:*
It takes nearly ten pounds of russet potatoes to make one bottle of Superfly Vodka.

*About:*
Superfly Distilling Company was opened in the spring of 2009 by Ryan Webster, who has an absolute love for what he does and has taken to the art with great passion and integrity. Focused on absolute quality and affordability, Superfly works to make the best product at the best price. Per Angusta ad Augusta!

Superfly Distilling Company
Brookings, Oregon

# Vinn Distillery

7990 SW Boeckman Road
Wilsonville, Oregon  97070

*Phone:*  503-427-0518

*Email:*  Michelle Ly, Owner:  michelle@vinndistillery.com
Quyen Ly, Owner:  quyen@vinndistillery.com
Vicki Ly, Owner:  vicki@vinndistillery.com
Lien Ly, Owner:  lien@vinndistillery.com
*Website:*  www.vinndistillery.com
*Facebook:*  Vinn Distillery
*Twitter:*  @vinndistillery
*Blog:*  www.vinncrowd.com

*Region:*  Pacific Northwest

*Type:*  Micro-distillery

*Opened:*  March 2009

*Tours:*  Tours are not available.

*Types of spirits produced:*  Rice vodka and fortified wine

*Names of spirits:*
- Vinn Mijiu (pronounced "Mee-Je-oh") Ice
- Vinn Mijiu (pronounced "Mee-Je-oh") Fire
- Vinn Baijiu (pronounced "By-Je-oh")

*Best known for:*  Vinn Baijiu

*Average bottle price:*  $15.99 to $24.95

*Distribution:*  Oregon grocery and liquor stores

*Highlighted spirits:*
**Vinn Baijiu**
Vinn Baijiu "Vodka" is distilled from brown rice. It is triple distilled and unfiltered, which means it retains a lot of the base rice grain characteristics. Baijiu is a classic Chinese spirit which translates literally into "white liquor." The nose has elements of white whiskey and unfiltered sake combining sweet high notes that smell slightly like buttered rice but are more savory.

**Vinn Mijiu Ice**
Vinn Mijiu Ice is made 100% from the purest brown rice.  Each sip delivers a unique sweet honey-pear aroma and finishes with a smooth, light taste of delicious almonds. Mijiu Ice is all natural and does not contain any added coloring or sulfites.

269

*Highlighted spirits:*

**Vinn Mijiu Fire**

Vinn Mijiu Fire is made 100% from the finest black "forbidden" rice. Every sip has the flavor of crushed berries trailed by a fiery hint of cinnamon. Mijiu Fire is all natural and does not contain added coloring or sulfites.

*Events and Celebrations:*

Vinn Distillery teams up with bars to launch events, specials and fundraisers.

*Interesting facts:*

- The recipe used to make all three of Vinn Distillery spirits is over 7 generations old.
- Baijiu - considered the national drink of China - is a Chinese distilled alcoholic beverage. The name baijiu literally means "white liquor."
- Vinn Distillery products are gluten free.

*About:*

Vinn Distillery, located in Wilsonville, OR, was the dream of the owner's father, Phan Ly. Ly was forced into retirement from the restaurant business by his children and was not very good at being retired. He had worked all his life so retiring was foreign to him. During the day, he would tinker with centuries old family recipes of making Mijiu (rice wine) and Baijiu (rice vodka) until he got it perfect. With some savings, a lot of family support, and hard work, the distillery opened and a dream came true.

Originally, Phan Ly wanted to call their products "5 siblings" (direct translation from the Chinese characters). Playing off that, one thing that the 5 siblings shared is the same middle name - Vinn.

Originating from southern China, the Ly family migrated from China to North Vietnam for a better life. In 1978, they were deported back to China where they later escaped from in March of 1979 and were welcomed into Hong Kong as refugees in April. On November 13, 1979, the entire family found themselves heading to Portland through the generosity and kindness of Frog Pond Church in Wilsonville, Oregon.

Vinn Distillery products are unique because of using two types of grains – black rice and brown rice. Everything is made in small batches because that is the way their ancestors did it, and the tradition continues today. Mijiu Fire and Mijiu Ice products retain all the nutrients found in black rice and brown rice (large molecules are kept through the fermentation process), making it a "healthy" drink.

Baijiu is normally served at room temperature or warm in a small ceramic bottle, then poured into a small cup or shot glass. It is traditionally consumed together with food rather than drunk on its own.

*Professional associations:* Oregon Distillers Guild

*Future business plans and goals:* Expanded product line and wider distribution

*Suggested recipes:*

**Vinn Dragon**
- 1 ½ oz Vinn Baijiu – Rice Vodka
- ½ oz Vinn Mijiu Fire – Red Port
- ½ oz of lemon juice

    Fill glass with pineapple juice.
    Garnish with basil.


**Fire and Ice -** Courtesy of Robbie Wilson of SnugBar, Corvallis, Oregon
- 2 oz Vinn Baijiu
- 2 pickled Thai chilis muddled into the Baijiu
- Juice from half a grapefruit
- Agave nectar to taste

    Shake it up and serve it in a cocktail glass.


Vinn Distillery
Wilsonville, Oregon

# Ye Ol' Grog Distillery

Lloyd Williams, Owner
Ken McFarland, Owner
Greg Scott, Owner
Marcus Alden, Owner

35855 Industrial Way, Unit C
Saint Helens, Oregon 97051

*Phone:* 503-366-4001
*Email:* info@yeolgrogdistillery.com
*Website:* www.yeolgrogdistillery.com, www.grogme.com
*Facebook:* Ye Ol Grog Distillery and Grog Wench Libations
*Twitter:* @YeOlGrog

*Region:* Pacific Northwest

*Type:* Micro-distillery producing approximately 350 cases of 750mls a week

*Opened:* September 2009

*Hours of operation:* Monday through Friday, 9:00am to 5:00pm. Sometimes Saturday

*Tours:* Tours are available by appointment.

*Types of spirits produced:*
Specialty distilled spirits and vodka

*Names of spirits:*
- Dog Watch Vodka
- Dutch Harbor Breeze (Grog)
- Good Morning Glory (Grog)

*Best known for:* Grog (both of them)

*Average bottle price:* Mid-range

*Distribution:* Oregon, Washington, and Alaska

*Highlighted spirits:*

## Dog Watch Vodka

To sailors, the words "dog watch" means that you have the easy watch and have more time to sit back and watch the world go by. At 80 proof, Dog Watch Vodka is clean and smooth. The unique distillation process removes the medicinal smell and taste that is typical of vodkas. So put your tired dogs up and enjoy premium Dog Watch Vodka.

## Dutch Harbor Breeze Grog

The Bering Sea has often been called a mistress to pirates, sailors and fisherman alike. She can kick up her heels with a "Dutch Harbor Breeze" that will find the lucky afloat and the less fortunate on the rocks. Named after Dutch Harbor, Alaska, where a stiff breeze starts at 80 knots, Dutch Harbor Breeze Grog has hints of cinnamon and spices, is sweetened with blue agave and is aged with oak. If you prefer whisky, then you'll enjoy the 100 proof, Dutch Harbor Breeze Grog.

## Good Morning Glory Grog

Named after a song that tells a story of going home with a 10 and waking up with a 2, Good Morning Glory Grog was designed to be a shooter. This 70 proof grain spirit is sweetened with blue agave nectar and is naturally flavored with citrus, cinnamon, spices, and other flavors not only for a great taste but also for an olfactory treat. Good Morning Glory Grog is wonderful mixed with any soda or fruit juice and is better served as a shot.

*Events and Celebrations:* Ye Ol' Grog Distillery participates in a number of annual events and festivals to promote its spirits.

*Services offered other than production:* A tasting room is open Monday through Friday from 1:00pm to 5:00pm and sometimes on Saturday.

*About:*

Located in western Oregon, Ye Ol' Grog Distillery was founded one evening by two friends sitting on a dock overlooking the Columbia River. They were talking about their dreams of a fun job that didn't involve working for billionaires. After that evening, Ken McFarland and Lloyd Williams brought on two more partners, Marcus Alden and Greg Scott, for additional financing as well as product and sales support.

Not satisfied with the commercially available distillation equipment, the four friends re-designed the classic pot still and the vodka reflux still. Keeping in mind the design needs of the classic Kentucky moonshiners, the stills at Ye Ol' Grog Distillery are easily and quickly reconfigured as production needs dictate. Not only does the equipment produce the highest quality drinking liquor, but it is also smart and efficient.

The reflux still column is a proprietary design and is the reason that Dog Watch Vodka is as pure and clean tasting as it is. The unique pot still used for the distillation of Dutch Harbor Breeze and Good Morning Glory Grogs resembles a 500 pound bomb and helps to give the Grogs their unique flavor.

273

You'll notice that most of Ye Ol' Grog products have an "FPC" brand that is their corporate take on political correctness. PC is for politically correct, the "F," well, you can figure that out for yourself.

*Management profile:*

## Marcus Alden

Marcus lived his first 18 years on a secret Navy test base in the middle of the California High Desert. Upon high school graduation, he wasn't exactly sure what he wanted to do but he did know that whatever it was it would not involve scorching sand, sun and lizards. It wasn't long until he found himself drawn to the sea and enrolled in the California Maritime Academy. Ships and sailing seemed to be his calling. Marcus eventually found himself working on aircrafts carriers and submarines. Ultimately he was drawn to the Alaskan fishing industry where he was asked to design and convert an oil field work boat into a King Crab catcher/processor. It was while fishing the waters of the Bering Sea that he and his wife fell in love with Alaska. A few years later, Marcus was asked to design and build a large fish processing plant in Dutch Harbor, Alaska. The plant was the Westward Seafood's plant that is often seen on the TV show "Deadliest Catch." As chief engineer of this small self-contained city, Marcus met a number of fascinating individuals including his future partners.

## Lloyd Williams

Lloyd started out in Bend, Oregon, where he left to join the Navy at his first opportunity. As a wide-eyed young man, he found himself in the "Black Gang" on the Navy "Tin Can" in the Gulf of Tonkin. He found he enjoyed the life at sea, except for all of the Navy rules and regulations. Lloyd also found that he liked shore leave and the bards and houses of ill repute. After a few years in the Navy, Lloyd was discharged and ashore. The Alaska King Crab boom was on and there were vessel owners who would pay a good price for an experienced engineer to man the crab catchers and processors in Alaska. He enjoyed the freedom and "open range" spirit of Alaska. Eventually Lloyd and his wife found themselves in Dutch Harbor at the Westward Seafood Plant where Lloyd was hired in the refrigeration department as a refrigeration engineer.

## Ken McFarland

Ken found his affinity for alcohol while attending the Colorado School of Mines. Late one night, he discovered that the school had a chemical engineering major that concentrated on how to make molecule ethanol. After the School of Mines, Ken spent 11 years as a chemical engineer for Archer Daniels Midland, an Illinois-based plant that creates millions of gallons of vodka. He later moved west and became operations manager at Cascade Grain Products. As the Cascade Grains plant opened up production, Ken and Lloyd found themselves working together. While doing the finale production run of fuel ethanol at the plant, the pair began talking about that was next for them after the plant shut down. One thing lead to the next and they found themselves talking about distillation of vodka, whiskey and rum.

## Greg Scott

Greg grew up in the Pacific Northwest. Driving boats and flying planes, Greg majored in rubber technology while attending Georgia University and later invented the elastrometric spongometer. Using inventions he created, the entire field of spongography revolutionized the use of rubber in everyday products. Had it not been for Greg's inventions, we would not have the everyday objects like the tuning knob on the radio, or waterproof rubber ducks. While on sales calls to Alaska, he would often find himself at the Westward Seafood's plant talking with Lloyd and Marcus.

*Future business plans and goals:* Continued growth and expanded distribution

*Suggested recipes:*
## Stormy Waters
In a 16oz pint glass filled with ice add:

- 1 oz of Good Morning Glory Grog
- 4oz of Sweet and Sour
- A splash of soda water
- A splash of cranberry juice
- A splash of Blue Curacao

When stirred it becomes "stormy" gray like the Bering Sea.

## Muddled Parley
- 4 pitted cherries
- ½ of a lime cut into slices
- 1 oz of simple syrup
- 2 oz Good Morning Glory Grog
- Top off with 7-Up or club soda

In a cocktail shaker, muddle simple syrup, cherries and limes to release the juices.
Add Good Morning Glory Grog and ice.
Shake vigorously and strain over an ice filled collins glass.
Top off with your taste preference of 7-Up or club soda.

## Deep Blue Plunder
In a glass filled with ice add:

- ½ oz Blue Curacao
- ½ oz Buttershots Schnapps
- 1 oz Good Morning Glory Grog
- 4 oz 7-Up

A light squeeze of lime or a lime slice slid into the cocktail gives it just a hint of lime flavor.

Ye Ol' Grog Distillery
Saint Helens, Oregon

## Pennsylvania Pure Distilleries LLC

# BOYD & BLAIR®
## POTATO VODKA

Barry L. Young, Owner
C. Prentiss Orr, Owner

1101 William Flinn Highway
Glenshaw, Pennsylvania 15116

*Phone:*  412-486-8666
*Fax:*  412-486-8820
*Email:*  info@boydandblair.com
*Website:*  www.boydandblair.com
*Facebook*:  Boyd and Blair Potato Vodka
*Twitter:*  @BoydBlairVodka

*Region:*  Western and Central Pennsylvania

*Type:*  Micro-distillery producing approximately 6,000 proof gallons per year

*Opened:*  March 2008

*Hours of operation:*  Weekdays from 9:30am to 6:00pm

*Tours:*  Only by appointment and, usually, only for restaurateurs, hospitality staff, or to support community, non-profit fundraisers. Based on pending Pennsylvania legislation, tastings and public tours may occur in 2012.  Updates will be posted on the website.

*Types of spirits produced:*  Potato vodka

*Names of spirits:*
* Boyd & Blair Potato Vodka  (80 proof)
* Boyd & Blair Professional Proof 151 Potato Vodka  (151 proof)

*Best known for:*  Boyd & Blair Potato Vodka

*Average bottle price:*
Boyd & Blair Potato Vodka retails at around $29.00 / 750 ml
Boyd & Blair Professional Proof 151 Potato Vodka, $49.00 / 750ml

*Distribution:*
Boyd & Blair Potato Vodka is currently available in more than 12 states, with the expectation of availability in 5 more states in 2012. Readily available from San Francisco to Newport, RI, and down the East Coast to Florida, the brand is often the featured vodka of craft spirit collections in fine wine and spirits stores as well as high-end or locavore restaurants.  Additionally, Boyd & Blair has an exclusive distribution agreement in Ontario, Canada.

276

**Boyd & Blair Potato Vodka**
- 5-Star "Highest Recommendation," Nov. 2010 F. Paul Pacult's Spirit Journal
- "The Top New Spirits for the Holidays," Food & Wine Magazine 2010
- "Four New Vodkas Are Down to Earth," Oct. 2010 article in Food Network Magazine
- "Four Brands Whose Founders Traded their CV for Aqua Vitae," article in Wall Street Journal Magazine, Dec. 2010
- "The Season's Top New Spirits," article in Food & Wine, Dec., 2010
- Five Star "Highest Recommendation," Spirit Journal, Dec. 2010
- The Top 140 Spirits in the World (ranked #22), Spirit Journal, June 2011
- "This Year, The Choice Is Clear," article in GQ magazine, Dec. 2011

*Highlighted spirits:*

**Boyd & Blair Potato Vodka**

Boyd & Blair Potato Vodka is distinctive in having a slightly sweet front, notable mouthfeel, and an inherently smooth back. Spirit Journal editor F. Paul Pacult's notes read, "Entry is nothing short of luscious, semisweet. Chewy and smooth; midpalate adds cocoa bean, maple, and honey. Aftertaste is graceful, solid, and simply delicious."

**Boyd & Blair Professional Proof 151**

Boyd & Blair Professional Proof 151 retains every bit of the semisweet character of the lower proof brand. In addition, for bartenders and mixologists who have had no choice but to create custom bitters from 151 rum, Boyd & Blair Professional Proof offers a more neutral palate to allow the true character of the bitters' ingredients to shine through.

*Events and Celebrations:* The distillery will occasionally host events, but only if they serve as a fundraiser for a local non-profit.

*Interesting facts:*
- The first vodka distillery in Pennsylvania

*About:*

Pennsylvania Pure Distilleries LLC was founded as Pennsylvania's first vodka distillery. Using only locally grown potatoes, each batch is distilled from mash in a single 1,200 liter pot still. The fermentation process was developed at Penn State University under a feasibility grant from the Pennsylvania Department of Community and Economic Development, employing a number of other state-funded agencies to discover a ready and stable source of locally grown produce and other Pennsylvania resources.

As one of the first craft distilleries in the U.S. since Prohibition, Pennsylvania Pure Distilleries set out to make a single spirit -- vodka -- distilled from locally grown potatoes. Unlike the vast majority of distilleries that have blossomed across the country in more recent years, Pennsylvania Pure still only makes one spirit, Boyd & Blair Potato Vodka, albeit the company now offers Boyd & Blair Professional Proof 151 Vodka and will soon launch a kosher for Passover certified brand of Boyd & Blair Potato Vodka.

Within the first six months of appearing in more than 250 Pennsylvania controlled liquor stores, Boyd & Blair Potato Vodka became the number 5 best-selling super premium vodka (out of 16 others) sold in the state. Today, it still commands its lead as the state's top selling craft vodka.

Boyd & Blair is made single batch by single batch from original mash, using only locally grown potatoes; that alone makes Boyd & Blair decidedly different from other distillers who are using NGS or blending multiple sources of bulk alcohol. However, what makes Boyd & Blair particularly sweet and smooth is

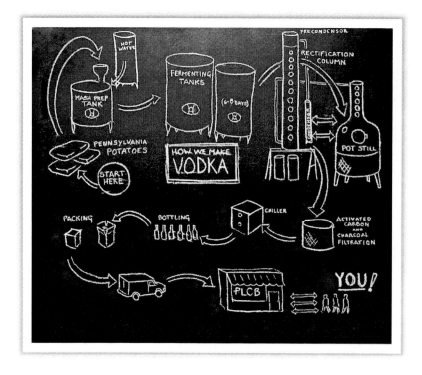

the exceptional cuts of the distillation process. No heads or tails are ever collected; only the hearts are bottled. Every distillation is taste tested for superior quality.

In addition to using only locally grown produce and sourcing all packaging materials and equipment through Pennsylvania suppliers, the bottles are manufactured within one hundred yards of where they are filled. Currently, the distillery is located in a 6,000 sq. ft. facility on property shared by Kelman Bottles (formerly Glenshaw Glass Co.). Every bottle is filled, corked, sealed and labeled by hand. Every label is batch numbered and hand signed by the still master.

*Professional associations:* Pennsylvania Craft Distillers Guild (founding member), US Bartenders Guild Pittsburgh Chapter

*Future business plans and goals:*
Expanded distribution and increased sales. Additionally, Pennsylvania Pure Distilleries aided in getting legislation changed to grant Pennsylvania craft distilleries many of the same privileges of wineries and breweries, including direct sales from the distillery, as well as an on-premise tasting room and other satellite retail sites.

*Suggested recipes:*

### A Glenshaw Rickshaw

- 2 oz of Boyd & Blair
- 2 oz of mango nectar
- ½ oz of simple syrup
- ½ oz of lemon juice

Shake over ice, strain and serve neat.

### Envy

- 1 oz Boyd & Blair Potato Vodka
- 2 ½ oz Lillet Blanc
- ½ oz simple syrup
- 5 basil leaves
- 3 slices of cucumber

Muddle cucumber in shaker.
Fill with ice and all other ingredients.
Shake vigorously.
Strain and serve in chilled martini glass.

### Twisted Cosmo

- 1 ½ oz Boyd & Blair Potato Vodka
- 2 oz cranberry juice
- 1 oz Cointreau
- ½ oz lime juice
- Splash of St-Germain Liqueur

Combine all ingredients in a cocktail shaker filled with ice and shake vigorously.
Strain into chilled martini glass.

Pennsylvania Pure Distilleries LLC
Glenshaw, Pennsylvania

# Philadelphia Distilling

Andrew Auwerda, President
Tim Yarnall, Vice President
Robert Cassell, Master Distiller

12285 McNulty Road #105
Philadelphia, Pennsylvania 19154

Phone:  215-671-0346
Fax:  215-671-0354

*Email:*  info@philadelphiadistilling.com
*Website:*  www.philadelphiadistilling.com, www.bluecoatgin.com
*Website:*  www.penn1681vodka.com, www.vieuxcarreabsinthe.com
*Website:*  www.shinewhiskey.com
*Facebook:*  Bluecoat American Dry Gin, Penn 1681 Rye Vodka
*Facebook:*  Vieux Carré Absinthe Supérieure, Shine Whiskey
*Twitter:*  @bluecoatgin, @vcabsinthe
*Twitter:*  @Penn1681Vodka, @shinewhiskey

*Region:*  Mid-Atlantic / Pennsylvania

*Opened:*  2005

*Hours of operation:*  Regular

*Tours:*  Tours are available.

*Products produced:*  Absinthe, gin, vodka, and white whiskey

*Names of spirits:*
- Bluecoat American Dry Gin
- Penn 1681 Rye Vodka
- Vieux Carré Absinthe Supérieure
- XXX Shine White Whiskey

*Best known for:*  Bluecoat American Dry Gin

*Average bottle price:*  $28.00

*Distribution:*  38 U.S. States, Bermuda, France, Spain, Italy, and East Africa

*Awards and Recognitions:*
**Bluecoat American Dry Gin**
- Double Gold Medal – Best Gin, 2009 & 2010 San Francisco World Spirits Competition
- Gold Medal – Best Gin, International Wine & Spirits Competition

*Highlighted spirits:*

## Bluecoat American Dry Gin

As the only American dry gin, Bluecoat is in a class by itself. What makes this different from other dry gins is the use of organic American citrus peels - sweet orange and lemon peel - combined with a proprietary blend of other American citrus notes. This gives Bluecoat its signature American dry gin taste profile. Bluecoat is also distilled to be an extremely smooth, pure spirit, without the harshness of impure alcohols often present in other gins. Finally, Bluecoat utilizes organic juniper berries which transmit spicy, earthy notes.

Bluecoat American Dry Gin is distilled using a small batch process. Only a small selection of the distillate meets purity requirements and matches the desired botanical flavors to be collected for bottling.

## Penn1681 Rye Vodka

Philadelphia Distilling proudly pays tribute to the founding of Pennsylvania by crafting a premium American spirit made with indigenous organic ingredients and artisan skill. Identifiable by its characteristically smooth and pure nature, it appeals to those with discriminating taste and is an excellent spirit for imbibers to enjoy straight or as the centerpiece of a favorite cocktail.

In 1681, King Charles II granted William Penn land which became the Commonwealth of Pennsylvania. Since then, Pennsylvania has ranked as a leading agricultural area and has produced surpluses for export. By the mid-18th century, an exceptionally prosperous farming area had developed in southeastern Pennsylvania with rye being one of the leading crops. The history of rye distilling in Pennsylvania dates back to before Prohibition, when many of the finest rye whiskies were distilled in Pennsylvania.

Packaging for Penn1681 includes a glass bottle which is partially made from recycled glass. The labels are made with organic inks and a biodegradable wood top was chosen to seal the pure spirit. The spent grains used to make the alcohol in Penn1681 Rye Vodka are exchanged with local farmers when new deliveries of organic rye are made. These spent grains are then used on farms as feed stock and fertilizer. By keeping sourcing, packaging and distribution local, consumers are also helping to protect the environment by choosing Penn1681 Rye Vodka.

281

### Vieux Carré Absinthe Supérieure

The French Quarter, locally known as Vieux Carré, is the soul of New Orleans, Louisiana. This city is replete with culture, architectural beauty and culinary arts. Philadelphia Distilling pays tribute to the unique and colorful history of absinthe in New Orleans with the release of Vieux Carré Absinthe Supérieure. The first batch of Vieux Carré was released on December 31, 2008.

Vieux Carré is batch distilled using a double maceration process featuring the mysterious grande wormwood and petite wormwood. Green and star anise, fennel doux provence, melissa, genepi, hyssop and spearmint complete the complex flavor profile. Vieux Carré's flavor and color are derived exclusively from 100% natural herbs. The flavor is complex with both familiar and intriguing notes. The deep green color is reminiscent of a vintage jewel. The spirit is not over filtered, preserving the flavors extracted through the natural coloring process.

The unique decanter protects the delicate spirit and the design portrays the ironwork prevalent in the Old Square in New Orleans.

### XXX Shine White Whiskey

XXX Shine White Whiskey is the real deal. Unaged and hard edged, XXX Shine *is* a whiskey without boundaries - a blend of hand selected American corn is distilled three times (XXX) in a copper-pot still. High proof yet surprisingly smooth, this white whiskey rocks. The traditions of the backwoods are combined with the talent and sophistication of the city to forge a truly exceptional spirit. As a shot, on the rocks, or with your favorite mixer, XXX Shine White Whiskey more than satisfies. This true American spirit is designed by the land and defined by the drinker.

*Events and Celebrations:* Participates in hundreds of charitable functions

*Interesting facts:*
- The first craft distillery in Pennsylvania since Prohibition
- The first spirit released was Bluecoat American Dry Gin
- The first East Coast distillery to distill authentic absinthe in over 100 years

*About:*
Custom made of pure, hand-hammered copper, the pot still is the only one of its design and size in the world. Batch distilling, using a pot still, is the traditional method of distillation. By taking advantage of modern technologies, Philadelphia Distilling is able to marry this traditional method to cutting edge design. A proprietary lye arm design allows for the greatest possible separation of alcohols, enabling the master distiller to create an ultra-smooth spirit. Additionally, a proprietary boil ball design aids in additional reflux, furthering the ability to separate the alcohol "fractions."

## Andrew Auwerda

President Andrew Auwerda (center) directs business and brand building functions. He graduated from the University of Maryland in 1990 with a BS Economics and has spent more than 20 years involved in the consumer business world. In the course of his career, Auwerda managed a multi-million dollar company, was a merchandiser responsible for all aspects of category development, and was a successful entrepreneur.

## Timothy Yarnall

Vice President Timothy Yarnall (left) directs sales and distribution. He graduated from the University of Pennsylvania in 1997 with a BA Communications and a minor in cognitive science. Prior to co-founding Philadelphia Distilling, Yarnall was a member of the corporate financial works in New York. He began his career as an applications analyst, an implementation specialist, and he held various sales roles with accounts in Canada, the Caribbean and New York.

## Robert J. Cassell

Master Distiller Robert J. Cassell (right) directs all aspects of the production facility as well as product development. Prior to PD, he had been in the brewing industry for more than 5 years. Robert is a member of the Master Brewers Association of America, American Society of Brewing Chemists, and the

Institute of Brewing and Distilling. Robert studied under Dr. Kris Berglund, a renowned American distiller and instructor at Michigan State. Cassell also majored in nuclear medicine at Wheeling Jesuit University and received his formal distilling education from programs at Michigan State and at Heriot-Watt University of Edinburgh in the U.K.

*Future business plans and goals:*
To continue to develop delicious handcrafted spirits in all spirit categories

Philadelphia Distilling
Philadelphia, Pennsylvania

Philadelphia Distilling photos courtesy of Jason Varney

# Newport Distilling Company

Brent Ryan, President and Head Distiller
Derek Luke, Founder and Brewmaster

293 JT Connell Road
Newport, Rhode Island 02840

*Phone:* 401-849-5232
*Email:* information@newportstorm.com
*Website:* www.thomastewrums.com
*Facebook:* Thomas Tew Rum

*Region:* Rhode Island

*Type*: Micro-distillery producing approximately 4,000 barrels annually

*Opened:* 2006

*Hours of operation:* Wednesday through Monday from 12:00pm to 5:00pm

*Tours:* Tours are available during regular hours of operation.

*Types of spirits produced:* Single barrel rum

*Names of spirits:*
- Thomas Tew Single Barrel Rum

*Best known for:* Thomas Tew Single Barrel Rum

*Average bottle price*: $30.00 to $35.00

*Distribution:* Rhode Island

*Awards and Recognitions:*
January 2011, Newport Distilling was featured on the Discovery Channel's "Dirty Jobs" with Mike Rowe

*Events and Celebrations:*
Special event space is available to rent.

*Services offered other than production:* Tastings and tours

*Interesting facts:*
- Newport Distilling Company received the first license to distill in the state since the close of the John Dyer distillery in Providence in 1872.

The Newport Distilling company was founded by the makers of Newport Storm Beer in 2006 to honor Newport, Rhode Island's, rich rum history. Since its colonial days, Newport's rum history and the Carribean's source of sugar cane and blackstrap mollasses have been intimately tied. The goal behind Newport Distilling was to recreate the rum that had been world famous 250 years ago. Using the same blackstrap molasses, local water, and pot still techniques, the end result is one single signature spirit, Thomas Tew Single Barrel Rum.

The Newport Distilling Company shares a building with its partner company, Coastal Extreme Brewing, the makers of Newport Storm beer. Brewers yeast from Newport Storm's Hurricane Amber Ale is used to ferment the blackstrap used in Thomas Tew Single Barrel Rum.

*Highlighted spirits:*
## Thomas Tew Single Barrel Rum
Thomas Tew Single Barrel Rum is slowly crafted in a small pot still to replicate the rum which would have been produced in Newport over a century ago. The still along with the dark molasses, temperate climate,

and local water combine to create a spirit that has slightly floral hints of molasses and oak.

*Future business plans and goals:* To expand distribution throughout New England

*Suggested recipe:*
## The Thomas Tew Dirty Mojito
- 1½ oz Thomas Tew Rum
- ½ oz lime juice
- 2 oz simple syrup
- 1½ oz club soda
- 2 mint leaves

The Thomas Tew Dirty Mojito was inspired by Newport Distilling's appearance on the Discovery Channel's "Dirty Jobs" with Mike Rowe.

Newport Distilling Company
Newport, Rhode Island

## Dark Corner Distillery

**DARK CORNER Distillery**
GREENVILLE, SC

Joe Fenten, Co-Founder
Richard Wenger, Co-Founder

241-B North Main Street
Greenville, South Carolina  29601

*Phone:*  864-631-1144
*Email:*  Joe Fenten:  joe@darkcornerdistillery.com
            Richard Wenger:  rich@darkcornerdistillery.com
*Website:*  www.darkcornerdistillery.com
*Facebook:*  Dark Corner Distillery
*Twitter:*  @DCDistillery

*Region:*  Northwestern South Carolina

*Type:*  Micro-distillery producing approximately 6,000 proof gallons per year

*Opened:*  September 21, 2011

*Hours of operation:*  Monday through Saturday, 10:00am to 7:00pm

*Tours:*  Tours are available by appointment.

*Types of spirits produced:*  Whiskey, beer schnapps, eau de vie, and brandy

*Names of spirits:*
- Moonshine
- Apple-achian Shine

*Best known for:*  Apple-achian Margarita

*Average bottle price*:  $32.00

*Distribution:*
Available at the distillery and throughout South Carolina

*Events and Celebrations:*  Dark Corner Distillery does host private events and holiday parties.

*Services offered other than production:*
Tastings, tours, training, on-site retail store, and event space

286

*Interesting facts:*

- The "Dark Corner" is a rugged, mountainous region in the northeastern corner of Greenville County, South Carolina, famous for nearly two centuries for its home-distilled moonshine whiskey, and infamous for countless fights, feuds, killings and other mayhem caused in part by misuse of the whiskey. It is an ironic, "dark" heritage in one of the state's most picturesque areas, and in perspective, delineates an area and a people among the Blue Ridge Mountains', and South Carolina's, finest.

While moonshine is produced from a basic recipe handed down from generation to generation, every moonshiner has his own unique twist in making his homemade whiskey. Dark Corner Distillery is in this tradition.

Hand-spirited encompasses four aspects of the word, spirit:

(1) It is spirits, a liquid containing alcohol and water, distilled from mash;

(2) It is spirited, meaning animated and full of spirit, or fire;

(3) It is spirituous, meaning refined and pure; and

(4) It is spirit of the maker, his temper or disposition of mind during the process.

*About:*

Dark Corner Distillery pays homage to South Carolina's upcountry heritage by hand-spiriting small batches of whiskey the way the settlers did; only this time its legal. Hidden in a dark corner of Main Street in downtown Greenville, the state's first legal whiskey distillery since Prohibition offers locals and tourists alike a glimpse into the past including a mini museum, storytelling and tours. Part of the distillery is a retail store chocked full of local mountain crafts, upcountry art, and moonshine-infused pantry goods. If that doesn't wet your whistle then step up to the tasting bar and have a swig of true Appalachian heritage.

*Future business plans and goals:* Expanded product line and broadened distribution

*Suggested recipe:*

**Apple-achian Margarita**
  Rim a rocks glass with caramel and salt.
  Fill with ice.
  Top with Apple-achian Shine.

Dark Corner Distillery
Greenville, South Carolina

## Firefly Distillery

Jim Irvin and Scott Newitt, Owners

6775 Bears Bluff Road
Wadmalaw Island, South Carolina 29487

*Phone:* 843-557-1405
*Fax:* 843-557-1068
*General Email:* info@fireflyvodka.com
*Website:* www.fireflyvodka.com
*Facebook:* The Official Firefly Sweet Tea Vodka Page
*Twitter:* @FireflyVodka

*Region:* Southeastern U.S.

*Type*: Micro-distillery

*Opened:* 2007

*Hours of operation:*
Production: Monday through Friday from 8:30am to 4:30pm
Retail: Wednesday through Saturday from 11:00am to 5:00pm
Closed January

*Tours:* A video tour is offered with tastings.

*Types of spirits produced:*
Rum, vodka, and blend bourbon

*Names of spirits:*
- Firefly Sweet Tea Vodka
- Firefly Lemon Tea Vodka
- Firefly Raspberry Tea Vodka
- Firefly Mint Tea Vodka
- Firefly Peach Tea Vodka
- Firefly Handcrafted Vodka
- Firefly Southern Lemonade Vodka
- Firefly Sweet Tea Bourbon
- Firefly Skinny Tea Vodka
- Sea Island Gold Rum
- Sea Island Java Rum
- Sea Island Spice Rum

*Best known for:* Firefly Sweet Tea Vodka

*Average bottle price*: Under $20.00

*Distribution:* Nationwide, in the US Virgin Islands, and at the tasting room

**Firefly Sweet Tea Vodkas**
- Medaled in the San Francisco World Spirits Competition

**Firefly Mint Tea Vodka**
- Double Gold Medal, 2009 San Francisco World Spirits Competition
- Firefly has also medaled in the New York Spirits Competition

*Highlighted spirits:*

**Firefly Sweet Tea Vodka**

Created in 2008, Firefly Sweet Tea Vodka is the original sweet tea vodka made with real Louisiana sugar cane and is the only tea produced in America.

**Firefly Sweet Tea Bourbon**

Firefly Sweet Tea Bourbon starts with Buffalo Trace Bourbon and is infused with a Firefly Sweet Tea mixture for a sweeter finish.

*Services offered other than production:* Tastings and retail store

*Interesting facts:*
- Firefly is the largest distillery in South Carolina.

*About:*

Jim Irvin (right) and Scott Newitt (left), two southern gentlemen with a passion for the South and all that makes it unique, opened Firefly Distillery in 2007 to produce world class southern spirits from the finest ingredients the South had to offer.

Jim crossed paths with Scott a few years after he and his wife moved to Wadmalaw Island in 2000 where they planted muscadine grape vines to produce South Carolina wine. Jim was out selling his wine when he met Scott who was a manager at a local liquor distributor. Scott told him that he made some nice southern wine and suggested they make some southern spirits. In 2007, they created a small batch of the first ever sweet tea vodka using South Carolina tea and Louisiana sugar cane. Firefly Sweet Tea Vodka, the original sweet tea vodka created with the only tea produced in America, is distilled four times, infused with tea grown on a plantation five miles from the distillery, and blended with real Louisiana sugar cane. Released in April 2008, Firefly Sweet Tea Vodka became an instant success in the South Carolina market and remains the highest seller and most widely distributed product for the company.

In 2009, Firefly Distillery took the original handcrafted sweet tea vodka and added a twist with the creation of four additional tea flavors - raspberry, peach, mint, and lemon. A year later, Jim and Scott expanded production to include Sea Island Rums and Firefly Sweet Tea Bourbon. 2011 brought the introduction of Sea Island Spiced Rum and Skinny Tea which will boast zero carbs and zero sugars.

Firefly Distillery is in a picturesque setting with an 11 acre vineyard, a pond, and oak trees covering the property. Its products are unique because Jim and Scott created a new segment in the industry; before Firefly, there were no other sweet tea vodkas.

Firefly Distillery uses tea from a plantation less than five miles from the distillery and sugar from Louisiana for the other products. The cane for Firefly Distillery Sea Island products is grown on Johns Island, 15 miles from distillery.

*Future business plans and goals:*
To constantly create and explore different flavors and options

*Suggested recipes:*
**Firefly Spiked Palmer**
- 1 part Firefly Sweet Tea Vodka
- 1 part fresh squeezed lemonade

**The Charleston Julep**
- 3 oz Firefly Sweet Tea Flavored Bourbon
- ¾ oz simple syrup

    Fill a highball glass half full with ice, mix Firefly and simple syrup. Top with mint sprig.

**Very Berry Sweet Tea**
- 1 ½ oz Firefly Raspberry Tea Flavored Vodka
- 1 ½ oz pomegranate liquor
- Splash of cranberry juice

    Shake with ice, strain into highball glass.

**Shoe Fly**
- 1 part Firefly Sweet Tea Flavored Vodka
- 1 part orange juice

    Mix Firefly and orange juice, serve.

Firefly Distillery
Wadmalaw Island, South Carolina

290

# Corsair Artisan Distillery

Darek Bell, Owner
Andrew Webber, Owner

Corsair Distillery Nashville
1200 Clinton Street #110
Nashville, Tennessee 37203

Corsair Distillery Kentucky
400 East Main Street #110
Bowling Green, Kentucky 42101

*Phone:* 615-200-0320

*Email:* Distillation / Management: andrew@corsairartisan.com
Owner: darek@corsairartisan.com
General Information and Sales: jason@corsairartisan.com
*Website:* www.corsairartisan.com
*Facebook:* Corsair Artisan Distillery
*Twitter:* @corsairartisan

*Region:* Mid-South

*Type:* Micro-distillery producing approximately 6,700 gallons per year

*Opened:*
Bowling Green, Kentucky facility opened in December of 2008
Nashville, Tennessee facility opened in April of 2010

*Hours of operation:*
Nashville
Monday through Wednesday, 9:00am to 6:00pm
Thursday and Friday, 9:00am to 8:00pm
Saturday, 2:00pm to 8:00pm
Bowling Green
Saturday, 10:00am to 6:00pm

*Tours:*
Nashville
Tours are available Thursday through Saturday from 4:00pm to 8:00pm.
Bowling Green
Tours are available Friday and Saturday from 10:00am to 6:00pm.

*Types of spirits produced:* Gin, rum, absinthe, vodka, and whiskeys

*Names of spirits:*
- Corsair Gin
- Corsair Spiced Rum
- Corsair Red Absinthe
- Corsair Vanilla Vodka
- Corsair Barrel Aged Gin
- Corsair Wry Moon Unaged Rye Whiskey
- Corsair Triple Smoke Single Malt Whiskey
- Corsair Pumpkin Spice Moonshine
- Corsair 100% Rye Aged Rye Whiskey

*Best known for:* Corsair Gin, Triple Smoke Whiskey, and Pumpkin Spice Moonshine

*Average bottle price*: $25.00 to $55.00

*Distribution:* Corsair tasting rooms in Nashville, TN, and Bowling Green, KY, as well as throughout Arkansas, California, Connecticut, Delaware, Florida, Illinois, Georgia, Kentucky, Maryland, Missouri, Nevada, New York, Oregon, Tennessee, Washington, and Washington DC. Coming soon: Colorado, Mississippi, New Jersey, North Carolina, Texas, and West Virginia

*Awards and Recognitions:*
**Corsair Gin**
- Silver Medal, 2011 MicroLiquor Spirit Awards
- Gold Medal, 2011 International Review of Spirits
- Gold Medal, 2009 San Francisco World Spirits Competition

**Corsair Barrel Aged Gin**
- Gold Medal, 2011 San Francisco World Spirits Competition

**Corsair Pumpkin Spice Moonshine**
- Bronze Medal, 2011 MicroLiquor Spirit Awards
- Bronze Medal, 2011 San Francisco World Spirits Competition

**Corsair Wry Moon Unaged Rye Whiskey**
- Silver Medal, 2010 ADI Conference
- Double Gold Medal, 2010 San Francisco World Spirits Competition

**Corsair Triple Smoke Single Malt Whiskey**
- Gold Medal, 2011 MicroLiquor Spirit Awards
- Bronze Medal, 2011 ADI Conference
- Silver Medal, 2010 ADI Conference
- Gold Medal, 2010 Beverage Testing Institute
- Gold Medal, 2010 San Francisco World Spirits Competition

**Corsair Rasputin Hopped Whiskey**
- Bronze Medal, 2011 ADI Conference

**Corsair Quinoa Whiskey**
- Silver Medal, 2011 New York International Spirits Competition

**Corsair 100% Rye Aged Rye Whiskey**
- Gold Medal, 2011 MicroLiquor Spirit Awards
- Silver Medal, 2011 ADI Conference
- Bronze Medal, 2010 ADI Conference
- Silver Medal, 2010 Beverage Testing Institute

*Highlighted spirits:*
## Corsair Triple Smoke Single Malt Whiskey
To craft this deeply complex, smokey and buttery whiskey, Corsair begins with fractions of malted barley, each smoked by a different fuel, including, cherry wood, peat, and beechwood. Pot distilled then barreled in new charred oak, Triple Smoke has the sweetness and barrel notes of an American whiskey and a single malt's rich smoke, broadened by tones of cherry and beech.

## Corsair Gin
Using an unusual mix of traditional botanicals and created in very small batches in a hand-hammered gin-head pot still, Corsair Gin is described as unique, citrusy and floral.

## Corsair Pumpkin Spice Moonshine
After creating a sweet malt whiskey, the pot still vapor basket is loaded with ginger, nutmeg, allspice, cinnamon and pumpkin, then is redistilled to infuse and marry all the flavors. The result is this Pumpkin Spice Moonshine

## Corsair Red Absinthe
Corsair tweaks traditional, 1800s absinthe recipes by adding unusual ingredients, including citrus, tarragon, and red hibiscus for floral tones and color.

*Services offered other than production:*
Corsair Artisan Distillery offers tastings, tours, and a gift shop at both distilleries.

*About:*
Corsair begins with classic spirit recipes, usually from the 1800s, and makes subtle changes with unusual ingredients to create an interesting and distinct taste.

*Management profile:* The management team at Corsair includes two pastors, a college professor, an automation expert, a video maker, and an archaeologist.

*Professional associations:*
American Distilling Institute and DISCUS

*Suggested recipe:*
## Pumpkin Pie Martini

- 1 oz Corsair Vanilla Vodka
- 1 oz Corsair Pumpkin Spice Moonshine
- ½ oz Bailey's Irish Cream
- Splash of butterscotch schnapps
- Ice

  Shake and then pour.
  For added "pie" effect, rim the glass with fresh lemon juice and crushed graham crackers.

Corsair Artisan Distillery
Nashville, Tennessee - Bowling Green, Kentucky

Corsair Artisan Distillery photos courtesy of Rodman Photography

## Ole Smoky Distillery, LLC

Justin King, Master Distiller

*Physical address:*
903 Parkway
Gatlinburg, Tennessee 37738

*Mailing address:*
236 E. Main Street #136
Sevierville, Tennessee  37862

*Phone:*  865-436-6995
*Fax:*  865-277-7746
*Email:* General info:  shine@osdistillery.com
　　　　Justin King:  justin@osdistillery.com
*Website:*  www.olesmokymoonshine.com
*Facebook:*  Ole Smoky Moonshine Distillery
*Twitter:*  @OleSmoky

*Region:*  East Tennessee

*Type:*  Micro-distillery

*Opened:*  July 2, 2010

*Hours of operation:*　Every day from 10:00am to 10:00pm
　　　　　　　　　　No alcohol sold on Sundays

*Tours:*　Self-guided tours are available. Guests can read the storyboards, see the working still, and speak with the distillers.

*Types of spirits produced:*  Moonshine

*Names of spirits:*
- Ole Smoky® Original Moonshine (Corn Whiskey)
- Ole Smoky® White Lightnin'™ (Neutral Spirits)
- Ole Smoky® Moonshine Cherries™
- Ole Smoky® Apple Pie Moonshine™
- Ole Smoky® Grape Moonshine™ (seasonal)
- Ole Smoky® Hunch Punch Moonshine™ (seasonal)
- Ole Smoky® Peach Moonshine™ (seasonal)

*Average bottle price*:  $24.95 to $34.95

*Distribution:* At the distillery and distributed in nearly 30 states
Check www.olesmokymoonshine.com/where/ for where to buy.

*Highlighted spirits:*
**Ole Smoky® Original Moonshine**
Ole Smoky's authentic moonshine is an unaged corn whiskey made from local farm grown corn in East Tennessee. The century-old recipe proclaims a grain bill of 80% corn with the remaining 20% a secret that gives Ole Smoky the distinct character and bold flavor of Tennessee moonshine.

**Ole Smoky® White Lightnin'™**
Ole Smoky's White Lightnin'™ is made from 100% grain neutral spirits that have been distilled six times for premium smoothness.

White Lightnin'™ is Ole Smoky's alternative to vodka, gin and tequila and is perfect for making apple pie, moonshine margaritas, moonshine mojitos or the mixed drink of your choice.

**Ole Smoky® Moonshine Cherries™**
Ole Smoky's Moonshine Cherries™ are an Appalachian party tradition. Each jar is hand-filled with fresh maraschino cherries soaked in Ole Smoky's 100 proof moonshine. Once the cherries have disappeared, enjoy the remaining cherry moonshine straight up or create the ultimate cherry coke or Shirley Temple.

**Ole Smoky® Apple Pie Moonshine™**
Americana in a jar. Ole Smoky® Apple Pie Moonshine™ captures the same delicious combination of flavors you'd find in grandma's baked apple pie. Made with pure apple juice, ground cinnamon and other spices blended with moonshine, this recipe has been loved for ages in Appalachia. At 40 proof, it's very drinkable and goes down as easy as a forkful of apple pie. Some like it cold, some like it hot, and some like it straight from the jar!

*Events and Celebrations:* Live bluegrass music on stage daily at the Ole Smoky Moonshine Holler. Guests can sit in rocking chairs and enjoy the music of days gone by.

*Services offered other than production:* Tasting station, retail shop and concession area

*Interesting facts:*
- Tennessee's first legal moonshine distillery
- The original, unaged corn whiskey is made from a 100-year-old family recipe

*About:*

Ole Smoky® Tennessee Moonshine is born in the fertile soil of East Tennessee farms where corn is raised and then transported to the family mill to be ground. At the distillery, you can see the grains converted into the clear corn liquor this part of the country is famous for.

Ole Smoky Distillery, the first federally licensed distillery in the history of East Tennessee, is locally owned and operated. When Tennessee's laws changed to allow the distillation of spirits, Ole Smoky saw an opportunity to showcase the art of superior mountain-made moonshine. The Ole Smoky recipes are the product of the hard work and experience of local families who have made moonshine in the mountains for the last two hundred years.

*Professional associations:* American Distilling Institute and DISCUS

*Future business plans and goals:* Continued growth and expanded distribution

*Suggested recipes:*

**Not So Cosmopolitan**
- 1 part Ole Smoky® White Lightnin'™
- 1 ½ parts cranberry juice
- ½ part triple sec

  Garnish with fresh lime.

**Smoky Mountain Apple**
- 1 part Ole Smoky® Original Moonshine
- 1 part Ole Smoky® Apple Pie Moonshine™
- 1 part cranberry juice

Ole Smoky Distillery, LLC
Gatlinburg, Tennessee

# Prichard's Distillery Inc.

Phil Prichard, President / Master Distiller

*Physical address:*
11 Kelso Smithland Road, Kelso, TN 37348

*Mailing address:*
Post Office Box 100, Kelso, TN 37348

*Phone:* 931-433-5454
*Fax:* 931-433-5488
*Email:* phil@pdspirits.com
*Website:* www.pdspirits.com
*Facebook:* Prichard's Distillery

*Region:* Southcentral Tennessee

*Type:* Micro-distillery producing approximately 15,000 nine liter cases per year

*Opened:* Incorporated in 1997, production began in 1999, sales began in 2001

*Hours of operation:* 8:00am to 4:00pm

*Tours:* Monday through Friday from 9:00am to 3:30pm, Saturday from 9:00am to 3:00pm

*Types of spirits produced:* Rum, whiskey and liqueurs

*Names of spirits:*
**Rums**
> Prichard's Fine Rum
> Prichard's Cranberry Rum
> Prichard's Crystal Rum
> Prichard's Key Lime Rum
> Prichard's Private Stock Rum
> Prichard's Sweet Georgia Bell

**Whiskey**
> Benjamin Prichard's Double Barreled Bourbon
> Benjamin Prichard's Double Chocolate Bourbon Whiskey
> Benjamin Prichard's Lincoln County Lightning
> Benjamin Prichard's Rye Whiskey
> Benjamin Prichard's Single Malt Whiskey
> Benjamin Prichard's Tennessee Whiskey

**Liqueurs**
> Benjamin Prichard's Cranberry Liqueur
> Benjamin Prichard's Sweet Lucy Bourbon Liqueur
> Benjamin Prichard's Sweet Lucy Bourbon Cream Liqueur

*Best known for:* Sweet Lucy

297

*Average bottle price*: $19.95 to $72.00

*Distribution:* 44 states and 8 European countries

*Awards and Recognitions:*

**Benjamin Prichard's Sweet Lucy**
- Gold Medal, Category: Flavored Whiskies & Whiskey-Based Liqueurs, 2010 ADI

**Benjamin Prichard's Tennessee Whiskey**
- Silver Medal, Category: Whiskey Idiosyncratic, 2010 ADI

**Benjamin Prichard's Single Malt Whiskey**
- Silver Medal, Category: Flavored Whiskies & Whiskey-Based Liqueurs, 2010 ADI

**Benjamin Prichard's Double Barreled Bourbon**
- Five Stars, Score 95 Ultimate Spirits Challenge, F. Paul Pacult

**Prichard's Key Lime Rum**
- Gold Medal, Category: Tasting Competition, 2009 International Rum Festival

**Prichard's Private Stock Rum**
- Silver Medal, Category: Tasting Competition, 2009 International Rum Festival

*Highlighted spirits:*

**Sweet Lucy Bourbon Liqueur** (70 Proof)

Sweet Lucy's legacy has been flowing up and down the Mississippi flyway for years warming the bodies and souls of outdoorsman for generations. Born in a duck blind and a frequent companion on duck hunts, variations of Sweet Lucy were generally homemade elixirs of peaches, oranges and apricots with lots of sugar and whiskey. Great pride would often be displayed by its maker as the bottle made its rounds for a sip among friends.

Although you may no longer find these same homemade remedies for the chill of a cold winter morning in a duck blind, Prichard's Distillery Inc. has captured the essence of the original Sweet Lucy. Benjamin Prichard's Sweet Lucy is an officially licensed product of Ducks Unlimited Inc.

Along with the noted Ducks Unlimited logo. the following statement is proudly printed on each bottle of Sweet Lucy: "With each purchase of Sweet Lucy, Prichard's Distillery will make a contribution to DUCKS Unlimited for their ongoing wetland conservation efforts throughout North America. Always remember, after the hunt, the best mixer for Sweet Lucy is...just good friends."

**Lincoln County Lightning** (90 Proof)

Benjamin Prichard's Lincoln County Lightning is a straight out of the still white lightning, and a wonderful flavor of white corn straight off the cob. Bold yet surprisingly mellow, Ben will be sure to take his place as an intriguing new flavor to add to a variety of new cocktails.

**Benjamin Prichard's Tennessee Whiskey** (80 Proof)

In celebration of over ten years of operation, Prichard's Distillery is pleased to announce the release of this fine ten-year-old whiskey. Benjamin Prichard's Tennessee Whiskey is distilled in the style of the traditional Tennessee whiskeys.

Original Tennessee whiskey, made during the Civil War, was distilled from white corn using a pot still. Benjamin Prichard's Tennessee Whiskey is made using similar pot still production techniques like Benjamin used back in the early 1800s, and white corn milled by the historic Falls Mill in nearby Old Salem, Tennessee. The resulting smooth whiskey is full of rich, bold character.

*Services offered other than production:* Tastings and retail store

*Interesting facts:*
- The first legal distillery in Tennessee in almost fifty years

*About:*

Five generations ago, when Benjamin Prichard of Davidson County, Tennessee, passed his "still, tubs and utensils thereto" to his son Enoch, his will of 1822 provided documentation of the last known "legal" distiller in the Prichard family. Ben made his whiskey with a high sugar content white corn, pure Tennessee spring water, and distilled it using ancient pot still techniques.

Prichard's Distillery has been producing handcrafted American spirits for more than a decade. Its spirits are an accurate recreation of America's first distilled beverages. The rums are made from Louisiana sweet molasses and the whiskies are made from white Tennessee corn. Distilled in traditional copper-pot stills using the techniques of the master distillers of an older time, Prichard's American spirits are most certainly nothing like the commercially produced spirits we have come to know today.

*Professional associations:* American Distilling Institute and DISCUS

*Future business plans and goals:* Continued growth

*Suggested recipes:*

**Brain Duster**
- 1 oz Prichard's Tennessee Whiskey
- 1 oz absinthe
- 1 oz sweet vermouth
- 1 dash bitters

    Combine all ingredients in a glass mixing pint. Stir well.
    Strain into a chilled cocktail glass.
    Garnish with a grated nutmeg and black pepper.

## Sleepy Hollow

- 1 ½ oz Double Barrel Bourbon
- 4 slices fresh ginger
- ¼ oz fresh lime juice
- 1 oz pumpkin purée

Muddle ginger and and lime juice in shaker.
Add all other ingredients and shake well.
Strain into a chilled cocktail glass.
Garnish with a toasted pumpkin seeds.

## Corn on the Collins

- 2 oz Lincoln County Lightning
- 1 ½ oz lemon juice
- 1 oz simple syrup
- 2 ½ oz club soda

Build in a highball glass with ice and stir.
Garnish with a lemon wheel.

Prichard's Distillery Inc.
Kelso, Tennessee

## Balcones Distillery

Chip Tate, President and Head Distiller

212 S. 17th Street and 225 S. 11th Street
Waco, Texas 76701

*Phone:* 254-755-6003
*Fax:* 888-859-0023
*Email:* info@balconesdistilling.com
*Website:* www.balconesdistilling.com

*Region:* Texas and the Southwest

*Type*: Craft-distillery producing and selling approximately 900 gallons per month

*Opened:* March 2008

*Hours of operation:*
Monday through Friday, 6:00am to 10:00pm

*Tours:* Available by appointment only

*Types of spirits produced:*
Whisky and rumble (rum/whisky/brandy hybrid)

*Names of spirits:*
- Baby Blue Whisky
- True Blue Whisky
- Rumble
- Rumble Cask Reserve
- '1' Texas Single Malt Whisky
- Brimstone Whisky

*Best known for:* Baby Blue Corn Whisky and '1' Texas Single Malt Whisky

*Average bottle price*: $35.00 to $65.00

*Distribution:* Texas, California, Illinois, New Mexico, Louisiana, Minnesota, Washington DC, Maryland, Kentucky, Connecticut, New York, New Jersey, Florida, Delaware, and the UK

*Awards and Recognitions:*
## Balcones Distillery
- "Icons of Whisky" 2012 Craft Whiskey Distillery of the Year, Whisky Magazine
- 2012 Good Food Award, Spirits Category - Regional Winner

### Baby Blue Whisky
- Double Gold Medal, San Francisco International Wine & Spirits Competition
- Gold Medal, 2010 American Distilling Institute Whiskey Competition
- Bronze Medal, New York International Spirits Competition
- 95 points Anthony Dias Blue, Tasting Panel Magazine
- 5 Stars, Highest Recommendation, December 2010 F. Paul Pacult's Spirit Journal
- Top 140, F. Paul Pacult's Spirit Journal, Top 140 5 Star spirits

### Rumble
- Silver Medal, San Francisco International Wine & Spirits Competition
- Bronze Medal, New York International Spirits Competition

### True Blue Whisky

- Bronze Medal, NY International Spirits Competition
- Silver Medal, 2011 San Francisco International Wine & Spirits Competition
- Silver Medal, 2011 ADI Whiskey Competition
- 4 Stars, Highly Recommended, F. Paul Pacult's Spirit Journal December 2010
- 88 Points, Very Good Strong Recommendation, 2011 Ultimate Beverage Challenge
- Silver Medal, 2011 New York World Wine & Spirits Competition

### '1' Texas Single Malt Whisky
- Double Gold Medal, Best Single Malt, 2011 NY World Wine and Spirits Competition
- Best Whiskey, 2011 NY World Wine & Spirits Competition
- Best in Show, Brown Spirit, 2011 New York World Wine & Spirits Competition

### Brimstone
- Gold Medal, 2011 New York World Wine & Spirits Competition

*Highlighted spirits:*

### Baby Blue Corn Whisky
Baby Blue is the first Texas whisky on the market since Prohibition, the only blue corn whisky, and it pays homage to the American whisky tradition.

### True Blue Whisky
True Blue Whisky is a cask strength version of Baby Blue Corn Whisky.

### Rumble
Rumble, a pioneered spirit, is a rum/whisky/brandy hybrid that has no official classification. Rumble is made entirely from turbinado sugar, wildflower honey and mission figs fermented together and distilled.

## Rumble Cask Reserve
Rumble Cask Reserve is a cask strength version of the Rumble.

## '1' Texas Single Malt Whisky
'1' Texas Single Malt Whisky is a unique style of malt whisky – Texas made, Texas proud. It has mellow notes of sautéed pears and ripe fruit mixed with a lingering toasty malt character.

## Brimstone
Brimstone is purification through fire – a Texas oak fire, that is. Rather than using Scottish peat smoke, this one of a kind whisky is smoked with sun-baked Texas scrub oak using the distiller's own secret process.

*Services offered other than production:* Tours

*Interesting facts*
- Producers of the first legal Texas whiskey since Prohibition, the only Blue Corn whisky, and Texas' first single malt

*About:*
Through a great deal of blood, sweat, and tears, as well as building equipment including stills and fermenters, Balcones Distillery was founded out of Chip Tate's love of creating fermented goodies, particularly whisky.

Balcones Distillery uses 100% Hopi blue corn sourced from New Mexico, one of the only places it is available in the world. All honey, sugar, and mission figs are sourced from within Texas.

Additionally, the distillery is energy efficient because it has specially designed condensers used to conserve water. Balcones gives all of its spent grain to a local organic farm for animal feed and compost.

*Management profile:*
## Chip Tate
Chip Tate (right), president and head distiller, has a master's in divinity, a background in engineering, and he welds copper.

*Professional associations:* American Distilling Institute

*Future business plans and goals:* Broaden distribution and expand into new facility

Balcones Distillery
Waco, Texas

# Garrison Brothers Distillery

Dan Garrison, Proprietor

Post Office Drawer 261
Hye, Texas 78635

*Phone:* 830-392-0246
*Fax:* 512-302-4144
*Email:* dan@garrisonbros.com
*Website:* www.garrisonbros.com
*Facebook:* Garrison Brothers Distillery

*Region:* Southcentral Texas

*Type:* Micro-distillery

*Opened:* 2008

*Types of spirits produced:* Bourbon

*Names of spirits:*
- Garrison Brothers Texas Straight Bourbon Whiskey

*Awards and Recognitions:*
**Garrison Brothers Texas Straight Bourbon Whiskey**
- Best in Category, 2011 American Distilling Institute
- Silver Medal, 2011 San Francisco International Wine & Spirits Competition

*Services offered other than production:* Tours are available.

*About:*
Garrison Brothers Texas Straight Bourbon Whiskey is handcrafted from fine ingredients including plump, organic yellow corn from the Texas Panhandle; premium, home-grown, organic winter wheat; and two-row barley from the Pacific Northwest and Canada.

Garrison Brothers Distillery
Hye, Texas

## Railean Distillers
Eagle Point Distillery

Kelly Railean, Owner / Master Distiller
Erik Bauer, EVP Sales

*Physical address:*
341 5th Street
San Leon, Texas  77539

*Mailing address:*
111 Pelican Court
League City, Texas  77573

*Phone:*  713-545-2742
*Fax:*  832-778-5061
*Email:*  Kelly Railean: krailean@railean.com
          Erik Bauer:  ebauer@railean.com
*Website:*  www.railean.com
*Facebook:*  Railean Handmade Texas Rum

*Region:*  Southeastern Texas along Galveston Bay

*Type:*  Micro-distillery producing approximately 4,000 cases per year

*Opened:*  2007

*Hours of operation:*  Railean Distillers is open to the public by appointment only and generally Monday through Saturday between 10:00am and 2:00pm.

*Tours:*  Tours are available by appointment only.

*Types of spirits produced:*
Rum (white and aged), 100% Blue Agave Spirit

*Names of spirits:*
- Railean Texas White Rum
- Railean Reserve XO Dark Rum
- Railean Small Cask Single Barrel Dark Rum
- Railean "El Perico" 100% Blue Agave Spirit

*Best known for:*  Reserve XO Dark Rum and Railean "Talk Like a Pirate" Rum Punch

*Average bottle price*:  $16.99 to $29.99

*Distribution:*  Available through distributors in Texas, California, and Arkansas. Railean Distillers is prohibited by law to sell its own products.

**Railean Small Cask Reserve Single Barrel Rum**
- Awarded 95 points, 2010 American Craft Spirits

**Railean Texas White Rum**
- Silver Medal, Miami International Rum Festival

**Railean Reserve XO Dark Rum**
- "Best Buy" Award, 2010

*Highlighted spirits:*

**Railean Texas White Rum**

Railean Texas White Rum is distilled multiple times to produce a pure, smooth spirit. It is crisp, clean, and perfect for making tropical drinks such as Mojitos, Rum Punch, and Daiquiris. It possesses an exceptionally dry taste and immediately comes alive on the palate with subtle notes of vanilla, sugar cookie, citrus and spice. The finish is smooth, clean and flavorful.

**Railean Reserve XO Dark Rum**

Railean Reserve XO Dark Rum is aged in small, new, double-charred, American oak barrels. It is aged to perfection making it smooth yet flavorful and perfect for a premium Cuba Libre. The Reserve XO has fabulous aromas of brown sugar, spice and oak. It is soft and well rounded and, as it opens up, it reveals an array of chocolate, caramel and toasted walnut notes. The finish is smooth, warm and relaxing.

**Railean Small Cask Reserve Single Barrel Rum**

Railean Small Cask Reserve Single Barrel Rum has at least twice the age of the Reserve XO. It is aged in small, new, double-charred, American oak barrels, just like the Reserve XO. The Small Cask Reserve is rich and sophisticated with notes of oak, leather, and mocha. The first sip reveals toasted sugar notes with hints of caramel and dark chocolate. The finish is long and full bodied with a delicious earthy and woodsy quality. This rum is perfect for sipping on the rocks or with just a splash of water or cola.

**Railean "El Perico" 100% Blue Agave Spirit**

Railean El Perico is made from 100% blue agave and is distilled multiple times resulting in a pure, smooth spirit. El Perico is perfect for authentic Texas margaritas or for sipping with a splash of lemon-lime soda. It possesses a silky, dry yet fruity taste, and it immediately comes alive on the palate with subtle notes of Meyer lemon and key lime, followed by a hint of dried pineapple. It opens up with traces of butterscotch, honey and white pepper. The finish is warming with a luscious texture and complex agave character.

*Events and Celebrations:* Railean Distillers hosts numerous events annually including tastings, cigar and rum pairing events, and open houses. Additionally, it hosts dinners, tastings, seminars, and festivals at various locations.

*Services offered other than production:* Tastings, tours, and small gift shop

*Interesting facts:*
- First and only distillery in the Houston / Galveston area
- First and only certified American made rum in the USA
- Blue Agave Spirits is certified "Made in America"

*About:*

Out of a fascination and passion for sailing, tropical islands, pirates, parrots, and rum, Kelly Railean discovered her destiny when she stumbled across some of the best rum she had ever tasted in the tropics.

Family, friends and co-workers thought Kelly was crazy to quit the daily grind and start up her own company, especially in a world of mass produced spirits where very few woman have ventured. However, she was committed to the craft and had a passion to produce an exceptional spirit.

Railean's Eagle Point Distillery is located along the shores of Galveston Bay in San Leon, Texas. Once a stronghold for the swashbuckling pirate Jean Lafitte, San Leon is now a small drinking community with a large fishing problem. The area is also home to a thriving population of wild parrots called monk parakeets.

*Management profile:*

**Kelly Railean**

Kelly Railean, founder, owner, master distiller is a first level wine sommelier with more than 15 years of wine and spirits experience. Additionally, she was the first woman to become a master distiller in the state of Texas and got interested in rum when she took up sailing and started collecting rum on rum distillery tours.

**Matthew Railean**

Matthew Railean, Kelly's husband, is a chemical engineer with a MS Finance.

*Future business plans and goals:* Facility expansion and broadened distribution
Spring 2012 release of Railean Spiced Rum & Railean "El Perico" 100% Blue Agave Reposado

*Suggested recipe:*

**Railean "Talk Like a Pirate" Rum Punch**
- 1 part pineapple juice
- 1 part orange juice
- 1 part ginger ale
- 1 part Railean Texas White Rum
- 1 part Railean Reserve XO Dark Rum
- Splash of grenadine and bitters

    Mix all ingredients and serve over ice in a tall glass.

Railean Distillers
San Leon, Texas

# Rebecca Creek Distillery LLC

Mike Cameron, Co-Founder and Owner
Steve Ison, Co-Founder and Owner

26605 Bulverde Road, Suite B
San Antonio, Texas 78260

*Phone:* 830-714-4581
*Fax:* 830-714-4582
*Email:* info@rebeccacreekdistillery.com
*Website:* www.rebeccacreekdistillery.com, www.rebeccacreekwhiskey.com
*Website:* www.texasvodka.com
*Facebook:* Enchanted Rock Vodka
*Twitter:* @TXvodka

*Region:* Central Texas Hill Country

*Type:*
Craft-distillery producing approximately 50,000 cases per year of Enchanted Rock Vodka
and approximately 50,000 cases annual whiskey production.

*Opened:* August 21, 2010

*Hours of operation:* Monday through Friday, 8:00am to 5:00pm.

*Tours:* Tours are held on Saturdays from 12:00pm to 5:00pm

*Types of spirits produced:*
Ultra-premium Texas vodka and fine Texas whiskey

*Names of spirits:*
- Enchanted Rock Vodka
- Rebecca Creek Fine Texas Whiskey

*Best known for:* Enchanted Rock Ultra-Premium Texas Vodka

*Average bottle price*: Enchanted Rock Vodka, $18.00 (750ml)
Rebecca Creek Whiskey, $35.00 (750ml)

*Distribution:*
Spirits are currently only available in Texas with plans for full nationwide
distribution by the end of 2012.

**Enchanted Rock Vodka**
- Bronze Medal, San Francisco World Spirits Competition
- First Place, 2010 Crewtini Mix Off
- Received "Strong Recommendation," Ultimate Beverage Challenge

*Highlighted spirits:*
**Enchanted Rock Vodka**
Inspired by its iconic Texas Hill Country namesake, Enchanted Rock Vodka is a true artisan-produced, corn based spirit with incredible clarity, a medium body and a creamy finish. Handcrafted in small batches with pure, naturally limestone-filtered water from the Trinity Aquifer, Enchanted Rock Vodka is crafted in a traditional copper-pot still.

**Rebecca Creek Fine Texas Whiskey**
Rebecca Creek Fine Texas Whiskey is distilled in Texas and it is produced from a proprietary blend of domestic malted barley and naturally limestone-filtered water. It is distilled in small batches in a traditional copper-pot still and matured in charred oak for maximum taste profiles.

*Events and Celebrations:* Hosts special events including conferences and meetings
*Services offered other than production:* Tastings, tours, and event venue

*Interesting facts:*
- Rebecca Creek Distillery was the first legal distillery in south Texas since Prohibition.

*About:*
Located in northern San Antonio, Rebecca Creek Distillery opened with the goal of creating the first ultra-premium Texas vodka as well as a fine Texas whiskey. The goal was also to use as many local Texas ingredients and products as possible and still get it to the shelf at an extremely reasonable sale price.

Rebecca Creek Distillery is one of North America's fastest growing craft distilleries. The first distillery ever built in south Texas, Rebecca Creek is a privately held "Spirited Texas Distillery" and is the brainchild of Steve Ison and Mike Cameron, two San Antonio entrepreneurs. With the launch of the ultra- premium Enchanted Rock Vodka and Rebecca Creek Whiskey, Ison and Cameron successfully took the distillery's plans from the drawing board to realization in less than two years.
Rebecca Creek Distillery was designed to host tastings, tours, entertainment and events.

Additionally, the founders sourced the best distillery equipment on the market and hired the best consultants with a focus on creating and crafting premium brands by investing in the necessary infrastructure up front.

The vodka is handcrafted by Texans with pure limestone-filtered water and distilled six times for maximum purity; but the distillation process is taken one step further. After the initial process through the copper pot still, the spirit is run into the copper distillation column through a series of 6 bubble plates to further distill and refine, resulting in extremely pure, superior tasting vodka.

*Management profile:*

**Mike Cameron**

Mike Cameron, co-founder and owner of Rebecca Creek Distillery, is a Southwest Texas State University graduate with a BS Organizational Communication and Business. Mike is also a graduate of TSTI in Waco, TX, and has a degree in airframe and power plant studies. Mike has always had a broad interest in mechanical applications and in the last 10 years has developed a true appreciation for fine handcrafted spirits. Mike is married with four boys and in his spare time enjoys spending time with his family, fishing, and playing golf.

**Steve Ison**

Steve Ison, co-founder and owner of Rebecca Creek Distillery, is a Texas State graduate with a BS Political Science and is the owner of an independent insurance agency, David Ison & Sons Insurance. Additionally, Steve owns Benefit Tree, a benefits company that provides a platform for large employers to offer voluntary benefits to their employees. Steve is married with three children and enjoys golf and tennis.

**Jeff Murphy**

Head Distiller Jeff Murphy has traveled the world to explore his passion for brewing and distilling and has been involved with multiple breweries and distilleries.

*Future business plans and goals:* Broaden distribution

*Suggested recipe:*

**Enchanted Tea**

- ½ oz Enchanted Rock Vodka
- ½ oz tequila
- ½ oz rum
- ½ oz Rebecca Creek Whiskey
- ½ oz Blue Curacao

  Pour into a pint glass filled with ice.
  Fill rest with 1/3 sweet & sour and 2/3 cola.
  Shake and add lime wedge.

Rebecca Creek Distillery LLC
San Antonio, Texas

## SAVVY Distillers L.P.

Chad Auler, Founder & President
Clayton Christopher, CEO
John Potts, VP of Sales
Brandon Cason, VP of Marketing
John Scarborough, CFO
Gary Crowell, Special Operations
Kevin Coles, Production Manager

*Physical address:*
13805 Quitman Pass
Austin, Texas  78728

*Mailing address:*
3601 S. Congress Avenue, Ste. C-104
Austin, Texas  78704

*Phone:*  512-476-4477
*Fax:*  512-476-6116
*Email:*  info@savvyvodka.com
*Website:*  www.savvyvodka.com
*Facebook:*  SAVVY Vodka
*Twitter:*  @SavvyMartini

*Region:*  Texas Hill Country

*Type:*  Micro-distillery producing approximately 10,000 gallons per year

*Opened:*  September 2007

*Hours of operation:*  Monday through Friday, 8:00 am to 5:00pm

*Tours:*  Tours are not available at this time.

*Types of spirits produced:*  Vodka

*Names of spirits:*  SAVVY Vodka

*Best known for:*  SAVVY Vodka

*Average bottle price:*  $20.00 to $25.00

*Distribution:*  Texas

*Awards and Recognitions:*
**SAVVY Vodka**
- Gold Medal, November 2010, BTI World Spirit Competition
- Gold Medal, 50 Best Domestic Vodkas Competition

*Highlighted spirits:*
## SAVVY Vodka

SAVVY combines the best of cutting edge technology with the best of Old World craftsmanship to produce vodka that is of the highest quality.

Handcrafted 400 gallons at a time, SAVVY Vodka is distilled at least 20 times in a state of the art, 20 foot column still yielding a much cleaner, smoother and better finished product than that of a traditional pot still and at a fraction of the energy use. Locally sourced and spring-fed, the water is charcoal filtered five times resulting in a silky smooth finish.

Beverage Testing Institute described SAVVY Vodka as, "Clear. Sweet pastry dough and cream aromas with a soft, satiny texture, a dry-yet-fruity medium body and a smooth, creamy mocha, pepper dust, powdered sugar and riverstone accented finish. A smooth and subtly flavorful vodka that will be great in martinis."

*About:*
Founder Chad Auler opened SAVVY after more than three years of due diligence and a desire to make the finest vodka on the planet. Auler's vision of producing premium vodka in Texas is aided by water sourced from the Fall Creek. Running through the Auler family ranch, Fall Creek empties into the Colorado River at Fall Creek Falls, a spectacular 85 foot waterfall.

Additionally, SAVVY is extremely conscious of conserving energy and resources.

Its state of the art column still not only yields a better distillate, but it also uses only a fraction of the energy required by a traditional pot still. In addition to saving huge amounts of energy, the water used during distillation is recycled.

The uniquely designed water reclamation system allows the distillery to recycle and reuse the same water in the distillation process over and over. It uses about 3,000 gallons to distill one 400-gallon batch of SAVVY, so instead of wasting that water, it reuses it indefinitely.

*Management profile:*
**Chad Auler**
Founder Chad Auler (right) is a lifelong resident of Austin, a University of Texas graduate and a sixth generation Texan. Since 1993, Auler has been active in the alcoholic beverage industry through his affiliation with Texas wine producer Fall Creek Vineyards and California's Perfect 10 Wines.

*Future business plans and goals:*
Broaden distribution

*Suggested recipe:*
**SAVVY Cucumber Martini**
- 2 oz SAVVY Vodka
- 1 oz lime juice
- ½ oz Licor 43 (or simple syrup)
- 1 tsp sugar
- 2 halfed cucumber coins

  Muddle cucumber and sugar.
  Add ingredients.
  Shake with ice and strain.

SAVVY Distillers L.P.
Austin, Texas

313

# Spirit of Texas LLC

Brad Haden, President
Shaun Siems, VP of Operations
Jason Malik, VP of Marketing and Sales

1715 Dalshank Street, Suite A
Pflugerville, Texas  78660

*Phone:*  512-789-1600

*Email:*  General info:   info@spiritoftx.com
       Brad Haden:  brad.haden@spiritoftx.com
       Shaun Siems:  shaun.siems@spiritoftx.com
       Jason Malik:  jason.malik@spiritoftx.com
*Website:*  www.spiritoftx.com , www.pecanstreetrum.com
*Facebook:*  Spirit of Texas Distillery, Pecan Street Rum
*Twitter:*  @Pecanstreetrum

*Region:*  Southeastern Texas

*Type:*  Micro-distillery producing approximately 1,500 gallons per year

*Opened:*  2010

*Hours of operation:*  Monday through Friday, 8:00am to 5:00pm

*Tours:*  No tours are offered.

*Types of spirits produced:*  Rum

*Names of spirits:*
- Pecan Street Rum
- Spirit of Texas Rum

*Best known for:*  Pecan Street Rum

*Average bottle price:*  $20.00

*Distribution:*
Spirit of Texas rums are carried in every major venue in Texas.  Many local chain and independent liquor stores carry these rums as well.

314

*Highlighted spirits:*
## Pecan Street Rum
Pecan Street Rum is distilled from the finest molasses and aged with oak and pecans creating a full-bodied texture. The butterscotch nose carries a tinge of orange, tempts the palate with a hint of sweetness and then follows with a sensation of pecans. This rum has been described as a cross between bourbon and rum.

## Spirit of Texas Rum
Especially smooth, Spirit of Texas Rum is white rum distilled to perfection and then bottled to capture the sweet aroma of molasses. With a slightly dry finish that is clean, this rum is perfect with any beverage.

*Interesting facts:*
- Pecan Street Rum is the first known rum to be aged in American oak barrels with Texas pecans.

*About:*
Spirit of Texas Distillery was opened in 2010 by three engineering and entrepreneurial friends who challenged each other to produce a spirit unlike anything on the market and to offer it for a reasonable price.

While working together as engineers at Samsung Austin Semiconductor on process improvement and defect reduction projects, Brad, Shaun, and Jason were oblivious to the fact that each was thinking about starting a distillery or brewery until it was mentioned in passing. After a number of weekly get togethers, the three developed a solid business plan and the Spirit of Texas was born.

Each knew that he didn't want to create just another distilled spirit disguised as something already on the shelf. They wanted something different, something they could enjoy and something that was top notch quality and enjoyable by itself.

After a lot of talking, experimenting, and some drinking - or maybe it was some talking and a lot of drinking - the trio produced their first product, Pecan Street Rum.

*Professional associations:* American Distilling Institute

*Future business plans and goals:*
Broaden distribution, expand production capabilities and develop new unique products

*Suggested recipes:*

## Pecan Pie

- 1 ½ oz Pecan Street Rum
- 5 oz hot water
- 1 tsp melted butter
- 1 tsp brown sugar

Stir in all ingredients and add a sprinkle of cinnamon.

## Pecan Sunset

- 1 ½ oz Pecan Street Rum
- 4 oz Sprite
- 1 oz orange juice

## Pecan Street Pineapple Punch

- ½ lime, cut in wedges
- 2 sugar cubes
  Muddle ingredients on bottom of rocks glass, then add:

- 1 ½ oz Pecan Street Rum
- ¾ oz pineapple juice

Fill with ice and shake hard.  Top off with Sprite.

## Blueberry Pomegranate Pecan Street Mojito

- 9 small blueberries
- 1 lime (wedge and squeeze)
- 4-6 mint leaves
  Muddle ingredients at bottom of pint glass, then add:

- ¾ oz simple syrup
- ½ oz pomegranate juice
- 2 oz Pecan Street Rum

Fill glass with ice, shake hard and top off with soda water.

Spirit of Texas LLC
Pflugerville, Texas

## Tito's Handmade Vodka

Fifth Generation, Inc.
Mockingbird Distillery

Tito Beveridge, Owner

Austin, Texas

*Phone:* 512-389-9011
*Email:* info@titosvodka.com
*Website:* www.titosvodka.com
*Facebook:* Titos Handmade Vodka
*Twitter:* @TitosVodka
*Flicker:* titosvodka

*Region:* Southcentral Texas

*Type:* Micro-distillery

*Opened:* 1995

*Hours of operation:* Monday through Friday, 8:00am to 5:00pm

*Tours:* Tours are not available.

*Types of spirits produced:* Vodka

*Names of spirits:*
- Tito's Handmade Vodka

*Best known for:* Tito's Handmade Vodka

*Average bottle price:* $20.00

*Distribution:* Throughout the U.S. and Canada

*Awards and Recognitions:*
**Tito's Handmade Vodka**
- First spirit to be Made in USA Certified™
- Double Gold, World Spirit's Competition
- Chairman's Trophy, 2010 Ultimate Cocktail Challenge for Best Vodka and Tonic
- Rated 95 out of 100 by Wine Enthusiast

*Highlighted spirits:*
**Tito's Handmade Vodka**
Tito's Handmade Vodka is made from 100% corn and is distilled six times in an old fashioned pot still.

*Events and Celebrations:* Tito's participates in a number of community and charity events, concerts and other events such as Austin City Limits, SXSW, and Lollapalooza.

317

*Services offered other than production:* Online store

*Interesting facts:*
- Tito's Handmade Vodka is Texas' first and oldest legal distillery.
- Tito's Handmade Vodka is gluten free.

*About:*
In the early 90s, Tito Beveridge, founder and owner of Tito's Handmade Vodka, bought and sampled 86 bottles of vodka. He picked the best two and set out to create something better.

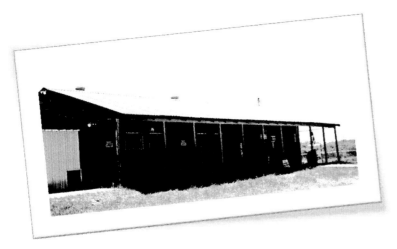

After all the permits were obtained, Tito built his one-man distillery (pictured) and production pot-still from scratch on the cheapest piece of land in the most liberal place in Texas. Once production had begun, he quickly discovered that his makeshift boiler didn't work as well as he had planned; he borrowed on a number of credit cards to fix the problem.

Although he had the help of a distributor, Tito started hand selling to liquor stores and, when he got paid, he would buy supplies and begin distilling again. His boot strapping, hand selling and shameless self-promoting finally paid off when Tito's Handmade Vodka won a Double Gold Medal at the World Spirits Competition for Best Vodka. Shortly

thereafter, Tito's won the Chairman's Trophy for Best Vodka and Tonic in the Ultimate Spirits Challenge and has since consecutively won numerous Fast Track and Impact awards.

Since his humble beginnings, Tito has slowly expanded production and broadened distribution to include all 50 states and parts of Canada.

*Management profile:*
**Tito Beveridge**
Tito Beveridge, founder and owner of Tito's Handmade Vodka, is a 40-something geologist with degrees in geology and geophysics from the University of Texas at Austin. After years of being in the oil and gas business in Texas, Venezuela and Colombia, Tito returned to Texas and started a drilling company in Houston. Getting tired of chasing the buck, he moved back to Austin and became an environmental groundwater scientist but got tired of going to waste dumps and mines. After giving that up, Tito got into

318

the mortgage business and started making flavored vodka for friends as Christmas presents. After receiving much praise for his vodka, he started thinking seriously about making and selling his vodka as a profession.

When rates went up a couple points in the mortgage business, he started going to liquor stores to ask if they would buy his flavored vodkas. They replied by saying, "No, go look at all the dust on the shoulders of those bottles there." They then told him that if he could make it smooth enough to drink straight then he might have something. Being very particular, Tito did just that, working diligently through trial and error until his formula was just right.

*Future business plans and goals:* Continued growth and having fun doing it

*Suggested recipes:*
### Tito's Passion
- 1½ oz Tito's Handmade Vodka
- 1 oz Grand Marnier
- 1 oz fresh sour
- 1½ oz fresh orange juice
- 1½ oz cranberry

Shake into a cocktail glass and add a lemon spiral.

### Moore Road Rendezvous
Muddle two large strawberries in ¾ oz simple syrup, then add:
- 2 oz Tito's Vodka
- ½ oz Martini Bianco
- ½ oz lemon juice
- ¼ Campari

Shake and fine strain over fresh ice in a double rocks glass. Garnish with a strawberry heart.

### The Texas Sipper
- 1½ oz Tito's Handmade Vodka
- ¼ oz St. Germain
- 2 oz fresh grapefruit
- 1 oz grapefruit soda

Garnish with a mint leaf.

Tito's Handmade Vodka
Austin, TX

## High West Distillery

David Perkins, Owner

703 Park Ave
Park City, Utah 84060

*Phone:* 435-649-8300
*Email:* info@highwest.com
*Website:* www.highwest.com
*Facebook:* High West Distillery

*Region:* Western U.S.

*Type:* Micro-distillery producing approximately 10,500 proof gallons per year

*Opened:* December 2009

*Hours of operation:* Open 7 days a week, 10:00am to 10:00pm

*Tours:* Tours of the facility are available.

*Types of spirits produced:* Whiskey and vodka

*Names of spirits:*
- High West Whiskey Rendezvous Rye
- High West Whiskey Bourye
- High West Whiskey Double Rye
- High West Silver Whiskey High Country Single Malt
- High West Silver Whiskey Western Oat
- High West Vodka 7000
- High West Vodka 7000 Peach
- High West Distillery Barreled Manhattan
- High West Whiskey Rocky Mountain Rye 16
- High West Whiskey Rocky Mountain Rye 21
- High West Double Rye
- High West Son Of Bourye
- High West OMG Pure Rye
- High West Valley Tan

*Best known for:* High West Whiskey Rendezvous Rye

*Average bottle price:* $30.00 to $130.00

*Distribution:* High West spirits are available in the distillery's general store as well as in Utah, California, Nevada, Arizona, Washington, Wyoming, Oregon, Pennsylvania, Illinois, Colorado, Missouri, Georgia, Washington DC, Maryland, Tennessee, Massachusetts, New York, the UK, Quebec, and Alberta.

320

**High West Whiskey Rendezvous Rye**
- 96 Points, Top 50 Spirits 2010, Wine Enthusiast
- Rated 95 points, 2008 John Hansell, Malt Advocate Magazine
- Top 10 New Whiskies of 2008

**High West Silver Whiskey Western Oat**
- 92 points, Exceptional, Beverage Testing Institute
- Tied for First, 2010 American Distilling Institute's Craft Whiskey Competition

**High West Whiskey Bourye**
- 90 Points, Whisky Advocate Magazine
- Best of Show, 2010 American Distilling Institute's Craft Whiskey Competition

**High West Double Rye**
- 90 Points, 2011 John Hansell, Malt Advocate Magazine
- Sourmash Manifesto 2011 Superb/ Outstanding, Jason Pyle

**High West Distillery & Saloon**
- Malt Advocate Magazine 2011 Whiskey Awards, High West "Pioneer of the Year"
- High West Saloon was just voted "Best Restaurant in Park City" by Salt Lake City Weekly, 2011 Best Of Guide.
- High West Saloon is Zagat rated, and one of only 20 restaurants in Utah listed in the printed Zagat guide.

*Highlighted spirits:*

**High West Whiskey Rendezvous Rye**
Having a spicy profile, Rendezvous Rye is a blend of two straight ryes- a young (2 year old) and an old (16 year old) whiskey. Rendezvous Rye celebrates the first recorded whiskeyfest out west in Utah. The "rendezvous" was the annual summer gathering of mountain men to exchange pelts for supplies. Alcohol was not one of the "supplies" at the first rendezvous. This oversight was corrected with a generous supply of whiskey at the second rendezvous in Utah's Cache Valley, resulting in a successful event and a tradition for all subsequent rendezvous.

**High West Whiskey Bourye**
Bourye is a blend of bourbon and straight rye. The name Bourye is a combination of "bou" for bourbon and "rye" for rye. Because combining bourbon and rye is a bit unusual, the creators of Bourye couldn't help thinking of the jackalope, the mythical creature native to the American West that is part rabbit and antelope, and they used the image on the label.

Western lore tells that when cowboys would gather by their campfires to sing at night, jackalopes would frequently be heard singing back, mimicking the voices of the cowboys. When chased, the jackalope would use its vocal abilities to elude capture. Legend suggests the best way to catch a jackalope is to lure it with whiskey, as they have a particular fondness for the brown liquid. Once intoxicated, the animal becomes slower and easier to hunt.

*Events and Celebrations:*
High West hosts a number of events including an annual Kentucky Derby party and an annual Repeal Day celebration.

*Services offered other than production:*
Full service restaurant and bar. High West Distillery also hosts whiskey classes for the Park City Food and Wine Classic held annually the second weekend of July. Classes include pairing whiskey with food, and survey of world whiskeys.

*Interesting facts:*
- High West Distillery became the first legal distillery in Utah since 1870.
- High West Distillery and Saloon is the only ski-in gastro-distillery in the world.

*About:*
Located in Old Town Park City, Utah, at exactly 7,000 feet high in elevation in the Wasatch Range of the Rocky Mountains, High West Distillery and Saloon offers a truly unique experience as the world's only ski-in distillery and gastro-distillery.

Founded by prospectors in the late 1860s, Park City became one of the richest silver mining towns in the West and the best watering hole in Utah.

High West's proprietor and distiller, David Perkins, married his background as a biochemist to his love of bourbon and cooking and to his passion for the American West in order to bring the craft of small-batch distilling back to Utah.

*Management profile:*
**David Perkins**
David Perkins, proprietor and distiller, moved to Park City in 2004 to pursue his passion to make whiskey. With a background in biochemistry, a love of bourbon as a result of being raised in Georgia, and a love of cooking, David knew he was fated to make whiskey. After learning the secrets of making good whiskey from distillers in Kentucky and Scotland, David decided to start a distillery and make whiskey. When asked why he chose Utah, Pekins said, "It's so beautiful and where I want to live."

**James Dumas**
Born in New York, James Dumas is a graduate of the Culinary Institute of America in Hyde Park, New York, and he trained in Switzerland. James specializes in combining regional and seasonal ingredients, as well as innovative approaches and classic cooking techniques. His hospitality mantra is to offer unique food from the freshest ingredients, exceptional service, and a comfortable ambiance all paired with great wine and spirits.

*Management profile:*
**Brendan Coyle**
Born and raised in Minnesota, Brendan came to Salt Lake City in 1999 where he began his career with Red Rock Brewing Company. After several years learning the art and science of brewing, Brendan headed to Edinburgh, Scotland, where he gained an appreciation for distilling and completed a Master of Science in Brewing and Distilling Sciences at Heriot - Watt University. With a love for skiing and the southern desert, Brendan was drawn back to Utah to join High West in early 2008.

*Professional associations:* American Distilling Institute

*Future business plans and goals:* Continued success and profits

*Suggested recipes:*
**Dead Man's Boots** – A High West Original
- 1 ½ oz Rendezvous Rye
- 1 oz tequila
- 2 lime wedges
- ¼ oz simple syrup
- Ginger beer
- Lime wedge

  Muddle lime wedges and simple syrup together in a shaker.
  Add Rendezvous Rye and tequila.
  Shake and strain into a collins glass and fill with ginger beer.
  Garnish with a lime wedge.

**Stone Fence** – A High West Original
- 1 ½ oz Rendezvous Rye
- Apple cider
- Lemon twist

  In a rocks glass, add ice and Rendezvous Rye.
  Fill with apple cider.
  Garnish with a lemon twist.

High West Distillery
Park City, Utah

# Flag Hill Farm

Sebastian Lousada and Sabra Ewing, Owners

*Address:*
135 Ewing Road
Post Office Box 31
Vershire, Vermont 05079

*Phone:* 802-685-7724
*Fax:* Same as above - call first
*Email:* flaghillfarm@wildblue.net
*Website:* www.flaghillfarm.com

*Region:* Vermont

*Type*: Micro-distillery producing approximately 300 gallons per year

*Opened:* Winery in 1986. Distillery in 2002.

*Hours of operation:* Open by appointment only

*Tours:* Tours by appointment only

*Types of spirits produced:* Brandy eau de vie

*Names of spirits:*
- Pomme de Vie - Vermont Apple Brandy
- Stair's Pear - Vermont Pear Brandy

*Best known for:* Apple Brandy

*Average bottle price*: $17.50 to $20.00

*Distribution:* Vermont

*Highlighted spirits:*
## Pomme de Vie
Pomme de Vie is inspired by the French apple brandy Calvados. Also known as an eau de vie or "water of life," Flag Hill Farm apple brandy is smooth, dry and made from its own unsprayed apples in dozens of varieties. Pomme de Vie is double distilled, slowly fermented, and barrelaged hard to produce a brandy with maximum flavor and aromatics.

*Interesting facts:*
- Produced the first legal Vermont brandies since Prohibition
- Flag Hill Farm Winery and Distillery is certified organic.

*About:*
Located in Vershire, Vermont, Flag Hill Farm produces handmade spirits on a 250 acre organic family farm. Founders Sabra Ewing and Sebastian Lousada planted acres of orchards with more than 80 varieties of cider apples for their wine and brandy. Additionally, the winery is insulated with straw bales and is 100% solar powered.

*Management profile:*
## Sebastian Lousada
Sebastian Lousada began making traditional country wines in England when he was 12 years old. He now oversees the entire wine making process, managing the winery and the orchards.

## Sabra Ewing
Sabra Ewing, the founder of VerShare, a community organization dedicated to improving life in the small town of Vershire, Vermont, has deep roots in sustainable rural living. Ewing manages Flag Hill Farm's sales and marketing and networks with retailers and restaurateurs throughout Vermont.

*Professional associations:* Distilled Spirits Council of Vermont

*Future business plans and goals:*
Expand production and broaden distribution

*Suggested recipes:*
### Vermont Honey Bee
- 2 oz Pomme de Vie
- 2 tsp lemon juice
- 1 Tbs Vermont honey

    Combine with ice.
    Shake well.
    Strain and serve.

### Champlain Royale
- ½ teaspoon sugar syrup
- 1 oz chilled Pomme de Vie

    Pour into a champagne flute.
    Top off with Flag Hill Farm Vermont Sparkling Cider.

Flag Hill Farm
Vershire, Vermont

## Vermont Spirits Distilling Co.

Steve Johnson, President and CEO
Harry Gorman, Vice President and Distiller
Mimi Buttenheim, General Manager

*Physical address:*
Quechee Gorge Village
5573 Woodstock Road
Quechee, Vermont 05059

*Mailing address:*
Post Office Box 443
Quechee, Vermont 05059

*Phone:* 866-998-6352
*Email:* info@vermontspirits.com
*Website:* www.vermontspirits.com
*Facebook:* VermontSpirits
*Twitter:* @VermontSpirits

*Region:* Vermont

*Type:*
Micro-distillery producing less than 50,000 proof gallons per year

*Opened:* 2012

*Hours of operation:*
Daily from 10:00am to 5:00pm.   Call for seasonal hours.

*Tours:*   Tours are not offered but the process is explained in the tasting room.

*Types of spirits produced:*   Vodka

*Names of spirits:*
- Vermont Gold Vodka
- Vermont White Vodka
- Vermont Spirits Limited Release Vodka

*Average bottle price:* $20.00 to $50.00

*Distribution:* NH, ME, MA, RI, CT, NY, NJ, TN, VA, DC, WA, OR, Vermont Agency Liquor Stores, and the distillery

# VERMONT SPIRITS
## DISTILLING COMPANY

### ARTISANAL VODKAS
*from* VERMONT

*Highlighted spirits:*

**Vermont Gold Vodka**

Vermont Gold Vodka is pure, delicate, unflavored vodka handmade in small batches from the sugar of maple sap, the very essence of Vermont. Each spring in New England, freezing nights and warm sunny days allow the mature maple trees to pump out the sugar which has been converted from starch and stored during the dormant winter season. The trees release this sugar as sap which flows for less than six weeks a year.

Vermont Gold is tripledistilled and lightly filtered to allow the distinct quality of the maple fermentation to come through. That quality combines a fragrant nose with smoothness in the mouth and a slight warmth that delights the true lover of vodka.

Vermont Gold is the "singl-malt" of vodka, a pure expression of the state of Vermont.

**Vermont White Vodka**

Vermont White Vodka is tripledistilled in small batches from pure milk-sugar and local spring water. The vodka is lightly charcoal filtered after the distiller selects the center cut of each distillation. Vermont White is crystal clear, smooth with a delicate nose. It is excellent straight with a twist, or lightly chilled in a favorite cocktail.

**Vermont Spirits Limited Release Vodka**

Limited Release Vodka is produced entirely from early run maple sap. As the annual "sugaring" season begins, the first few flows of sap are referred to as "early run sap." This delicate liquid is light in color with a subtle, sweet flavor. It is this first harvest which has been prized for generations and is used to make the highest quality and most sought after maple syrup. This unique natural sugar coupled with proprietary distilling methods produces a vodka unlike any other. Limited Release Vodka is truly a connoisseur's vodka.

*Services offered other than production:* Tasting and retail sales

*Interesting facts:*
- Vermont White Vodka is lactose free.
- Both vodkas are gluten free.

*About:*

Vermont Spirits vodkas are handcrafted in New England's Green Mountain State. Originally established in 1998, the company has made steady strides over the years and its vodkas are now available throughout New England and New York state. While the business has grown, the approach to distilling has remained unchanged. Every stage in the production process is engineered in-house and hand-built, frequently employing simple gravity to transfer the evolving spirits between stages of production. The still was hand constructed by Vermont Spirits' own distiller, Harry Gorman.

Fractionating columns ordinarily used in industrial continuous flow stills are used in the batch-distilling process, leaving the most flavorful and smoothest alcohol from the "heart of the run." By combining this technology with the artisan techniques of batch distillation, Vermont Spirits is able take the purification to a new level. The result is a smoother, distinctly American-style vodka.

"Our goal is to produce vodkas with flavor....not flavored vodkas, and we distill each batch with the spirits connoisseur and lover of fine food in mind," says Harry.

*Professional associations:*   Distilled Spirits Council of Vermont and DISCUS

*Future business plans and goals:*   Expanded product line and broadened distribution

*Suggested recipes:*
**Chocolate Martini**
- 2 oz Vermont White Vodka
- 1 oz Godiva® Liqueur
- Dash of Bailey's® Irish Cream
- Hershey's® chocolate syrup

Swirl a ring of chocolate syrup around the inside of a martini glass.
In a mixing glass, add ingredients.
Shake with ice, and strain into the chocolate-swirled martini glass.

**Illumination**
- 1 ½ oz Vermont Gold Vodka
- ¾ oz Navan® Vanilla Liqueur
- ½ oz Cointreau®

Chill over ice.
Strain and serve up in a martini glass.
Garnished with a twist of orange.

Vermont Spirits Distilling Company
Quechee, Vermont

# A. Smith Bowman

One Bowman Drive
At Deep Run
Fredericksburg, Virginia 22408

*Phone:* 540-373-4555
*Fax:* 540-371-2236

*Website:* www.asmithbowman.com

*Type:* Micro-distillery

*Opened:* 1935, moved in 1988

*Hours of operation:*
The distillery is open from 7:00am to 3:30pm.
The gift shop is open from 10:00am to 3:00pm.

*Tours:* Tours of the facility are available at 10:00am, 2:00pm, and also by appointment.

*Types of spirits produced:* Whiskey (bourbon and special editions) gin, rum, and vodka

*Names of spirits:*
- Bowman Brothers Small Batch Virginia Straight Bourbon Whiskey
- John J. Bowman Single Barrel Virginia Straight Bourbon Whiskey
- Abraham Bowman Limited Edition Whiskey
- George Bowman Colonial Era Dark Caribbean Rum
- Deep Run Virginia Vodka
- Sunset Hills Virginia Gin
- Virginia Gentleman

*Awards and Recognitions:*

**Abraham Bowman Limited Edition Rye**
- Two Gold Medals, San Francisco World Spirits Competition

**Abraham Bowman Limited Edition 18 Year Old Bourbon, 138.6 proof**
- Gold Medal, MicroLiquor Spirit Awards

**John J. Bowman Single Barrel Bourbon**
- Silver Medal, San Francisco World Spirits Competition
- Double Gold Medal, San Francisco World Spirits Competition
- Triple Gold Medal, MicroLiquor Spirit Awards

**Bowman Brothers Bourbon**
- Gold Medal, San Francisco World Spirits Competition
- Silver Medal, San Francisco World Spirits Competition
- Triple Gold, MicroLiquor Spirit Awards

**Sunset Hills Gin**
- Gold Medal, MicroLiquor Spirit Awards

329

**Bowman Brothers Virginia Straight Bourbon Whiskey**

John, Abraham, Joseph and Isaac Bowman were Virginia militia officers in the American Revolutionary War. In 1779, they led thirty pioneer families to Madison County, Kentucky, and established Bowman's Station. Later, the brothers helped establish and settle Fayette County. They were legends, admired and respected by fellow settlers for their courage and bravery. This handcrafted bourbon whiskey is a tribute to these four heroic Bowman Brothers.

This small batch bourbon has been distilled three times using the finest corn, rye and malted barley. A unique copper still produces a distinct flavor. After many years of aging in new charred oak barrels, this 90 proof Virginia bourbon whiskey has hints of vanilla and oak while the finish is smooth and mellow.

**George Bowman Colonial Era Dark Caribbean Rum**

During the late 17th century, imported rum became exceedingly popular in colonial America. Early estimates of rum consumption in those colonies suggested every settler drank an average of three imperial gallons of rum each year. To support this demand, a substantial trade was developed between the Caribbean and the American colonies. The Sugar Act in 1764 disrupted this trade; nevertheless, the popularity of rum continued. This dark imported rum commemorates George Bowman and other early American colonists.

This special, pot-still rum has been distilled, aged and blended much like it was centuries ago. Imported from a small rum maker, this rum spent years aging in the Caribbean heat to garner its dark color and full flavor. The subtle aroma of coconut and vanilla are followed by the rich flavors of molasses, honey and brown sugar. Drink straight, over ice, or in your favorite rum cocktail.

**Deep Run Virginia Vodka**

Deep Run Lake rests quietly in central Virginia. However, Deep Run was once the site of defining conflicts during the War of Northern Aggression, like the Battle of Fredericksburg involving such generals as Robert E. Lee, Thomas J. Jackson and Ambrose E. Burnside. Today this scenic lake borders the A. Smith Bowman Distillery.

Deep Run Virginia Vodka is handcrafted for a smooth, clean taste in honor of its namesake. It is distilled seven times in very small batches to guarantee the utmost quality as well as a smooth, clean taste. It is then bottled at the distillery in Spotsylvania County near Fredericksburg, VA.

**Sunset Hills Virginia Gin**

Nestled among the hills of the rural northwestern section of Fairfax County lies the original seat of the Bowman Family called Sunset Hills Farm. The origin of the farm dates back to 1649 when King Charles II of England granted the land between the Potomac and the Rappahannock Rivers. In 1852, the 8,210 acre tract was deeded as Sunset Hills Farm.

The Bowman family embraced Sunset Hills as a home, farm and distillery for many years. This small batch gin is a tribute to this historic site and its link to old England.

Meticulously distilled in small batches with juniper and other botanicals, Sunset Hills Gin has an amazingly light and smooth taste.

*Services offered other than production:* Visitors center and tours

*About:*
A. Smith Bowman's distilling roots date back to the years before Prohibition. In 1927, Abram Smith Bowman and his sons relocated to Virginia, and in 1935 with the repeal of Prohibition they continued the family tradition with the distillation of bourbon. The original distillery, located on the Bowman family homestead in Fairfax County, Virginia, was called Sunset Hills Farm.

In response to the rapid growth of northern Virginia, the distillery was moved in 1988 and is now nestled in Spotsylvania County near the city of Fredericksburg, 60 miles away from the original location.

A. Smith Bowman Distillery is located on Deep Run, a tributary of the Rappahannock River. The distillery site is less than ¼ mile from the river at a place referred to as "Franklin's Crossing." It was at this location that the Union Army built the third set of pontoon bridges to cross the Rappahannock and assault the Confederate troops. The Union troops would have crossed this site on their way to the Confederate fortifications just to the west.

As a small, privately owned company, A. Smith Bowman Distillery continues the time-honored traditions on which it was founded. A. Smith Bowman produces an assortment of handcrafted spirits distilled from fine natural ingredients using the latest technology. This micro-distillery focuses on the production of premium spirits honoring the legacy of Virginia's first settlers.

The distillery site is picturesque and with many large trees along the banks of Deep Run, several of which were there during the Civil War. The buildings are classic post-Depression industrial architecture. Most are built with red brick on the outside as well as on the inside. Some are made with tile blocks on the inside. All of this provides a relaxed atmosphere in a very historic setting. Four major battlefields are within 17.7 miles of the distillery. The closest is only one mile away and houses the National Park Service Fredericksburg Battlefield Visitors Center.

A. Smith Bowman
Fredericksburg, Virginia

# Belmont Farms Distillery

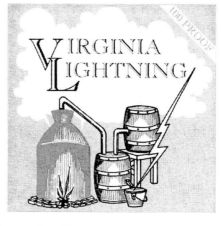

Chuck and Jeanette Miller, Owners

13490 Cedar Run Road
Culpeper, Virginia 22701

*Phone:* 540-825-3207
*Email:* jtmiller46@aol.com
*Website:* www.virginiawhiskey.com

*Region:* Virginia

*Type:* Micro-distillery producing approximately 10,000 proof gallons per year

*Opened:* 1987

*Hours of operation:* Tuesday through Saturday, 10:00am to 5:00pm

*Tours:* Tours are available from April 1st through December 15th Tuesday through Saturday, from 10:00am to 5:00pm

*Types of spirits produced:* Virginia whiskey and corn whiskey

*Ingredients:* All grains are grown on the Miller's farm.

*Names of spirits:*
- Kopper Kettle Virginian Whiskey
- Virginia Lightning Whiskey

*Average bottle price:* $14.95 to $19.95

*Distribution:* On-site gift shop and at Virginia ABC stores

*Highlighted spirits:*

## Virginia Lightning Whiskey
Virginia Lightning Whiskey is a true home grown beverage. It is produced in an American tradition, using an old family recipe and corn grown on the family farm. Quality and care go into every batch to ensure a timely delivery of fresh, twice-distilled corn whiskey.

## Kopper Kettle Virginian Whiskey
Kopper Kettle Virginian Whiskey is a triple-grain whiskey, double wood, and twice distilled. Beginning with a secret formula of corn, wheat, and barley, Kopper Kettle Virginian Whiskey is mashed and then fermented in the all-copper fermentation tanks and is then double distilled in a unique pot still. Kopper Kettle is then charcoal filtered and presoaked with oak and apple wood chips before it is aged in barrels for three years. Before bottling, the barrels are hand selected in three barrel batches to preserve its uniqueness.

*Events and Celebrations:* Hosts a farm show every October

*Services offered other than production:* Tours and gift shop

*Interesting facts:*
- Belmont Farms Distillery has appeared on "How It's Made" on the Science Channel and has been featured on "The History Channel" and "The National Geographic Channel." Additionally, Author Patricia Cornwell visited the still and did her own filming.

*About:*
Belmont Farms Distillery, a family owned and operated distillery located in Culpeper, Virginia, takes great pride in preserving a national tradition of copper-pot still fresh corn whiskey - "Virginia Lightning."

Until about 20 years ago, corn whiskey for popular consumption had been made in column stills handling thousands of gallons per hour. At Belmont Farms, the whiskey is produced in a genuine solid copper-pot still and handled with care to preserve all of the aroma and taste of a fine, fresh corn whiskey.

Belmont Farms Distillery follows a unique family recipe to cook the corn mash. Once the mash is cooked, it is sent to copper fermentation tanks for four days and is then distilled in a 2000 gallon copper-pot still that was constructed in 1933.

Although this form of whiskey production had been abandoned in the United States, Belmont Farms dedicates itself to the continuation of pot-still whiskey.

Once the whiskey leaves the pot still, it proceeds to the doubler where it is further distilled to increase the proof and ensure a quality product. The whiskey is then ready to be bottled and is sent to the bottling room where it is prepared for shipment.

Belmont Farms Distillery
Culpeper, Virginia

# Catoctin Creek Distilling Co. LLC

Scott and Becky Harris, Owners

37251C East Richardson Lane
Purcellville, Virginia  20132-3505

*Phone:*  540-751-8404
*Fax:*  540-751-3060
*Email:*  info@catoctincreek.com
*Website:*  www.catoctincreek.com
*Facebook:*  Catoctin Creek Distilling Company
*Twitter:*  @catoctincreek
*YouTube:*  Catoctin Creek Distilling Company
*LinkedIn:*  Catoctin Creek Distilling Company

*Type:*  Micro-distillery producing approximately 40-80 gallons per month

*Opened:*  February 2009

*Hours of operation:*
Monday through Friday, 8:00am to 3:00pm, and Saturday 11:00am to 4:00pm

*Tours:*  Tours and tastings daily

*Types of spirits produced:*  Rye whiskey (aged and unaged), gin, and fruit spirits

*Names of spirits:*
- Catoctin Creek Organic Roundstone Rye™
- Catoctin Creek Organic Mosby's Spirit™
- Catoctin Creek Organic Watershed Gin®
- Catoctin Creek Pearousia®
- Catoctin Creek 1757 Virginia Brandy™

*Best known for:*
Catoctin Creek Organic Roundstone Rye™

*Average bottle price*:  $38.90

*Distribution:*  Stores and restaurants in Virginia, Maryland, District of Columbia, Tennessee, California, Kentucky, and Washington, and at the distillery.

*Awards and Recognitions:*
**Catoctin Creek Organic Watershed Gin™**
- Silver Medal,
  2011 New York International Spirits Competition
- Gold Medal, 2011 Beverage Testing Institute

Photo by: Ed Felker, Mayfly Design

**Catoctin Creek Organic Mosby's Spirit™**

- Strong Recommendation 87 Point Rating, 2011 Ultimate Beverage Challenge
- Bronze Medal, 2010 American Distilling Institute Whiskey Competition
- Silver Medal, 2010 New York International Spirits Competition
- Silver Medal, 85 Pts. Highly Recommended, 2011 Beverage Testing Institute
- Very Good, 87 Pts. Strong Recommendation, 2011 Ultimate Spirits Challenge

**Catoctin Creek Organic Roundstone Rye™**

- Silver Medal, 2010 New York International Spirits Competition
- Scored 88 "Wise beyond their age," 2010 American Craft Spirits
- Silver Medal, 87 Pts. Highly Recommended, 2011 Beverage Testing Institute

*Highlighted spirits:*

**Catoctin Creek Organic Mosby's Spirit™**

Catoctin Creek Organic Mosby's Spirit™ is a multiple award winning, delicious rye "white whisky." It has a velvety smooth, sweet and undeniably pleasing cereal taste with floral notes and citrus. This spirit is reminiscent of the tradition of clear grain spirits common in the 19th century, and hearkens back to the fierce independence that forged our nation despite the conflict that almost destroyed it.

John S. Mosby was a Civil War colonel and leader of a local band of rangers called Mosby's Raiders. Called the "Gray Ghost" for his elusiveness during the war, Mosby was fiercely independent and ever loyal to his beloved Virginia.

**Catoctin Creek Organic Roundstone Rye™**

Catoctin Creek Organic Roundstone Rye™ is one of the only organic whiskeys in the entire nation. Aged in new Minnesota white oak casks, Roundstone Rye has a woody taste with notes of caramel, rich butter toffee, and a hint of lemon in the nose.

**Catoctin Creek Organic Watershed Gin®**

Catoctin Creek Organic Watershed Gin® pays respect to the Chesapeake Bay watershed which the Catoctin Creek flows into. Distilled from organic rye grain with a secret recipe of organic herbs and spices, Catoctin Creek Organic Watershed Gin® is amazingly complex with a rye base that shines through subtle citrus and cinnamon notes, essences of fresh cut hay, and a crisp juniper character.

**Catoctin Creek Pearousia®**

Pearousia® is a very special collaboration between Fabbioli Cellars and Catoctin Creek. Doug Fabbioli, owner and vintner at Fabbioli Cellars, produces a pear wine that Catoctin Creek distills into brandy and casks in oak. This pear brandy maintains the fresh aroma of the fruit as well as the caramel and vanilla of the oak.

*Services offered other than production:* Tastings and tours

Four times a year, Catoctin Creek Distilling Company offers an all-day seminar and hands on workshop teaching the fundamentals of operating a craft distillery. Anyone interested in the art of craft distilling, anyone thinking of starting their own distillery, or anyone who's just really interested in distilled spirits are encouraged to attend. More information on this limited seating workshop can be found on the website.

*Interesting facts:*
- First legal distillery in Loudoun County, Virginia since Prohibition
- Certified organic and kosher

*About:*

Located in Purcellville, Virginia, Catoctin Creek Distilling Company was founded by Becky and Scott Harris in 2009. Loudoun County, often called Washington D.C.'s Wine Country, is home to more than twenty vineyards, wineries, and now a distillery.

Photo by: Sarah Hauser, Virginia Tourism Corporation

"Catoctin" is a regional name. Pronounced Ka-TOCK-tin, the name is derived from the Indian tribal name "Kittocton" which, legend has it, meant "place of many deer." Catoctin describes a range of mountains and the creek which flows into the Potomac River and Chesapeake Watershed. Catoctin Creek® uses all organic raw material and is certified kosher by the Star-K certification agency; it is proud to offer one of the nation's only lines of kosher spirits.

Catoctin Creek Distillery is also environmentally friendly. Spent rye mash is collected and given away freely to farmers as an organic and nutrient-rich livestock feed minimizing the impact on landfill and sewage systems. Additionally, the distillery buys inventory and services from local farms, orchards, vineyards and businesses. This not only reduces shipping and transportation costs, but also reduces the carbon footprint.

*Management profile:*

**Scott Harris**

Scott Harris, co-owner, graduated with honors from Georgia Tech. He spent years building a software career in telecommunication systems and government IT solutions, then he traded it all for the chance to run his own distillery. Liquors of all types are his greatest love (besides Becky, of course).

**Becky Harris**

Becky Harris, co-owner and master distiller, graduated with honors from the University of

Photo by: Mark Rhodes

336

Wisconsin, Madison. As a chemical engineer, she worked at Amoco, YDK America, and CIBA, specializing in industrial processes and production systems. Becky applied this knowledge to something she loved - making fine distilled spirits. If there is a fruit, vegetable, tuber or root with starch or sugar in it, you can bet that Becky will try to distill it.

*Professional associations:* American Distilling Institute and DISCUS

*Future business plans and goals:* Facility expansion

*Suggested recipes:*

**Virginia Grasshopper** - Courtesy of Stephanie Wolf

- *1 oz Catoctin Creek Roundstone Rye Whisky*
- *1 oz Creme De Menthe*
- *1 oz Creme de Cacao*
- *½ oz Limoncello*
- *1 oz cream or half and half*

Shake over ice (shaking the cream gives it a nice frothy head).

**Raspberry Collins -** Courtesy of Stephanie Wolf

- 1 oz Catoctin Creek Organic Watershed Gin
- ½ oz lemon juice
- ½ oz simple syrup
- 6 raspberries

Shake over ice.
Pour in tall glass.
Top with soda water.

Catoctin Creek Distilling Company LLC
Purcellville, Virginia

# Copper Fox Distillery

COPPER FOX DISTILLERY

Richard Wasmund, Owner / Master Distiller

9 River Lane
Sperryville, Virginia  22740

*Phone:*  540-987-8554
*Email:*  rwasm@aol.com
*Website:*  www.copperfox.biz
*Facebook:*  Copper Fox Distillery
*Twitter:*  @cufoxdistillery
*YouTube:*  Copper Fox Distillery

*Region:*  Northern Virginia

*Type:*  Micro-distillery producing approximately 400 gallons per month

*Opened:*  2005

*Hours of operation:*  Monday through Saturday, 10:00am to 6:00pm

*Tours:*  Tours of the facility are available.

*Types of spirits produced:*  Single malt whisky and rye whisky

*Names of spirits:*
- Wasmund's Single Malt Whisky
- Wasmund's Single Malt Spirit
- Copper Fox Rye Whisky
- Wasmund's Rye Spirit

*Average bottle price*:  $22.00 to $46.00

*Distribution:*  Available in 24 states across the U.S.

*Awards and Recognitions:*
**Wasmund's Single Malt Whisky**
- Gold Medal 92 Points, 2011 Beverage Testing Institute
- Gold Medal 93 Points, 2009 Beverage Testing Institute
**Copper Fox Rye Whisky**
- Gold Medal 94 Points, 2011 Beverage Testing Institute

*Highlighted spirits:*
**Wasmund's Single Malt Whisky**
Introduced in the fall of 2006, Wasmund's Single Malt Whisky combines the best of the grand tradition of single malt whisky with creative and unique innovations for aging and flavoring.

338

### Wasmund's Single Malt Spirit

Wasmund's Single Malt Spirit is Wasmund's Single Malt Whisky bottled at barrel strength prior to aging. Single Malt is handcrafted from 100% thoroughbred barley developed and grown locally and exclusively for Copper Fox Distillery. Single Malt was introduced in December of 2007.

### Wasmund's Rye Spirit

Wasmund's Rye Spirit is Wasmund's Rye Whisky bottled at barrel strength prior to aging. It was introduced in February of 2008.

### Copper Fox Rye Whisky

Copper Fox Rye Whisky, introduced in the fall of 2008, is made with an extraordinarily generous amount of smoked malt. The mash bill is 2/3 Virginia rye and 1/3 Virginia thoroughbred hand-malted barley. It's kiln dried with applewood and cherry wood smoke. Copper Fox is double- pot stilled to between 150 and 160 proof and aged with a progressive series of new and used applewood and oak chips inside used bourbon barrels.

*Services offered other than production:* Tours and retail

*About:*
The Copper Fox Distillery, located at the foot of the Blue Ridge Mountains in Sperryville, Virginia, is the brainchild of Founder Richard Wasmund.

In early 2000, he began thinking about how he could make a distinct whisky by using special fruitwood peat and fruitwood barrels in the traditional whisky making process.

He explored most of the distilleries in the U.S. then traveled to Scotland where he gained a greater appreciation for the skill, passion and dedication needed to craft distill. His experience further reinforced a conviction that his ideas were in fact new to the whisky world, and were unique enough that he could make a commercially viable, distinct product. During a six week internship at Bowmore Distillery on Islay, Richard worked each of the three shifts, six days a week. He absorbed all he could, took notes, and talked to all the men who, combined, held more than a century of whiskey making experience.

After Scotland, Richard continued experimenting at home, formed a business plan and turned that plan into action. The distillery was built in 2005.

*Future business plans and goals:* Increased production

Copper Fox Distillery
Sperryville, Virginia

# Reservoir Distillery

David Cuttino, General Manager and Co-owner
James H. Carpenter, Master Distiller and Co-owner

1800 A Summit Avenue
Richmond, Virginia 23230

*Phone:* 804-912-2621
*Website:* www.reservoirdistillery.com

*Region:* Northeast U.S.

*Type:* Micro-distillery producing less than 5,000 proof gallons per year

*Opened:* 2009

*Hours of operation:* Around the clock operation

*Tours:* No tours are offered.

*Types of spirits produced:*
Bourbon, rye and wheat whiskey (all 100 proof)

*Names of spirits:*
Reservoir Bourbon, Rye and Wheat Whiskey

*Best known for:* Bourbon

*Average bottle price:*
$40.00 per 375ml, $80.00 per 750ml

*Distribution:*
Virginia, Maryland, Delaware, Florida, and
Washington DC

*About:*
Reservoir Distillery embraces the principles of a traditional southern handcrafted whiskey. It's grain is locally sourced and ground on site for cooking and fermentation. The mash is distilled twice and aged in small, new American oak barrels. Each batch, from its southern bourbon, (a spicier cousin to bourbon in a rye whiskey) to its pioneering true wheat whiskey, is tasted regularly until it is perfect. Every bottle is carefully hand filled, waxed and signed by the distillers to demonstrate their commitment to authenticity and accountability. Reservoir Distillery bottles at 100 proof because of the flavor of high quality spirits transition relative to proof and ambient temperature. Founders David Cuttino and Jay Carpenter, childhood friends from Richmond, Virginia, have finally given the Commonwealth a classic quality bourbon of its own.

340

*Management profile:*
**David Cuttino**
David Cuttino, general manager and co-owner of Reservoir Distillery, is a former bond trader and graduate of Virginia Tech and Columbia University. While the financial markets were slipping into crisis mode, he began to think about his next step in life.

After reading an article about George Washington's distillery at Mount Vernon, the wheels started to turn and he began to research the distilling industry. A short time later, he quit his job and spent the next six months interning at Tuthilltown Spirits in Gardiner, New York. Realizing early that the startup process was too daunting for a single individual to handle, he partnered with his childhood friend, Jay Carpenter, who shared his enthusiasm and vision for bringing hand-crafted bourbon back to the Old Dominion. Since Carpenter grew up surrounded by Goochland County's rich farm country and history of distilling, it was the perfect partnership to make Reservoir Distillery a reality.

*Future business plans and goals:* Increased production and distribution

Reservoir Distillery
Richmond, Virginia

## Virginia Distillery Company

George Moore, Chairman
John McCray, President

299 Eades Lane
Post Office Box 509
Lovingston, Virginia  22949

*Phone:*  434-325-1299
*Email:*  info@vadistillery.com
*Website:*  www.vadistillery.com
*Facebook:*  Virginia Distillery Company, Eades Whisky
*Twitter:*  @VADistillery

*Region:*  Virginia

*Type*:  Craft-distillery

*Opened:*  2010

*Types of spirits produced:*  Whisky

*Names of spirits:*
- Eades Double Malt Whisky
- Virginia Single Malt Whisky
- Virginia New Make Spirit
- Virginia Highland Malt Whisky

*Best known for:*  Eades Double Malt Whisky

*Average bottle price*:  $70.00

*Distribution:*  Eades Double Malt whiskies are currently available in Virginia ABC stores as well as restaurants and retail stores in Washington DC, Maryland, Delaware, and Chicago.

*Awards and Recognitions:*
**Eades 2nd Edition Islay Double Malt Whisky**
- Gold Medal Score of 93, 2011 Beverage Testing Institute

**Eades 2nd Edition Speyside Double Malt Whisky**
- Gold Medal Score of 92, 2011 Beverage Testing Institute

**Eades 2nd Edition Highland Double Malt Whisky**
- Gold Medal Score of 91, 2011 Beverage Testing Institute

*Highlighted spirits:*

## Virginia Single Malt

Virginia Single Malt is double distilled using authentic, Scottish-made copper-pot stills and is aged in charred American white oak casks previously used to age bourbon in nearby Kentucky; these are the same types of casks preferred in Scotland and in single malt distilleries worldwide. After a minimum of four years, the spirit will turn from clear to an amber color and will develop a nuanced flavor.

## Eades Double Malt Whisky

Named for the founder's home in Eades (rhymes with "needs") Hollow near Lovingston, Virginia, Eades Double Malt Whiskies represent the quintessential malt whisky experience from each of Scotland's major distilling regions – Islay ("EYE-lah"), Speyside and Highland.

*About:*

Located in Virginia's Blue Ridge Mountains, Virginia Distillery Company (VDC) is committed to producing high quality single malt whisky by employing traditional distilling techniques, including an authentic copper-pot still from Scotland and proper aging of its whiskies.

Based on the experience of single malt distilleries in warm climates such as Singapore, VDC expects that some of its whisky will age faster in Virginia's hot summers. The sharp change from summer to winter may also accelerate the interaction of the wood with the whisky. It will be monitoring the whisky to determine the effect and, with luck, will have more fine whisky earlier than the current timeline.

Ingredients for Virginia Distillery's products are sourced from the upper Midwest. Additionally, Virginia Distillery repurposes waste products such as the draff from the malted barley for cattle feed and the spent lees for pig feed. It installed an extensive drain field to return the water used in production to the same ground.

*Management profile:*
John McCray (pictured top right), Pat Jones (pictured center left) and Joe Hungate (pictured lower right) comprise the management team. Friends for decades and early single malt enthusiasts, they took over the management of the distillery bringing extensive business and marketing experience to the operation. With experienced project management and financing from new investors, they are in the process of completing the vision of distilling single malt whisky in central Virginia. When fully operational, the distillery will have the capacity to produce 100,000 cases of spirits. This size puts it on the high end of the craft distilling category.

Key to the Virginia Distillery Company's commitment to authenticity are its authentic Scottish copper-pot stills. These stills are critical to the double distillation and small batch characteristics that single malt is famous for which you don't get with continuous operation stills and ones suitable for rum and other spirits. The adherence to Scottish tradition is strong but the Virginia terroir will be evident in this New World whisky.

Building an authentic distillery is a substantial investment and a complex design task. That meant they needed not only the best copper-pot stills and finest ingredients, but also the right expertise. For that task, VDC brought in one of the world's leading experts, Harry Coburn. Harry Coburn spent many years managing distilleries and has overseen the building of them in such diverse places as Cape Breton, Bhutan, and in Korea. Coburn oversaw the purchase of the equipment, the layout of the building, and the design of the intricate stills, mashtuns, pumps and piping.

*Future business plans and goals:* To continue to produce quality spirits

*Suggested recipe:*
## Gov. Nelson's Signature
- 1oz Eades Double Malt Speyside
- 1oz fresh squeezed orange juice (strained)
- ¾ oz sweet vermouth
- ¾ oz Cherry Heering cherry brandy

    Shake all ingredients over ice.
    Strain into a chilled cocktail glass.
    Garnish with a maraschino cherry.

Virginia Distillery Company
Lovingston, Virginia

# Bainbridge Organic Distillers

Keith Barnes and Patrick Barnes, Owners

9727 Coppertop Loop NE, Unit 101
Bainbridge Island, Washington  98110

*Email:* General info:  info@bainbridgedistillers.com
          Mr. Barnes:  barnes@bainbridgedistillers.com
*Website:* www.bainbridgedistillers.com
*Facebook:* Bainbridge Organic Distillers

*Region:*  Washington

*Type:*  Craft-distillery producing approximately 36,000 – 46,000 liters annually

*Opened:* 2009

*Hours of operation:* Monday through Friday, 10:00am to 5:00pm
                      Saturday, 10:00am to 3:00pm and closed Sundays

*Tours:*  Tours are available.

*Types of spirits produced:*
Vodka, whiskey, gin, and bourbon

*Names of spirits:*
- Bainbridge Legacy Organic Vodka
- Bainbridge Battle Point Organic Whiskey
- Bainbridge Heritage Organic Gin
- Bainbridge Rolling Bay Organic Rye
- Bainbridge Anthem Organic Applejack

*Average bottle price:*  $32.95 to $46.95

*Distribution:*
Products are distributed through Washington liquor stores, online retailers and at the distillery.

*Awards and Recognitions:*
**Bainbridge Legacy Organic Vodka**
- #3 Vodka 92 Rating, 2011 Ultimate Spirits Competition

**Bainbridge Battle Point Organic Whiskey**
- 91 Rating, The Tasting Panel Magazine

*Highlighted spirits:*

### Bainbridge Legacy Organic Vodka

Bainbridge Legacy Organic Vodka is distilled from organic wheat from Walla Walla County in Washington. The grain is ground and fermented in small batches and distilled slowly to retain its subtle flavor. The final product is distilled six times and has a subtle and pleasing toasty grain taste, hints of citrus and vanilla, and a smooth and soft finish.

### Bainbridge Battle Point Organic Whiskey

Bainbridge Battle Point Organic Whiskey is distilled from wheat grown in the Dungeness River Delta near where the Straights of Juan De Fuca empty out into the Pacific Ocean. This grain has a truly unique character and pedigree that is a good match to the distillery's island location. The whiskey is aged in small, new, white oak barrels specially selected for the qualities and structure of the wood. ·The final whiskey presents a subtle grain profile backed with vanilla, caramel and eucalyptus notes, a little char, and a hint of high fruit.

### Bainbridge Heritage Organic Gin

Bainbridge Heritage Organic Gin starts with the same wheat as is used in Bainbridge Legacy Organic Vodka, but it is fermented using a different yeast creating a more subtle flavor base. The final distillate is infused with an all-organic blend of juniper, cardamom, orris, licorice and angelica root, citrus peel, fennel, and local spruce. The nose is fresh and full, and the flavor palate is classic dry gin but with a freshness and evergreen note that makes it uniquely delicious.

*Services offered other than production:*
Tasting, tours, and workshops

*Interesting facts:* First distillery producing USDA Certified Organic spirits

*About:*
Bainbridge Organic Distillers was founded with the goal of creating organic luxury spirits made from local grains.

Keith and Patrick Barnes, a father and son team, began operations in May of 2009 by installing custom built Vendome distilling equipment in their 3,600 square foot distillery. Over the next several months, they perfected their skills of operating the equipment, grain handling and mashing, distilling, and barrel maturation.

346

Late fall 2009 saw the first stocks of whiskey distilled and laid into new oak barrels. The distillery released its first product, Bainbridge Legacy Organic Vodka, in May of 2010, and released its first whiskey, Bainbridge Battle Point Organic Whiskey, in November of 2010. In January 2011, the first batch of gin, Bainbridge Heritage Organic Gin, was started, as well as the first bourbon, Bainbridge Rolling Bay Bourbon.

The Barnes strive to present the tastes of their area's grains in a way that observes product type standards while treating the drinker to subtle, unique and delicious variations on the standard themes.

Bainbridge Organic Distillers
Bainbridge Island, Washington

# Dry Fly Distilling

Don Poffenroth, Owner
Kent Fleischmann, Owner

1003 E. Trent, Suite 200
Spokane, Washington 99202

*Phone:* 509-489-2112
*Fax:* 509-489-3245
*Email:* don@dryflydistilling.com, kent@dryflydistilling.com
*Website:* www.dryflydistilling.com
*Facebook:* Dry Fly Distilling
*Twitter:* @dryflydistiller

*Region:* Pacific Northwest

*Type*: Micro-distillery selling approximately 10,000 cases per year

*Opened:* May 2007

*Hours of operation:*
Monday through Friday, 8:00am to 5:00pm
Saturday, 10:00am to 3:00pm

*Tours:* Tours are available.

*Types of spirits produced:* Vodka, gin, and multiple whiskies

*Names of spirits:*
- Dry Fly Washington Wheat Vodka
- Dry Fly Washington Wheat Gin
- Dry Fly Washington Wheat Whiskey
- Dry Fly Washington Bourbon Whiskey
- Dry Fly Washington Triticale Whiskey

*Best known for:*
A "PMD" - Dry Fly Vodka from the freezer and a splash of cranberry juice

*Average bottle price*: $29.95 to $49.95

*Distribution:* Available at the distillery and in more than 30 U.S. states, Europe and the Caribbean.

*Awards and Recognitions:*
**Dry Fly Washington Wheat Vodka**
- Double Gold Medal, 2009 San Francisco World Spirits Competition
- Best in Show, 2009 San Francisco World Spirits Competition

*Awards and Recognitions:*

**Dry Fly Washington Wheat Whiskey**
- Triple Gold Medal, 2011 MicroLiquor Spirit Awards
- Silver Medal, 2011 New York World Wine & Spirits Competition
- Bronze Medal, 2010 San Francisco World Spirits Competition

**Dry Fly Distilling**
- Distillery of the Year, 2011 American Distilling Institute

*Highlighted spirits:*

**Dry Fly Washington Wheat Vodka**
Caramel overtones, a butterscotch nose, and vanilla on the finish.

**Dry Fly Washington Wheat Gin**
Six NW botanicals - juniper, fuji apple, coriander, lavender, mint, and hops are combined in this gin.

*Events and Celebrations:* Hosts numerous events

*Services offered other than production:* Tasting, retail sales, and distilling school

*Interesting facts*
- Dry Fly Distillery is Washington's first craft distillery producing vodka, gin, and whiskey.
- The "Dry Fly" company name stemmed from Kent and Don's mutually shared passion for fly fishing.

*About:*
While knee-deep in Montana's Gallatin River, it occurred to co-founders Kent Fleischmann and Don Poffenroth how privileged they were to live, work, and fish in one of the most amazing places on Earth. They felt so fortunate that they wanted to find some way to share the natural beauty and purity of the great Northwest. What better way than by producing fly fishing-inspired distilled spirits made from only the purest locally grown ingredients?

With less than 100 distilleries in domestic operation, Kent and Don recognized an opportunity to create a locally owned and operated craft distillery. Located in Spokane, Washington, Dry Fly Distilling produces vodka, gin, and whiskey utilizing Christian Carl pot stills manufactured in Goppingen, Germany.

*Management profile:*
Patrick Donovan (left), lead distiller; Don Poffenroth (on ladder), co-owner; and Kent Fleischmann (right), co-owner.

*Future business plans and goals:* Increased production

Dry Fly Distilling
Spokane, Washington

# Ezra Cox Distillery

Ezra Cox III, Owner/Manager

719 N. Tower Avenue
Centralia, Washington   98531

*Email:* ezracoxiii@gmail.com
*Website:* www.ezracox.com
*Facebook:* Ezra Cox Distillery

*Region:* Pacific Northwest

*Type:* Micro-distillery producing approximately 1,000 gallons per year

*Opened:* December 2011

*Hours of operation:* Friday evenings and weekends

*Tours:* Tours are available.

*Types of spirits produced:* Moonshine and whiskey

*Names of spirits:*
- Ezra Cox Moonshine
- Ezra Cox Whiskey
- Ezra Cox Smoked Whiskey

*Average bottle price:* $20.00 to $30.00

*Distribution:*
Tasting room and Washington state liquor store network

*Highlighted spirits:*
**Ezra Cox Moonshine**
This is an unaged white whiskey made from 100% malted barley.

**Ezra Cox Whiskey**
This is an oak aged whiskey made from 100% malted barley.

**Ezra Cox Smoked Whiskey**
This whiskey made from 100% malted barley, a portion of which has been smoked.

*Events and Celebrations:*
The distillery hosts a variety of community and group events.  Situated on the main commercial street in old downtown Centralia, Ezra Cox Distillery has a large tasting room with full visibility and access to the production area.  It is well suited for entertaining large groups to include tasting, food service and tours.

*Services offered other than production:* Tours and tastings

*About:*
Ezra Cox Distillery is a family business built by a small group of friends and entrepreneurs committed to long-term success. They focus on spirits produced from 100% malted barley in the single malt Scotch tradition and do not include adjuncts such as corn or other grains, flavorings, etc.

Only three ingredients are used in their spirits. The water is snow-melt from the Cascade Mountain range, the brewing barley is 100% sourced from Washington state farms, and the yeast strain is from Scotland. The process begins by brewing an exceptional beer using a time-tested process. The beer is then distilled into the finest spirit possible, preserving the flavor contribution of the malt and yeast from the mash and fermentation.

*Management profile:*
**Ezra Cox III**
Ezra Cox was brewmaster and production manager of a microbrewery for 12 years. During this time the brewery grew from a local start-up to a recognized brand with regional distribution. Cox left that position to pursue the challenge of building his own brewery and brand. While in the business planning stages of this new venture, Washington state enacted new legislation regarding distilling. Cox changed his focus to building a distillery, foreseeing this as a new industry with a greater opportunity for growth and creative potential. He assembled a small team of key individuals with the skills to finance, build and operate a growing distillery and brand.

*Future business plans and goals:* National branding and increased production

Ezra Cox Distillery
Centralia, Washington

# Golden Distillery

Bob Stilnovich and Jim Caudill, Owners

9746 Samish Island Road
Bow, Washington 98232

*Phone:* 360-542-8332
*Email:* goldendistillery@gmail.com
*Website:* www.goldendistillery.com

*Region:* Skagit Valley Washington

*Type:* Micro-distillery producing approximately 2,000 gallons per year

*Opened:* October 2010

*Hours of operation:* Friday and Saturday, 11:00am to 5:00pm

*Tours:* Tours are available.

*Types of spirits produced:* Whiskey and brandy

*Names of spirits:*
- Golden Samish Bay Whiskey
- Golden Samish Bay Whiskey Reserve
- Golden White Gold Whiskey
- Golden Apple Brandy

*Best known for:* Single malt whiskey

*Average bottle price:* $40.00 to $50.00

*Distribution:* Spirits are available at the distillery and in Washington state liquor stores.

*Awards and Recognitions:*
**Golden Apple Brandy**
- Nationwide Tasting Medal

*Highlighted spirits:*
**Golden Samish Bay Whiskey**
Golden Samish Bay Whiskey is a single malt whiskey with deep smokey flavors made from 100% Washington-grown premium grain and pure filtered water.

**Golden White Gold Whiskey**
Golden White Gold Whiskey is a single malt whiskey with light flavors that capture the sweetness of Washington barley.

352

*Services offered other than production:* Tastings, tours, and retail sales

*Interesting facts:*
- Golden Distillery is the first distillery to open in Skagit County.

*About:* Golden Distillery is a small micro-distillery located just west of the Chuckanut Mountains on the quaint hideaway of Samish Island.

"Golden Boys" Jim Caudill (left) and Bob Stillnovich (right) opened the distillery in 2010 for the challenge of producing top notch spirits. Jim and Bob use 100% Washington grain and fruit to create local artisan-style spirits.

*Management profile:*
Jim Caudill and Bob Stillnovich are both retired restaurant owners who adopted a common passion for distilling. They live on Samish Island with their wives, who introduced them.

*Future business plans and goals:* Expand product line and broaden distribution

Golden Distillery
Bow, Washington

# It's 5 O'clock Somewhere

Colin Levi, Owner

207 Mission Avenue
Cashmere, Washington 98801

*Phone:* 509-679-9771
*Email:* 5oclock@5oclocksomewheredistillery.com
*Website:* www.5oclockdistillery.com

*Region:* Central Washington

*Type:* Craft-distillery producing approximately 8,000 gallons per year

*Opened:* December 2009

*Hours of operation:*
Call for an appointment on Monday, Tuesday and Sunday;
Wednesday through Friday, 10:00am to 5:00pm; Saturday, 1:00pm to 5:00pm

*Tours:* Tours are available by appointment.

*Types of spirits produced:*
Eau de vie, brandy, grappa, whiskey, gin and fruit liqueurs

*Names of spirits:*
- Block and Tackle Moonshine 100% Corn Whiskey Unaged
- Block and Tackle Sunshine 100% Corn Whiskey Aged
- Northwest Dry Gin
- Grappa
- Eaux de Vie: Voignier, Apple, Pear, Apricot, Cherry, and Plum
- Liqueur: Raspberry, Blueberry, Elderberry, Blackberry, Pear, Apricot, and Cherry

*Best known for:* Block and Tackle Moonshine

*Average bottle price:* $30.00 and up

*Distribution:* Tasting room and liquor stores

*Highlighted spirits:*
## Block and Tackle Moonshine
Block and Tackle Moonshine is 100% corn whiskey with an unmistakable smell and taste of corn followed by green apple, pepper, and caramel.

## Northwest Dry Gin
Northwest Dry Gin is a unique gin made from the finest botanicals sourced from around the world.

*Services offered other than production:* Tastings, tours and retail store

*Interesting facts*
- North Central Washington's seventh craft distillery since Prohibition

*About:*
It's Five O'clock Somewhere was established in December 2009 by Colin Levi, a chef with a vision of creating high quality spirits from the fruits and grains available in Washington. Since then, Levi has crafted a Chilean-style brandy made from grapes, a pear brandy, a moonshine (an unaged corn whiskey), and a couple of other styles of grain-based whiskeys. It currently has an 8,000 square foot production facility in Cashmere. Colin is always on the hunt for high quality ingredients. All possible ingredients are sourced from within Washington state.

*Professional associations:*
Washington Distillers Guild

*Future business plans and goals:*
Continued growth

*Suggested recipes:*
**The Cashmere Corny Apple**
- 1 oz Block & Tackle Moonshine
- 1 oz Apple Eau de Vie
- ½ oz caramel syrup

Stir and serve over ice.


**Northwest Dry Martini**
- 2 oz frozen Northwest Dry Gin
- 1 dash absinthe
- ½ a fresh lime juiced

Stir and serve in a frozen martini glass.
Garnish with a cocktail onion, green olive, or both.



It's 5 O'clock Somewhere
Cashmere, Washington

# J.P. Trodden Small Batch Bourbon

Mark Nesheim, Owner and Distiller
Jennifer Seversen, Owner

18646 142nd Ave NE
Woodinville, Washington  98072

*Phone:*  206-399-6291
*Fax:*  425-908-7741
*Email:*  Mark Nesheim:  mark@jptroddendistilling.com
            Jennifer Seversen:   jennifer@jptroddendistilling.com
*Website:*  Under construction
*Facebook:*  JP Trodden, JP Trodden Distilling

*Region:*  Pacific Northwest

*Type:*  Micro-distillery producing approximately 800 cases per year

*Opened:*  May 2011

*Hours of operation:*   Monday through Friday, 7:00am to 5:00pm
                          Saturday, 8:00am to 1:00pm

*Tours:*   Tours are available by appointment.

*Types of spirits produced:*  Bourbon

*Names of spirits:* JP Trodden Small Batch Bourbon

*Average bottle price*:  $62.00

*Distribution:*  Bourbon will start selling in September 2013 from the tasting room and at liquor outlets in Washington state.

*Highlighted spirits:*
**JP Trodden Small Batch Bourbon**
This bourbon has a caramel nose and the aroma of toasted bread and nuts with a whisp of smoke and leather.

*Events and Celebrations:*  Release party September 2013

*Services offered other than production:*  Tasting room with retail merchandise in 2013

*About:*
J.P. Trodden is named after Owner/Distiller Mark Nesheim's grandfather (right), who lived in Chesaw, Washington, several miles south of Canada. J.P.'s father was the first mail carrier in the region and, after a time, J.P. took over his route which happened to be during Prohibition. Legend has it that old J.P. was known to stick a few bottles of whiskey in his mailbag and bring it back over the border to share with his friends. Not bootlegging, just sharing in the great spirit of J.P. Trodden, Mark is making bourbon to share, too.

Production began in June 2011 and the first barrel was filled in August.

Part of what makes JP Trodden Small Batch Bourbon unique is that the owners are only making one product - bourbon. Their bourbon is 100% American. The copper still was made by a coppersmith in Eugene, Oregon, and the corn and winter wheat are grown on a small family farm in Washington.

*Future business plans and goals:*
Releasing a 6 year aged bourbon, JP Trodden Reserve

J.P. Trodden Small Batch Bourbon
Woodinville, Washington

357

# Pacific Distillery LLC

Marc Bernhard, Owner and Master Distiller

18808-142nd Avenue NE #4B
Woodinville, Washington 98072

*Phone:* 425-350-9061
*Fax:* 425-645-7941
*Email:* mbernhard@pacificdistillery.com
*Website:* www.pacificdistillery.com
*Facebook:* Pacific Distillery
*Twitter:* @PacificDistill

*Region:* Northwestern Washington

*Type:* Micro-distillery producing less than 60,000 gallons per year

*Opened:* 2008

*Tours:* Tours are offered.

*Types of spirits produced:* Absinthe and gin

*Names of spirits:*
- Voyager Single Batch Distilled Gin
- Pacifique Absinthe Verte

*Average bottle price:* $30.00 to $63.00

*Distribution:*
Pacific Distillery spirits are mainly sold in Washington liquor stores with limited distribution in Oregon, California, Illinois, New York, Connecticut, Montana, and Louisiana. Licensing prohibits on-site tastings or product sales.

*Awards and Recognitions:*
**Voyager Single Batch Distilled Gin**
- Double Gold Medal, 2011 San Francisco International Spirits Competition
- Gold Medal, 2010 Beverage Testing Institute

**Pacifique Absinthe Verte**
- Gold Medal, 2011 San Francisco International Spirits Competition
- Recognized as one of the "Top 50 Spirits of 2010" by Wine Enthusiast Magazine

**Voyager Single Batch Distilled Gin**

Voyager Single Batch Distilled Gin is a handcrafted American gin in the London dry style. Artisan distilled using only the finest grain spirits and select, all-organic plants, herbs and spices from around the globe, Voyager Gin is a world class product that carries forward the traditions of 19th century craft distillers.

The ingredients are placed into a hand-hammered copper alambic-pot still and carefully distilled to ensure that the finished flavor and aromas are fully integrated and complementary. The result is an ultra-premium spirit.

**Pacifique Absinthe Verte Supérieure**

Pacifique Absinthe Verte Supérieure is a super-premium absinthe, handcrafted in the historic Franco-Swiss style. Made in exact accordance with a classic 1855 French recipe, Pacifique is reminiscent of the kind of absinthe one would drink in 19th century France.

Pacifique is artisan distilled using historic distilling techniques in a hand-hammered copper alambic-pot still, the finest grain spirits, and selected botanicals chosen from around the globe.

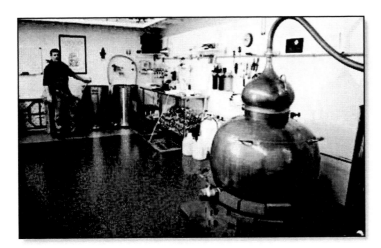

*About:*
Pacific Distillery is a small, family owned and operated distillery located in the heart of Woodinville, Washington's, wine country, just north of Seattle.

Specializing in making world-class hand-made spirits using Old World methods, recipes and equipment, Pacific Distillery products are distilled in a genuine direct-fired 500 liter copper alambic-pot still using all- organic botanicals.

*Professional associations:* American Distilling Institute

*Future business plans and goals:* Contract distillation projects

Pacific Distillery LLC
Woodinville, Washington

# Sidetrack Distillery

Larry Person, Partner
Linda Person, Partner
David O'Neal, Partner

27010 78th Ave S.
Kent, Washington 98032

*Phone:* 206-963-5079
*Email:* info@sidetrackdistillery.com
*Website:* www.sidetrackdistillery.com
*Facebook:* Sidetrack Distillery

*Region:* Green River Valley, Kent, Washington

*Type:* Micro-distillery

*Opened:* July 2011

*Hours of operation:*
Tasting Room hours
      Saturdays 11:00am to 5:00pm
      Sundays 11:00am to 4:00pm
      Weekdays by appointment

*Tours:* Tours are offered by appointment.

*Types of spirits produced:*
Fruit liqueurs and brandies

*Names of spirits:*
- Sidetrack Distillery Raspberry Liqueur
- Sidetrack Distillery Strawberry Liqueur
- Sidetrack Distillery Blackberry Liqueur
- Sidetrack Distillery Blueberry Liqueur
- Sidetrack Distillery Strawberry Brandy
- Sidetrack Distillery Blueberry Brandy
- Sidetrack Distillery Blackberry Brandy

*Best known for:* Raspberry Liqueur

*Average bottle price*: Liqueurs $24.95, 375ml; Brandies $49.95, 375ml

*Distribution:* Tasting room, Washington state liquor stores and several restaurants and bars in the Seattle area.

*Highlighted spirits:*
The liqueurs are the most popular spirits produced here. Not overly sweet or heavy, these liqueurs are made by macerating our own hand-picked berries in alcohol distilled on location. From this point on very little else is added to them, resulting in a clean and flavorful liqueur which captures the full essence of the berry.

*Services offered other than production:*
There is a tasting room for the beverages plus on-site sales for merchandise, plants and u-pick berries. Additionally, the farm will soon be available as a venue for outdoor summer events.

*About:*
Sidetrack Distillery is a family owned and operated distillery using fruits and herbs naturally grown on the estate farm.

The owners, David O'Neal (left), Linda Person (center) and Larry Person (right) have always appreciated fine fermented and distilled beverages. Having developed an all-natural fruit and berry farm, it was only natural to step into preserving the farm fresh fruit into spirits. Being a true estate distillery, the main focus is to capture the full quality and essence of the fruit in every bottle produced. The liqueurs are not overly sweet and heavy, remaining true to the natural flavor and acidity of the fruit. Sidetrack Distillery is also a destination spot, giving people a chance to escape the city and view the beautiful, serene farmland as they walk up to the tasting room.

*Professional associations:*
Washington Distillers Guild

*Future business plans and goals:*
Broaden distribution

Sidetrack Distillery
Kent, Washington

Sidetrack Distillery photos courtesy of Jeffery Noble

# Soft Tail Spirits

Dennis Robertson, Owner
Tammy Robertson, Owner

Cameron Robertson, Distiller
Matthew Farmer, Distiller

*First location:*
12280 NE Woodinville Drive, Suite C
Woodinville, Washington  98072

*Second location:*
14356 Woodinville Redmond Road
Redmond, Washington  98052

*Mailing address:*
Post Office Box 2174
Woodinville Washington  98072

*Phone:*  425-770-1154, 425-770-1158
*Fax:*  425-488-6922
*Email:*  Dennis Robertson:  dennis@softtailspirits.com
         Tammy Robertson:  tammy@softtailspirits.com
         Matthew Farmer:  matthew@softtailspirits.com
*Website:*  www.softtailspirits.com
*Facebook:*  Soft Tail Spirits
*Twitter:*  @softtailspirits

*Region:*  Pacific Northwest

*Type:*
Micro-distillery producing approximately 2,400 gallons per year

*Opened:*
Woodinville Distillery (DSP-WA15018) Opened October 31, 2008
Redmond Distillery (DSP-WA15065) Opened April 18, 2011

*Hours of operation:*
Woodinville, Monday through Saturday, 12:00pm to 5:00pm
Redmond, Friday through Sunday, 12:00pm to 5:00pm

*Tours:*  Tours are available during business hours by appointment.

*Types of spirits produced:*  Grappa and vodka

362

*Names of spirits:*
- Soft Tail Vodka
- Soft Tail Blanco Grappa
- Giallo Grappa
- Sangiovese Grappa

*Best known for:* Soft Tail Martini

*Average bottle price:* $32.00 to $38.00

*Distribution:* Tasting room as well as Washington and Oregon liquor stores

*Awards and Recognitions:*
**Soft Tail Vodka**
- Bronze Medal, 2010 San Francisco World Spirits

**Saniovese Grappa**
- Silver Medal, 2010 San Francisco World Spirits

*Highlighted spirits:*
**Soft Tail Vodka**
A departure from the ordinary, Soft Tail Vodka offers warmth and smoothness that is sure to warrant a second sip. Part of the unique character of Soft Tail Vodka comes from the high quality fruit sugars that are found naturally within a Washington state apple.

**Soft Tail Giallo**
Soft and golden color, Soft Tail Giallo spends six months in French oak barrels. It has aromas of straw and hay with soft pear and apple flavors similar to a light lowland Scotch whiskey.

**Sangiovese Grappa**
Made exclusively from Sangiovese pomace, this traditional single varietal grappa is one of Soft Tail Spirits' most popular. It has fresh aromas of strawberry and hay with a pleasent grainy mouthfeel that warms the throat. It's a remarkably good match with chocolate covered espresso beans.

*Events and Celebrations:* Special group events are hosted at both facilities.

*Services offered other than production:* Tours, tastings, and retail

*About:*
Located in Woodinville, WA, Soft Tail Spirits started distilling in 2008 and set out to produce the finest spirits possible using the most traditional equipment available.

Surrounded by western Washington's largest collection of wineries, Soft Tail Spirits capitalizes on its wasted pressings destined for land fill. These pressings are used to produce three grappas - Blanco, Giallo and Reserve distilled from a blend of Merlot, Syrah, and Cabernet wine grapes. Additionally, the distillery produces two single varietal grappas - a wonderful Sangiovese and a hearty Cabernet Sauvignon.

The grappa still is an Old World, hammered copper alambic from Portugal - a design time tested in Europe for centuries. Nicknamed "Maggie" the design is perfectly suited for making grappa. With Maggie's 58,000 BTU burners lit, it takes little more attention than the computerized stills being used routinely today.

The vodka still is a perfect match for Maggie. Nicknamed "Tumwater," it is a beautiful 200L alambic modified to feed the copper column for reflux. Gas fired as well, the balance of heating and cooling is personally scrutinized during the distillation process giving the distiller total control of the finished vodka.

Soft Tail Vodka, made from Washington state apples, is a clean, premium vodka that is also gluten free. Through a multiple distillation process, the apple flavors are gone and what's left is a crisp, fresh premium vodka.

*Professional associations:* Washington Distillers Guild

*Future business plans and goals:* Expanded distribution

*Suggested recipes:*
**Soft Tail Saint** - Courtesy of Dan Minjares (Sky City – The Space Needle)
- 2 oz Soft Tail Vodka
- 1 oz St. Germain Elderflower Liqueur
- ¾ oz yuzu citrus juice

   Shake and serve in a martini glass.
   Add a "sink" of Chambord at the bottom of the glass.
   Garnish with a long orange twist.

**The Pink Rottweiler**
- 1 cup fresh squeezed grapefruit juice
- A sprig of fresh mint leaves
- 6 ice cubes

   Muddle until ice is crushed, then add:
- 1 ounce Soft Tail Grappa Reserve
- 1 ounce Soft Tail Vodka

   Shake and pour with cheese cloth filter.
   Serve in martini glass with mint leaf garnish.

Soft Tail Spirits
Woodinville and Redmond Washington

# Sound Spirits

Steven Stone, Founder / Head Distiller

1630 15th Avenue West
Seattle, Washington 98119

*Phone:* 206-651-5166
*Email:* info@drinksoundspirits.com
*Website:* www.drinksoundspirits.com
*Facebook:* Sound Spirits

*Region:* Washington

*Type:* Micro-distillery producing approximately 300 gallons per month

*Opened:* September 17, 2010

*Hours of operation:* Usually open every day. Check the website

*Tours:* Tours are available.

*Types of spirits produced:* Vodka, gin, old tom gin, and aquavit

*Names of spirits:*
- Ebb+Flow Vodka
- Ebb+Flow Gin
- Sound Spirits – Old Tom Gin
- Sound Spirits – Aquavit

*Average bottle price:* $33.00

*Distribution:* Sound Spirits' products are available in the tasting room and in Washington state liquor stores.

*Highlighted spirits:*
**Ebb+Flow Vodka**
Ebb+Flow Vodka is handcrafted from 100% single malt barley. Made in small batches, it has the barest touch of natural flavor and sweetness.

**Ebb+Flow Gin**
Ebb+Flow Gin was inspired by a recipe from the 1800s and offers a wonderful balance of flavors - herbal, citrus and spice.

**Sound Spirits Aquavit**
Sound Spirits Aquavit is a true small batch gem inspired by Seattle's Scandinavian heritage.

**Sound Spirits Old Tom Gin**
Sound Spirits Old Tom Gin is gently rested on oak, bringing lovely tones of vanilla and caramel to a floral and spicy gin.

*Services offered other than production:* Tastings and tours

*Interesting facts:*
- Sound Spirits is Seattle's first craft distillery since Prohibition.

*About:*
Located in Seattle Washington, Sound Spirits produces handcrafted artisanal spirits from fine local ingredients including Washington barley and pure water that hails from the Cascades. Most ingredients are sourced from within Washington state.

*Professional associations:*
American Distilling Institute and Washington Distillers Guild

*Future business plans and goals:*
Expand product line to include whiskey and liqueurs

Steven Stone – Founder
Photo by: Thomas Barwick

*Suggested recipes:*
**Ebb+Flow Last Word**
- ½ oz Ebb+Flow Gin
- ½ oz maraschino
- ½ oz green chartreuse
- ½ oz lime juice

Shake with ice, strain and serve up.

**Ebb and Flower Vesper**
- 2 oz Ebb+Flow Gin
- 1 oz Ebb+Flow Vodka
- ¼ oz St. Germaine

Shake with ice, strain and serve up with lemon twist.

Sound Spirits
Seattle, Washington

# The Ellensburg Distillery

1000 N Prospect Street
Ellensburg, Washington  98926

*Phone:*  509-925-1295
*Fax:*  509-925-1295
*Email:*  info@theellensburgdistillery.com
*Website:*  www.theellensburgdistillery.com
*Facebook:*  The Ellensburg Distillery
*Twitter:*  @GoldBuckleClub

*Region:*  Pacific Northwest

*Type*:  Micro-distillery

*Opened:*  November 1, 2008

*Hours of operation:*  By appointment

*Tours:*  VIP tours and tastings are available by appointment

*Types of spirits produced:*  Whisky and brandy

*Names of spirits:*
- Gold Buckle Club Malt Whisky
- El Chalán Pisco-style Brandy
- Wildcat White Whisky

*Average bottle price*:  $28.00 to $110.00

*Distribution:*  Washington

*Awards and Recognitions:*
**Gold Buckle Club Malt Whisky**
- Gold Medal and Best Spirit Trophy, 2010 NorthWest Wine & Spirits Summit
**El Chalán Brandy**
- Gold Medal and Best Spirit Trophy 2009 NorthWest Wine & Spirits Summit

*Services offered other than production:*  VIP tours and tastings

*Interesting facts:*
- The Ellensburg Distillery is Washington's second licensed distillery.
- It's known for making brandy and whisky.

*Management profile:*

**Berle W. Figgins, Jr.**

Berle W. Figgins, Jr., owner and operator of Ellensburg Distillery, has been a career winemaker and viticulturist since growing up in the family winery operation and gaining his Bachelor of Applied Science degree in Viticulture and Enology from an Australian university. He also earned the Master Distiller's Professional Certification from the Institute of Brewing and Distilling in London. Most recently, Berle headed the Cave B Estate Winery near Quincy, Washington.

*Future business plans and goals:* Expanded distribution

Pictured are Lola and Esmeralda, the hardworking twin sisters who deliver fine, award winning spirits to The Ellensburg Distillery.

The Ellensburg Distillery
Ellensburg, Washington

# Wishkah River Distillery

Susan Watts, Owner

2210 Port Industrial Road
Post Office Box 415
Aberdeen, Washington 98520

*Phone:* 360-589-1829
*Fax:* 360-532-3753
*Email:* sue@wishkahriver.com
*Website:* www.wishkahriver.com
*Facebook:* Wishkah River Distillery
*Twitter:* @WRDistillery

*Region:* Pacific Northwest

*Type:* Micro-distillery producing approximately 1,200 gallons per year

*Opened:* January 2011

*Hours of operation:* Daily

*Tours:* Tours will be offered. Exact times are TBA.

*Types of spirits produced:* Vodka, whiskey, and brandy

*Names of spirits:*
- Wishkah River Distillery Vodka, made from 100% honey
- Wishkah River Distillery Vodka, grain
- Wanigan Small Batch Whiskey

*Average bottle price:*
$20.00 to $30.00 for 375ml, $30.00 to $50.00 for 750ml

*Distribution:* Tasting room and Seattle, Washington area.

*Highlighted spirits:*
**Wishkah River Distillery Vodka**
80 and 100 proof versions of this vodka are made from honey.

**Wanigan Small Batch White Whiskey**
This is made from barley and wheat.

*Services offered other than production:* Tasting room

*About:*
Wishkah River Distillery, located in Grays Harbor, Washington, is a craft distillery of ultra-premium, small batch spirits that include Washington state themed, pot-distilled vodkas (neutral and flavored), whiskey, brandy, and liqueurs.

From the selection of the most flavorful grains to the freshness of the fruits and spices, Wishkah River Distillery focusses on locally produced, sustainable agriculture to produce uniquely flavored, quality spirits. The honey originates in western Washington and the grains originates in eastern Washington.

*Management profile:*
Sue Watts is a graduate of the University of Washington with a degree in pulp and paper science and engineering.

*Professional associations:*
American Distillers Institute and Washington Distillers Guild

*Future business plans and goals:* Expand product line and increase distribution

Wishkah River Distillery
Aberdeen, Washington

## Woodinville Whiskey Co.

# WOODINVILLE
— · handcrafted small-batch spirits · —
# WHISKEY CO.

Orlin Sorensen, Owner and Operator
Brett Carlile, Owner and Operator

16110 Woodinville Redmond Road NE, Suite 3
Woodinville, Washington 98072

*Phone:* 425-486-1199
*Fax:* 877-634-7547
*Email:* Orlin Sorensen: orlin@woodinvillewhiskeyco.com
        Brett Carlile: brett@woodinvillewhiskeyco.com
*Website:* www.woodinvillewhiskeyco.com
*Facebook:* Woodinville Whiskey Co.

*Region:* Washington and the Pacific Northwest

*Type:* Micro-distillery producing approximately 40,000 to 60,000 gallons annually

*Opened:* July 2010

*Hours of operation:* Monday through Sunday, 5:00am to 6:00pm
Tasting room is open Wednesday through Sunday, 12:00pm to 5:00pm

*Tours:* Tours are available Wednesday through Sunday at 4:00pm.

*Types of spirits produced:* Bourbon, rye whiskey, American whiskey, and vodka

*Names of spirits:*
- The Microbarreled™ Collection - Bourbon and Rye Whiskey
- Headlong™ White Dog Whiskey
- Peabody Jones™ Vodka
- Age Your Own™ Whiskey Kit

*Best known for:* The Microbarreled™ Collection

*Average bottle price:* $29.95 to $39.95

*Distribution:* WA, OR, CA IL, ID, and NV

*Awards and Recognitions:*
**Peabody Jones™ Vodka**
- Silver Medal, 2011 San Francisco World Spirits Competition
- Bronze Medal, 2010 NY International Spirits Competition
**Headlong™ White Dog Whiskey**
- "92 Points - Exceptional" Beverage Testing Institute
**Woodinville Whiskey Company**
- Best of 2010, Seattle Magazine

*Highlighted spirits:*

## Headlong™ White Dog Whiskey

Made from a true bourbon whiskey mash bill and 100% organic corn, wheat and malted barley, Headlong™ White Dog Whiskey is unaged and slowly distilled with precise cuts and handcrafted quality. Gentle aromas of banana and citrus lead to a buttery mouthfeel on the tongue followed by an unexpectedly smooth finish with hints of malt, nutmeg and oatmeal cookies.

## Peabody Jones™ Vodka

Distilled by Northwest legend Peabody Jones from 100% organic soft winter wheat grown exclusively in Washington, Peabody Jones™ Vodka is uncharacteristically smooth.

## The Microbarreled Collection

This collection is crafted entirely by hand in very small batches from Washington state grains and aged to maturity in new, charred, American oak microbarrels. This demanding process results in an extremely rich and full-bodied bourbon and rye whiskey.

*Events and Celebrations:* Hosts "Whiskey After Dark" and "The Whiskey Experience"

*Services offered other than production:* Tasting room and tours

*About:*
Woodinville Whiskey Company, a grain to bottle craft distillery located in Woodinville, Washington was founded by two longtime friends committed to delivering the best whiskey while making new friends along the way.

As with many other stories, the Woodinville Whiskey Company story started over whiskey. In 2009, best friends Orlin Sorensen (right) and Brett Carlile (left) concocted an idea so bold and crazy that it had to have started over whiskey. They pondered a number of questions. Could they really do it better? Could they handcraft a whiskey and vodka so smooth, so flavorful, and so different that it changed what people would come to expect out of a bottle? They decided they could and it became their mission to do just that.

372

A year later, Orlin and Brett set up shop in Washington, and it wasn't because they couldn't find a map to Kentucky. Pure ingredients, pristine water and unique aging conditions make Washington an ideal place for distilling. They brought together state of the art distilling equipment, quailty grain grown in Washington state, and the expertise of an industry giant to deliver unrivaled quality and flavor characteristics to true whiskey and vodka drinkers.

A 14 year veteran of whiskey making as master distiller at Maker's Mark, David Pickerell's (center) recipes and mentorship were brought to life using the finest ingredients available - pure Washington mountain water, advanced distilling technology from Germany, and the finest new American oak whiskey barrels from the northern forest.

The still was engineered and built in Germany and it represents the beauty that can be achieved when old world tradition is melded with modern day innovation.

*Professional associations:* American Distilling Institute and DISCUS

*Future business plans and goals:*
Continue to produce world class spirits and broaden distribution

*Suggested recipe:*
**The Green Trellis**
- 3 slices peeled cucumber
- 10-12 mint leaves muddled together

After muddled, add:
- 1½ oz Headlong™ White Dog Whiskey
- 1 oz apple cider
- ½ oz simple sugar (1 part sugar, 1 part water, heated until sugar dissolves)

Shake all ingredients well with ice and strain into a cocktail glass.

Woodinville Whiskey Co.
Woodinville, Washington

# Smooth Ambler Spirits Company

John Little, John Foster, Owners
TAG Galyean, Greg Parseghian, Owners

745 Industrial Park Road
Maxwelton, West Virginia 24957

*Phone:* 304-497-3123
*Fax:* 304-497-3124
*Email:* sales@smoothambler.com
*Websites:* www.smoothambler.com
*Facebook:* Smooth Ambler Spirits

*Region:* Southeastern West Virginia

*Type:* Micro-distillery producing approximately 1,200 gallons

*Opened:* April 2010

*Hours of operation:* Monday through Friday, 10:00am to 6:00pm
Saturday, 11:00am to 3:00pm

*Tours:* Thursday and Friday, 2:00pm and 4:00pm, Saturday, 12:00pm and 2:00pm

*Types of spirits produced:* Vodka, gin, white whiskey, and bourbon

*Names of spirits:*
- Smooth Ambler Old Scout
- Smooth Ambler Greenbrier Gin
- Smooth Ambler Whitewater Vodka
- Smooth Ambler Yearling Bourbon
- Smooth Ambler Exceptional White Whiskey
- Smooth Ambler Old Scout Straight Bourbon Whiskey

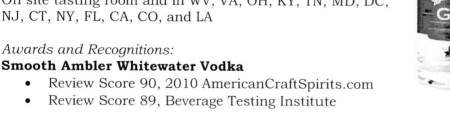

*Best known for:*
Gin and ginger ale, and Baptist martinis (house favorites)

*Average bottle price:* $28.00 to $30.00

*Distribution:*
On site tasting room and in WV, VA, OH, KY, TN, MD, DC,
NJ, CT, NY, FL, CA, CO, and LA

*Awards and Recognitions:*
**Smooth Ambler Whitewater Vodka**
- Review Score 90, 2010 AmericanCraftSpirits.com
- Review Score 89, Beverage Testing Institute

**Smooth Ambler Greenbrier Gin**
- Review Score 91, AmericanCraftSpirits.com
- Review Score 89, 2010 Beverage Testing Institute

**Smooth Ambler Exceptional White Whiskey**
- Review Score 93, Blue Reviews

*Highlighted spirits:*
**Smooth Ambler Old Scout**
Aged in 5 and 6 year old barrels with a high rye content of 36%, this fine whiskey has exceptional taste and smoothness. It's non-chill filtered, non-carbon filtered. A robust 99 proof, it's strong but deliciously drinkable like all of Smooth Ambler's offerings. This spirit is bold, with sweet-spicy flavors and with a subtle apple, cherry and tobacco aroma.

**Smooth Ambler Greenbrier Gin**
With serious citrus, a bit of black pepper spice, and light and pleasant juniper notes, Smooth Ambler Greenbrier Gin exudes the cool smoothness the brand name implies. Greenbrier Gin is designed to have a rich and luxurious mouthfeel without being overly "piney" like a typical, dry gin. Smooth Ambler Greenbrier Gin is named for its home embedded in the rolling Appalachian hills of Greenbrier County, WV.

**Smooth Ambler Whitewater Vodka**
Clean and crisp with a sweet, buttery, caramel undertone, Smooth Ambler Whitewater Vodka is made from the finest American grains and some of the same mountain water responsible for the rush and exhilaration of the world-renowned rapids it's named after. Whitewater Vodka is triple distilled in a pot and column still, carbon filtered, chill filtered, and guided completely by hand until each bottle is filled and numbered.

**Smooth Ambler Exceptional White Whiskey**
Exceptional White Whiskey is a sophisticated moonshine made using the same recipe and process as the bourbon that is barreled for aging. The whiskey is cut to 100 proof and is very smooth with early and bold notes of the sweet corn and wheat that, after time in white oak barrels, become mellow and caramel-tinged.

*Events and Celebrations:*
Smooth Ambler Spirits Company frequently hosts special events and tastings at the distillery as well as tasting and charity events in the market.

*Services offered other than production:*
Tasting room and on-site retail sales of spirits, apparel, and other goods

*About:*

In 2009, TAG Galyean (left) and John Little (right) founded Smooth Ambler to produce fine artisan spirits by combining patient Appalachian know-how with the finest of American ingredients. Located in the rolling Appalachian hills of Greenbrier Valley in West Virginia, Smooth Ambler uses state of the art distillery equipment in conjunction with natural resources of the region - high-valley mountain air, natural waters, ideal temperature variations and friendly folks.

Smooth Ambler Spirits is a true grain-to-glass distillery. Using the finest whole American grains milled onsite and carefully combined with the local mountain water, products are crafted with quality in mind and with a passion that is taken deeply to heart. The spirits are produced with talent and skill informed by hundreds of years of distilling excellence. Additionally, TAG and John are guided by the desire to acquire the purest and best ingredients, and to do the best with them one slow step at a time.

Smooth Ambler Spirits constantly strives to improve its green efforts. Currently it uses a hot water tank to store cooling water. Also, all of the stillage is picked up by a local farmer and used as cattle feed, and the distillery recycles all boxes and cardboard.

*Professional associations:* American Distilling Institute

*Future business plans and goals:* Smooth Ambler Spirits anticipates a 120% increase in production following the purchase of two more fermenters and a second Vendome still for making whiskey and for stripping. Additionally, it plans to build a new barrel house.

*Suggested recipe:*

**The Baptist Martini**
- 1½ ozs of Whitewater Vodka
- 3 ozs of lemonade (Real Simple Fresh Lemonade)
- Fresh lemon

  Mix over ice in a tumbler with a little club soda on top *or* mix it in a shaker, pour into a martini glass, and then add a splash of soda for a fancier, martini-looking drink.

  Add fresh lemon to either when done.

Smooth Ambler Spirits Company
Maxwelton, West Virginia

# WV Distilling Co. LLC

Payton Fireman, Owner

1380 Fenwick Avenue
Morgantown, West Virginia 26505

*Phone:* 304-599-0960
*Email:* pfireman@frontier.com
*Website:* www.mountainmoonshine.com

*Region:* West Virginia

*Type:* Micro-distillery producing approximately 5,000 gallons per year

*Opened:* 1999

*Hours of operation:* No set hours

*Tours:* Tours are not available

*Types of spirits produced:* Corn whiskey

*Names of spirits:*
- Mountain Moonshine Spirit Whiskey
- Mountain Moonshine Old Oak Recipe

*Average bottle price:* $15.00

*Distribution:*
WV Distilling products are carried in 100 of the 150 liquor stores in WV.

*Awards and Recognitions:*
**Mountain Moonshine Old Oak Recipe**
- Gold Medal, American Craft Distillers Awards, American Distilling Institute

**Mountain Moonshine -** 100 Proof
- Bronze Medal, American Craft Distillers Awards, American Distilling Institute

*Interesting facts:*
- WV Distilling Company was West Virginia's first legal distilled spirits company since the repeal of Prohibition.

*About:*

In 1999, Payton Fireman decided to create a legal moonshine distillery.

West Virginia's distilling history goes back to the first pioneers who crossed the Allegheny Mountains in the late 1700s. These settlers brought their distilling traditions and equipment from Scotland and Ireland. Usually six to ten homesteaders would share a still to distill their surplus rye and corn for sale back east in exchange for axes, needles, cloth and other essential finished goods. It was easier to haul a gallon of whiskey back east than it was to haul the corn it took to make the whiskey.

Using whiskey as a form of currency ended after the Whiskey Rebellion of 1791-94. The excise tax structure created by George Washington and Alexander Hamilton to pay Revolutionary War debts regulated the industry. Many distillers moved their operations to Kentucky where corn grew better and they could continue their trade without government supervision.

West Virginia's distilling tradition continued as a back woods affair, away from the prying eyes of revenue agents. Colorful stories of bootleggers outsmarting and outrunning the law and the Prohibition agents that eventually caught them are a part of West Virginia's heritage as well. Until now, moonshine has been hard to find. Almost all of it was distilled in the back woods away from the prying eyes of tax revenue officers out to stop the illegal business of non-tax paid whiskey.

WV Distilling Company makes only legal corn whiskey that is not only licensed and taxed, but is hand bottled as well.

*Suggested recipe:*

**Moonshine Manhattan**
- 3 parts Mountain Moonshine Old Oak Recipe
- 1 part sweet vermouth
- Splash of Angostura bitters
- 1 maraschino cherry

WV Distilling Co. LLC
Morgantown, West Virginia

# 45th Parallel Spirits LLC

Werni Family owned
Paul Werni Sr., Co-owner
Paul Werni Jr., Master Distiller and Co-owner
Deb Hale, Sales and Co-owner
Tom Gunn and Scott Davis, Distillers

1570 Madison Avenue
New Richmond, Wisconsin  54017

*Phone:*  715-246-0565
*Fax:*  715-246-4566
*Email:*  Paul Werni Jr.:  paul@45thparallelspirits.com
            Deb Hale:  deb@45thparallelspirits.com
*Website:*  www.45thparallelspirits.com
*Facebook:*  45th Parallel Vodka

*Region:*   Upper Midwest

*Type*:
Micro-distillery producing approximately 1,000 gallons a month

*Opened:*  April 2007

*Hours of operation:*
        Monday through Friday, 8:00am to 6:00pm
        Saturday, 12:00pm to 4:00pm

*Tours:*   Tours are conducted Monday through Friday from 4:00pm
to 6:00pm and on Saturday from 12:00pm to 4:00pm.

*Types of spirits produced:*
Vodka, gin, whiskey, bourbon, and a horseradish infused vodka

*Names of spirits:*
- 45th Parallel Vodka
- Midwest Vodka
- Midwest Gin
- Referent Vodka
- Madison Avenue Lemoncello

*Average bottle price:*  $19.00 to $30.00

*Distribution:*  On-site retail and through distributors in WI, MN, IL,
UT, CA, and NC

*Awards and Recognitions:*
- 45th Parallel Vodka ranked #1 by The Spirit Journal in 2009 and 2010

*Highlighted spirits:*
## 45th Parallel Vodka
The distilling method for 45th Parallel Vodka embraces the natural flavors extracted from the grains and has no additives. The result is a sweeter aroma and a clean and balanced taste, an artisan alternative to other mass produced varieties.

*Events and Celebrations:* Hosts private events by reservation

*Services offered other than production:*
Tastings, tours, retail shop, and monthly distilling classes

*Interesting facts:*
- 45th Parallel Spirits is also the location.

*About:*
A marker on the side of old Highway 51 in Wisconsin, north of Wausau, south of Merrill, informs passersby they are at the 45th parallel (half-way between the equator and the North Pole).

45th Parallel Vodka is crafted on a small, family owned distillery in the western Wisconsin town of New Richmond, situated about 50 minutes east of downtown Minneapolis. Using 100% local grain and a hands-on approach, every drop in every bottle of 45th Parallel Vodka is produced and bottled entirely within the facility.

Spent grain is returned to neighboring cattle farm to be used as feed.

*Management profile:*
## Paul Werni Jr.
Paul Werni Jr., (pictured) founder, owner, and master distiller of 45th Parallel Spirits LLC, wanted to create world class vodka with a manageable staff and facility in the Midwest where the grain is grown.

After nearly a decade of running a successful construction business, Paul felt it was time to move on. Being relatively secure, he figured he could stay home for a few years to spend more time with his kids while he decided what to do next. Within a few months, the idea of 45th Parallel came to be.

Paul read everything he could find on distillation. He attended workshops in New Hampshire and traveled to Germany and Austria to tour and gain more knowledge about small distilleries. He learned with the help of Christian Carl's Alexander Plank and Nicholas Haase. They answered more questions than they probably thought could be asked.

Admittedly, Paul is more self-taught than formally trained in distillation methods. He found that, with time and study, creating high quality premium vodka is reasonably achievable. The only thing in his way was fear. Starting a distillery is expensive, relatively rare and risky. With his wife and family approving of the gamble, he set out to build 45th Parallel Spirits LLC.

## Scott Davis

Living only blocks from one another, Scott Davis (pictured right) met Paul over 20 years ago while loading trucks at UPS. While they were having breakfast at Brownies Café in northeast Minneapolis, Scott first learned of Paul's desire to start a distillery. Scott followed 45th Parallel's progress with the anticipation of someday joining it. Today, Scott brings to 45th Parallel a passion for the spirits and food industry as well as another creative mind. After helping his wife Erin open Toast Wine Bar & Café in the North Loop Warehouse District, Scott felt it was time to add his skills to the distillery.

His inspiration to help create a high quality product like 45th Parallel is only equaled by his desire to beat Paul in cribbage.

## Paul Werni Sr.

Paul Werni Sr. (pictured left) is a retired phone man. Being of German heritage and born in Serbia at the beginning of WWII, he lost his father and home to the war. After the war, Paul Sr., his mother, brother and one sister came to the U.S. on a boat with few belongings. They settled in Milwaukee where they worked hard, assimilated, sacrificed and provided opportunities for their kids. Paul Sr. is presently lending his "golden" time to his son and the distillery. When the distillery is in production, he drives three hours each way every week to help out. He usually stays a few days, helping to work the fermenters and distilling equipment. Carol, his wife of almost 50 years, supports his time away.

*Professional associations:* Wisconsin Distillers Association

*Future business plans and goals:* Expand product line and distribution

*Suggested recipe:*
## 45th Tomatini
- 2 ½ ozs 45th Parallel Vodka
- 1 oz tequila
- ½ oz tomato juice

  Combine all ingredients in cocktail shaker with ice.
  Shake for 30 seconds.
  Strain into martini glass.
  Garnish with lemon twist.

45th Parallel Spirits LLC
New Richmond, Wisconsin

# AEppelTreow Winery & Distillery

Charles and Milissa McGonegal, Owners

1072 288th Avenue
Burlington, Wisconsin 53105

*Phone:* 262-878-5345
*Email:* cider@appletrue.com
cpm@appletrue.com
*Website:* www.appletrue.com
*Facebook:* AEppelTreow Winery Artisan Ciders

*Region:* Southeastern Wisconsin

*Type:* Micro-distillery producing approximately 100 gallons per year

*Opened:* Cidery 2001, Distillery 2009

*Hours of operation:* Open seasonally, May through December. Visit website for details.

*Tours:* Tours of the facility are available.

*Types of spirits produced:* Apple brandy and hard cider

*Names of spirits:*
- AeppelTreow WI Apple Brandy
- Brown Dog Whiskey

*Best known for:* Sparkling cider

*Average bottle price*: $20.00 to $30.00

*Distribution:*
On-site retail and distribution in Wisconsin

*Highlighted spirits:*

**Apple Brandy**
Apple Brandy is aged in new charred Wisconsin oak. It's spicy and aromatic.

**Brown Dog Whiskey**
Brown Dog is local sorghum distilled and aged with oak, chestnut, apple and cherry wood. It is reminiscent of a light whiskey and has hints of nuts and banana bread.

382

*Events and Celebrations:* Does not host events or celebrations

*Services offered other than production:* Tours, tastings, and retail shop

*About:*
AEppelTreow (pronounced Apple True) Winery & Distillery specializes in Wisconsin grown and produced artisan hard cider, brandy and specialty spirits to make craft beverages from heirloom apples.

*Management profile:*
**Charles McGonegal**
Charles McGonegal is a trained biochemist and petrochemical research chemist.

**Milissa McGonegal**
Milissa McGonegal is a chemical engineer and graphic artist.

*Suggested recipe:*
- 1 oz WI Apple Brandy
- ½ oz pommeau
- Dash orange bitters

  Mix ingredients.
  Top with Appely Doux champagne-method cider.

AeppelTreow Winery & Distillery
Burlington, Wisconsin

# Death's Door Spirits

Brian Ellison, President
John Jeffery, Distiller

2220 Eagle Drive
Middleton, Wisconsin  53562

*Phone:*  608-441-1083
*Email:*  Brian Ellison (President):  brian@deathsdoorspirits.com
John Kinder (National Sales Director):  john@deathsdoorspirits.com
Mike Reiber (Director of Operations): mike@deathsdoorspirits.com
John Jeffery (Head Distiller): johnny@deathsdoorspirits.com
*Website:*  www.deathsdoorspirits.com
*Facebook:*  Death's Door Spirits
*Twitter:* @deathsdoor

*Region:*  Wisconsin

*Type*:  Distilled spirits company selling approximately 15,000 gallons per year

*Opened:*  2007

*Hours of operation:*  Not open to the public

*Tours:*  Tours are not available.

*Types of spirits produced:*  Gin, vodka, and white whisky

*Names of spirits:*
- Death's Door Gin
- Death's Door Vodka
- Death's Door White Whisky

*Best known for:*  Exceptional taste, eye-catching packaging and sustainable practices

*Average bottle price:*  $29.99 to $34.99

*Distribution:*  Distributed in 34 states and the UK.  Visit website for specific locations and distributors.

*Awards and Recognitions:*
**Death's Door Gin**
- "What could be the finest American-made craft gin", Dec. 2011, Wall Street Journal
- Named "Spirit of the Year," 2009 by Wine and Spirits Magazine
- Rated 93 by the Tasting Panel
- "Best Tasting," September 2009 Cooking Light Magazine

*Awards and Recognitions:*

**Death's Door White Whisky**
- Winner, Spirits Category by 2012 Good Food Awards
- #4 in Top 10 American Spirits, June 2010 Wine Enthusiast Magazine
- Rated 91 by the Tasting Panel

**Death's Door Vodka**
- "Pure as they come" January 2011 by GQ Magazine
- Rated 92 by the Tasting Panel

*Highlighted spirits:*

**Death's Door Gin**

Death's Door Gin has a surprisingly simple botanical mix of organic juniper berries, coriander and fennel. Combining juniper berries that grow wild on Washington Island with coriander and fennel sourced from within the state, Death's Door Spirits is able to showcase how complimentary and complex simple expressions can be. Death's Door Gin employs a mix of organic Washington Island wheat and organic malted barley from Chilton, Wisconsin. Death's Door Gin has a full London dry flavor without all of the bitterness because of the distillation process and the grains used.

**Death's Door Vodka**

Death's Door Vodka employs a mix of organic Washington Island wheat and organic malted barley from Chilton, Wisconsin. Death's Door Vodka is triple distilled and hand cut, resulting in a spirit that's smooth and rich with subtle notes of vanilla.

**Death's Door White Whisky**

A pioneer in the whisky category, Death's Door White Whisky is made up of a mash bill of an 80:20 ratio of organic Washington Island Wheat to organic malted barley from Chilton, Wisconsin. The spirit is then double distilled up to 160 proof (80% ABV), rested in stainless steel, and finished in uncharred Minnesota oak barrels to help bring the "white whisky" together and to meld this unique spirit's flavors. The bouquet is one part "South of the Border" (artisanal cachaça, tequila) and one part "Eastern" (sweet potato shochu/soju and earthy sake), yet the palate is unmistakably whisky (a smooth double-distilled varietal with vanilla, chocolate covered raisin, and dark cherry flavor).

*Events and Celebrations:* The distillery hosts several events, including an annual Juniper Harvest Festival each fall on Washington Island, Wisconsin.

*About:*
Washington Island, Wisconsin, is at the heart and soul of everything produced by Death's Door Spirits. This 22 square mile island hosts 700 year-round residents and all the amenities of a quaint town. Washington Island also has miles of beautiful uninterrupted shoreline, protected coves and inlets, and acres upon acres of open land with rolling hills and hardwood stands.

385

Death's Door takes its name from the body of water between Door County peninsula and Washington Island. Potowatami and Winnebego tribesmen originally named the waterway, while the French called it Port de Morts when trading in the area to ward off other traders.

In 2005, a small group of like-minded people began exploring the possibility of restoring farming on Washington Island, which had been dormant since the early 1970s when the potato was the chief crop. Armed with enough seed to plant five acres and enough know-how to get it done, brothers Tom and Ken Koyen began growing wheat on the island. What started as wheat to use as flour at the Washington Island Hotel has grown into a select specialty grain for use in Capital Brewery's Island Wheat Ale and all of Death's Door Spirits products.

Since 2005, Death's Door Spirits and Capital Brewery have supported the farmers' efforts on Washington Island to expand the acreage of hard red winter wheat from five to over 1,000 under cultivation. Also, three years ago, organic certification was achieved for all of the crops.

*Management profile:*

**Brian Ellison**

Death's Door Spirits was the brainchild of Brian Ellison (right), president and CEO, while he was employed at a land planning and economic development firm in Madison, Wisconsin.

Through his work in economic development, Brian recognized that the protection of small and medium scale family farms in rural Wisconsin would require high value-added products to provide stable and healthy returns to families to compete in the global marketplace.

Ellison holds a bachelor's degree (cum laude) from the University of Georgia and an MBA from ISES in Barcelona, Spain. Brian lives with his wife, Christine, and two children, Otto and Phoebe, in Madison, Wisconsin.

**John Kinder**

John Kinder is the National Sales Director for Death's Door Spirits. John joined Brian in November of 2009 to help grow the brand in the Midwest. John's extensive experience in mixology and the spirits industry has helped propel sales and brand exposure. Prior to Death's Door, John was national brand ambassador and director of education for Mystique Brands. John honed his mixology skills while working at MK restaurant and the Pump Room in Chicago. John's mixology accolades include, Star Chefs "2008 Rising Star Bar Chef," one of 10 national "Up and Coming Mixologists" by the Beverage Media Guide in 2007, and one of Chicago's top five mixologists by NewCity in 2007.

John holds an MBA from the University of Illinois-Chicago and a bachelor's degree in public relations from the University of Florida. He lives with his wife, Jamie, and three children, Veronica, Jack and Parker, on Madison's west side.

386

## Mike Reiber

Michael Reiber is the Director of Operations for Death's Door Spirits. Mike joined the team in June of 2011 to increase production capacity while improving supply chain and manufacturing systems to support Death's Door Spirits' rapid growth. Mike brings a wide and deep level of supply chain and manufacturing experience to the team. He recently served as Vice President of Manufacturing for a premium pet food company, a role he carried after ten (10) years of progressive supply chain & operations experience with Interstate Brands Corp. (i.e., Hostess Brands).

In addition, to his role at Death's Door Spirits, Mike co-facilitates the "Operations Management" class at the American Institute of Baking and is a past member of the American Society of Baking Executive Committee. Mike holds a MBA from Benedictine College and a Bachelor Degree in Criminal Justice from Kansas State University. Mike currently resides on the southwest side of Madison with his wife, Tiffany, and three children: Madison, Shelby and Colton.

## John Jeffery

John Jeffery is the Head Distiller for Death's Door Spirits. John completed his Master of Science Degree in Food Science at Michigan State University where his research focused on barrel aging dynamics, fermentation optimization, yeast byproducts and other fermentation and distillation processes. He is a graduate of the Artisan Distilled Spirits Program of MSU. John managed distillery operations for three years at MSU, and helped to build a production and R&D portfolio for the program that not only funded distillery operations, but in 2011 produced some process optimizations for Death's Door Spirits. This lead to his move to Death's Door to begin an aging program for the brand's wheat whiskey in addition to helping build and run the new distillery.

John has presented his research at the 2011 American Chemical Society proceedings and at distilling workshops nationwide. He has designed and produced spirits for artisan start-ups across the country while consulting on both production and aging.

John also holds a Bachelor's Degree in Kinesiology from University of Illinois at Chicago. He lives with his wife Dorota, and his two children, Malina and Kasper, in Madison, Wisconsin.

*Future business plans and goals:*
To increase production and meet the needs of existing markets in the Great Lakes region and the country by building the largest distillery in Wisconsin. Moreover, looking to increase the brand's exports to the United Kingdom and other markets around the world.

*Suggested recipe:*
## Negroni
- 1 ½ oz Death's Door Gin
- 1 oz Campari
- 1 oz sweet vermouth

    Stir and garnish with an orange peel.

Deaths Door Spirits
Middleton, Wisconsin

## Great Lakes Distillery LLC

Guy Rehorst, Owner

616 W. Virginia Street
Milwaukee, Wisconsin 53204

*Phone:* 414-431-8683
*Fax:* 414-431-1637
*Email:* info@greatlakesdistillery.com
*Website:* www.GreatLakesDistillery.com
*Facebook:* Great Lakes Distillery
*Twitter:* @GtLksDistillery

*Region:* Wisconsin

*Type:* Micro-distillery producing approximately 4,000 gallons per year

*Opened:* 2004

*Hours of operation:* Monday through Saturday, 12:00pm to 6:00pm

*Tours:* Tours are available Monday through Saturday.

*Types of spirits produced:*
Vodka, flavored vodka, gin, rum, European style fruit brandy, absinthe, whiskey

*Names of spirits:*
- Rehorst Premium Milwaukee Vodka
- Rehorst Citrus Honey Flavored Vodka
- Rehorst Premium Milwaukee Gin
- Roaring Dan's Rum
- Kinnickinnic Whiskey
- Great Lakes Seasonal Pumpkin Spirit
- Amerique 1912 Absinthe Verte
- Amerique 1912 Absinthe Rouge
- Great Lakes Artisan Series Grappa
- Great Lakes Artisan Series Pear Eau-de-Vie
- Great Lakes Artisan Series Kirschwasser
- Various extremely small batch whiskeys

*Best known for:* Rehorst Premium Milwaukee Vodka

*Average bottle price:* $29.00

*Distribution:* Great Lakes Distillery spirits are available in the tasting room, in stores, and inbars in Wisconsin, Illinois, Minnesota, California, Colorado and Arizona.

*Awards and Recognitions:*

**Rehorst Premium Milwaukee Vodka**
- Silver Medal, 2007 San Francisco World Spirits Competition

**Rehorst Premium Milwaukee Vodka**
- Silver Medal, 2008 Beverage Testing Institute

**Rehorst Premium Milwaukee Gin**
- Double Gold Medal, 2008 San Francisco World Spirits Competition
- Gold Medal, 2008 Beverage Testing Institute

**Rehorst Citrus Honey Flavored Vodka**
- Gold Medal, 2009 San Francisco World Spirits Competition
- Gold Medal, 2008 Beverage Testing Institute

**Amerique 1912 Absinthe Verte**
- Bronze Medal, 2011 San Francisco World Spirits Competition
- Gold Medal, 2010 Beverage Testing Institute

**Amerique 1912 Absinthe Rouge**
- Gold Medal, 2010 Beverage Testing Institute

*Highlighted spirits:*

**Rehorst Premium Milwaukee Vodka**
Rehorst Premium Milwaukee Vodka is made with Wisconsin-grown red wheat.

**Rehorst Citrus and Honey Flavored Vodkas**
Rehorst Citrus and Honey Flavored Vodkas are made from hand zested lemons and a very pure Wisconsin honey.

**Rehorst Premium Milwaukee Gin**
Rehorst Premium Milwaukee Gin is made with nine botanicals including two not used in any other gins - sweet basil and Wisconsin ginseng.

**Great Lakes Pumpkin Spirit**
Great Lakes Pumpkin Spirit is a seasonal spirit made by distilling Milwaukee's Lakefront Brewery Pumpkin Lager which is brewed using Thomas Jefferson's recipe. Pumpkin Spirit is aged in charred oak barrels. Bottling is very limited and it's available in October of every year.

## Roaring Dan's Rum

Roaring Dan's Rum, named for the only man ever charged with piracy on the Great Lakes, is a golden maple flavored rum made from top quality molasses. During the second distillation, pure Wisconsin maple syrup is added to the still giving Roaring Dan a very creamy finish. Roaring Dan is aged in a combination of used bourbon barrels and new charred oak barrels.

## Kinnickinnic Whiskey

Kinnickinnic Whiskey is a blend of Kentucky Straight Bourbon that is sourced from one of Kentucky's finest distilleries and a malt whiskey produced at Great Lakes Distillery.

*Events and Celebrations:*
Great Lakes Distillery hosts several events throughout the year including Wisconsin's Largest Bloody Mary benefit, an annual Repeal Day celebration commemorating the repeal of Prohibition and its annual Festivus Celebration (Dec 23rd).

*Services offered other than production:* Tours, tastings, and retail shop

*Interesting facts:*
- Great Lakes Distillery is Wisconsin's first distillery since Prohibition.

*Management profile:*
### Guy Rehorst

Founder Guy Rehorst realized that, while he could go to any bar or restaurant and order an excellent craft beer, all the spirits came from a small handful of large distilleries or from overseas. As a home brewer/wine maker, distilling peaked his curiosity to the point that he wondered if he was getting the best spirits. After some experimentation, he realized he could make better spirits than the big distilleries and spent the next few years learning about distillation. He then decided to open Great Lakes Distillery. Guy previously founded a high tech manufacturing company which was one of INC Magazines 500 fastest growing companies in the U.S. for two years in a row. Guy was also instrumental in getting tasting room laws changed in Wisconsin, thus enabling the sampling and sale of spirits in Wisconsin distilleries and wineries.

*Professional associations:* American Distilling Institute and DISCUS

*Future business plans and goals:* Expand product line and broaden distribution

*Suggested recipes:*
### The Mooncusser
- 1 ½ oz Roaring Dan's Rum
- Sprecher Cream Soda
- Angostura bitters

    Mix in a rocks glass filled with ice, add rum and bitters, top with cream soda.

Great Lakes Distillery LLC
Milwaukee, Wisconsin

390

## Lo Artisan Distillery LLC

Po Lo, Owner
Chong Va Lo, Operations Supervisor

1607 South Stevenson Pier Road
Sturgeon Bay, Wisconsin  54235

*Phone:*  337-660-1600
*Email:*  poclo@lo-artisandistillery.com
*Website:*  www.lo-artisandistillery.com
*Facebook:*  Lo Artisan Distillery

*Region:*  Wisconsin

*Type*:  Craft distillery

*Opened:*  2011

*Tours:*  Tours are available by appointment

*Types of spirits produced:*  Hmong Rice Spirits

*Names of spirits:*  Yerlo Rice Spirits

*Best known for:*  Hmong Rice Spirits

*Distribution:*
On-site retail shop and numerous locations in Wisconsin, California, and Minnesota

*Highlighted spirits:*
**Yerlo Rice Spirits**
Yerlo Rice Spirits is a sweet yet strong spirit rich with tradition and passion.
(Yerlo 120 Proof, Yerlo Reserve 130 Proof)

*Services offered other than production:*  Tours, tastings and a gift shop

*Interesting facts:*
- Lo Artisan Distillery uses all-natural rice grains, no additives or neutral spirits are added.

*About:*
Lo Artisan Distillery is a family-run distillery producing a genuine handcrafted rice spirit named Yerlo.  Rice spirits are used in all traditions and celebrations among the Hmong people.

Yerlo is created using a centuries-old family recipe with all-natural ingredients that are enhanced by modern technologies. Lo Artisan Distillery's rice spirit has no additives or artificial flavors; this gives a smoother, cleaner, and more balanced taste.

Beginning with the best grains of sweet (glutinous) and long grain rice to produce an authentic traditional flavor, Yerlo is produced in small, carefully handcrafted batches in a custom German still pot. Additionally, the distillery creates its own yeast that is mixed with the cooked rice and then fermented up to four months in its 225 gallon tanks. The result is a sweet jasmine fragrance and a sweet aftertaste.

*Management profile:*
**Po Lo**
For many years, Po had visions of creating a product that would reflect his passion for sharing the Hmong people's rich heritage. After years of perfecting and distilling the traditional rice spirit with his mother and attending distilling seminars and workshops, Po used his dedication and knowledge to start his own artisan distillery. Being a business owner for nearly a decade, he is highly energized to create a long lasting product and establishment that the public will enjoy.

*Future business plans and goals:* Continue producing and sharing Yerlo

*Suggested recipe:*
**Chili**
Serves 3 (best served on cold or chilly days)

- 1 cup apple cider
- 1 cup apple juice
- 1 cinnamon stick
- 3 oz Yerlo Rice Spirits

  Mix all liquids in small pot and stir until it begins to boil.
  (Note: DO NOT bring pot to full boil.)
  Remove pot from heat and place on cool surface.
  Stir with cinnamon stick for 1 to 2 minutes.
  Best served hot or warm.

Lo Artisan Distillery LLC
Sturgeon Bay, Wisconsin

# Old Sugar Distillery

Nathan Greenawalt, Owner / Distiller

931 East Main Street, Suite 8
Madison, Wisconsin 53703

*Phone:* 608-260-0812
*Email:* madisondistillery@gmail.com
*Website:* www.madisondistillery.com
*Facebook:* Old Sugar Distillery

*Region:* Wisconsin

*Type*: Micro-distillery producing approximately 100 gallons per month

*Opened:* 2010

*Hours of operation:* Thursday and Friday, 4:00pm to 10:00pm
Saturdays, noon to 10:00pm

*Tours:*
Tours are available Thursday through Saturday.

*Types of spirits produced:*
Sorghum whiskey, rum, honey liqueur, ouzo, and seasonal grappa and brandy

*Names of spirits:*
- Cane and Abe Freshwater Rum
- Old Sugar Factory Honey Liqueur
- Americanaki Ouzo
- Queen Jennie Sorghum Whiskey
- Brandy Station
  (brandy distilled from Wisconsin grapes)

*Average bottle price*: $30.00 to $35.00

*Distribution:* Wisconsin, Illinois, New York, New Jersey, Connecticut, Delaware, Maryland, Florida, and Washington, D.C.

*Highlighted spirits:*
## Cane and Abe Freshwater Rum
Cane and Abe Freshwater Rum is an un-sweetened, golden rum made exclusively from domestically-grown dark brown cane sugar. It is fermented and distilled in-house, and aged in a blend of both new and used American oak barrels in order to achieve its characteristic smooth, robust flavor. Cane and Abe Freshwater Rum is named for Old Abe, the legendary bald eagle that was the mascot for Wisconsin's 8th Infantry during the Civil War.

## Old Sugar Factory Honey Liqueur

Old Sugar Factory Honey Liqueur is distilled from Midwestern grown, dark brown beet sugar which is fermented in-house. It is distilled in a copper-pot still and then aged in lightly charred oak barrels. Pure Wisconsin honey is also added.

## Americanaki Ouzo

Americanaki Ouzo is twice distilled and twice infused in order to achieve its smooth, licorice-like taste. Distilled from a fermented mash of Mid-western grown, dark brown beet sugar, the spirit is infused with star anise and seed anise. It is then redistilled with anise in the head of the still, and then infused again with star anise prior to bottling.

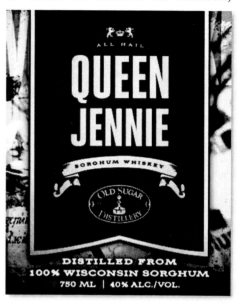

## Queen Jennie Sorghum Whiskey

Queen Jennie is made from 100% Wisconsin sorghum. It is aged in small charred oak barrels from Minnesota. Fantastically smooth, it has a mildness similar to a Canadian whiskey; however the sorghum provides a unique character deserving of its name. Queen Jennie Sorghum Whiskey is currently only available at the distillery.

*Events and Celebrations:*
The distillery can be rented for private parties.

*Services offered other than production:*
Tours, tastings, cocktail bar, bottle sales

*Future business plans and goals:* Increased production and broadened distribution

*Suggested recipe:*
**Honey-Cap**
- 1 oz fresh squeezed lime juice
- 1 oz honey (or more if you want it sweeter)
- 4 medium lime slices
- 2 oz Old Sugar Factory Honey Liqueur

In a mixing glass, stir lime juice and honey until dissolved.
Add lime slices and muddle.
Add Old Sugar Factory Honey Liqueur.
Add ice and then pour into another glass (to get lime on top).
Top with about 3 or 4 ounces of club soda and stir.

Old Sugar Distillery
Madison, Wisconsin

## Wyoming Whiskey Distillery

Brad Mead, Owner
Kate Mead, Owner
David DeFazio, Owner / COO

100 South Nelson
Kirby, Wyoming   82430

*Phone:* 307-864-2116
*Website:* www.wyomingwhiskey.com
*Facebook:* Wyoming Whiskey

# WYOMING WHISKEY

*Region:*  Big Horn Basin

*Type*:   Craft-distillery producing approximately 5,000 gallons per month

*Opened:*  July 2009

*Hours of operation:*   Monday, Tuesday, Thursday, and Friday from 10:00am to 4:00pm

*Tours:*   Tours are conducted during operating hours.

*Types of spirits produced:*  Bourbon

*Names of spirits:*
- Wyoming Whiskey (not yet bottled, still maturing)

*Best known for:*  Wyoming Whiskey

*Average bottle price:*  The price has not yet been set.

*Distribution:*  Distribution has not yet begun, but will begin in Wyoming only.
As supplies allow, distribution will expand to choice markets across the United States.

*Highlighted spirits:*
**Wyoming Whiskey**
Made from corn, wheat, and malted barley, it has a rich color and smooth flavor.

*Events and Celebrations:*  Events will take place in the visitor's center.

*Services offered other than production:*  Tours, tastings and retail shop

*Interesting facts:*
- First legal distillery in Wyoming

*About:*

Wyoming Whiskey Distillery opened as a result of the combined efforts of Brad and Kate Mead, and David DeFazio. Brad and David have shared an appreciation of bourbon for over a decade and the three decided that they wanted to expand their horizons and branch out from their careers as lawyers and ranchers. The Big Horn Basin offered all of the natural resources that are necessary for bourbon making: grain, limestone water, workforce, and land. The distillery was constructed on the Mead Ranch at the end of the road in Kirby, Wyoming, which is the resting place for Butch Cassidy and his gang. The distillery was built from the ground up and includes a Vendome copper and brass custom made 18" copper still, doubler and four 2,500 gallon fermenters. The facility was built to resemble the grain elevators that can be observed around Wyoming.

All of the grains have been selected especially for distillation by working with the growers. Growing at elevation requires careful consideration of the species of corn, wheat, and barley, none of which is genetically modified. The water comes from a deep artisanal well that draws water from a limestone layer nearly a mile below the surface. Twice a week, the tanker is sent to retrieve 6,000 gallons of this water that could not be more perfect for cooking the mash. The still was custom made for the distillery's needs and the distillery itself was designed for the sole purpose of making bourbon. All barrels are selected based upon the distiller's specifications.

The Meads are fourth generation Wyoming ranchers who run cattle in Kirby and in Jackson. Brad's grandfather, Cliff Hansen, was a US senator and governor. Brad's brother, Matt, is the current governor.

*Management profile:*

**Steve Nally**

Steve Nally (right), the master distiller and distillery manager, worked at Makers Mark for 33 years and served as its master distiller for 15 years. He is a member of the Kentucky Bourbon Hall of Fame.

**Donna Nally**

Donna Nally, the director of tourism and public relations, worked for Makers Marks for 10 years and ran its tourism department.

*Future business plans and goals:*

The goal is to make Wyoming proud by releasing approximately 90 proof bourbon within the next couple of years.

Wyoming Whiskey Distillery
Kirby, Wyoming

Wyoming Whiskey Distillery photos courtesy of Jay McLaurin, Colter Productions

397

## Cidrerie Michel Jodoin

Michel Jodoin, Owner

1130, Petite Caroline
Rougemont, Québec
Canada  JOL 1M0

*Phone:* 450-469-2676
*Fax:* 450-469-1286
*Email:* info@micheljodoin.ca
*Website:* www.micheljodoin.ca
*Facebook:* Cidrerie Michel Jodoin
*Twitter:* @cidrerie

*Region:*  Québec, Canada

*Type:*  Micro-distillery producing approximately 1,700 gallons per year

*Opened:* The cider mill opened in 1988.  The micro-distillery opened in 1999.

*Hours of operation:*   Monday through Friday, 9:00am to 5:00pm
Saturday and Sunday, 10:00am to 4:00pm

*Tours:*  Guided tours and tastings are available year-round.

*Types of spirits produced:*
Apple liquor, brandy, eau de vie, and fortified cider

*Names of spirits:*
- Calijo
- Calijo XO
- Fine Caroline
- Pom de vie
- Ambre de pomme (fortified cider)

*Average bottle price:* $33.00

*Distribution:*  SAQ only for the spirits

*Awards and Recognitions:*
In 2008, Michel Jodoin was named Agri-marketing Personality 2008 by the CAMA (Canadian Agri-Marketing Association) for his contribution to the development of the cider industry.

### Calijo
- Silver Medal, 2007 Finger Lakes International Wine Competition
- Bronze Medal, 2008 Finger Lakes International Wine Competition
### Pom de vie
- Bronze Medal, 2008 Finger Lakes International Wine Competition

*Highlighted spirits:*

## Calijo / Apple Brandy

Calijo is a blend of different apple ciders (Cortland, Lobo, and Empire) distilled in a German-made still. It then matures three years in new 200 litre oak barrels.

## Fine Caroline / Apple Liquor

Made with McIntosh apples, this liqueur is crafted from a blend of apple eau de vie and fresh apple juice.

## Pom de vie / Apple Eau de vie

This Eau de vie is made from McIntosh cider, then is distilled in a German-made still.

*Services offered other than production:* Tours and tastings

*Interesting facts:*

- In 1999, the cidrerie became the first micro-distillery of apples in Canada.

*About:*

Michel Jodoin is a descendant of a long line of apple growers. In 1901, the family patriarch, Jean-Baptiste Jodoin, bought an orchard of approximately 100 apple trees at a Sunday auction on the front steps of the local church. His son, Ernest Jodoin, inherited the family orchard in 1937 and, during his lifetime, acquired more land which he later sold to his sons. Sixteen years later, Jean Jodoin bought part of the orchard and, in 1980 he gave a section of it to his son, Michel.

At first Michel Jodoin sold apples on the market but, little by little, he moved towards transforming his crop into cider. In 1988, he was one of the first people in Québec to obtain a cider-making license. During the first six months, however, he sold only 150 bottles. Since the 1970s, the reputation of cider had declined in Québec; its image had to be repositioned and cider had to regain its popularity with the public. Undaunted, Jodoin succeeded in gaining media attention and attracting tourists to his site. Public reaction was conclusive. The next year, production climbed to 5,000 bottles and then sky rocketed off the chart. In 2010, over 400,000 bottles were produced, making Michel Jodoin one of the largest producers of cider in Québec.

First introduced to cider-making by his father and grandfather who, like so many other apple growers, were making cider on the sly before cider production was legalized, Jodoin then perfected his skills in Brittany, Normandy, and at Épernay in the Champagne region.

*Management profile:*
**Michel Jodoin**

As ambitious in life as he is in business, Michel has always had a penchant for adventure travel, particularly running. In 2007, for his 50th birthday, he ran his first marathon and was hooked. His passion for the sport would subsequently take him twice to the Moroccan dessert to run the Marathon des Sables, a seven day, 240 km supermarathon, and to the Polar Circle Marathon in Greenland.

*Future business plans and goals:*

To focus on agrotourism and bring more people to the cidrerie, as well as developing new products and expanding market activities throughout Canada and in other countries.

Cidrerie Michel Jodoin
Rougemont, Québec

# Glenora Distillery

Lauchie MacLean, President and CEO

13727 Route 19, Glenville
Cape Breton, Nova Scotia
Canada  B0E 1X0

*Phone:*  902-258-2662, 1-800-839-0491
*Fax:*  902-468-3704
*Email:*  info@glenora1.ca
*Website:*  www.glenoradistillery.com
*Facebook:*  Glenora Inn & Distillery
*Twitter:*  @GlenBreton

*Region:*  Nova Scotia, Canada

*Type*:  Micro-distillery producing approximately 50,000 litres per year

*Opened:*  1990

*Hours of operation:*  Open May through October

*Tours:*  Tours are available on the hour from 9:00am to 5:00pm.

*Types of spirits produced:*  Single malt whisky

*Names of spirits:*
- Glen Breton Canadian Single Malt Whisky
- Glen Breton Ice
- Battle of the Glen

*Average bottle price*:  $50.00 to $300.00

*Distribution:*  Canada, U.S., and Europe

*Awards and Recognitions:*
**Glen Breton Canadian Single Malt Whisky  (Rare)**
- Rated in Top 50 Spirits by Wine Enthusiast Magazine 2006
- Gold Medal, 95 Pts., International Review of Spirits

**Glen Breton Ice**
- Silver Medal, 2006 World Whisky Competition San Francisco
  **Glenora Distillery**
- Canadian Distillery of the Year, Canadian Whisky Awards Group

*Services offered other than production:*
A nine room inn, six highland chalets, a pub, dining room, and gift shop

*About:*
The Glenora Inn and Distillery is located on a 600 acre site in Glenville, Inverness County, Nova Scotia, Canada.

It was the dream of founder Bruce Jardine to craft a single malt whisky made in traditional authentic Scottish copper-pot stills using barley, yeast, and water from MacLellan's Brook. The distillery and tourism facilities were constructed between 1988 and 1990 in traditional post and beam style, similar in nature to distilleries found in Scotland. Additionally, the two copper-pot stills were made by Forsyth & Sons of Speyside, Scotland.

Glenora Distillers partnered with Jost Vineyard, an award winning Nova Scotia winery, to produce the world's first ice wine finished single malt whisky.

*Future business plans and goals:*
To continue to produce and sell a world class, single malt whisky

*Suggested recipe:*
**Angel's Share**

- 1oz Glen Breton Canadian Single Malt Whisky
- ½ oz Cointreau
- 12-15 torn mint leaves
- Juice from half a lemon
- Lemon iced tea

Add all ingredients in a tall glass and top with lemon ice tea.
Garnish with lemon or blueberries.

**The Glen Breton Toast**
by Bryan Finlay

So the word is now out for all to see
A single malt from this side of the sea
A lowland taste, or a highland smile, or the tang of the sea,
Like a malt from the Isle

These secrets reside in the walls of the cask,
And those bouquets and flavours are with us at last.
Ten years in a complex of oak and of smoke,
Now we reach for the glass,
For the cask has awoke

And we'll toast with Glen Breton,
With more than a dram,
For the dream of Glenora has captured our land

From the shores of Cape Breton to our mountainous west
Canadians now toast with their very own best

Glenora Distillery
Cape Breton, Nova Scotia

# Myriad View Artisan Distillery Inc.

Dr. Paul and Angie Berrow, Owners
Ken and Danielle Mill, Owners

1336 Route 2
Rollo Bay, Prince Edward Island
Canada C0A 2B0

*Phone:* 902-687-1281
*Fax:* 902-687-1546
*Email:* info@straitshine.com
*Website:* www.straitshine.com

*Region:* Rollo Bay, Prince Edward Island

*Type*: Craft-distillery producing approximately 20,000 bottles per year

*Opened:* Spring 2007

*Hours of operation:* Hours vary. Refer to website.

*Tours:* Tours of the facility are available.

*Types of spirits produced:* Moonshine, rum, gin, whisky, and vodka

*Names of spirits:*
- Strait Shine
- Strait Lightning
- Strait Rum (historic 100 proof 57.1%)
- Strait Rum (40%)
- Strait Vodka
- Strait Gin
- Strait Pastis
- Strait Whisky

*Best known for:* Strait Shine

*Average bottle price*: $26.00 to $42.00

*Distribution:*
Myriad View Artisan products are available in the retail shop, in all Prince Edward Island Liquor Stores, and in Calgary, Alberta.

*Awards and Recognitions:*
Myriad View Artisan Distillery doesn't bother to enter competitions as that is not in keeping with the spirit of moonshining. The experience teaches the owners that awards do not equate to product quality.

*Highlighted spirits:*

**Strait Shine**

Bringing a novel product like Shine to the commercial market was the driving force behind the birth of Myriad View Artisan Distillery. Strait Shine pays homage to the era of Prohibition and illegal moonshining. Prince Edward Island endured Prohibition longer than other provinces in Canada and played an active role in illegal shine production and its illicit shipment to the USA. Consequently PEI and Shine have a rich, interwoven and largely untold history. Strait Shine is fermented on site from pure cane sugar and high grade molasses, and it is carefully distilled through a state of the art copper still.

**Strait Rum**

Produced from pure cane sugar and molasses, Strait Rum is fermented, distilled and aged on site in select American oak barrels.

**Strait Vodka**

Strait Vodka begins with a Canadian pure grain alcohol. This vodka grade spirit is further distilled twice, creating a triple distilled and pure vodka. Strait Vodka has an exceptionally smooth and neutral flavor with hints of natural sweetness that show its Canadian grain origins.

**Strait Gin**

In crafting Strait Gin, Strait Vodka is distilled a fourth time through a unique blend of botanicals. These eight hand-picked organically grown herbs and spices gathered from five continents are gently wrapped and suspended in a separate and specially designed stainless steel botanicals vessel.

*Services offered other than production:* Tastings, tours and retail shop

*Interesting facts*
- Prince Edward Island's first distillery

*About:*

Overlooking the Northumberland Strait, it was this beautiful and ever-changing myriad view of nature's moods that inspired the name "The Myriad View."

Founded in 2006 by Paul and Angela Berrow who were joined shortly thereafter by Ken and Danielle Mill, Myriad View Artisan Distillery was established with the express intention of producing spirits with a history and heritage unique to Prince Edward Island and the Maritimes.

From the outset, their vision has been to handcraft high quality, unique distilled spirits. Each of the owners have a background in science and public service; these skills have adapted well to the art and science of distillation.

Each product is carefully crafted from the owners' unique and historical recipes in a time honored authentic manner. Their state of the art copper still, handcrafted in Germany by Christian Carl, allows them to capture the individual essence and flavors unique to each of their products.

*Future business plans and goals:* Continue to make small batches of high quality, handcrafted spirits

*Suggested recipes:*

**Lemon Drop**

- Lemon wedge
- Superfine sugar
- 1½ oz Strait Vodka
- 1½ oz Cointreau or triple sec
- 1½ oz fresh lemon juice
- ½ oz fresh orange juice
- Lemon peel spiral

Rub rim of chilled large cocktail glass with lemon wedge.
Rim with superfine sugar. Shake liquid ingredients vigorously with ice.
Strain into prepared glass and garnish with lemon peel spiral.

**Maple Lightning**

- 1 oz Strait Lightning
- 1½ oz Strait Gin
- 2 oz lime juice
- 2 oz maple syrup
- Lime wedge

Shake liquid ingredients vigorously with ice and strain into a chilled cocktail glass.
Garnish with lime.

**Strait Chocolate Martini**

- 1½ oz Strait Vodka
- ¼ oz Godiva Chocolate Liquer or Dark Crème de Cacao
- ¼ oz White Crème de Cacao
- Dark chocolate shavings

Shake the liquid ingredients vigorously with ice.
Strain into a chilled cocktail glass.
Sprinkle with the dark chocolate shavings.

Myriad View Artisan Distillery Inc.
Rollo Bay, Prince Edward Island

## Still Waters Distillery

Barry Bernstein and Barry Stein, Owners

150 Bradwick Drive, Unit # 26
Concord, Ontario (Toronto area)
Canada  L4K 4M7

*Phone:*  905-482-2080
*Fax:*  416-913-1954
*Email:*  info@stillwatersdistillery.com
*Website:*  www.stillwatersdistillery.com
*Facebook:*  Still Waters Distillery
*Twitter:*  @StillWatersD

*Region:*  Ontario, Canada

*Type*:  Micro-distillery producing approximately 5,000 cases per year

*Opened:*  March 2009

*Hours of operation:*  Monday through Friday, 10:00am to 5:00pm and weekends by appointment

*Tours:*  Tours of the facility can be arranged by appointment.

*Types of spirits produced:*
Vodka, single malt whisky, rye whisky, and "traditional" Canadian whisky

*Names of spirits:*
- Still Waters Single Malt Vodka

*Best known for:*  Still Waters S'mortini and The Dam Pub Tom Cat Martini

*Average bottle price:*  $30.00 to $40.00

*Distribution:*  Liquor Control Board of Ontario and across Canada as well as through Purple Valley Imports for the U.S.

*Awards and Recognitions:*
**Still Waters Single Malt Vodka**
- Gold Medal, 2011 International SIP Award
- Silver Medal, 2010 Beverage Testing Institute
- Bronze Medal, 2010 San Francisco World Spirits Competition

406

*Highlighted spirits:*

**Single Malt Vodka**

Single Malt Vodka is made from only the finest 100% premium Canadian two-row malted barley, yeast and water. These are the only ingredients used. No other grains, additives or preservatives are ever used. Made by hand in a pot still, each batch is tripled distilled and then filter polished to produce a clean, smooth, crystal clear vodka with subtle and unique flavors. The nose has hints of malt and a subtle sweetness as well as a mix of tropical fruits and green grapes. The taste has a subtle sweetness and a soft, fruity roundness with a hint of vanilla. The finish is buttery smooth with no burn.

*Services offered other than production:* Tours and retail store

*Interesting facts:*
- The first micro-distillery in Ontario

*About:*

After years of enjoying fine whiskies and other spirits together, Barry Stein (left) and Barry Bernstein (right) decided that their future lie in the alcoholic beverage industry. In 2006, they embarked on a journey that established them as Canada's first independent bottlers of whisky. They sourced unique single malt scotches of varying

ages from different distilleries. They imported the casks and bottled the products themselves, selling their exclusive offerings across Canada.

Three years later, they applied their more than 50 years of combined business experience to this industry and decided to satisfy their desire to distill their own spirits. After a year of planning, training and education, Still Waters Distillery opened for business in January and the first alcohol flowed in March.

Still Waters Distillery makes its vodka and whiskies by hand in small batches. This ensures that each individual batch meets the highest standards for quality. Additionally, the men bottle and pack each of their products by hand and believe that pride in their products extends from selection of ingredients through the distillation process and right through to the finished product.

*Professional associations:* American Distilling Institute

*Suggested recipes:*
## The Dam Pub Tom Cat Martini
- 2 oz of Still Waters Single Malt Vodka
- Spritz (burn) of Drambuie
- 1 maraschino cherry

Shake vodka and Drambuie long on ice.
Strain into a chilled martini glass.
Drop in 1 maraschino cherry.


## Kathy's Kosmo
- 2 oz Still Waters Single Malt Vodka
- 1 oz triple sec
- ½ oz fresh lime juice
- 4 oz cranberry juice

Add all ingredients to shaker, add ice to fill.
Shake until well chilled. Pour into martini glasses.
Garnish with lime wedges.

For a taste twist on this Kosmo, use 4 oz of pomegranate juice instead of cranberry juice.


## Still Waters S'mortini

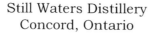

- 2 Graham cracker squares, finely crushed
- 2 oz Still Waters Single Malt Vodka
- 1 oz Crème de cacao
- 2 tsp brown sugar cinnamon syrup
- Handful mini marshmallows for garnish

Brown Sugar Cinnamon Syrup
- 2 Tbs brown sugar
- ¼ tsp ground cinnamon
- 2 Tbs water

Combine sugar, cinnamon and water in small glass bowl.
Microwave 30 seconds. Let cool.
(Makes 4 servings. Save extra for encores.)

For S'mortini, moisten rim of martini glass and dip into plate covered in graham cracker crumbs. In cocktail shaker, shake alcohol and 2 teaspoons brown sugar cinnamon syrup with ice. Pour into martini glass. Garnish with marshmallows.

Still Waters Distillery
Concord, Ontario

# Victoria Spirits

Valerie and Bryan Murray, Owners
Peter Hunt, Distiller

6170 Old West Saanich Road
Victoria, British Columbia
Canada  V9E 2G8

*Phone:*  250-544-8217
*Website:*  www.victoriaspirits.com
*Twitter:*  @victoriaspirits

*Region:*  Victoria, British Columbia

*Type*:  Micro-distillery producing approximately 12,000 liters annually

*Opened:*  January 2008

*Hours of operation:*  Distillery is open Tuesday through Saturday, 10:00am to 6:00pm
Tasting room is open Saturday and Sunday, 11:00am to 5:00pm from Easter to Thanksgiving

*Tours:*  Tours are available during tasting room hours or by prior arrangement.
Tours are $5.00 which includes complimentary tasting.

*Types of spirits produced:*
Gin, vodka, oak barrel aged gin, whisky, and bitters

*Names of spirits:*
- Victoria Gin
- Left Coast Hemp Vodka
- Oaken Gin
- Craigdarroch Whisky
- Twisted and Bitter Bitters

*Best known for:*  Victoria Gin

*Average bottle price:*  $50.00

*Distribution:*  Tasting room at the distillery, in Provincial Government Liquor Stores, and independent retail outlets in British Columbia, Alberta, Saskatchewan, Manitoba, Quebec, and Ontario

*Awards and Recognitions:*
**Victoria Gin**
- Silver Medal, 2010 Los Angeles International Wine and Spirits Show
- Silver Medal, 2009 San Francisco International Spirits Competition
- Gold Medal, 2008 Northwest Wine and Spirits Competition

*Highlighted spirits:*

**Victoria Gin**

Victoria Gin uses ten natural and wild botanicals to create a powerful but elegant spirit. Those botanicals are juniper berries, coriander, angelica, orris root, lemon peel, orange peel, star anise, cinnamon bark, rose petals, and a secret ingredient.

**Left Coast Hemp Vodka**

Left Coast Hemp Vodka is distilled with fine locally grown organic hemp seed. The rich silky texture is elicited by the smooth oils of the hemp hearts. Notes of hazelnut and a hint of spice are present and the finish is long, clean and refreshing.

**Oaken Gin**

Oaken Gin is Victoria Gin matured in new American oak barrels until it is amber in color and beautifully smooth. Behind the portrait of a more mature Queen Victoria is a spirit that's softened with vanilla notes from the oak and that is full and buttery with a caramel sweetness.

**Twisted & Bitter Aromatic Bitters**

Bitters have been used for centuries as a cooking ingredient and as flavoring in drinks. While bitters aren't technically a spirit, they are produced in the still.

**Craigdarroch Whisky**

Without alluding to a heavy dose of local history, Craigdarroch means "oak of the rocks" and will be ready in 2013.

*Events and Celebrations:*

Hosts private parties and group tastings

*Services offered other than production:*

Tastings, tours and on-site sales

*Interesting facts:*

• First artisan producer of premium gin in Canada

*About:*

Located in Victoria, British Columbia, Victoria Spirits is the first artisan producer of premium gin in Canada using a small single batch wood fired pot still. Pictured with the still is Master Distiller Peter Hunt.

*Future business plans and goals:*

Continue developing strong brand recognition in Canada and establishing international markets

*Suggested recipes:*

**Blue Moon**

- 2 oz Vic Gin
- 1 oz dry vermouth
- Dash of Twisted & Bitter Orange Bitters
- Dash of Crème de violette

Shake with ice.
Pour into a champagne flute.
Top with sparkling wine.

**The Prickly Pear**

- 1 oz Victoria Gin
- 1 oz  scotch whisky (or whatever is around)
- 2½ oz pear juice (or nectar)
- ½ oz  simple syrup (optional)
- 1/3 oz fresh lemon juice

Combine ingredients and shake well.
Garnish with a slice of pear.

**Pre-Prohibition Martini**

- 1 oz Vic Gin
- 1 oz sweet vermouth
- Dash of Twisted & Bitter Orange Bitters

Stir with ice and strain.
Garnish with a maraschino cherry.

Victoria Spirits
Victoria, British Columbia

# Yukon Spirits

Alan Hansen and Bob Baxter, Owners

102A Copper Road
Whitehorse, Yukon
Canada   Y1A 2Z6

*Phone:*  867-668-4183
*Fax:*  867-633-5669
*Email:*  bob@yukonbeer.com
*Website:*  www.yukonbeer.com, www.yukonspirits.ca
*Facebook:*  Yukon Spirits

*Region:*  Yukon, Canada

*Type*:   Micro-distillery producing approximately 200 gallons per month

*Opened:*  Brewery opened in 1997.  Distillery opened in 2010.

*Hours of operation:*  Monday through Sunday, 8:00am to 6:00pm

*Tours:*   Tours are available.

*Types of spirits produced:*  Vodka and whisky (still aging)

*Names of spirits:*  Solstice Infused Vodka

*Best known for:*  Solstice

*Average bottle price*:  $44.95

*Distribution:*  Distillery's store and in liquor stores and bars around the Yukon

*Highlighted spirits:*
## Solstice Infused Vodka
Solstice is a 40% abv (80 proof) infusion from a wheat based alcohol that is infused with all-natural raspberry, rosehip, and sage; no artificial flavors are added.

*Services offered other than production:*  On-site retail store

*About:*  Located in Whitehorse, Yukon, Yukon Spirits uses all natural ingredients in its still combined with pure Yukon water to produce its unique spirits.

*Management profile:*  The owners are both engineers.

*Future business plans and goals:*  Continue growing while producing fine spirits

Yukon Spirits
Whitehorse, Yukon

412

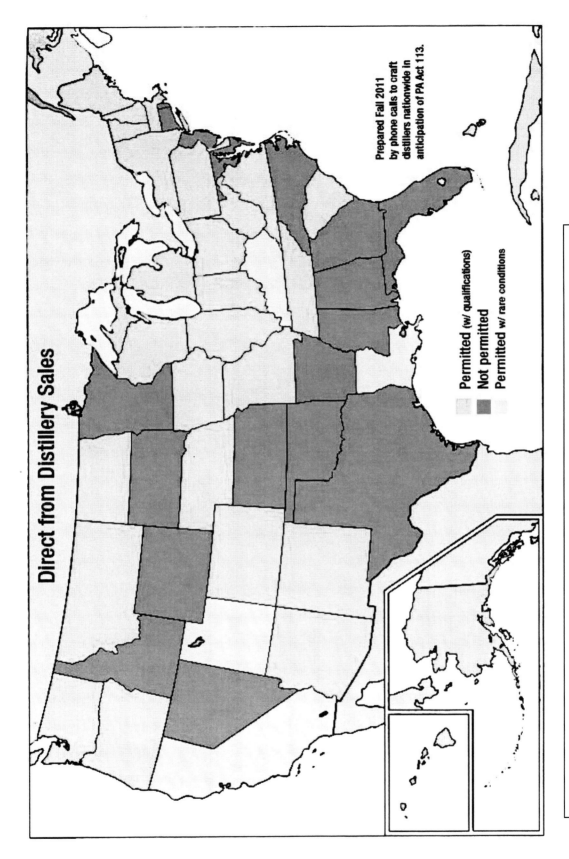

**Direct from Distillery Sales**

Prepared Fall 2011 by phone calls to craft distillers nationwide in anticipation of PA Act 113.

Permitted (w/ qualifications)
Not permitted
Permitted w/ rare conditions

Graphic courtesy of C. Prentiss Orr, Pennsylvania Pure Distilleries LLC
(c) 2011 C. Prentiss Orr

413

# Distilling Associations and Guilds

**American Distilling Institute**
Box 577
Hayward, California  94543
510-886-7418

*Email:* bill@distilling.com
*Website:* www.distilling.com
*Facebook:* American Distilling Institute

**Colorado Distillers Guild**
P.O. Box 17862
Boulder, Colorado  80308
720-635-8511

*Email:* aspengold1@comcast.net
*Website:* coloradodistillersguild.publishpath.com
*Facebook:* Colorado Distillers Guild

**Distilled Spirits Council of Vermont**
7627 Vermont Route 9
Wilmington, Vermont  05363
802-380-5600

*Facebook:* Distilled Spirits Council of Vermont

**Distillery Row Association**
Portland, Oregon

*Website:* www.distilleryrowpdx.com

**Distilled Spirits Council of the United States (DISCUS)**
1250 Eye Street, NW - Suite 400
Washington, D.C. 20005
202-628-3544

*Website:* www.discus.org
*Facebook:* Distilled Spirits Council of the United States

**Kentucky Distillers' Association (Kentucky Bourbon Trail)**
612-A Shelby Street
Frankfort, Kentucky  40601
502-875-9351
Fax: 502.875.9354

*Email:* enjoy@kybourbon.com
*Website:* www.kybourbon.com
*Website:* www.kybourbontrail.com
*Facebook:* Kentucky Bourbon Trail
*Twitter:* KentuckyBourbonTrail

**Midwest Distillers Guild**
Chicago, Illinois

*Email:* info@kovaldistillery.com
*Website:* www.midwestdistilling.com

**New York Craft Distillers Guild**
New York

*Email:* site_distiller@burningstill.com
*Website:* www.burningstill.com

**Oregon Distillers Guild**

*Email:* director@oregondistillersguild.org
*Website:* www.oregondistillersguild.org
*Facebook:* Oregon Distillers Guild
*Twitter:* OR Distillers Guild

**Washington Distillers Guild**
Washington

*Website:* www.washingtondistillersguild.org

**Wisconsin Distillers Association**
Wisconsin

*Website:* www.widistillers.org

# Resources & Information

**Alcohol and Tobacco Tax and Trade Bureau**
Distilled Spirits

*Website:* www.ttb.gov/spirits

**American Craft Spirits**
Reviews & Interviews

*Email:* info@americancraftspirits.com
*Website:* www.americancraftspirits.com
*Facebook:* American Craft Spirits

**BevX**
Beverage & Lifestyle Magazine

*Email:* sean@bevx.com
*Website:* www.bevx.com
*Facebook:* BevX.com

**Cigars & Spirits Magazine**

*Email:* customerservice@cigarandspirits.com
*Website:* www.cigarandspirits.com

**Drink Me**
Lifestyle Beyond The Glass

*Email:* info@drinkmemag.com
*Website:* www.drinkmemag.com
*Facebook:* Drink Me Magazine
*Twitter:* Drink Me Magazine

**Imbibe**
Liquid Culture

*Email:* info@imbibemagazine.com
*Website:* www.imbibemagazine.com
*Facebook:* Imbibe Magazine
*Twitter:* Imbibe Magazine

**Micro Liquor**
Liquor Entrepreneurship + Innovation

*Email:* contact@MicroLiquor.com
*Website:* www.microliquor.com
*Facebook:* MicroLiquor
*Twitter:* MicroLiquor

**Modern Distillery Age**
Spirits Business e-newsletter

*Email:* gregg@distilleryage.com
*Website:* www.distilleryage.com
*Facebook:* Modern Distillery Age

**F. Paul Pacult's Spirit Journal**

*Email:* mail@spiritjournal.com
*Website:* www.spiritjournal.com

**The Tasting Panel**
Connection for Beverage Trends

*Email:* mmay@tastingpanelmag.com
*Website:* www.tastingpanelmag.com
*Facebook:* The Tasting Panel Magazine
*Twitter:* Tasting Panel Mag

**Whisky Advocate**

*Email:* info@maltadvocate.com
*Website:* www.whiskyadvocate.com

**Wine & Spirits Magazine**

*Email:* info@wineandspiritsmagazine.com
*Website:* www.wineandspiritsmagazine.com
*Facebook:* Wine & Spirits Magazine
*Twitter:* Wine & Spirits Mag

# Spirit Events and Festivals

| | |
|---|---|
| Art of the Cocktail – Victoria BC, Canada | www.artofthecocktail.ca |
| Cocktail Camp – Portland, OR | www.cocktailcamp.net |
| Craft Spirits Conference (US cities change) | www.distilling.com |
| Great American Distillers Festival – Portland, OR | www.distillersfestival.com |
| Independent Spirits Expo (US cities change) | www.indiespiritsexpo.com |
| Kentucky Bourbon Festival – Bardstown, KY | www.kybourbonfestival.com |
| Manhattan Cocktail Classic – New York, NY | www.manhattancocktailclassic.com |
| Midtown Cocktail Week – Sacramento, CA | www.midtowncocktailweek.org |
| NW Food and Wine Festival – Portland, OR | www.nwwinefestival.com |
| Pittsburgh Wine and Fine Spirits Festival | www.pittsburghwhiskeyfestival.com |
| Portland Cocktail Week – Portland, OR | www.portlandcocktailweek.com |
| San Francisco Cocktail Week – Bay Area, CA | www.sfcoctailweek.com |
| Tails of the Cocktail – New Orleans, LA | www.talesofthecocktail.com |
| Ultimate Blast – New York, NY | www.ultimate-beverage.com |
| Whisky & Fine Spirits Expo – Indianapolis, IN | www.eatdrinkevolve.com |
| Whisky Live – Canada | www.whiskylive.com/canada |
| Whisky Live – (US cities change) | www.whiskylive.com/usa |

# Museums

| | |
|---|---|
| Museum of the American Cocktail<br>New Orleans, LA | www.museumoftheamericancocktail.org |

# Index by Spirit Type

**Absinthe**
Corsair Artisan Distillery – TN     *Corsair Red Absinthe*
Fat Dog Spirits LLC – FL     *Artemisia Superior Absinthe Verte*
Flag Hill Winery and Distillery – NH     *Edward III Modern Absinthe*
Germain-Robin – CA     *Germain-Robin Absinthe Superieure*
Great Lakes Distilling LLC – WI     *Amerique 1912 Absinthe Rouge*
    *Amerique 1912 Absinthe Verte*
Greenway Distillers Inc. – CA     *Germain-Robin Absinthe Superieure*
Maison De La Vie Ltd. – CO     *Redux Absinthe, Redux Absinthe No. 2*
Pacific Distillery LLC – WA     *Pacifique Absinthe Verte*
Philadelphia Distilling – PA     *Vieux Carre Absinthe Superieure*
Quincy Street Distillery – IL     *Strindberg™*
St. George Spirits – CA     *St. George Absinthe Verte*

**Agave / Tequila Blanco**
Bainbridge Organic Dist. – WA     *Bainbridge Anthem Organic Applejack*
Charbay Winery & Distillery – CA     *Charbay Tequila Blanco*
Colorado Gold Distillery – CO     *Colorado Gold's Own Agave Spirits*
Railean Distillers – TX     *Railean "El Perico" 100% Blue Agave Spirit*
Square One Brewery and Dist. – MO     *Agave Blue*
St. George Spirits – CA     *Agua Azul*

**Applejack**
Dry Fly Distilling – WA     *Dry Fly Washington Wheat Vodka*
Harvest Spirits LLC – NY     *Cornelius Applejack*

**Aquavit**
Sound Spirits Distillery – WA     *Sound Spirits Aquavit*

**Bitters**
Breckenridge Distillery – CO     *Turin-Style Bitters*
Maison De La Vie Ltd. – CO     *Cocktail Bitters*
Victoria Spirits – Victoria, BC     *Twisted and Bitter Bitters*

**Bourbon**
Ballast Point Spirits – CA     *Devils' Share Bourbon*
Breckenridge Distillery – CO     *Seasonal Spiced Bourbon*
Don Quixote Dist. & Winery – NM     *Don Quixote Blue Corn Bourbon*
Eastside Distlling – OR     *Burnside Bourbon*
Entente Spirits LLC – MI     *DiVine Bourbon*
Firefly Distillery – SC     *Firefly Sweet Tea Bourbon*
Heartland Distillers – IN     *Heartland Distiller's Reserve Bourbon*
Journeyman Distillery – MI     *Featherbone Bourbon*
J.P. Trodden Sm. Batch Bourbon – WA     *J.P. Trodden Small Batch Bourbon*
Reservoir Distillery – VA     *Reservoir Bourbon*
Smooth Ambler Spirits Co. – WV     *Smooth Ambler Yearling Bourbon*
St. George Spirits – CA     *Breaking & Entering Bourbon*
Stoutridge Distillery – NY     *Northern Threat Yankee Bourbon*

## Brandy

| | |
|---|---|
| AEppelTreow Winery & Distillery – WI | AeppelTreow WI Apple Brandy |
| Brandy Peak Distillery – OR | Brandy Peak Aged Grape Brandy, Brandy Peak Aged Muscat Brand, Brandy Peak Aged Pear Brandy, Brandy Peak Aged Pinot Noir Brandy, Brandy Peak Natural Pear Brandy, Brandy Peak Spirit of Muscat Brandy |
| Catoctin Creek Distilling Co. LLC – VA | Catoctin Creek 1757 Virginia Brandy Catoctin Creek Pearousia® |
| Cedar Ridge Distillery – IA | Cedar Ridge Apple Brandy Cedar Ridge Grape Brandy |
| Charbay Winery & Distillery – CA | Charbay Black Walnut Liqueur Charbay Brandy No. 83 Folle Blanche |
| Chateau Chantal – MI | Chateau Chantal Brandy |
| Churchill Vineyards LLC – NV | Nevada Brandy |
| Cidrerie Michel Jodoin – Quebec | Ambre de pomme, Calijo, Calijo XO, Fine Caroline, Pom de vie |
| Corey Lake Orchards – MI | Hubbard's Peach Brandy, Hubbard's Pear Brandy, Hubbard's Apple Brandy, Hubbard's Cherry Brandy, Hubbard's Grape Brandy |
| Don Quixote Distillery & Winery – NM | Don Quixote Pisco, Don Quixote Qalvados Apple Brandy, Spirit of Santa Fe Brandy |
| Flag Hill Farm – VT | Pomme de Vie – Vermont Apple Brandy Stair's Pear - Vermont Pear Brandy |
| Flag Hill Winery and Distillery – NH | Josiah Bartlett Barrel Aged Apple Brandy |
| Germain-Robin – CA | Germain-Robin Apple Brandy, Germain-Robin Brandy |
| Golden Distillery – WA | Golden Apple Brandy |
| Great Lakes Distillery LLC – WI | Great Lakes Artisan Series Kirschwasser |
| Harvest Spirits LLC – NY | Rare Pear Brandy |
| Hidden Marsh Distillery – NY | Apple Brandy |
| Koenig Distillery – ID | Koenig Apricot Brandy, Koenig Cherry Brandy, Koenig Pear Brandy, Koenig Plum Brandy |
| Koval, Inc. – IL | KOVAL Apple Brandy, KOVAL Pear Brandy |
| Lil'bit Distillery Inc. – OR | MiLi BiT Țuică |
| Long Island Spirits – NY | Sono Rinata Brandy |
| Napa Valley Distillery – CA | Napa Brandy |
| Old Sugar Distillery – WI | Brandy Station |
| Old World Spirits LLC – CA | Kuchan Alambic Brandy |
| Santa Fe Spirits – NM | Santa Fe Apple Brandy |
| Sidetrack Distillery – WA | Sidetrack Distillery Blackberry Brandy, Sidetrack Distillery Blueberry Brandy, Sidetrack Distillery Strawberry Brandy |
| Spirits of Maine Distillery – ME | Fine Apple Brandy, Raspberry Geist |
| StilltheOne Distillery LLC – NY | COMB Blossom Brandy |
| Stringer's Orchard Winery – OR | Plum Brandy (Slivovitz) |
| The Ellensburg Distillery – WA | El Chalán Pisco-style Brandy |
| Warwick Valley Distillery – NY | American Fruits™ Apple Brandy, American Fruits™ Pear Brandy |

## Cordial

| | |
|---|---|
| Warwick Valley Distillery – NY | American Fruits™ Black Currant Cordial, American Fruits™ Sour Cherry Cordial |

## Eau de Vie

| | |
|---|---|
| Chateau Chantal – MI | Chateau Chantal Cerise, Chateau Chantal Cerise Noir, Chateau Chantal Cherry Eau de Vie, Chateau Chantal Entice, Chateau Chantal Pear Eau de Vie, Chateau Chantal Plm Eau de Vie |
| Don Quixote Dist. & Winery – NM | Don Quixote Mon Cherie Cherry Eau de Vie |
| Essential Spirits Alambic – CA | Classick Pure Pear Eau-de-Vie |
| Great Lakes Distillery LLC – WI | Great Lakes Artisan Series Pear Eau de Vie |
| Harvest Spirits LLC – NY | Apple Eau de Vie, Pear Eau de Vie |
| Immortal Spirits and Dist. Co. – OR | Eau de Vie Poire |
| It's 5 o'clock Somewhere – WA | Apple Eau de Vie, Apricot Eau de Vie, Cherry Eau de Vie, Pear Eau de Vie, Plum Eau de Vie, Voignier Eau de Vie |
| Old World Spirits LLC – CA | Indian Blood Peach, Kuchan Eaux De Vie Poire Williams |
| Quincy Street Distillery – IL | Taliesin™ |
| Spirits of Maine Distillery – ME | Honey Eau-De-Vie, Peach Eau-De-Vie, Pear Eau-De-Vie |
| St. George Spirits – CA | Aqua Perfecta |

## Gin

| | |
|---|---|
| 47th Parallel Spirits LLC – WI | Midwest Gin |
| A. Smith Bowman – VA | Sunset Hills Virginia Gin |
| Alaska Distillery – AK | Alaska Distillery Gin, Permafrost Alaska Gin |
| Arizona High Spirits Distillery – AZ | Desert Dry Gin |
| Bainbridge Organic Dist. – WA | Bainbridge Heritage Organic Gin, Bainbridge Rolling Bay Organic Rye |
| Ballast Point Spirits – CA | Old Grove Gin |
| Bardenay Inc. – ID | Bardenay London Dry Gin |
| Bendistillery – OR | Cascade Mountain Gin |
| Brandon's Rock Town Dist. Inc. – AR | Brandon's Gin |
| Breuckelen Distilling Co. Inc. – NY | Gin |
| Cascade Peak Spirits Distillery – OR | Oldfield Rye Whiskey |
| Catoctin Creek Dist. Co. LLC – VA | Catoctin Creek Organic Watershed Gin® |
| Cedar Ridge Distillery – IA | Clear Heart Gin |
| Colorado Gold Distillery – CO | Colorado Gold Premium Gin |
| Corsair Artisan Distillery – TN | Corsair Barrel Aged Gin, Corsair Gin |
| Death's Door Spirits – WI | Death's Door Gin |
| Distillery No. 209 – CA | No. 209 Gin, No. 209 Kosher for Passover Gin |
| Don Quixote Dist. & Winery – NM | Don Quixote Gin, Spirit of Santa Fe Gin |
| Dry Fly Distilling – WA | Dry Fly Washington Wheat Whiskey |
| Fat Dog Spirits LLC – FL | Nicholas Gin |
| Few Spirits – IL | American Gin |
| Flag Hill Winery and Distillery – NH | Karner Blue Gin |
| Great Lakes Distillery LLC – WI | Rehorst Premium Milwaukee Gin |
| Heartland Distillers – IN | Prohibition Gin |
| It's 5 o'clock Somewhere – WA | Northwest Dry Gin |
| Journeyman Distillery – MI | Bilberry Black Heart's Gin |
| Maison De La Vie Ltd. – CO | Golden Old-Fashioned Distilled Gin |
| Mississippi River Distilling Co. – IA | River Rose Gin |
| Myriad View Dist. – PEI | Strait Gin |
| Mystic Mountain Distillery LLC - CO | Colorado Fog Gin |
| New Deal Distillery – OR | Clawfoot Gin, Gin No. 3, Gin No.1 |

| | |
|---|---|
| Northern United Brewing Co. & Dist. – MI | *Civilized Gin* |
| Old World Spirits LLC – CA | *Blade California Small Batch Gin, La Sorciere Absinthe Verte and Bleue, Rusty Blade, Barrel Aged Gin* |
| Pacific Distillery LLC – WA | *Voyager Single Batch Distilled Gin* |
| Philadelphia Distilling – PA | *Bluecoat American Dry Gin* |
| Pinckney Bend Distilling Co. – MO | *Pinckney Bend American Dry Gin* |
| Quincy Street Distillery – IL | *Old No. 176* |
| Ransom Spirits – OR | *Old Tom Gin, Small's Gin* |
| Rogue Spirits – OR | *Rogue Pink Gin, Rogue Spruce Gin* |
| Roundhouse Spirits – CO | *Imperial Barrel Aged Gin, Roundhouse Gin* |
| Ryan & Wood Inc. – MA | *Knockabout Gin* |
| Smooth Ambler Spirits Co. – WV | *Smooth Ambler Greenbrier Gin* |
| Sound Spirits Distillery – WA | *Ebb+Flow Gin, Sound Spirits Old Tom Gin* |
| Spring 44 – CO | *Spring44 Gin* |
| Square One Brewery and Dist. – MO | *Regatta Bay Gin* |
| St. George Spirits – CA | *St. George Botanivore Gin, St. George Dry Rye Gin, St. George Terroir Gin* |
| StilltheOne Distillery LLC – NY | *COMB 9 Gin* |
| Stoutridge Distillery – NY | *Stoutridge Gin* |
| Stringer's Orchard Winery – OR | *Pacific Plum Gin* |
| Sweetgrass Farm Winery & Dist. – ME | *Back River Gin* |
| Tahoe Moonshine Dist. Inc. – CA | *Jagged Peaks Gin* |
| Triple Eight Distillery – MA | *Gale Force Gin* |
| Victoria Spirits – BC | *Oaken Gin, Victoria Gin* |
| Warwick Valley Distillery – NY | *Warwick Rustic American Gin* |

## Grappa

| | |
|---|---|
| Brandy Peak Distillery – OR | *Brandy Peak Grappa* |
| Cedar Ridge Distillery – IA | *Cedar Ridge Grappa* |
| Charbay Winery & Distillery – CA | *Charbay Grappa di Marko* |
| Don Quixote Dist. & Winery – NM | *Don Quixote Grappa, Don Quixote Malvasia Bianca Grappa* |
| Essential Spirits Alambic – CA | *Classick Grappa di Cabernet* |
| Fiore Winery & Distillery – MD | *Fiore Grappa* |
| Flag Hill Winery and Distillery – NH | *Graham's Grappa* |
| Germain-Robin – CA | *Germain-Robin Grappa* |
| Great Lakes Distillery LLC – WI | *Great Lakes Artisan Series Grappa* |
| Harvest Spirits LLC – NY | *Grappa* |
| It's 5 o'clock Somewhere – WA | *Grappa* |
| Koenig Distillery – ID | *Koenig Grappa* |
| Ransom Spirits – OR | *Gewürztraminer Grappa* |
| Soft Tail Spirits – WA | *Giallo Grappa, Sangiovese Grappa Soft Tail Blanco Grappa* |

## Grog

| | |
|---|---|
| Ye Ol' Grog Distillery – OR | *Dutch Harbor Breeze, Good Morning Glory* |

## Lemoncello / Limoncello

| | |
|---|---|
| 45th Parallel Spirits LLC – WI | *Madison Avenue Lemoncello* |
| Fiore Winery & Distillery – MD | *Fiore Limoncello* |
| Ventura Limoncello Company – CA | *Ventura Limoncello Crema, Limoncello Originale* |

420

## Lightning / White Lightning

Brandon's Rock Town Dist. Inc. – AR     *Arkansas Lightning*
Myriad View Distillery – PEI     *Strait Lightning*
Stoutridge Distillery – NY     *Wagner's White Lightning*

## Liqueur

Arizona High Spirits Distillery – AZ     *Prickly Pear Liqueur*
Brandy Peak Distillery – OR     *Brandy Peak Blackberry Liqueur*
Breckenridge Distillery – CO     *Wild-Harvested Genepi Liqueur*
Cedar Ridge Distillery – IA     *Cedar Ridge Lamponcella, Cedar Ridge Lemoncella*
Eastside Distlling – OR     *Holiday Spiced Liqueur*
Elixir, Inc. – OR     *Calisaya*
Flag Hill Winery and Distillery – NH     *Blueberry Liqueur, Cranberry Liqueur, Raspberry Liqueur, Strawberry LiqueurSugar Maple Liqueur*

Germain-Robin – CA     *Germain-Robin Creme de Poete Liqueur*
Greenway Distillers Inc. – CA     *Crispin's Rose Liqueur*
Hidden Marsh Distillery – NY     *Maple Liqueur, Raspberry Liqueur*
It's 5 o'clock Somewhere – WA     *Apricot Liqueur, Blackberry Liqueur, Blueberry Liqueur, Cherry Liqueur, Elderberry Liqueur Pear Liqueur, Raspberry Liqueur*

Koval, Inc. – Chicago, IL     *KOVAL Chrysanthemum Honey Liqueur, KOVAL Coffee Liqueur, KOVAL Ginger Liqueur, KOVAL Jasmine Liqueur, KOVAL Orange Blossom Liqueur, KOVAL Rose Hip Liqueur*

Long Island Spirits – NY     *Sorbetta*
Myriad View Distillery – PEI     *Strait Pastis*
Napa Valley Distillery – CA     *Napa Liqueur*
New Deal Distillery – OR     *Coffee Liqueur, Ginger Liqueur*
Old Sugar Distillery – WI     *Old Sugar Factory Honey Liqueur*
Old World Spirits LLC – CA     *Kuchan Nocino Black Walnut Liqueur, O'Henry Oak Aged Peach (Kuchan Eau de Vie)*
Prichard's Distillery Inc. – TN     *Benjamin Prichard's Cranberry Liqueur, Benjamin Prichard's Sweet Lucy Bourbon Cream Liqueur, Benjamin Prichard's Sweet Lucy Bourbon Liqueur*

Roundhouse Spirits – CO     *Corretto Coffee Liqueur*
Sidetrack Distillery – WA     *Sidetrack Distillery Blackberry Liqueur, Sidetrack Distillery Blueberry Liqueur, Sidetrack Distillery Raspberry Liqueur, Sidetrack Distillery Strawberry Liqueur*

Square One Brewery and Dist. – MO     *Vermont Night Whiskey Liqueur*
St. George Spirits – CA     *Firelit Coffee Liqueur, Qi*
Stringer's Orchard Winery – OR     *Pacific Plum Liqueur*
Sweetgrass Farm Winery & Dist. – ME     *Maple Smash Liqueur*
Tahoe Moonshine Dist. Inc. – CA     *Dream Bean Coffee Liqueur, VanHees' Mean Irish Cream*

Warwick Valley Distillery – NY     *American Fruits™ Bartlett Pear Liqueur, American Fruits™ Bourbon Barrel Aged Apple Liqueur*

## Moonshine / Shine

Barrel House Distilling Co. – KY     *Devil John Moonshine*
Corsair Artisan Distillery – TN     *Corsair Pumpkin Spice Moonshine*
Crown Valley Distilling Co. – MO     *Missouri Moonshine*
Dark Corner Distillery – SC     *Apple-achian Shine, Moonshine*

| | |
|---|---|
| Ezra Cox Distillery – WA | *Ezra Cox Moonshine* |
| Flag Hill Winery and Distillery – NH | *Moonshine* |
| Hard Times Distillery LLC – OR | *Sweet Baby Moonshine* |
| Indian Creek Distillery – OH | *Lady Liberty Moonshine* |
| MB Roland Distillery – KY | *Apple Pie Kentucky Shine, Barrel Aged Kentucky Shine, Blueberry Kentucky Shine, Kentucky Mint Julep, Kentucky Pink Lemonade, Strawberry Kentucky Shine, True Kentucky Shine* |
| Myriad View Distillery – PEI | *Strait Shine* |
| Mystic Mountain Distillery LLC - CO | *Rocky Mountain Moonshine* |
| New Deal Distillery – OR | *Distiller's Workshop Moonshine* |
| Ole Smoky Moonshine Dist. LLC – TN | *Apple Pie Moonshine, Grape Moonshine, Hunch Punch Moonshine, Moonshine Cherries, Peach Moonshine, White Lightnin' Moonshine* |
| Onyx Spirits Company LLC – CT | *Onyx Moonshine* |
| Piedmont Distillers – NC | *Catdaddy Carolina Moonshine, Junior Johnson's Midnight Moon* |
| St. Julian Winery – MI | *Moonshine Bandits Outlaw Moonshine* |
| Valley Spirits LLC – CA | *Moonshine Bandits Outlaw Moonshine* |

**Orangecello**

| | |
|---|---|
| Ventura Limoncello Company – CA | *Ventura Orangecello Blood Orange* |

**Ouzo**

| | |
|---|---|
| Old Sugar Distillery – WI | *Americanaki Ouzo* |

**Rum**

| | |
|---|---|
| A. Smith Bowman – VA | *George Bowman Colonial Era Dark Caribbean Rum* |
| Arizona High Spirits Distillery – AZ | *Pieces of Eight Spiced Rum* |
| Ballast Point Spirits – CA | *Three Sheets Barrel Aged Rum, Three Sheets White Rum* |
| Bardenay Inc. – ID | *Bardenay Small Batch Rum* |
| Barrel House Distilling Co. – KY | *Kentucky Honey* |
| Breckenridge Distillery – CO | *Dark Spiced Naval Rum* |
| Bull Run Distilling Company – OR | *Pacific Rum* |
| Cedar Ridge Distillery – IA | *Cedar Ridge Dark Rum, ClearHeart Light Rum* |
| Celebration Distillation – LA | *Old New Orleans Amber Rum, Old New Orleans Cajun Spice Rum, Old New Orleans Crystal Rum* |
| Charbay Winery & Distillery – CA | *Charbay Tahitian Vanilla Bean Rum* |
| Corsair Artisan Distillery – TN | *Corsair Spiced Rum* |
| Eastside Distlling – OR | *Deco Coffee Rum, Deco Ginger Rum, Deco Silver Rum* |
| Downslope Distilling – CO | *Downslope Gold Rum, Downslope Spiced Rum, Downslope Vanilla Rum, Downslope White Rum, Downslope Wine Barrel Aged Rum* |
| Entente Spirits LLC – MI | *DiVine Rum* |
| Essential Spirits Alambic – CA | *Sgt. Classick Hawaiian Rum* |
| Firefly Distillery – SC | *Sea Island Gold Rum, Sea Island Java Rum, Sea Island Spice Rum* |
| Great Lakes Distillery LLC – WI | *Roaring Dan's Rum* |
| Immortal Spirits and Dist. Co. – OR | *State of Jefferson Rum* |
| Journeyman Distillery – MI | *Road's End Rum* |

| | |
|---|---|
| Kōloa Rum Company – HI | *Kaua`i Dark Rum, Kaua`i Gold, Kaua`i Spice Rum, Kaua`i White* |
| Montanya Distillers – CO | *Montanya Oro Rum, Montanya Platino Rum* |
| Myriad View Distillery – PEI | *Strait Rum* |
| New Deal Distillery – OR | *Distiller's Workshop Rum* |
| Newport Distilling Company – RI | *Thomas Tew Single Barrel Rum* |
| Northern Unit. Brewing Co. – MI | *Civilized Rum* |
| Old Sugar Distillery – WI | *Cane and Abe Freshwater Rum* |
| Prichard's Distillery Inc. – TN | *Prichard's Crystal Rum, Prichard's Fine Rum, Prichard's Cranberry Rum, Prichard's Key Lime Rum, Prichard's Private Stock Rum, Prichard's Sweet Bell* |
| Railean Distillers – TX | *Railean Reserve XO Dark Rum, Railean Small Cask Single Barrel Dark Rum, Railean Texas White* |
| Rogue Spirits – OR | *Rogue Dark Rum, Rogue Hazelnut Spiced Rum, Rogue White Rum* |
| Ryan & Wood Inc. – MA | *Folly Cove Rum* |
| Sòlas Distillery – NE | *Chava Rum* |
| Spirit of Texas LLC – TX | *Pecan Street Rum, Spirit of Texas Rum* |
| Spirits of Maine Distillery – ME | *Dark Rum, Light Rum* |
| Square One Brewery and Dist. – MO | *Island Time Amber Rum* |
| St. George Spirits – CA | *Agua Libre Rum* |
| Sweetgrass Farm Winery & Dist. – ME | *Three Crow Rum* |
| Tahoe Moonshine Dist. Inc. – CA | *California Dreamin Rum, Jug Dealer Rum* |
| The Richland Distillery Co. – GA | *Richland Rum* |
| Triple Eight Distillery – MA | *Hurricane Rum* |
| Tuthilltown Spirits Distillery – NY | *Rogen's Rum* |

## Spirit

| | |
|---|---|
| Balcones Distilling – TX | *Rumble, Rumble Cask Reserve* |
| Catoctin Creek Dist. Co. LLC – VA | *Catoctin Creek Organic Mosby's Spirit™* |
| Copper Fox Distillery – VA | *Wasmund's Rye &, Wasmund's Single Malt Spirit* |
| Great Lakes Distillery LLC – WI | *Great Lakes Seasonal Pumpkin Spirit* |
| Hidden Marsh Distillery – NY | *Queen's Flight* |
| Hum Spirits Company – IL | *Hum Botanical Spirit* |
| Koval, Inc. – IL | *KOVAL Bierbrand* |
| Lo Artisan Distillery LLC – WI | *Yerlo Rice Spirit* |
| Mississippi River Distilling Co. – IA | *River Baron Artisan Spirit* |
| Nahmias et Fils – NY | *Mahia* |
| St. Julian Winery – MI | *Prohibition Spirits* |
| Valley Spirits LLC – CA | *Prohibition Spirits* |
| Vinn Distillery – OR | *Vinn Baijiu, Vinn Mijiu Fire, Vinn Mijiu Ice* |
| Virginia Distillery Company – VA | *Virginia New Make Spirit* |

## Vodka

| | |
|---|---|
| 45th Parallel Spirits LLC – WI | *45th Parallel Vodka, Midwest Vodka, Referent Vodka* |
| A. Smith Bowman – VA | *Deep Run Virginia Vodka* |

| | |
|---|---|
| Alaska Distillery – AK | *Alaska Distillery Birch Syrup Vodka, Alaska Distillery High Bush Cranberry, Alaska Distillery Low Bush Blueberry, Alaska Distillery Red Raspberry Vodka Alaska Distillery Rhubarb Vodka, Alaska Distillery Smoked Salmon Vodka, Alaska Distillery Wild Blackberry Vodka, Frostbite Alaska Vodka, Permafrost Alaska Vodka, Purgatory Hemp Seed Vod.* |
| Arizona High Spirits Distillery – AZ | *American Vodka, Chili Vodka, Prickly Pear Vodka* |
| Bainbridge Organic Distillers – WA | *Bainbridge Legacy Organic Vodka* |
| Ballast Point Spirits – CA | *Fugu Vodka* |
| Bardenay Inc. – ID | *Bardenay Vodka* |
| Barrel House Distilling Co. – KY | *Pure Blue Vodka* |
| Bendistillery – OR | *Cofia Hazlenut Expresso Vodka, Crater Lake Vodka, Diamond 100 Vodka, Mazama Infused Pepper Vodka* |
| Blackwater Distilling Inc. – MD | *Sloop Betty* |
| Brandon's Rock Town Distillery Inc. – AR | *Brandon's Vodka* |
| Breckenridge Distillery – CO | *Rocky Ford Watermelon Vodka* |
| Bull Run Distilling Company – OR | *Medoyeff Vodka* |
| Cal-Czech Distillery – CA | *Vodka Morava* |
| Cascade Peak Spirits Distillery – OR | *Organic Nation Gin* |
| Cathead Distillery LLC – MS | *Cathead Vodka* |
| Catskill Distilling Company LTD – NY | *Peace Vodka* |
| Cedar Ridge Distillery – IA | *ClearHeart Vodka* |
| Charbay Winery & Distillery – CA | *Charbay Vodka* |
| Churchill Vineyards LLC – NV | *Nevada Vodka* |
| Colorado Gold Distillery – CO | *Colorado Gold Premium Vodka* |
| Corsair Artisan Distillery – TN | *Corsair Vanilla Vodka* |
| Crown Valley Distilling Company – MO | *Crown Valley Vodka* |
| Death's Door Spirits – WI | *Death's Door Vodka* |
| Don Quixote Distillery & Winery – NM | *Blue Corn Vodka, Spirit of Santa Fe Vodka* |
| Downslope Distilling – CO | *Downslope Cane Vodka, Downslope Grain Vodka, Downslope Pepper Vodka* |
| Dry Fly Distilling – WA | *Dry Fly Washington Wheat Gin* |
| Entente Spirits LLC – MI | *DiVine Vodka* |
| Fat Dog Spirits LLC – FL | *Touch Key Lime Flavored Vodka, Touch Red Grapefruit Flavored Vodka, Touch Valencia Orange Flavored Vodka, Touch Vodka* |
| Firefly Distillery – SC | *Firefly Handcrafted Vodka, Firefly Lemon Tea Vodka, Firefly Mint Tea Vodka, Firefly Peach Tea Vodka, Firefly Raspberry Tea Vodka, Firefly Skinny Tea Vodka, Firefly Southern Lemonade Vodka, Firefly Sweet Tea Vodka* |
| Flag Hill Winery and Distillery – NH | *General John Stark Vodka* |
| Good Spirits Distilling – KS | *Clear10 Vodka, Miss Kitty's Velvet Vod., Twister Vod.* |
| Grand Traverse Distillery – MI | *True North Cherry Flavored Vodka, True North Chocolate Flavored Vodka, True North Vodka, Wheat Vodka* |
| Great Lakes Distillery LLC – WI | *Rehorst Citrus Honey Flavored Vodka, Rehorst Premium Milwaukee Vodka* |
| Hard Times Distillery LLC – OR | *Green Geisha, Sugar Momma* |
| Harvest Spirits LLC – NY | *Core Vodka* |
| Heartland Distillers – IN | *Heartland Distiller's Reserve Vodka, Indiana Vodka* |

| | |
|---|---|
| Hidden Marsh Distillery – NY | BEE Vodka |
| High Sea Spirits LLC – HI | Ocean Vodka |
| High West Distillery – UT | High West Vodka 7000, High West Vodka 7000 Peach |
| Island Distillers Inc. – HI | COCONUT Hawaiian Vodka, Hawaiian Vodka |
| Journeyman Distillery – MI | Red Arrow Vodka |
| Koenig Distillery – ID | Koenig Huckleberry Flavored Vodka, Koenig Potato Vodka |
| | |
| Lake Placid Spirits LLC – NY | 46 Peaks Potato Vodka, P3 Placid Vodka |
| Las Vegas Distillery – NV | Las Vegas Distillery Nevada Vodka |
| Long Island Spirits – NY | LiV Vodka |
| Mississippi River Distilling Co. – IA | River Pilot Vodka |
| Myriad View Distillery – PEI | Strait Vodka |
| Mystic Mountain Distillery LLC - CO | BOHICA Vodka, Colorado Blue Vodka, Colorado Crystal Vodka |
| | |
| Napa Valley Distillery – CA | Napa Vodka |
| New Deal Distillery – OR | Hot Monkey Pepper Vodka, Mud Puddle Chocolate Vodka, New Deal Vodka, Portland 88 Vodka |
| | |
| Northern United Brewing Co. & Dist. – MI | Civilized Sakura, Civilized Vodka |
| Pennsylvania Pure Distilleries LLC – PA | Boyd & Blair Potato Vodka, Boyd & Blair Prof. 151 Potato Vodka |
| | |
| Philadelphia Distilling – PA | Penn 1681 Rye Vodka |
| Ransom Spirits – OR | The Vodka |
| Rebecca Creek Distillery LLC – TX | Enchanted Rock Vodka |
| Ryan & Wood Inc. – MA | Beauport Vodka |
| SAVVY Vodka Distillers LP – TX | SAVVY Vodka |
| Smooth Ambler Spirits Company – WV | Smooth Ambler Whitewater Vodka |
| Soft Tail Spirits – WA | Soft Tail Vodka |
| Sòlas Distillery – NE | Joss Vodka |
| Sound Spirits Distillery – WA | Ebb+Flow Vodka |
| Spring 44 – CO | Spring44 Honey Vodka, Spring44 Vodka |
| St. George Spirits – CA | Hangar One Vodka |
| St. Julian Winery – MI | Grey Heron Vodka |
| Still Waters Distillery – Ontario | Still Waters Single Malt Vodka |
| StilltheOne Distillery LLC – NY | COMB Vodka |
| Stoutridge Distillery – NY | Stoutridge Vodka |
| Sub Rosa Spirits – OR | Sub Rosa Saffron Vodka, Sub Rosa Tarragon Vodka |
| Syntax Spirits LLC – CO | Class V Vodka |
| Tahoe Moonshine Distillery Inc. – CA | Hot Stinkin Garlic Vodka, Peanut Butter Vodka, Snowflake Vodka |
| Tito's Handmade Vodka – TX | Tito's Handmade Vodka |
| Treasure Island Distillery – CA | Baker Beach San Francisco Vodka, China Beach San Francisco Vodka, Ocean Beach San Francisco Vodka |
| | |
| Triple Eight Distillery – MA | Triple Eight Vodka |
| Tuthilltown Spirits Distillery – NY | Heart and Spirit of the Hudson Vodka |
| Valentine Distilling Company – MI | Valentine Vodka, White Blossom |
| Valley Spirits LLC – CA | Cold House Vodka |
| Vermont Spirits Distilling Company – VT | Vermont Gold Vodka, Vermont White Vodka |
| Victoria Spirits – BC | Left Coast Hemp Vodka |
| Virtuoso Distillers LLC – IN | 18 Vodka |

| | |
|---|---|
| Wishkah River Distillery – WA | *Wishkah River Distillery Vodka, Grain,* *Wishkah River Distillery Vodka, Honey* |
| Woodinville Whiskey Co. – WA | *Peabody Jones™ Vodka* |
| Woodstone Creek – OH | *Woodstone Creek Vodka* |
| Ye Ol' Grog Distillery – OR | *Dog Watch Vodka* |
| Yukon Spirits – Yukon | *Solstice* |

## Whiskey / Whisky / White Dog

| | |
|---|---|
| A. Smith Bowman – VA | *Abraham Bowman Limited Ed. Whiskey, Bowman Brothers Small Batch Virginia Straight Bourbon Whiskey, John J. Bowman Single Barrel Virginia Straight Bourbon Whiskey* |
| Adam Dalton Distillery – NC | *White Widow* |
| AEppelTreow Winery & Distillery – WI | *Brown Dog Whiskey* |
| Alaska Distillery – AK | *Bear Creek Alaska Whiskey* |
| American Craft Whiskey Distillery – CA | *Low Gap Clear Whiskey* |
| Arizona High Spirits Distillery – AZ | *Single Malt Mesquite Smoked Whisky* |
| Bainbridge Organic Distillers – WA | *Bainbridge Battle Point Organic Whiskey* |
| Balcones Distilling – TX | *'1' Texas Single Malt Whisky, Baby Blue Whisky, Brimstone Whisky, True Blue Whisky* |
| Ballast Point Spirits – CA | *Devil's Share Whiskey* |
| Belmont Farms Distillery – VA | *Kopper Kettle Virginia Whiskey, Virginia Lightning Whiskey* |
| Brandon's Rock Town Distillery Inc. – AR | *Arkansas Hickory Smoked Whiskey* |
| Bull Run Distilling Company – OR | *Oregon Whiskey, Temperance Trader KY Straight Bourbon Whiskey* |
| Cascade Peak Spirits Distillery – OR | *Organic Nation Vodka* |
| Catoctin Creek Dist. Co. LLC – VA | *Catoctin Creek Organic Roundstone Rye™* |
| Cedar Ridge Distillery – IA | *Cedar Ridge Iowa Bourbon Whiskey* |
| Charbay Winery & Dist. – CA | *Charbay Doubled & Twisted Light Whiskey, Charbay Whiskey - Release II* |
| Churchill Vineyards LLC – NV | *Nevada Single Malt Whiskey* |
| Colorado Gold Distillery – CO | *Colorado Gold Straight Bourbon Whiskey, Colorado's Own Corn Whiskey* |
| Copper Fox Distillery – VA | *Copper Fox Rye Whisky, Wasmund's Single Malt Whisky* |
| Corsair Artisan Distillery – TN | *Corsair 100% Rye Aged Rye Whiskey, Corsair Triple Smoke Single Malt Whiskey, Corsair Wry Moon Unaged Rye Whiskey* |
| Death's Door Spirits – WI | *Death's Door White Whisky* |
| Downslope Distilling – CO | *Downslope Double Diamond Whiskey, Downslope Malt Whiskey* |
| Dry Fly Distilling – WA | *Dry Fly Washington Bourbon Whiskey, Dry Fly Washington Triticale Whiskey* |
| E.H. Taylor, Jr. Old Fashion Copper Distillery – KY | *E.H. Taylor, Jr. Straight Kentucky Bourbon Whiskey* |
| Ernest Scarano Distillery – OH | *Old Homicide, Whiskey Dick* |
| Ezra Cox Distillery – WA | *Ezra Cox Smoked Whiskey, Ezra Cox Whiskey* |
| Few Spirits – IL | *White Whiskey* |
| Florida Farm Distillers – FL | *Palm Ridge Reserve Micro Batch Florida Whiskey* |
| Garrison Brothers Distillery – TX | *Garrison Brothers Straight Texas Bourbon Whiskey* |

| | |
|---|---|
| Glacier Distilling Company – MT | *Bad Rock Rye, Glacier Dew, North Fork Flood Stage Whiskey, Wheatfish Whiskey* |
| Glenora Distillery – Nova Scotia | *Glen Breton Canadian Single Malt Whisky* |
| Golden Distillery – WA | *Golden Samish Bay Whiskey, Golden Samish Bay Whiskey Reserve, Golden White Gold Whiskey* |
| Grand Traverse Distillery – MI | *Bourbon Whiskey, Ole George Whiskey* |
| Great Lakes Distillery LLC – WI | *Kinnickinnic Whiskey* |
| High West Distillery – UT | *High West Distillery Barreled Manhattan, High West Double Rye, High West OMG Pure Rye, High West Silver Whiskey High Country Single Malt, High West Silver Whiskey Western Oat, High West Son Of Bourye, High West Valley Tan, High West Whiskey Bourye, High West Whiskey Double Rye, High West Whiskey Rendezvous Rye, High West Whiskey Rocky Mountain Rye 16, High West Whiskey Rocky Mountain Rye 21* |
| Indian Creek Distillery – OH | *Staley Rye Whiskey* |
| It's 5 o'clock Somewhere – WA | *Block and Tackle Moonshine 100% Corn Whiskey UA Block and Tackle Sunshine 100% Corn Whiskey Aged* |
| Journeyman Distillery – MI | *Buggy Whip Wheat Whiskey, Michigan Spirit Whiskey, Ravenswood Rye Whiskey, Three Oaks Single Malt, W.R. Whiskey* |
| Koval, Inc. – IL | *KOVAL American Oat White Whiskey, KOVAL Levant Spelt White Whiskey, KOVAL Midwest Wheat White Whiskey, KOVAL Raksi Millet White Whiskey, KOVAL Rye Chicago White Whiskey, Lion's Pride Dark Millet Aged Whiskey, Lion's Pride Dark Oat Aged Whiskey, Lion's Pride Dark Rye Aged Whiskey, Lion's Pride Dark Spelt Aged Whiskey, Lion's Pride Dark Wheat Aged Whiskey, Lion's Pride Millet Aged Whiskey, Lion's Pride Oat Aged Whiskey, Lion's Pride Rye Aged Whiskey, Lion's Pride Spelt, Aged Whiskey, Lion's Pride Wheat Aged Whiskey* |
| MB Roland Distillery – KY | *Black Dog Whiskey, Black Patch Whiskey, Bourbon Whiskey, Malt Whiskey, White Dog Whiskey, X Barrel Whiskey* |
| Mississippi River Distilling Co. – IA | *Cody Road Bourbon Whiskey* |
| Myriad View Distillery – PEI | *Strait Whisky* |
| Mystic Mountain Distillery LLC - CO | *Blackjack Aces High Whiskey* |
| Nahmias et Fils – NY | *Legs Diamond Whiskey* |
| Napa Valley Distillery – CA | *Napa California Cowboy Whiskey* |
| New Deal Distillery – OR | *Distiller's Workshop Whiskey* |
| Northern United Brewing Co. – MI | *Civilized Single Malt Whiskey, Civilized Whiskey, Civilized White Dog* |
| Old Sugar Distillery – WI | *Queen Jennie Sorghum Whiskey* |
| Old World Spirits LLC – CA | *Goldrun Rye Whiskey* |
| Ole Smoky Moonshine Dist. LLC – TN | *Original Corn Whiskey* |
| Philadelphia Distilling – PA | *XXX Shine White Whiskey* |

| | |
|---|---|
| Prichard's Dist. Inc. – TN | *Benjamin Prichard's Double Barreled Bourbon Whiskey, Benjamin Prichard's Double Chocolate Bourbon Whiskey, Benjamin Prichard's Lincoln County Lightning Whiskey, Benjamin Prichard's Rye Whiskey, Benjamin Prichard's Single Malt Whiskey, Benjamin Prichard's Tennessee Whiskey* |
| Quincy Street Distillery – IL | *Water Tower White Whiskey* |
| Ransom Spirits – OR | *Whippersnapper Oregon Spirit Whiskey* |
| Rebecca Creek Distillery LLC – TX | *Rebecca Creek Fine Texas Whiskey* |
| Reservoir Distillery – VA | *Reservoir Rye Whiskey, Reservoir Wheat Whiskey* |
| Rogue Spirits – Newport, OR | *Rogue Dead Guy Whiskey, Rogue Oregon Single Malt Whiskey* |
| Ryan & Wood Inc. – MA | *Ryan & Wood Straight Rye Whiskey, Ryan & Wood Straight Wheat Whiskey* |
| Santa Fe Spirits – NM | *Santa Fe Silver Coyote Pure Malt Whiskey* |
| Smooth Ambler Spirits Co. – WV | *Smooth Ambler Exceptional White Whiskey, Smooth Ambler Old Scout, Smooth Ambler Old Scout Straight Bourbon Whiskey* |
| Sòlas Distillery – NE | *Sòlas Single Malt Whisky* |
| Square One Brewery and Dist. – MO | *JJ Neukomm American Malt Whiskey* |
| St. George Spirits – CA | *St. George Single Malt Whiskey* |
| Tahoe Moonshine Dist. Inc. – CA | *Stormin' Corn Whiskey* |
| Templeton Rye Distillery – IA | *Templeton Rye Whiskey* |
| The Ellensburg Distillery – WA | *Gold Buckle Club Malt Whisky, Wildcat White Whisky* |
| Triple Eight Distillery – MA | *Notch Single Malt Whisky* |
| Tuthilltown Spirits Distillery – NY | *Baby Bourbon Whiskey, Four Grain Bourbon Whiskey, Manhattan Rye Whiskey, New York Corn Whiskey, Single Malt Whiskey* |
| Victoria Spirits – British Columbia | *Craigdarroch Whisky* |
| Virginia Distillery Company – VA | *Eades Double Malt Wsky., Virginia Single Malt Wsky.* |
| Wishkah River Distillery – WA | *Wanigan Small Batch Whiskey* |
| Woodinville Whiskey Co. – WA | *Headlong™ White Dog Whiskey* |
| Woodstone Creek – OH | *Woodstone Creek 5 Grain Straight Bourbon Whisky, Woodstone Cr. Single Barrel Peated Single Malt Whi.* |
| WV Distilling Co. LLC – WV | *Mountain Moonshine Old Oak Recipe, Mountain Moonshine Spirit Whiskey* |
| Wyoming Whiskey Distillery – WY | *Wyoming Whiskey* |